The United Nations Human Rights Council

C000101950

The United Nations Human Rights Council was created in 2006 to replace the UN Commission on Human Rights. The Council's mandate and founding principles demonstrate that one of the main aims, at its creation, was for the Council to overcome the Commission's flaws. Despite the need to avoid repeating its predecessor's failings, the Council's form, nature and many of its roles and functions are strikingly similar to those of the Commission.

The book examines the creation and formative years of the United Nations Human Rights Council and assesses the extent to which the Council has fulfilled its mandate. International law and theories of international relations are used to examine the Council and its functions. Council sessions, procedures and mechanisms are analysed in-depth, with particular consideration given to whether the Council has become politicised to the same extent as the Commission. Whilst remaining aware of the key differences in their functions, Rosa Freedman compares the work of the Council to that of treaty-based human rights bodies. The author draws on observations from her attendance at Council proceedings in order to offer a unique account of how the body works in practice.

The United Nations Human Rights Council will be of great interest to students and scholars of human rights law and international relations, as well as lawyers, NGOs and relevant government agencies.

Dr. Rosa Freedman is a Lecturer at the University of Birmingham and a member of the English Bar. Specialising in International Law and International Human Rights, she has published articles in, amongst others, the *Netherlands Quarterly of Human Rights* and the *International Journal of Human Rights*. She has worked for various NGOs and contributes to *The Guardian* online.

Routledge Research in Human Rights Law

The United Nations Human Rights Council

A Critique and Early Assessment

Rosa Freedman

Routledge
Taylor & Francis Group

LONDON AND NEW YORK

First published 2013
by Routledge
2 Park Square, Milton Park, Abingdon, Oxfordshire OX14 4RN

Simultaneously published in the USA and Canada
by Routledge
711 Third Avenue, New York, NY 10017

First issued in paperback 2014

Routledge is an imprint of the Taylor & Francis Group, an informa business

British Library Cataloguing in Publication Data
A catalogue record for this book is available from the British Library

Library of Congress Cataloguing in Publication Data
Freedman, Rosa.
    The United Nations Human Rights Council : a critique and early
assessment / Rosa Freedman.
    pages cm
    ISBN 978-0-415-64032-9 (hardback) – ISBN 978-0-203-07473-2 (e-book)
(print)   1. United Nations Human Rights Council.   2. Human rights.
I. Title.
    K3241.F74 2013
    341.4′8–dc23

                                                            2012034242

ISBN 13: 978-0-415-64032-9 (hbk)
ISBN 13: 978-1-138-82889-6 (pbk)

Typeset in Garamond
by Graphicraft Limited, Hong Kong

For Alfie and 'his' Lily

Contents

Acknowledgement

I am extremely fortunate to have been taught and guided by Professor Eric Heinze. This monograph would not have been possible without Eric's hard work and infinite patience. Eric has been a constant source of support, insight and provocation. Above all, he constantly encouraged me to think; any failure to do so falls squarely on my shoulders.

I am indebted to Professor Walter Kälin and Professor Philippe Sands for their constructive criticism and suggestions at the most crucial point in this project. My thanks also go to Professor Merris Amos, Professor Malgosia Fitzmaurice, Professor Dominic McGoldrick, Ruth Houghton and the three anonymous reviewers for their insightful comments at various stages of this work. I am grateful to the UN staff and government delegates who have been so generous with their time (always on condition of anonymity), and to Ophelie Namiech and Leon Saltiel for all of their help during my initial visits to Palais des Nations.

Parts of this book have been published, in somewhat different form, as: 'Improvement on the Commission?: The UN Human Rights Council's Inaction on Darfur', 16 (1) *University of California-Davis J. of Int'l Law & Policy* (2009), 81–129; 'The United States and the Human Rights Council: An Early Assessment,' 23 (1) *St Thomas Law Review* (2010), 23–70; 'New Mechanisms of the UN Human Rights Council', 29 (3) *Netherlands Quarterly of Human Rights* (2011), 289–323.

Table of abbreviations

AI	Amnesty International
AMIS	African Union Mission in Sudan
CAT	Committee Against Torture
CCPR	Human Rights Committee
CED	Committee on Enforced Disappearances
CEDAW	Convention on the Elimination of Discrimination against Women
CERD	Committee for the Elimination of Racial Discrimination
CESCR	Committee on Economic, Social and Cultural Rights
CHR	United Nations Commission on Human Rights
CIA	Central Intelligence Agency
CMW	Committee on Migrant Workers
CPA	Comprehensive Peace Agreement
CRC	Committee on the Rights of the Child
CRPD	Convention on the Rights of Persons with Disabilities
DPA	Darfur Peace Agreement
DPRK	Democratic People's Republic of Korea (North Korea)
DRC	Democratic Republic of Congo
ECOSOC	United Nations Economic and Social Council
ECtHR	European Court of Human Rights
EU	European Union
G-77	The Group of 77
GA	United Nations General Assembly
GAOR	General Assembly Official Records
GRULAC	Group of Latin American and Caribbean Countries
HRC	United Nations Human Rights Council

IBP	Institution Building Package of the United Nations Human Rights Council
ICC	International Criminal Court
ICCPR	International Covenant on Civil and Political Rights
IDP	Internally Displaced Persons
IHL	International Humanitarian Law
ILO	International Labour Organisation
ISHR	International Service for Human Rights
IWC	International Whaling Commission
LBGT	Lesbian, Bisexual, Gay and Transsexual
NAM	Non-Aligned Movement
NATO	North Atlantic Treaty Organisation
NGO	Non-Governmental Organisation
OHCHR	Office of the High Commissioner for Human Rights
OIC	Organisation of the Islamic Conference
OPT	Occupied Palestinian Territories
SC	United Nations Security Council
SLA	Sudan Liberation Army
SPT	Subcommittee on Prevention of Torture
SR	United Nations Special Rapporteur
TEU	Treaty of the European Union
UDHR	Universal Declaration of Human Rights
UK	United Kingdom of Great Britain and Northern Ireland
UN	United Nations
UNESCO	United Nations Educational, Scientific and Cultural Organisation
UNHCHR	United Nations High Commissioner for Human Rights
UNICEF	United Nations Children's Fund
UPR	Universal Periodic Review
US/USA	United States of America
USSR	Union of Soviet Socialist Republics
WEOG	Western European and Others Group

Introduction

The United Nations Human Rights Council was created in 2006 to replace the UN Commission on Human Rights. Despite the need to overcome the Commission's failings, the Council's form, nature, and many of its roles and functions are not markedly different to its predecessor. The Council's mandate and founding principles, however, demonstrate that a main aim for the body was that it should overcome the Commission's flaws. The purpose of this work is to assess the extent to which the Council has achieved that aim. Assessing the body requires examination of the Commission's demise, the Council's creation, its mandate, and finally the body's work during its formative years. In 2011, the Council conducted an internal review of its initial five years. This work offers a scholarly assessment of the Council's formative years.

Key for the present assessment is a focus on the body's responsibilities and duties, as well as the impact of the body's intergovernmental form on its work and proceedings. The work seeks to identify the Council's problems and weaknesses rather than proposing reforms. Although proposals for major reform will not be a central part of this book, the Council is constantly honing new mechanisms and procedures. Potential minor reforms that may change and improve Council procedures will be noted throughout.

The final nail in the coffin for the Commission was Kofi Annan's damning 2005 report,[1] which condemned its selectivity and politicisation. The report recommended abolishing the Commission; advising the creation of the Human Rights Council as its replacement body. That move was welcomed by many states and organisations who argued that the only way for the UN to move forward on human rights would be with a clean slate. The Commission had achieved numerous successes, such as the preliminary drafting of the Universal Declaration of Human Rights,[2] the International Covenant on Economic, Social and Cultural Rights,[3] and the International Covenant on

---

1 General Assembly, 'In Larger Freedom; Towards Development, Security and Human Rights for All', *Report of the Secretary-General*, 21 March 2005, UN Doc. A/59/2005.
2 GA Res. 217A (III), 'Universal Declaration of Human Rights', 1948, UN Doc. A/810, 71.
3 GA Res. 2200A (XXI), 'International Covenant on Economic, Social and Cultural Rights', 16 December 1966, UN Doc. A/6316, *entered into force* 3 January 1976.

Civil and Political Rights.[4] The Commission nevertheless became politicised in its final years and that politicisation has widely been cited as key to the body's dissolution. The Commission was accused, amongst other things, of hypocrisy; an accusation that was exemplified when Muammar Gadaffi's Libya, with its own blotted human rights record,[5] was elected to chair the Commission in 2003. The Council's founding principles[6] aim to eliminate such problems.

Current scholarship on the Council is lacking, resulting in the need for a detailed assessment of the body prior to work commencing on possible reforms. Many observations are drawn from the author's attendance at Council proceedings during its first five years. United Nations documents, such as resolutions and decisions, are utilised, as well as scholarship on the Council's creation and early proceedings. Other works cited include commentary on the Commission, articles on international human rights, and scholarship on the theories of international organisations.

One technique deployed for evaluating the Council's work is to compare it to that of the treaty-based human rights committees. There are key differences between the Council and the treaty-based bodies. The Council is universal whereas the committees deal only with states' parties to each treaty. The treaty-based bodies are limited to each treaty's substantive norms, whereas the Council deals with all aspects of international human rights. The treaty-based committees generate a steady flow of written documentation grounded firmly within the interpretative frameworks of their respective treaties, officially comprised of experts who seek to maintain independence from the politics of their sending state governments. The Council, by contrast, lacks any such normative strictures. A simple comparison with treaty bodies is not sufficient; the Council requires a different analytic framework.

Accordingly, considerable attention will be paid to international relations theories, specifically designed for the analysis of an intergovernmental political body. Previously, international law and international relations have been dealt with separately by scholars. However, if a thorough assessment of the Council is to be made, it cannot stop at an analysis of the legal documents and a consideration of the dichotomy between idealism and realism. Rather, and as this work aims to do, the processes and procedures of the Council's work need to be included in such an assessment. To do this, international theories must be considered alongside international law. Analysis based on the intersection of international law and international relations will show that there is a difference between the Council envisaged in its constituent instrument and the Council in practice.

---

4 GA Res. 2200A (XXI), 'International Covenant on Civil and Political Rights', 16 December 1966, UN Doc. A/6316 (1966), *entered into force* 23 March 1976.

5 See, for example, UN Human Rights Committee, 'Concluding Observations of the Human Rights Committee, Libyan Arab Jamahiriya', (1998), UN Doc. CCPR/C/79/Add.101, paras 6–22.

6 GA Res. 60/251, 'Human Rights Council', 15 March 2006, UN Doc. A/RES/60/251.

Other sources used when assessing the Council's work are well established non-governmental organisations, including Amnesty International, Human Rights Watch and Reporters Without Borders. NGOs provide helpful information on human rights violations, particularly about the most egregious abusers, who tend not to be party to human rights treaties.

Part 1 examines the Council's legal basis and its mandate under General Assembly Resolution 60/251, which created the body. It focuses on GA Res. 60/251, negotiations leading up to its drafting and adoption, the mandate that it sets out for the new body, and the powers it confers on to the body. In order to explore the Council's creation, form and mandate, Chapter 1 sets out the background by examining the Commission and the reasons for its demise. The Commission's demise is discussed in order to examine the main criticisms that led to its abolition. Academic scholarship and comments from other observers are used to explore the Commission's failings, allowing later assessment as to whether the Council has overcome its predecessor's flaws. This background is built upon, with particular focus on comparing the two bodies throughout the book. Chapter 2 explores the reform proposals for the UN human rights body in order to examine the positions taken by various state and non-state actors. Many of the recommended reforms, intended to address the problems that beset the Commission, were not implemented in the Council's creation. The failure to implement those recommendations will be examined. Chapter 3 then examines the Council's creation, looking in detail at its founding Resolution[7] and comparing it with the proposed reforms, in order to analyse how effective it might be as a replacement body. In order to allow later assessment of the Council's fulfilment of its mandate, Chapter 3 explores the body's constituent instrument with a particular focus on the Council's legal mandate and powers.

Part 2 puts forward the criteria by which the Council will be assessed. Beyond the body's express mandate, there are three broad areas which provide criteria for assessing the Council: Theories of international relations, theories on the roles and functions of international organisations, and theories of politicisation. These theories enable a broader understanding of the Council's mandate, and how the duties are discharged in practice, by providing an interdisciplinary approach to this intergovernmental, political body.

Chapter 4 sets out five main international relations theories, applying them to international organisations in order to shed light on the Council's proceedings and the problems it faces. This is key to understanding how states operate within the Council, as well as for identifying the various discourses used by states, groups and blocs. Chapter 5 then turns to roles and functions of international organisations, applying these concepts to the Council. Finally, Chapter 6 explores the concept of politicisation, examining its different forms across the UN and at human rights bodies. Politicisation

---

7 *Ibid.*

was a major cause of the Commission's demise and is crucial for understanding the problems already identified at the Council.

Part 3 provides the assessment of the Council's formative years using three case studies. The book will not give a detailed appraisal of Special Procedures as the nature of the system, which runs concurrent to the Council and other UN bodies, is outside the scope of this work, although aspects of the system will be explored in context. Critiquing the Council entails comparisons with the Commission in order to ascertain whether it has overcome its predecessor's failings. In order to make this evaluation in relation to politicisation of the Council, Chapters 7 and 8 focus on two different aspects of politicisation that were direct causes of the Commission's demise, exploring whether, and to what extent, they are prevalent at the new body.

Chapter 7 focuses on politicisation through lack of even-handedness and disproportionate scrutiny of certain states. Those issues are explored by examining the Council's relationship with the US. The US had voiced serious concerns at the time of the Council's creation as to whether the body's mechanisms and structure were sufficient to eliminate many of the Commission's failings, especially the membership of known human rights abusers. The US, widely perceived as the sole superpower, despite emerging powers such as China and India becoming increasingly stronger on the global stage,[8] arguably allowed its position in international affairs to impact upon its relationship with the new body. Registering its protest, the US chose not to stand for election to the Council, instead maintaining a permanent observer status. Ongoing problems during the Council's first two years, as explored in-depth in Chapter 7, resulted in the US withdrawing from the body altogether. Examination of the relations between the Council and the US permits analysis of whether issues such as selectivity and bias remain at the new body, as well as the possible reasons, including the pursuit of national agendas, for such politicisation.

The Council's inaction on certain human rights situations mirrors similar inaction at the Commission that was heavily criticised by states and observers. Chapter 8 looks specifically at the Council's inaction on Darfur, and the methods by which Sudan was protected by its allies. The form of politicisation examined is regionalism. Regionalism, and the other tactics used by groups seeking to dominate proceedings and exert collective influence, is explained in relation to the Council through the example of Darfur. Comparisons are drawn with similar problems at the Commission.

Chapter 9 explores two innovative Council mechanisms set up to deal with some of the Commission's main flaws. A key reform proposal taken up at the Council's creation was the Universal Periodic Review (UPR) mechanism. The mechanism examines the human rights record of each UN member state. The chapter explains how the review works, analyses discussions creating the

8 See, for example, B. Emmott, *Rivals: How the Power Struggle Between China, India and Japan Will Shape Our Next Decade*, Boston, MA: Houghton Mifflin Harcourt, 2009.

mechanism, and assesses the extent to which UPR can address the Commission's weaknesses. Early UPR cycles are examined to ascertain its usefulness in the Council's fulfilment of its mandate. Another new mechanism is the Council's ability to convene Special Sessions dealing with crises situations. The Council's initial Special Sessions will be examined in detail, including who called the sessions, what positions were adopted, and the outcome. Analysis of these sessions will focus on their contribution to the Council's fulfilment of its mandate, as well as their use of states or regional groups for political motives.

Part 1

The Human Rights Council's mandate

1 Background: from Commission to Council

1.0. Introduction to part

The Council's predecessor, the UN Commission on Human Rights, was the first international organisation mandated to deal with international human rights. Created in 1946,[1] the Commission operated for 60 years before being disbanded and replaced by the Council in 2006. Much has been written about the Commission's demise by human rights scholars, practitioners and experts. Various positions on the Commission were put forward by states, regions, and observers.

Understanding the Commission's flaws, especially those contributing to its ultimate failure, lays foundations for analysing the new Human Rights Council. Reform of the Commission has led to significant changes, reflected in the Council's mechanisms and proceedings. Other features of the old body remain in place at the HRC. In order to analyse the composition of the new body, I shall first explore the issues raised regarding the Commission, the reform proposals, and the impact upon the new body.

1.1. History of the Commission on Human Rights

1.1.1 Human rights organisations background

Human rights present problems different from other international matters. Traditionally, human rights have been viewed as a domestic issue, not based on material interdependencies between states.[2] Some observers argue that international human rights derive from moral interdependencies between states.[3] However, in practice, human rights remains almost exclusively a domestic issue. It is because human rights are considered to be a domestic issue that the temptation exists for states to limit resources and expenditures on this

---

1 ECOSOC Resolution 5(I), 'Commission on Human Rights', 16 February 1946, UN Doc. E/Res/5(I).
2 J. Donnelly, *International Human Rights*, 2nd edn., Boulder, CO: Westview, 1998, p. 55.
3 V. Rittberger and B. Zangl, *International Organization: Polity, Politics and Policies*, Houndsmills: Palgrave Macmillan, 2006, pp. 193–208.

area. Typically, poorer states devote fewer resources and place less emphasis on human rights than richer countries. Where resources are scarce, human rights are less likely to be a priority. Corruption and authoritarianism are more likely to exist within poorer, especially developing, nations. Autocratic regimes often pay scant attention to human rights. Owing to the disparate attention given to human rights issues, international attention is required in order to ensure state compliance with human rights standards. The reasons behind the need for international supervision are also its weakness; compliance with international standards is easier to organise amongst richer democratic states than poorer authoritarian countries, despite the greater need to implement human rights within the latter group.[4]

Conflicts on human rights issues are often presented as conflicts between states' values. Governments frequently use cultural or religious values to justify taking positions that conflict with human rights norms.[5] Resolving such conflicts becomes politically sensitive, and compromise often appears unfeasible.[6] Invocations of cultural differences may be legitimate, for example when states rely on those differences during the setting of an educational curriculum. Such invocations, however, typically relate to uncontroversial human rights matters upon which the Council may undertake work, but which seldom arise within Council discussions. Franck argues that, although cultural sensitivities can affect the way a fact is perceived, it is more likely that 'disagreement over the facts merely reflects wishful thinking or wilful deception, a hypocritical avoidance of the fundamental rules of international conduct by lying'.[7] One example is where questionable claims about 'cultural sensitivities' are invoked to justify oppression of homosexuals.[8] Although some states, particularly those heavily influenced by faiths such as Roman Catholicism or Islam, might disagree with homosexual rights, recent events in some African states, such as Uganda and Malawi, have demonstrated the misuse of 'cultural sensitivities' to oppress homosexuals.[9] Divergence between developing and developed states, under the guise of 'cultural sensitivities', hampers efforts to take action on many human rights issues.[10]

4 A. Moravcsik, 'The Origins of Human Rights Regimes: Democratic Delegation in Postwar Europe', *International Organization*, Vol. 54(2), 2000, 217–52.

5 B. Kausikan, 'A Universal Definition of Human Rights Ignores Cultural Diversity', in M. E. Williams (ed.), *Human Rights: Opposing Viewpoints*, Greenhaven Press Inc., 1998, pp. 21–24.

6 Rittberger and Zangl, *International Organization*, pp. 193–208.

7 T.M. Franck, 'Of Gnats and Camels: Is there a double standard at the United Nations?', *The American Journal of International Law*, Vol. 78 (4), 1984, 831–2.

8 E. Heinze, 'Sexual Orientation and International Law: A study in the Manufacture of Cross-Cultural Sensitivity', *Michigan Journal of International Law*, Vol. 22 (2), 2001, 283–309.

9 See, for example, G. Mapondera and D. Smith, 'Human Rights campaigners attack Malawi gay couple conviction', *The Guardian*, 19 May 2010; X. Rice, 'Gay activists attack Ugandan preacher's porn slideshow', *The Guardian*, 19 February 2010; Editorial, 'The Church must not be complicit in gay persecution in Africa', *The Observer*, 23 May 2010.

10 R. Jolly, L. Emmerij and T.G. Weiss, *UN Ideas That Changed The World*, Bloomington, IN: Indiana University Press, 2009, p. 61.

International human rights organisations with broader global representation have greater overall potential for conflicts under the guise of 'cultural sensitivities' in comparison to regional organisations. An organisation like the European Court of Human Rights deals with states that may have cultural differences, but enjoy a relatively greater level of agreement on human rights. In comparison, the UN's global membership represents all cultures, which can give rise to diametrically opposing views on some human rights issues. All European Union states are party to the European Convention on Human Rights, binding them to these norms. UN members are not all party to the same human rights treaties, nor are they subject to enforcement mechanisms such as the European Court of Human Rights. States at international organisations can, therefore, more easily manipulate regional differences and use them as a tactic to justify non-compliance with human rights.

The African and American human rights courts encounter more difficulties than the European Court. Within developing countries, state capacity is far lower and this impacts upon the implementation of human rights. That limitation in turn creates internal conflicts between the institution and its members. Tensions also arise within developing states regarding the Western-influenced human rights, which arguably creates conflicts that do not exist within the Western world. Many non-Western states lack the natural rights traditions that led to today's human rights regimes. Developing states also label human rights as 'Western imperialism'. Weiss argues that this 'inability to move beyond a simplistic and ritualized North–South pattern is definitely a debilitating ailment'[11] at the UN and non-homogeneous regional institutions.

Politicisation of international organisations is a complex concept. The very nature of international organisations is political, and therefore some degree of politicisation will always exist. Lyons *et al.* define politicisation of international organisations as the introduction of unrelated controversial issues by countries seeking to further their own political objectives.[12] The term 'politicisation' is used where political discussions unrelated to the particular debate occur at an organisation or body. Politicisation of that particular kind was not commonplace throughout all of the Commission's existence. It did, however, increase towards the end, and contributed to its demise. Heinze adds that politicisation does not just occur at the discursive level, although that level may make the politicisation more overt.[13] State actions at the Commission, for example voting in blocs and selectivity regarding country-specific human rights situations, demonstrate politicisation in the body's work.[14]

11 T.G. Weiss, *What's Wrong with the United Nations and How to Fix It*, Cambridge: Polity Press, 2008, p. 61.
12 G.M. Lyons, D.A. Baldwin and D.W. McNemar, 'The "Politicization" Issue in the UN Specialized Agencies', *Proceedings of the Academy of Political Science*, Vol. 32 (4), 1977, 89.
13 E. Heinze, 'Even-handedness and the Politics of Human Rights', *Harvard Human Rights Journal*, Vol. 21 (7), 2008, 41.
14 *Ibid.*

Overt and subtle forms of politicisation are both capable of affecting a body's ability to fulfil its mandate. Keohane and Nye foresaw the threat to an organisation's existence where extreme politicisation occurs.[15] Such bodies may lose credibility, become ineffective, or even undermine the legitimacy of their own processes. Organisations that deal with controversial issues are more likely to become politicised than those involving less sensitive matters. Cultural sensitivities and geographical differences give rise to varying stances on controversial issues. States seek to further their own interests and may politicise proceedings in order to achieve their aims.

Many states accused of violations, however justifiably, complain of being victimised by a 'politicised' process. Accusations of politicisation – often, but not always justified – are more likely to occur when states' foreign policy goals conflict with each other, leading to criticism where a controversial issue is raised. Where there is agreement between state members, the organisation's actions will be viewed as routine or non-political and they will be non-controversial to all countries. However, where states take conflicting positions to each other, particularly on controversial or sensitive issues, those countries are vulnerable to charges of politicisation.

Regionalism is a form of politicisation that played a key role in the Commission's failure. It continues to dominate the Council's proceedings. States tend to form alliances with other countries from the same region. Odum claimed that a region should be relatively homogeneous across various purposes or benchmarks.[16] At the UN there are five regional groups: the African Group; the Asian Group; the Latin American and Caribbean Group (GRULAC); the Western European and Others Group (WEOG); and the Eastern European Group. Member states join the appropriate regional group based on their geographic location.[17] The five regional groups were established in 1963 and are used by the UN to ensure proportionate geographic representation when apportioning seats or membership to UN bodies.[18] However, geographic regional groups are not the only form of alliances at the UN.

Political coalitions have, over time, become as influential as the geographically linked groups.[19] Developing nations have formed subgroups, within or across

15 R.O. Keohane and J.S. Nye, 'World Politics and the International Economic System', in C. Fred Bergsten (ed.), *The Future of International Economic Order: An Agenda for Research*, Lexington, MA: Lexington Books, 1973, pp. 116–18.

16 H.W. Odum, 'A Sociological Approach to the Study and Practice of American Regionalism', *Social Force*, Vol. 20 (4), 1942, 425–36.

17 The only state not to be a member of a regional group is Israel. Arab states within the Asian Group, particularly Iraq and Saudi Arabia, consistently blocked Israel's attempts to join that regional group.

18 See, for example, R. Thakur, *What is Equitable Geographical Distribution in the 21st Century*, New York: United Nations University, 1999.

19 D. Nicol, 'Interregional Co-ordination Within the United Nations: The Role of the Commonwealth', in B. Andemicael (ed.), *Regionalism and the United Nations*, Dobbs Ferry, NY: Oceana Publications Ltd, 1979, p. 102.

regional groups, asserting collective strength to pursue collective aims. Weiss maintains that 'the various roles on the international stage and in the global theater are played by actors from the two major troupes, North and South'.[20] He argues that the end of East–West tensions, with the fall of the Soviet Union, saw a shift to another world rift, this time between the North and the South.[21] Quoting Black that 'axis descriptors – developing/developed, non-industrialized/industrialized, rich/poor – are crude and value-laden',[22] Weiss argues that membership of the South/North has nothing to do with geographic location but is rather about economic, social and other similar factors.[23]

The UN's main political groups give strength to Weiss' argument. Political groups form alliances between either developed or developing states. Furthermore, developing states have formed much stronger political alliances than developed nations owing to far greater need for collective strength on their part. The UN was designed and created by colonial powers and strong states. With the increasing self-determination of former colonies, political alliances were needed for new states' interests to be collectively represented at the body. Strong alliances between developing countries allowed them to challenge the world economic order as set out by industrialised nations,[24] and to secure methods for trade, development, and economic growth.

Use of regional groups and, even to some extent, political alliances is not surprising within an intergovernmental body. Although these groupings can confer benefits, the impact of regionalism is not always positive. As will be shown throughout the book, groups, blocs and alliances can hinder the effectiveness of the discussions at the Council, hamper the discharge of the body's mandate and undermine its credibility.

1.1.2 The UN Commission on Human Rights

Human rights ceased to be predominantly viewed as a fundamentally domestic concern after the Second World War.[25] The atrocities committed during the Second World War underscored the need for international guarantees for human rights protection. That process began during the war; in 1941 the Atlantic Charter was enacted between the UK and the US.[26] The League

---

20 Weiss, *What's Wrong with the United Nations*, p. 50.
21 *Ibid.*, pp. 50–51.
22 M. Black, *The No-Nonsense Guide to International Development*, 2nd edn., Oxford: New Internationalist, 2007, p. 16.
23 Weiss, *What's Wrong with the United Nations*, p. 50.
24 J.S. Nye, 'UNCTAD: Poor Nations' Pressure Group', in Robert W. Cox and Harold K. Jacobson (eds.), *The Anatomy of Influence: Decision Making in International Organization*, New Haven, CT and London: Yale University Press, 1973, pp. 334–70.
25 See, for example, H. Lauterpacht, *International Law and Human Rights*, London: Stevens & Sons Limited, 1950, pp. 416–31.
26 F.D. Roosevelt and W. Churchill, *The Atlantic charter: the eight-point declaration of President Roosevelt and Prime Minister Churchill, August 14, 1941*, Commission to study the organization of peace, 1941.

of Nations' failure to prevent the Second World War, and the violations committed during those years, demonstrated the weaknesses in normative idealism as related to international organisations. The use of an international organisation to protect human rights reflected the social constructivist theory that emerged after the Second World War.[27]

The second aim stated in the preamble to the UN Charter[28] is 'to reaffirm faith in fundamental human rights' (preamb. para. 2). The Charter did not, however, establish a principal organ to deal with human rights issues. Instead, Article 68 specifically mandated ECOSOC, one of the UN's principal organs, to set up a Commission on Human Rights: 'The Economic and Social Council shall set up commissions in economic and social fields for the protection and promotion of human rights, and such other commissions as may be required for the performance of its functions.' The Commission was a subsidiary Charter-based body. Human rights bodies created pursuant to the UN Charter have jurisdiction over all UN members and may deal with any aspects of human rights.[29] In contrast, treaty-based bodies are established pursuant to specific conventions, and monitor implementation of the respective treaties by state parties.[30]

There is a strong case that maintenance of international peace and security is the UN's primary purpose, with development coming a close second. The argument fails to acknowledge that, under the UN Charter, human rights are the organisation's 'third pillar'.[31] The failure to create a human rights organ, as opposed to a subsidiary Charter-based body, does indicate that human rights remained a secondary issue from the outset.

The Commission was created as a functional ancillary of ECOSOC. It was hoped that power struggles and national agendas, found in organs such as the Security Council and General Assembly, could be eliminated from the Commission and that the body would be allowed to focus solely on protecting and promoting human rights. Initial recommendations called for member states to send experts as delegates to the Commission rather than government representatives. That would have allowed the Commission to provide human rights expertise, as well as technical and practical assistance, without national agendas dominating proceedings. That proposal was not followed, for reasons discussed below, and the Commission indeed became a political body.

Initially the Commission had 18 members. Membership increased to 21 states in 1962, 32 states in 1967, 43 states in 1980, and 53 states in 1992. Membership increases reflected the growing number of states joining the UN due to decolonisation. Farer and Gaer comment that developing nations

27 See Chapter 4, Section 4.3.
28 United Nations Charter (1945).
29 cf. W. Kälin and J. Künzli, *The Law of International Human Rights Protection*, Oxford: Oxford University Press, 2009, p. 239.
30 *Ibid.*, pp. 206–8.
31 cf. United Nations Charter, 1945, preamb. para. 1 (2); Articles 1(2), 1(3), 13(1), 55, 56, 62, 68, 76.

sought expansion of the Commission in order to gain control of the body.[32] Indeed, composition of the Commission changed as a result of increased membership. In 1946 the Commission reflected Western dominance, but as it grew the body became more representative. Increased membership allowed for a more representative membership, in many ways legitimising that body through greater geographical representation encompassing different governance. However, concerns were expressed repeatedly that enlargement would result in the Commission's sessions being more difficult and complex.[33] Change in composition, whilst allowing greater representation and countering Western dominance, resulted in more national political agendas being raised at proceedings and increased power struggles between states and regions.

Commission sessions were popular among state and non-state actors keen to engage with human rights issues. Sessions were viewed as an opportunity to discuss human rights issues in a representative and public forum. Many non-member states sought to, and indeed did, participate in Commission proceedings. It also became established practice for NGOs to address that body on human rights issues.[34] Despite increasing participation from state and non-state actors, the Commission only held one annual six-week session. That limited the number of agenda items that could be discussed and the depth of any such debates. The transparency of the Commission's work was also affected, owing to many discussions and negotiations needing to occur at other times throughout the year. The Commission had limited facilities, such as meeting rooms and translators, amongst others, which again impacted upon the breadth and depth of its work. However, the Commission's work covered many major areas and it had many accomplishments before its eventual demise.

1.1.3 The Commission's work

The Commission's mandate was safeguarding and promoting international human rights. Its work can be divided into two main areas: standard-setting and the protection and promotion of human rights. Standard-setting was the Commission's primary focus during the body's first 20 years. From 1967, when ECOSOC authorised the Commission to deal with human rights violations, its work extended to human rights monitoring, implementing, and promoting, amongst others. Rahmani-Ocora comments that, having been

32 T.J. Farer and F.D. Gaer, 'The UN and Human Rights: At the end of the beginning', in A. Roberts and B. Kingsbury (eds), *United Nations, Divided World*, 2nd edn., Oxford: Oxford University Press, 1993, p. 261.

33 M. Lempinen, *The United Nations Commission on Human Rights and the Different Treatment of Governments*, Abo: Abo Akademi University Press, 2005, pp. 20–21; cf. M. Nowak, 'Country-Orientated Human Rights Protection by the UN Commission on Human Rights and its Sub-Commission', *Netherlands Yearbook of International Law*, Vol. 22, 1991, 90.

34 N. Schrijver, 'The UN Human Rights Council: A New "Society of the Committed" or Just Old Wine in New Bottles', *Leiden Journal of International Law*, Vol. 20 (4), 2007, 812.

given the task of standard-setting, during its early years the Commission focused on universal human rights as well as specific thematic issues such as racial discrimination, torture, and women's rights, amongst others.[35]

The Commission's first task was creating the Universal Declaration of Human Rights[36] in 1948.[37] Although not an international treaty,[38] and thus not binding, it has been universally accepted[39] and many states have incorporated its provisions into national law.[40] Two legally binding treaties were adopted in 1966, the International Covenant on Economic, Social and Cultural Rights,[41] and the International Covenant on Civil and Political Rights.[42] These Commission documents comprise the so-called International Bill of Human Rights,[43] and reflect different positions towards human rights taken, at the time, by the West, Eastern Europe and developing nations.[44] Farer and Gaer note that the USSR delegate abstained from the vote on the Universal Declaration of Human Rights.[45] The delegate's argument that 'a number of articles completely ignore the sovereign rights of democratic governments'[46] appears to be at odds with the USSR's approach to statehood and sovereignty of countries, other than Russia, belonging to the Soviet Union.

From the 1960s, the Commission began monitoring standard implementation, often undertaken by mandate holders, treaty bodies, and the Sub-Commission. State self-determination changed the Commission's focus. Until then, the Commission was set up and run by Western states, many of which

35 L. Rahmani-Ocora, 'Giving the Emperor Real Clothes: The UN Human Rights Council', *Global Governance*, Vol. 12 (1), 2006, 15.

36 GA Res. 217A (III), 'Universal Declaration of Human Rights', (1948), UN Doc. A/810, p. 71.

37 See, for example, J.P. Humphrey, *Human Rights and the United Nations: A Great Adventure*, New York: Transnational Publishers Inc, 1984, pp. 25–36, providing a first-hand account of the drafting of the Universal Declaration of Human Rights.

38 'Mrs. Roosevelt made it very clear in her leadership (and in her statement before the General Assembly in December 1948) that the declaration was not to be a treaty but a declaration of general principles of human rights and freedoms to serve as a common standard', Jolly *et al.*, *UN Ideas That Changed The World*, p. 56.

39 See, for example, J.V. Bernstorff, 'The Changing Fortunes of the Universal Declaration of Human Rights', *European Journal of International Law*, Vol. 19 (5), 2008, 903.

40 See, for example, I. Brownlie, *Principles of Public International Law*, 6th edn., Oxford: Oxford University Press, 2003, pp. 534–5.

41 GA Res. 2200A (XXI), 'International Covenant on Economic, Social and Cultural Rights', 16 December 1966, UN Doc. A/6316, *entered into force* 3 January 1976.

42 GA Res. 2200A (XXI), 'International Covenant on Civil and Political Rights', 16 December 1966, UN Doc. A/6316 (1966), *entered into force* 23 March 1976.

43 See, for example, P. Meyer, 'The International Bill: A Brief History', in P. Williams (ed.), *The International Bill of Rights*, Glen Ellen, CA: Entwhistle Books, 1981.

44 See, for example, D. Evans, *Before the War: Reflections in a New Millennium*, Kelowna, BC, Canada: Wood Lake Publishing Inc., 2004, pp. 122–4; R. Normand and S. Zaidi, *Human Rights at the UN: The Political History of Universal Justice*, Bloomington, IN: Indiana University Press, 2008, pp. 216–17.

45 Farer and Gaer, 'At the end of the beginning', p. 248.

46 GAOR, 3rd Session, part 1, plenary meetings, 10 December 1948, 923–4.

were still colonial powers, applying double standards between human rights aspirations and the treatment of peoples under their control.[47] Decolonised countries, as a result of recent colonial practices, tended to distrust the largely westernised UN human rights machinery. Mechanisms including Working Groups, Special Rapporteurs, and independent experts, were created and used by the Commission to monitor states' implementation of human rights. As worldwide concern for human rights grew, and violations became more publicised, the Commission's work expanded to undertake specific investigations of human rights situations. In 1967 the Commission was empowered to investigate human rights practices in individual states without their permission, through confidential complaints being made under the 1235 Procedure.[48] That procedure enabled an annual public debate between states on country-specific human rights violations. The 1503 Procedure,[49] created in 1970, went further. It enabled a confidential complaints procedure open to states, NGOs and individuals.[50] Countries could be investigated and Commission action taken even without national cooperation. As cross-border violations became a 'major phenomena of human rights violations world-wide',[51] country-specific mandates were unable adequately to deal with all human rights situations. The Commission responded by creating thematic mandates to examine human rights issues across a number of states or regions. The Commission was able to address widespread violations of a specific right as well as dealing with gross and systemic abuses of a number of rights within a specific country. Expansion of the Commission's mechanisms and work enabled it to respond to human rights violations and to implement the standards that it had originally been created to set. However, the Commission's failure adequately to respond to human rights situations, especially in its final years, was a main reason for the body's eventual demise.

1.2. The Commission's demise

The Commission's dissolution has widely been attributed to the body's increasing failings. The Commission's final years were steeped in controversy and criticism as the body's increasing deficiencies undermined its ability to fulfil its mandate. The expansion of international human rights to cover ever more issues, coupled with the body's increasing loss of credibility in the eyes of states and observers, resulted in the Commission widely being deemed to be unable to fulfil its mandate. Schrijver comments that as, the general interest in human rights grew, there were heightened expectations of the

---

47 See, for example, B. Ibhawoh, *Imperialism and Human Rights: Colonial Discourses of Rights and Liberties in African History*, Albany, NY: SUNY Press, 2008, p. 17.

48 ECOSOC Res. 1235 (XLII), 6 June 1967, UN Doc. E/4393.

49 ECOSOC Res. 1503 (XLVIII), 27 May 1970, UN Doc. E/4832.

50 See, for example, Farer and Gaer, 'At the End of the Beginning', p. 279.

51 P. Alston, *The United Nations and Human Rights: A Critical Appraisal*, Oxford: Clarendon Press, 1995, p. 126.

Commission's work, and criticisms therefore ensued when those expectations were not met.[52] The Commission became a target for more general attacks against the UN by neo-conservatives, governments, and even some NGOs, owing to perceptions that it was not fulfilling its mandate.[53]

Criticisms came from different, and sometimes diametrically opposing, perspectives. Alston observes that:

> [w]hile many of the critics called for a conciliatory approach that would avoid confrontation with governments, others impugned its credibility precisely because it had failed to condemn governments that they considered to be responsible for egregious cases of human rights violations.[54]

As attacks on the Commission came from different angles, the body's ability to deal effectively with the criticisms waned.

A number of specific issues were raised by states, non-state actors, and observers. Redondo lists major criticisms of the Commission, including: membership of known abuser states; 'naming and shaming' of countries through country-specific resolutions, which developing nations viewed as a neo-colonial tool; protection of states through group-blocking action; absence of membership criteria; and 'bad practice' of the Commission, for example use of 'technical cooperation' rather than taking stronger measures against abusers, or political use of 'non-action' to avoid country-specific resolutions.[55] I shall examine five areas which address and build upon key aspects of those criticisms: Commission membership, inaction, country-specific resolutions, insufficient time for dealing with human rights issues, and regionalism. Exploring these themes, which are broader than Redondo's criticisms, will provide a framework for analysing reform proposals, negotiations and indeed for assessing the Council's founding Resolution.

It is important to note that not all states or observers expressed, or even agreed with, criticisms of the Commission. Recent scholarship demonstrates that some observers still view criticism of the Commission as unnecessary and undeserved, arguing that the body was not flawed and did fulfil its mandate.[56] Some observers maintain that the Commission's disbanding resulted from a more general reformation atmosphere at the UN rather than due to an

---

52 Schrijver, 'A "New Society of the Committed"', 812.

53 *Ibid.*

54 P. Alston, 'Reconceiving the UN Human Rights Regime: Challenges Confronting the New UN Human Rights Council', *Melbourne Journal of International Law*, Vol. 7, 2006, 188.

55 E.D. Redondo, 'The Universal Periodic Review of the UN Human Rights Council: An Assessment of the First Session', *Chinese Journal of International Law*, Vol. 7 (3), 2008, 721–34.

56 See, for example, J.H. Lebovic and E. Voeten, 'The Politics of Shame: The Condemnation of Country Human Rights Practices in UNCHR', *International Studies Quarterly*, Vol. 50 (4), 2006, 861–88.

inherent need to end that body. Ghanea asserts that in all of the general UN reform proposals, the Commission's potential to fulfil its mandate appeared to have been forgotten.[57] Since the Commission's demise, arguments have been made that the body's failure is attributable not to its flaws but rather to the UN's political atmosphere whereby many member states and administrative staff sought to reform various aspects of the organisation.

Some observers insist that the weaknesses identified could be viewed as strengths. For example, Ghanea argues that use of the Commission to advance national political agendas made the body relevant to individual states.[58] She asserts that politicisation was the Commission's 'greatest asset as well as its greatest liability'. Amnesty International's 2005 report provided a nuanced view on the Commission, which highlighted the body's good work and provided constructive reform proposals.[59] That report distanced Amnesty International from other NGOs which, at that time, solely attacked the Commission. Amnesty reported, for example, that the Commission had always been 'a unique international forum for human rights discourse'.[60] Defending many aspects of the Commission, the report argued that some parts of the Commission's work should be preserved and strengthened at the new body as, despite criticisms of the Commission, the body did have valuable aspects.[61] The report listed Commission accomplishments, and argued that states' behaviour in attempting to avoid Commission scrutiny can be used as evidence of the body's reputation and impact on human rights.[62]

1.2.1 *Membership issues*

The main, or at least the most voiced, reason for the Commission's demise was the presence of known human rights abusers as members of the Commission. Moss comments that membership of known and grave human rights abusers severely damaged the Commission's credibility.[63] Similar sentiments were expressed by many scholars seeking to explain the reasons for the Commission's failure.

57 N. Ghanea, 'From UN Commission on Human Rights to UN Human Rights Council: One Step Forwards or Two Steps Sideways?', *International and Comparative Law Quarterly*, Vol. 55 (3), 2006, 704–5.

58 *Ibid.*, 702.

59 Amnesty International, 'Meeting the Challenge: Transforming the Commission on Human Rights into a Human Rights Council', 12 April 2005, AI Index IOR 40/008/2005.

60 *Ibid.*

61 *Ibid.*

62 'Although it can be difficult to measure the impact of the Commission's actions, especially at the national level, the lengths to which states go to evade Commission scrutiny are a clear indication of their sensitivity to criticism by that body.' Amnesty International, 'Meeting the Challenge'.

63 L.C. Moss, 'Will the Human Rights Council have Better Membership than the Commission on Human Rights?', *Human Rights Brief*, Vol. 13 (3), 2006, 11.

Initially, at the Commission's creation,[64] it was recommended that the body should consist of 'highly qualified persons', and that 'members should serve as non-governmental representatives'.[65] Highly qualified persons would have been experts or jurists from the human rights field. Such persons are distinguished from government representatives as they hold a specialist knowledge in the subject area, and have a high degree of independence from their sending states' government, allowing them to engage in impartial and non-bias activities. Those recommendations reflect the functionalist theory[66] that states ought to grant powers to the organisation, minimising national political roles in international human rights issues. The recommendations were not adopted in practice. A compromise required all members to be confirmed by ECOSOC in order to ensure they were of a high calibre and expertise. Although nominally followed, ECOSOC did not reject any nominations, resulting in the Commission's membership soon becoming 'governmentalised' despite some states sending human rights experts as their representatives, such as Eleanor Roosevelt of the US and René Cassin from France.[67] The impact was the creation of a political rather than expert body. Delegates advanced national agendas rather than solely focusing on the Commission's mandate.

Power struggles occurred between states at the UN even before its creation, with countries seeking to exert influence even during its formation. During negotiations on the UN, many states sought to limit the power held by the five 'great powers', for example, through permanent seats and vetoes at the Security Council. All UN members sought to retain and exert influence at the new organisation, and the Commission was another opportunity for inter-state power struggles. That opportunity resulted in governments' reluctance to send experts rather than delegates to the Commission. Governments' insistence on sending delegates rather than expert representatives underscores arguments that the Commission was viewed by most states as a political arena. State representatives advanced national policies and objectives, whereas experts would have had a high degree of autonomy and independence from their countries of origin. States' insistence on creating a political forum came at the expense of ensuring that the body focus solely on advancing human rights.

Weaker states' positions towards the Commission can be understood when light is shed on the importance of bargaining power across the range of issues dealt with by an international organisation. Weak states recognised that Commission membership would afford them greater influence and bargaining power regarding other UN issues. Weaker states at ECOSOC, sensing the

---

64 Humphrey, *A Great Adventure*, p. 17.
65 ECOSOC Res. 38, 'Report of the Commission on Human Rights to the Second Session of the Economic and Social Council', 21 June 1946, UN Doc. E/38, 230–1.
66 See Chapter 4, Section 4.5.
67 Alston, 'Reconceiving the UN Human Rights Regime', 190.

ability to exert influence at the Commission through bargaining power, therefore rejected proposals[68] to send independent experts who would not advance national agendas and were outside the sphere of government control. They instead preferred to send representatives that were controlled by their sending states and who would further national policies and objectives.

Another interpretation is that states' continuing reluctance to relinquish control was an attempt to preserve autonomy over human rights. Having seen human rights enter the international arena, many states were keen to ensure a degree of control over monitoring of countries' compliance with international human rights standards. Even powerful, democratic states would have been reticent about allowing a national issue to become international without seeking to retain some control. Alston argues that, had the recommendations regarding members been accepted, problems regarding grave human rights abusers being Commission members would have been far less significant.[69] Experts on human rights would not have been bound by national policies in the manner that government representatives have been. Alston further argues that it would be easier to enforce minimum human rights criteria for such nominees than it was for state members.[70]

Presence of known abusers as Commission members may be attributed to a lack of membership criteria at that body.[71] Membership criteria could have ensured that grave violators were excluded from such a position. Alston comments that the Commission's membership criteria were solely concerned with its geographic composition, ensuring that different cultures and regions were represented along the usual UN divide amongst the five regional groupings.[72] Equitable distribution of seats is of central importance at an organisation with universal membership, as evidenced through the emphasis placed on this requirement at most UN organs and bodies. However, lack of any other membership criteria resulted in states with dubious human rights records being allowed membership. Scholars, such as Ramcharan, expressed concerns that emphasis on equitable geographic representation rather than on membership criteria resulted in increasing numbers of known abusers being able to secure membership of that body.[73] Indeed, throughout the Commission's existence, grave human rights violators were members of

68 ESC Res. 9(II), UN ESCOR, 2nd Session, Annex 14, 21 June 1946, UN Doc. E/RES/9(II).

69 Alston, 'Reconceiving the UN Human Rights Regime', 189–90.

70 *Ibid.*, 190.

71 cf. Lempinen, *The United Nations Commission on Human Rights and the Different Treatment of Governments*, pp. 24–7.

72 P. Alston, 'Richard Lillich Memorial Lecture: Promoting the Accountability of Members of the New UN Human Rights Council', *Journal of Transnational Law and Policy*, Vol. 15, 2005–2006, 60.

73 B.G. Ramcharan, 'Strategies for the International Protection of Human Rights in the 1990s', in R.P. Claude and B.H. Weston (eds.), *Human Rights and the International Community: Issues and Action*, Philadelphia, PA: University of Pennsylvania Press, 1992, p. 271.

the body, and this disproportionately increased with each enlargement of the Commission.[74]

Tolerance of known abusers at the Commission has been attributed to the Cold War politics that engulfed the UN until the USSR's dissolution. According to Alston, states viewed as human rights violators by one side 'were the other side's champions of resistance'.[75] He argues that membership problems surfaced after the Cold War owing to a shift in the international political atmosphere.

Use of human rights as part of the Cold War power struggle demonstrates the realist approach towards international organisations. With the fall of the USSR, the US used its position as the remaining superpower to champion democracy, exerting its influence against non-democratic regimes that had previously been allied with the Soviet Union. The shift in global politics from an East–West to a North–South divide resulted in membership problems increasing at the Commission as states and alliances from the South became stronger. The US considered a number of Commission members, many of whom were from the Global South, to be human rights abusers, and was critical of their membership and ability to play an active role in the Commission's decision-making and work.[76]

Criticism of the Commission's membership became a greater issue after the US failed in its 2001 re-election bid, a failure largely attributable to North–South politics. That was the first time the US had failed to be re-elected since the body's creation. Although membership was already recognised as a serious flaw, this event provided a catalyst for criticisms especially from US observers. Schoenbaum comments that the Commission's failure to elect the US in 2001, giving its seat to Austria, was portrayed in the media, and widely seen, as 'a slap in the face for the new Bush administration at the United Nations'.[77] Austria, at the time of replacing the US, had been subject to international scrutiny and criticism regarding human rights owing to Austria's Freedom Party, widely perceived as racist, anti-immigrant and sympathetic to Nazism, recently joining its governing coalition.[78]

Alston comments that, although there had been some criticism of 'pariah' states' membership at the Commission, the issue came to the fore when the US began to consider seriously the issue of membership criteria, after it failed to be re-elected in 2001 for the first time in the Commission's existence.[79]

---

74 cf. Lempinen, *The United Nations Commission on Human Rights and the Different Treatment of Governments*, pp. 24–5.

75 Alston, 'Reconceiving the UN Human Rights Regime', 58.

76 Alston, 'Richard Lillich Memorial Lecture: Promoting the Accountability of Members of the New UN Human Rights Council', 60.

77 T.J. Schoenbaum, *International Relations – The Path Not Taken: Using International Law to Promote World Peace and Security*, Cambridge: Cambridge University Press, 2006, p. 250.

78 *Ibid.*

79 Alston, 'Richard Lillich Memorial Lecture: Promoting the Accountability of Members of the New UN Human Rights Council', 59.

Condoleezza Rice, at that time US National Security Adviser, condemned the vote. She described Sudan's election, whilst the US had failed in its bid, as 'an outrage'.[80] Critical of non-democratic regimes, the US argued that those regimes were incompatible with human rights principles.

That event offers an example of an alliance of states from the Global South fighting Western imperialism and hegemony by refusing to re-elect the sole superpower. States used their combined strength to exert influence over the strongest country as part of an ongoing power struggle. The US position, immediately after the Cold War, as the most powerful and influential country had resulted in attacks from groups of weaker states at other UN bodies. Indeed Schoenbaum suggests that the non-election of the US whilst Sudan – 'in the midst of committing [. . .] "genocide"' – retained its seat, was simply a display of power politics by 'the African-Muslim block at the United Nations, demonstrating its disdain for Western sensibilities'.[81] That power politics had surfaced against the US is difficult to reconcile with the Commission's aims, yet should come as no surprise bearing in mind the international atmosphere and the body's political nature.

A number of reasons have been cited for the failed re-election bid. General ill-will towards the Bush administration undoubtedly played a role. Even prior to the terrorist attacks of September 11, 2001, and the subsequent US response, the Bush administration had become unpopular within the international community, owing to increasing US exceptionalism and unilateralism. Steiner, Alston and Goodman insist that China's lobbying against the US re-election played a large role in the outcome.[82] Chinese representatives said that the US had failed to be re-elected because it had used 'human rights as a tool to pursue its power politics and hegemony in the world'.[83] While the US did engage in power politics, by lobbying for collective action against China, China arguably acted in the same manner. Tactics employed by China and her allies in ousting the US were most likely a result of national power struggles. Undeniably, the Commission's work, and the US contribution to it, were not at the fore of this decision. Politicisation, regardless of the reason, was clearly the motivating factor.

The US regained election the following year, using tactics to ensure that it could not fail to be elected, including threatening to withhold its dues and ensuring a closed regional slate. A closed slate occurs where a regional group proposes only the same number of candidates as seats available. Closed slates ensure that all candidates are elected owing to no other options being available through which inappropriate states' nominations might be countered.[84]

80 *Ibid.*
81 Schoenbaum, *International Relations*, p. 252.
82 H.J. Steiner, P. Alston and R. Goodman, *International Human Rights in Context*, 3rd edn., Oxford: Oxford University Press, 2008, p. 793.
83 Opinion, 'Vote for Justice, Embarrassment for US', *People's Daily (China)*, 4 May 2001.
84 Moss, 'Will the Human Rights Council have Better Membership'.

Dennis notes that the US only announced its candidacy once Spain and Italy had withdrawn from election.[85] He argues that the US wished to ensure a closed slate for the Western European and Other States Group, that is, nomination for election of only as many states as there were seats in order to ensure that those countries gain membership. Withdrawal of those two countries was, according to Dennis, due in part to US pressure as well as a widespread belief amongst states from the Global North that the Commission would only maintain credibility with the US as a member.[86]

Despite the US regaining its Commission seat, debate on membership continued. Proposals by Human Rights Watch in 2003 called for membership criteria, which demonstrated growing dissatisfaction with the lack of membership rules. Although that NGO did subsequently change its position, retracting its endorsement of formal membership criteria altogether, Human Rights Watch originally proposed that membership should require ratification of core human rights treaties, compliance with reporting obligations, and that no recent condemnations of that country had been issued by the Commission.[87]

Discussions were exacerbated in 2003 by the election of Libya as Chair of the Commission.[88] That state was known for its grave abuses, and its election undermined the Commission's credibility. Dennis outlined reasons for the decision.[89] The African Group, whose turn it was to nominate a chairperson, unanimously endorsed Libya. Weiss comments that states from the South view 'state sovereignty or cultural solidarity [as] routinely trump[ing] UN efforts to protect rights'.[90] The African Group emphasised that it was its turn to nominate, encouraging other states to accept the nomination based on the need for friendly relations with the Group's members.[91]

No UN body had ever rejected the candidate endorsed by the region whose turn it was to nominate. The US insisted a vote was called owing to Libya's poor human rights record. The vote failed to overturn the nomination, although a number of states abstained rather than endorse Libya. Weiss reports that many EU members, despite being 'shocked' by Libya's nomination, abstained from the vote in order not to offend the African states who had nominated that country.[92] EU states' behaviour demonstrates

85 M. Dennis, 'Human Rights in 2002: The Annual Sessions of the UN Commission on Human Rights and the Economic and Social Council', *American Journal of International Law*, Vol. 97 (2), 2003, 385.

86 *Ibid.*

87 Human Rights Watch, 'UN Human Rights Body in Serious Decline', *Human Rights News, (US)*, 25 April 2003.

88 Despite the controversy in 2003, in 2010 Libya was elected to the Human Rights Council with 155/192 votes.

89 Dennis, 'Human Rights in 2002', 385.

90 Weiss, *What's Wrong with the United Nations*, p. 38.

91 *Ibid.*

92 *Ibid.*

national agendas, regarding political and other relations with the African states, being prioritised over human rights principles. Interstate relations were arguably more important to those abstaining countries than acting in accordance with the values that stopped them being able to endorse Libya's candidacy.

US failure to be elected, followed by Libya becoming chair of the Commission, meant that states finally confronted the membership issues that had been quietly debated for some time.[93] Sudan's re-election in 2004, at a time when grave violations were occurring within that state and especially in Darfur, led to strong protests, especially from the US.[94] During the Commission's 2004 annual session, US Ambassador Richard S. Williamson said that the body 'should not be allowed to become a protected sanctuary for human rights violators who aim to pervert and distort its work', arguing that only democratic countries be allowed membership.[95] The US position reflects its general approach towards non-democratic regimes. Strong language by its representative demonstrates the severe criticism of the Commission within that country at that time.

Ghanea notes the involvement of non-state actors in membership discussion.[96] She comments that those NGOs who had criticised membership of known abusers were particularly supportive of the increasing calls for membership criteria. NGO criticisms were at times more severe even than state criticisms. Human Rights Watch Executive Director, Kenneth Roth, wrote a particularly damning article in 2001 in which he observed:

> Imagine a jury that includes murderers and rapists, or a police force run in large part by suspected murderers and rapists who are determined to stymie investigation of their crimes. Sadly, such spectacles are not far from reality at the United Nations Commission on Human Rights [. . .] It features the sordid ritual of the world's despots and tyrants scrambling to join a commission that is tasked with investigating and condemning the world's despots and tyrants [. . .] Dictatorships are as free as democracies to serve. The latest batch of new members illustrates how poorly this system works. They include such dubious paragons of human rights virtue as Algeria, the Democratic Republic of the Congo, Kenya, Libya, Saudi Arabia, Syria and Vietnam. Needless to say, such governments do not seek membership out of a commitment to promote human rights abroad or to improve their own abysmal human rights records. Rather they join the commission to protect themselves from criticism and to undermine its work.[97]

93 Alston, 'Reconceiving the UN Human Rights Regime', 192.
94 E. Leopold, 'Sudan Elected to UN Rights Group, US Walks Out', *Reuters*, 5 May 2004.
95 Oral statement of US delegate, Commission on Human Rights, 60th Session.
96 Ghanea, 'From UN Commission on Human Rights to UN Human Rights Council', 699.
97 K. Roth, 'Despots Pretending to Spot and Shame Despots', *New York Times*, 17 April 2001.

Similar observations were made, sometimes in less strident fashion, by renowned human rights scholars.[98] For example Dennis wrote:

> Unfortunately, many UN member states, where human rights are not properly accepted and implemented, have realised that the best way to protect oneself from scrutiny is to be elected to the Commission and divert attention from implementation to the ever greater elaboration of new rights and principles. Largely through their efforts, the 58th session of the Commission saw an unprecedented erosion of its prestige and credibility and regression of human rights norms.[99]

Criticism of Commission membership, then, came mainly from Western states, NGOs and observers. Many human rights abusers that sought membership to protect themselves from scrutiny were non-Western states, and those countries were therefore unlikely to criticise the lack of membership criteria.

1.2.2 *Commission inaction*

Criticism of the Commission's failure to take action on grave human rights situations emphasised serious failings that significantly contributed to its demise. Lack of action in protection of human rights led to accusations that it failed adequately to address human rights issues. In 2005, for example, the Commission adopted four resolutions against Israel and four against other states (Belarus, Cuba, Democratic People's Republic of Korea (North Korea), and Myanmar).[100] The Commission ignored ongoing grave violations in other countries such as Sudan, Zimbabwe, or the Democratic Republic of Congo, amongst others, largely owing to the regional and political objectives of Commission members.

States, groups and blocs used various tactics to ensure that the Commission failed to take action on particular human rights situations. Ghanea comments that abuser states used increasingly 'ingenious' methods to avoid Commission action.[101] Those methods included withdrawal of draft resolutions, blocking action through voting against resolutions, and through misuse of the 'no-action motion', which was a procedural mechanism used by members to vote against taking action on a specific agenda item. All were forms of politicisation whereby the Commission was used to advance objectives other than its mandated protection and promotion of human rights. Regionalism affected the Commission by groups blocking action against

---

98 See, for example, Schoenbaum, *International Relations*, p. 250.

99 Dennis, 'Human Rights in 2002', 385–6.

100 ECOSOC, 'Commission on Human Rights: Report on the Sixty-First Session', 22 April 2005, UN Doc. E/CN.4/2005/135, xiv.

101 Ghanea, 'From UN Commission on Human Rights to UN Human Rights Council', 697.

members. Inaction also occurred because political alliances exerted collective strength and influence over proceedings to protect known abusers.

Powerful states allegedly avoided scrutiny at the Commission owing to difficulties in holding them accountable for human rights abuses. Power politics played a role in ensuring that the most powerful states, especially Russia, China and the US, were able to commit violations without Commission condemnation. This was illustrated by events in the 2004 session, when a draft resolution against Russia regarding grave abuses in the Chechen Republic was rejected;[102] China successfully proposed a no-action motion on a draft resolution regarding its own record;[103] Cuba withdrew a draft resolution against the US regarding Guantanamo when it became clear that it lacked support from other states despite approval from experts.

Moss attributes the lack of action taken at the Commission to broad political relations between states.[104] He argues that even liberal democratic states failed to condemn human rights abuses in other countries where to do so could harm interstate relations. Moss comments that economic, security, religious, cultural, and other ties, prevented states from insisting upon action being taken against human rights violators.[105] In support of this argument, Moss gives the example of the US encouraging resolutions against China, Iran, Sudan and Cuba, while simultaneously refusing to condemn gross violations in countries with whom it had important relations, such as Iraq in 1989.[106]

Rule 65(2) of the Rules of Procedure of the Functional Commissions of ECOSOC[107] allowed states to circumvent country-specific resolutions by proposing a no-action motion. If passed, this precluded discussion about the substance of the draft resolution. Despite criticism of its use, the no-action motion remained, and increasingly was misused by states seeking protection from Commission scrutiny or action.[108] Rahmani-Ocora argues that state misuse of that mechanism impeded the Commission's fulfilment of its mandate, and encouraged selectivity by allowing states to block discussions on gross and systemic violations in, for example, China and Sudan.[109] Providing members with a tool for blocking action where sufficient votes could be

---

102 CHR Draft Resolution, 'Situation of Human Rights in the Republic of Chechnya of the Russian Federation', 8 April 2004, UN Doc. E/CN.4/2004/L.29, rejected by 23 votes to 12, with 18 abstentions.
103 CHR Draft Resolution, 'Situation of Human Rights in China', 9 April 2004, UN Doc. E/CN.4/2004/L.37.
104 Moss, 'Will the Human Rights Council have Better Membership', pp. 10–11.
105 *Ibid.*
106 *Ibid.*
107 ECOSOC Res. E/5975/Rev.1, 'Rules of Procedure of the Functional Commission of the Economic and Social Council', 1983, UN Doc. E/5975/Rev.1
108 cf. Lempinen, *The United Nations Commission on Human Rights and the Different Treatment of Governments*, pp. 159–66.
109 Rahmani-Ocora, 'Giving the Emperor Real Clothes', 16.

garnered encouraged abuser states to take collective action protecting each other. Misuse of this mechanism by known violators was arguably inevitable once such states had gained membership.

Human Rights Watch Executive Director Roth criticised the Commission's inaction:

> Abusive governments can usually be counted on to reject efforts to criticize other abusive governments. For example, each year when China lobbies against condemnation of its repressive rule it can count on a sympathetic ear from the many other abusive countries on the com-mission. [. . .] That, in part, is why, even in the aftermath of the 1989 Tiananmen Square crackdown, the commission never mustered enough votes to condemn China, and why the Iraqi dictator Saddam Hussein could gas and execute tens of thousands of Kurds with impunity before his ill-fated invasion of Kuwait.[110]

NGOs viewed inaction with frustration, arguing that the Commission had become a forum for legitimising human rights abuses rather than to take action against such situations. Another respected NGO, Reporters Without Borders, was similarly critical of the Commission's inaction. In its 2003 report, that NGO criticised the political allegiances that blocked the Com-mission from taking needed action against Russia, Zimbabwe, Sudan, Cuba, and Iran, for example, where gross violations of human rights had occurred. It reported that NGOs had condemned the 2002 session, but then commented that 2003 was even worse.[111] Inaction arose from politicisation of the Com-mission and misuse of its procedures. As a result of that politicisation, the body increasingly was unable to fulfil its mandate.

1.2.3 Country-specific issues

Country-specific discussions were introduced to allow the Commission to deal with specific human rights situations. Such discussions and resolutions allowed the Commission to focus on gross and systemic situations and gener-ally poor human rights practices within one state. Despite heavy criticism, that practice led to human rights improvements within some states. The Working Group on Chile, for example, resulted in greater protection from human rights abuses such as enforced disappearances. However, successes tended to occur where a state sought assistance, as was the case with Chile, or where a state was politically isolated and had few allies to shield it from scrutiny, as occurred with South Africa during apartheid. Since the Com-mission's demise, some observers have continued to express support for its

110 Roth, 'Despots Pretending to Spot and Shame Despots'.
111 J.C. Buhrer, 'UN Commission on Human Rights Loses All Credibility', *Reporters Without Borders*, 2003.

country-specific mechanisms. Scannella and Splinter comment that some governments and many NGOs regarded country-specific mechanisms as fundamental to the Commission's work.[112]

There has been some defence of these resolutions, including a recent study by Lebovic and Voeten examining which states were the targets of country-specific resolutions in the years following the Cold War.[113] Lebovic and Voeten conclude that country-specific resolutions resulted from Commission members seeking governmental accountability regarding human rights norms. The problem with their argument is that many Commission members were themselves not upholding the norms and standards that they officially sought to promote through country-specific resolutions. Indeed, Lebovic and Voeten's argument becomes untenable when examining the human rights records of some member states.

Lebovic and Voeten's study seeks to prove that, using country-specific mechanisms, 'the Commission went after the worst offenders' in the post-Cold War years.[114] Indeed the authors argue that country-specific resolutions were not used primarily to pursue political objectives, but that the Commission targeted states due to their human rights practices rather than according to national political motivations. Of course, states targeted under this mechanism can be shown to have committed human rights abuses, but so had many other countries that were not subject to that scrutiny. Lempinen documents instances of the Commission's late action, including on Idi Amin's Uganda and Saddam Hussein's Iraq, as well as its refusal to deal with certain gross and systemic violations, for example in Zimbabwe.[115] Powerful states such as China, Russia and the US blocked the Commission from scrutinising their own human rights records. Moreover, grave situations in many other states – such as Cote d'Ivoire, Libya, and Sri Lanka – flew under the Commission's radar altogether. Delegates articulated valid human rights reasons for targeting specific states, but it is naïve to take at face value the rationales put forward by governments, especially those which altogether ignored other similar or graver situations. Governments' official positions for seeking country-specific resolutions must be read alongside their national policies and objectives. Moreover, even where the Commission did target known abusers, that does not entail the conclusion that all, or even most, abusers were targeted.

Lebovic and Voeten attribute the rise in country-specific resolutions in the 1990s to the emergence of new states following the USSR's dissolution. Many of the new states still had oppressive governments that failed to comply with international human rights standards. The number of country-specific

---

112 P. Scannella and P. Splinter, 'The United Nations Human Rights Council: A Promise to be Fulfilled', *Human Rights Law Review*, Vol. 7 (1), 2007, 50.

113 Lebovic and Voeten, 'The Politics of Shame', 861–88.

114 Lebovic and Voeten, 'The Politics of Shame', 884.

115 Lempinen, *The United Nations Commission on Human Rights and the Different Treatment of Governments*, pp. 146–58.

resolutions rose in order to deal with this increase in the number of states with gross and systemic violations. The authors fail to deal with the more obvious reason for the rise in country-specific resolutions, namely that, following the end of the Cold War, states and groups used this mechanism to demonstrate their strength during the power struggles occurring within the new international atmosphere.

The authors argue that a country's record for repression directly impacted upon whether it was punished by the Commission. However, they fail to deal with those countries that were not targeted at all, choosing only to look at the ones that were raised at the Commission's sessions. Therefore, the authors do not deal with the biased motives for selecting certain states for country-specific resolutions yet simultaneously ignoring other similar, grave situations. Similarly, they recognise that the Commission failed to deal with human rights abuses in known abuser states, but defend it by arguing that the country-specific mechanisms were used against some known abusers.[116] This argument misses the point that use of the mechanisms was politicised and selective, as only a small number of known abuser states were targeted. 'In practice the Human Rights Commission advanced only with studied caution beyond Southern Africa and the territories occupied by Israel'.[117] The Commission's selection of a few states was inadequate as the body altogether ignored so many other human rights abusers.

Support for country-specific resolutions was not widespread. Despite some scholarship, such as Lebovic and Voeten's study, it has widely been accepted that states did indeed often misuse that procedure to attack countries for political purposes. Two main criticisms of that mechanism led to two very different approaches about its contribution to the Commission's demise. One argument, proposed mainly by Western states, NGOs and observers, is that this mechanism was used for political purposes to take a disproportionate amount of action against politically isolated states.[118] The other argument, put forward by China and its allies in the Like-Minded Group, an alliance of developing nations led by China, criticised this mechanism as a neo-colonial tool used against developing nations. Both views will be further explored as weaknesses contributing to the Commission's demise.

Donnelly echoes other writers in observing that 'certain countries are singled out, for partisan purposes, to the exclusion of other, no less reprehensible regimes'.[119] Use of country-specific discussions and resolutions to attack particular states was exemplified through their use against Israel. Although most observers recognise serious human rights problems in the

116 Lebovic and Voeten, 'The Politics of Shame', 884.
117 Farer and Gaer, 'At the End of the Beginning', 276.
118 For example, Franck examines issues of double standards, in particular regarding the Commission's treatment of Israel (Franck, 'Of Gnats and Camels: Is there a Double Standard at the United Nations?', 819–25).
119 J. Donnelly, 'Human Rights at the United Nations 1955–85: The Question of Bias', *International Studies Quarterly*, Vol. 32 (3), 1988, 288.

Israeli Occupied Territories, politicisation in this regard occurred to emphasise strength of feeling against that country. In particular, many states favoured the return of occupied territories to Syria and the creation of a Palestinian state. The disproportionate focus on Israel ensured that the Commission spent time focusing on that one state in order to shield other countries from scrutiny owing to limited time at Commission sessions.

Dennis noted that:

> Israel remains the only country that is subjected to multiple resolutions and for which a rapporteur has an open-ended mandate (all the other mandates are for one year). It is also the only UN member that remains barred from a seat on the Commission (or any other UN body except the General Assembly) since it is not a member of a regional group.[120]

Israel has been denied membership of the Asian Group by Arab members of that group. Although Israel was afforded temporary membership of the Western European and Others Group in 2000, conditions of that membership include not seeking membership of key rotating seats at bodies including ECOSOC and the Human Rights Council. Therefore, despite known abusers having the opportunity to sit on the Security Council, hold membership of other UN bodies, and generally participate in international affairs, Israel is effectively excluded from those bodies where membership is proportionately distributed amongst the regional groups. As a result, Israel is regularly reproached in international institutions, especially through bodies, such as the Commission, where it is effectively barred from membership.

Ghanea argues that the only countries targeted under country-specific resolutions were those sufficiently removed from global and regional alliances as to allow the international community to take a strong position against them without serious repercussions in interstate relations.[121] Power and influence was used to focus the Commission's attention disproportionately on one state, whilst deflecting attention away from other abusers. Misuse in this manner was heavily criticised by observers, for example Scannella and Splinter argue that politicisation and selectivity, two of the Commission's main flaws, were at the heart of country-specific discussions.[122] These characteristics took precedence over human rights issues during country-specific considerations.

The second criticism of country-specific resolutions came from developing states who argued that the resolutions were used by powerful, Western states to ostracise and oppress developing nations. Alston comments that developing countries, led by China, actively sought to eliminate country-specific

---

120 Dennis, 'Human Rights in 2002', 384.
121 Ghanea, 'From UN Commission on Human Rights to UN Human Rights Council', 697.
122 Scannella and Splinter, 'The United Nations Human Rights Council: A Promise to be Fulfilled', 45.

resolutions.[123] The Like-Minded Group viewed country-specific resolutions as a form of oppression used by the 'West against the rest'.[124] Lempinen demonstrates that the West was the main initiator of country-specific resolutions and that 'the rest' were disproportionately targeted.[125] However, the reasons for this go beyond simply applying a post-colonial discourse, and include, for example, the fact that human rights violations occur more frequently, and with more gravity, in developing than developed states.[126]

China, deploying a Third World discourse, encouraged her allies, especially developing and ex-colonial states, to join China's fight against powerful, rich countries seeking to repress poorer, weaker states. China reasoned that use of country-specific resolutions against developing states was made worse because that mechanism had been introduced, ostensibly, to enable developing nations to fight human rights violations by colonial powers.[127] That discourse was taken up by other states from the South, including Pakistan, Egypt and Cuba,[128] who complained that developing nations were 'the defendants' in the Commission.[129]

Despite China's reasoning, and the support of at least some states who took a post-colonial approach,[130] China's position against the West, specifically the US, arguably resulted from an ongoing power struggle. China's statement to the Commission in 1997 alleged that, since the Cold War, almost all of the country resolutions focused on developing nations.[131] China commented that this caused resentment because Western countries themselves had terrible historic human rights records, so they ought not to judge developing nations. It further argued that Western nations are responsible for world poverty which leads to human rights violations. China proposed that the Commission should encourage democracy, not impose it, and that it should abide by principles of equality and mutual respect through dialogue and cooperation, not allow bullying and oppression by dominant strong states.[132] China's arguments not only attacked Western states, but also sought to weaken the

123 Alston, 'Reconceiving the UN Human Rights Regime', 196.

124 *Ibid.*, 203–5.

125 Lempinen, *The United Nations Commission on Human Rights and the Different Treatment of Governments*, pp. 167–72.

126 Ramcharan, 'Strategies for the International Protection of Human Rights in the 1990s', 271.

127 R. Wheeler, 'The United Nations Commission on Human Rights, 1982–1997: A Study of "Targeted" Resolutions', *Canadian Journal of Political Science*, Vol. 32 (1), 1999, 75–6; Steiner, Alston, and Goodman, *International Human Rights*, p. 754.

128 See, for example, Alston, 'Reconceiving the UN Human Rights Regime', pp. 205–6.

129 For Cuban delegate's oral remarks, see CHR, 'Commission on Human Rights Opens Sixty-First Session', 14 March 2005, UN Doc. HR/CN/1107.

130 Franck examines the transposition of Western human rights laws on non-Western states, exploring issues of such human rights laws in developing nations (T.M. Franck, *Human Rights in Third World Perspective*, Dobbs Ferry, NY: Oceana Publications Inc, 1982).

131 Steiner, Alston and Goodman, *International Human Rights*, p. 791.

132 *Ibid.*, pp. 791–2.

application of universal human rights, thus undermining the Commission's work and mandate.

Powerful states had long used country-specific resolutions for political motives. Alongside allegations of neo-colonialism was the proposition that powerful countries used this mechanism to further Cold War political agendas. The US attacked Cuba both during and after the Cold War. The USSR focused on US allies, such as Chile, while ignoring graver situations within the Soviet Union itself. Despite diverging views on the misuse of country-specific resolutions, the main criticisms attacked their selective and politicised use. Misuse of country-specific considerations undermined the Commission's role and function. States' misuse of this mechanism to achieve political aims affected the body's credibility and ability to fulfil its mandate.

1.2.4 *Commission's lack of resources*

A main Commission flaw was insufficient time allocated to deal with human rights issues. The Commission held one annual six-week session during which it dealt with increasing numbers of agenda items each year due to emergence of ever more human rights issues. The volume of agenda items precluded many members from participating in all discussions owing to delegations lacking resources to engage with all of the matters raised. Moreover, the Commission's annual session was criticised for being too brief. Scannella and Splinter emphasise the impact of insufficient time on the Commission's work.[133] Sessions did not allow sufficient time to address all items on the agenda, let alone to deal adequately with the issues raised.

The Commission was ill-equipped to respond to human rights crises as it was not a standing body with its own permanent resources. Crisis situations could not adequately be addressed, and sometimes could not even be raised, at an already packed regular session. Indeed, Rahmani-Ocora comments that the Commission could not devote sufficient time or attention even to preventative measures and strategies.[134] In 1990, the Commission was given the possibility of intersessional meetings,[135] but this rarely occurred in practice; only four intersessionals were convened during the 15 years that the mechanism existed.[136]

---

133 Scannella and Splinter, 'The United Nations Human Rights Council: A Promise to be Fulfilled', 46.

134 Rahmani-Ocora, 'Giving the Emperor Real Clothes', 16.

135 ECOSOC Resolution 1990/48, 'Enlargement of the Commission on Human Rights and the Further Promotion of Human Rights and Fundamental Freedoms', 25 May 1990, UN Doc. E/CN.4/1990/94, authorised the Commission to agree by majority to meet exceptionally for special sessions in order to be able to deal with urgent and acute human rights situations.

136 It met in 1992 regarding the situation in the former Yugoslavia; in 1994 regarding Rwanda; in 1999 regarding East Timor; in 2000 regarding the Palestinian people.

It could be argued that the overwhelming amount of human rights issues presented to the Commission impeded its work. A different approach was taken by Human Rights Watch's Executive Director Roth who suggested that the problem was not a lack of resources, but rather politicisation and the refusal of some states to engage with the Commission and the resources that body made available:

> Abusive governments have become quite creative in proposing 'reforms' that would impair the commission's ability to generate pressure on behalf of human rights [. . .] The abusive governments that flock to the commission frequently refuse to cooperate with UN investigators. Cuba refused for years to allow a visit by the rapporteur assigned to monitor its human rights record. China and Algeria are stonewalling on requests for visits by the rapporteur on torture. Russia has blocked visits to Chechnya by the rapporteurs on torture and extrajudicial execution. The most egregious case was Sudan. When a rapporteur denounced its violations of religious freedom, it called him an 'enemy of Islam'. Yet Sudan was later rewarded for this rejectionism with the deputy chairmanship of the commission.[137]

That position demonstrates that the impact of the Commission's insufficient resources on its ability to fulfil its mandate was often made worse by those countries who were most worried about becoming focal points of its work. Scarce resources coupled with politicisation resulted in a level of inaction that was heavily criticised in the Commission's final years.

1.2.5   Regionalism

Politicisation in the form of regionalism occurred throughout the Commission's existence, but was a growing concern during the body's later years owing to it increasingly overshadowing the Commission's proceedings and work. Regionalism has been identified as one of the Commission's main problems.[138] Rahmani-Ocora comments that the body 'came to resemble a club where friendships easily overlooked wrongdoing'.[139]

Humphrey recounts that such politicisation took place even during the Commission's first session.[140] He notes that the Cold War had already started 'and all the uncertainties inherent in a new undertaking were compounded by political controversy and recrimination'. According to Dennis, regionalism occurred at the Commission throughout the Cold War.[141] He argues that

137 Roth, 'Despots Pretending to Spot and Shame Despots'.
138 cf. H. Tolley, *The U.N. Commission on Human Rights*, Boulder, CO: Westview Press, 1987, pp. 199–203.
139 Rahmani-Ocora, 'Giving the Emperor Real Clothes', 16.
140 Humphrey, *A Great Adventure*, p. 24.
141 Dennis, 'Human Rights in 2002', 374.

Western states pushed for liberal, democratic institutions that mirrored their political ideology, whereas Communist states, following a Marxist discourse, viewed capitalism as the main source of human rights violations. That division still exists in the UN human rights machinery, although it now takes the form of a North–South divide.

Weiss argues that during the Cold War, developing nations would stand at the sidelines, supporting whichever superpower appeared to be winning.[142] Indeed some developing states' political affiliations led them to participate actively in the Cold War. The result, according to Weiss, was 'mainly a shouting match' with little emphasis placed on providing practical assistance for national human rights issues.

The Commission was accused of allowing ever greater politicisation through regional politics. After the Cold War, regionalism focused solely on protecting group members from scrutiny. Wheeler, commenting on resolutions about grave situations, reports on regional pressure to protect group members.[143] He notes that Commission members were regularly encouraged, especially by regional allies, to vote against resolutions. Harris cites examples of regional politics protecting states such as Libya, Sudan and Zimbabwe, enabling them to become members and indeed leaders at the Commission.[144] The impact of those states gaining membership went further than affecting the body's credibility, extending to affect NGOs working in those countries. Regionalism impacted on the Commission and also on the ability to protect and promote human rights on the ground in grave situations.

Scannella and Splinter describe regionalism at the Commission as conducting business using regional groups and other blocs.[145] The impact on Commission proceedings resulted in the lowest common denominator being reached within each group, and then a further lowest common denominator negotiated between the groups. The authors cite the Commission's final session as a 'pathetic illustration' of regionalism whereby work 'was negotiated through regional groups and was totally devoid of substance'.[146]

Schrijver sets out the Commission's main regional alliances in its latter years in terms of politicisation of that body.[147] He identifies the importance of The Group of 77, the Non-Aligned Movement, and the Organisation of the Islamic Conference (OIC) as newer groups opposing the established European Union or the Western bloc. Weiss notes that India and the Philippines, both

---

142 Weiss, *What's Wrong with the United Nations*, pp. 63–4.
143 Wheeler, 'The United Nations Commission on Human Rights, 1982–1997', 81.
144 H. Harris, 'The Politics of Depoliticization: International Perspectives on the Human Rights Council', *Human Rights Brief*, Vol. 13 (3), 2006, 8–9.
145 Scannella and Splinter, 'The United Nations Human Rights Council: A Promise to be Fulfilled', 68–9.
146 *Ibid.*
147 Schrijver, 'A "New Society of the Committed"', 812.

during and after Marcos's rule, constantly opposed initiatives which placed protection of individuals over state sovereignty, seeking to encourage alliances between developing nations and promote the collective Southern agenda of avoiding human rights criticisms from Western nations.[148] Schrijver similarly argues that the Commission's increased politicisation resulted in almost regional battles of 'the Rest against the West'.[149] Dennis, writing about the 2002 Commission session where the US was an observer for the first time, also singles out The Group of 77 as demonstrating regionalism, observing that many members supported Cuba's position on resolutions out of solidarity with that state rather than based on the resolution itself.[150] Weiss similarly comments that Latin American states sought to shield Cuba, and other repressive Latin American regimes, from Commission scrutiny.[151]

Regionalism did not just occur in relation to groups and blocs from the Global South. Western states significantly contributed to the rise of regionalism at the Commission. After the adoption, in 1993, of the require-ment for a common foreign policy, the EU's ability to negotiate and compromise with other groups and blocs was significantly reduced. That common foreign policy required all EU member states to adhere to an often fragile compromise between members of that bloc.[152] As a result, positions taken by the EU were difficult to amend within the Commission without revisiting internal group discussions. Although the EU did not abuse its group tactics by advancing political agendas in direct conflict with the Com-mission's mandate, the impact of the common foreign policy was significant at the Commission. By closing the door to negotiations with non-EU members, that bloc paved the way for other groups and blocs to adopt similar, if less needed, tactics.

The impact of regionalism, according to Roth, was to create a farcical body where human rights abusers used alliances to block scrutiny:

> [A] mafia-like code of silence reigns in Geneva, with one abuser covering for another, knowing that, when necessary, the favor will be reciprocated. It would be a mistake to attribute responsibility for this sorry state of affairs to the United Nations itself. Secretary-General Kofi Annan and the human rights commissioner, Mary Robinson, have spoken out with unprecedented candor on behalf of human rights. Rather, blame lies with the member states, the governments that allow this farce to continue year after year.[153]

148 Weiss, *What's Wrong with the United Nations*, pp. 37–8.
149 Schrijver, 'A "New Society of the Committed"', 812.
150 Dennis, 'Human Rights in 2002', 366.
151 Weiss, *What's Wrong with the United Nations*, pp. 37–8.
152 U. Khaliq, *Ethical Dimensions of the Foreign Policy of the European Union: A Legal Appraisal*, Cambridge: Cambridge University Press, 2008, pp. 88–9.
153 Roth, 'Despots Pretending to Spot and Shame Despots'.

Regionalism may attract heavy criticism, but any political body consisting of proportionate geographic representation will find that its members divide into regional groups and alliances. However, those groupings become a problem when they are misused by their own member states. Regionalism is a form of power struggle, and also a method by which states with similar positions on issues can support each other. Regionalism is a form of politicisation. Commission mechanisms, such as the no-action motion, allowed regionalism to dominate proceedings and to politicise that body to such an extent as to attract severe criticism from states and observers.

2 Reforming the UN principal Charter-based human rights body

2.1. Reform proposals

Reforms were proposed, and implemented, at various points throughout the Commission's existence. More concerted reform efforts occurred during its final decade. Focus on human rights magnified after the Cold War. Previously, human rights issues were used as a pawn in that conflict or were marginalised as security issues were prioritised. Intensified attention on human rights ensured that major Commission reform became a key goal for certain states and observers. Debate on major criticisms of the Commission was ignited after the US failed in its 2001 re-election bid. Those discussions paved the way for increasing numbers of more concrete reform proposals.

Proposals were generated through various methods during the Commission's final years. The UN as a whole was debating reform proposals as the organisation neared its 60th anniversary. The Secretary General set out more specific proposals regarding the Commission, as part of these general reforms. Of course, there were states, non-state actors, and observers, including legal scholars, who set out complementary or competing proposals. Reform proposals occurred within a relatively short timeframe, providing impetus for change that had not previously existed, despite reform discussions being part of the public discourse for some time.[1]

Reform proposals are key to understanding the Council because they demonstrate the main issues to be dealt with in disbanding the Commission and creating the Council.[2] Some radical proposals display the impetus for definitive change that could have altered the UN human rights machinery. However, many reform proposals were ignored or diluted, leaving issues unresolved, much to the Council's detriment. Reform proposals will be examined in three stages: recurring Commission reforms, general UN reform proposals affecting the Commission, and specific proposals that led to the HRC's creation.

1 P. Alston, 'Reconceiving the UN Human Rights Regime: Challenges Confronting the New UN Human Rights Council', *Melbourne Journal of International Law*, Vol. 7, 2006, 223.
2 cf. F.J. Hampson, 'An Overview of the Reform of the UN Human Rights Machinery', *Human Rights Law Review*, Vol. 7 (1), 2007, 7–27.

2.1.1 *Recurring reforms*

Over six decades the Commission underwent major reforms. The changes included increased membership and new mechanisms. Reform processes were not always coherent; instead they often occurred on an ad hoc basis. The body, therefore, was not always in a position to consider fully, or to be able to implement, the reforms at the time when they were proposed. As a result, not all reform proposals were acted upon; even where to do so would have improved that body's work. Ghanea observes that reform of the Commission had taken place at the body for some time, but that those reforms had been sporadic and focused on procedural issues rather than dealing with the salient issues.[3]

One main reform that did take place was expansion of the Commission's membership. The Commission originally had 18 members. As the organisation expanded, so too did its membership. States were keen to be involved at the Commission, reflecting both the importance of its work, but also states' reticence to relinquish control over domestic human rights issues to a few, non-geographically representative countries. Alston notes that the Commission membership expanded gradually, with each increase citing the need for more equitable geographic representation.[4] Increased membership allowed a cross-section of political systems to gain access to the Commission. Failure to increase membership, especially as the Commission predominantly consisted of Western states, would have appeared as attempts by developed states to interfere with the internal affairs of newly self-determined nations.

Increased membership had negative impacts on the body's work. Representation of various cultures and systems made the Commission's work more difficult, owing to competing positions being taken by governments on human rights issues. Politicisation increased with the number of members, as more national agendas were brought into proceedings. Regionalism increased, as the more members there were, the more countries belonged to groups and alliances. Tolley described Commission efforts at institutional developments as 'largely futile' due to 'irreconcilable differences between the blocs about both means and ends'.[5]

Two procedural reforms had significant impact both on the Commission's work and on its demise. Two separate complaints mechanisms were created: the 1235 Procedure in 1967[6] and the 1503 Procedure in

---

3   N. Ghanea, 'From UN Commission on Human Rights to UN Human Rights Council: One Step Forwards or Two Steps Sideways?', *International and Comparative Law Quarterly*, Vol. 55 (3), 2006, 695.

4   P. Alston, 'The Commission on Human Rights', in P. Alston (ed.), *The United Nations and Human Rights, A Critical Appraisal*, Oxford: Clarendon Press, 1992, p. 194.

5   H. Tolley, *The U.N. Commission on Human Rights*, Boulder, CO: Westview Press, 1987, p. 154.

6   'In 1967 the Commission was empowered to investigate human rights practices in individual states without their permission, through confidential complaints being made under the 1235 Procedure'. See Chapter 1, Section 1.1.3.

1970.[7] The 1235 Procedure authorised the Commission to hold an annual, public debate on country-specific violations (para. 1). The ECOSOC Resolution establishing the Procedure authorised the Commission to examine information on 'gross' human rights violations (para. 2), and to respond to situations with a 'consistent pattern' of abuses (para. 3). That language, first mentioned in Resolution 1235, increasingly became central to the Commission's mission and to human rights generally. Although there is no legally defined category of 'gross and systemic' human rights violations,[8] the language has widely been used when identifying particularly grave human rights situations. ECOSOC Resolution 1503 enabled confidential complaints to be made about 'a consistent pattern of gross' violations committed by a state (para. 1). The 1503 Procedure authorised the Commission to undertake country-specific investigations where necessary (paras 6 and 7).

These procedural developments allowed the Commission to circumscribe the original decision, in 1947, not to take action on, nor complaints relating to, country-specific human rights. At the Commission's outset, Western states had insisted that focusing on individual states would undermine the Commission's work and could result in bias and politicisation. Many of those states were themselves imperial powers which, arguably, sought to avoid scrutiny of violations occurring within their colonies. As the Commission expanded to include decolonised states, the body faced increasing pressure to address country-specific human rights violations and condemn colonial abuses. Scholars have attributed creation of the 1235 and 1503 Procedures to that pressure from new developing nations supported by Eastern European states.[9] As weak states, these countries required tools to counter human rights violations, especially in Southern Africa. ECOSOC Resolution 1235 referred to 'the policy of apartheid' and identifying the government of South Africa in two out of six paragraphs. The procedures were created 'to pursue the struggle against racist and colonialist policies'.[10] Many developing states used a post-colonial discourse to underscore the struggle between nations and their former empirical masters. The 1235 and 1503 procedures allowed public scrutiny of violations committed by colonial powers in the developing world. Indeed, these mechanisms were seen as providing tools to be used in power struggles by new, weak states against established, powerful nations.

---

7 'The 1503 Procedure, created in 1970, went further. It enabled a confidential complaints procedure open to states, NGOs and individuals'. See Chapter 1, Section 1.1.3.

8 cf. H. Rombouts, *Victims Organizations and the Politics of Reparations: A Case Study on Rwanda*, London: Intersentia, 2004, p. 10.

9 cf. R. Wheeler, 'The United Nations Commission on Human Rights, 1982–1997: A Study of "Targeted" Resolutions', *Canadian Journal of Political Science*, Vol. 32 (1), 1999, 75–6.

10 H.J. Steiner, P. Alston and R. Goodman, *International Human Rights in Context*, 3rd edn., Oxford: Oxford University Press, 2008, p. 754.

Scrutiny extended to all states, not just colonial territories, at the insistence of Western nations who sought to deflect the spotlight away from colonial practices.[11] Western states also sought to ensure that the Commission scrutinised human rights violations occurring within decolonised states which, typically, had limited capabilities for human rights compliance. Ultimately the Special Procedures system stemmed from individual mandates established under those procedures. These mechanisms were eventually misused, with politicisation, bias and selectivity, particularly prevalent with regard to the country-specific mandates established under the 1503 Procedure.

Several states and observers insisted that the UN and its organs should be used to enable emerging nations in their struggle against oppressive powers and assist in their capacity-building, as opposed to focusing on criticising underdeveloped national human rights systems. UN emphasis on capacity-building took hold in the 1990s, and increasing provision of assistance with capacity-building has continued since that time. Former High Commissioner for Human Rights, Mary Robinson, insisted that capacity-building was key for preventing human rights violations.[12] The United Nations Development Programme defines capacity-building as 'the process through which individuals, organizations and societies obtain, strengthen and maintain the capabilities to set and achieve their own development objectives over time'.[13] Capacity-building provides a strong mechanism through which states may exercise their right to development.[14] Known human rights abusers, however, have increasingly called for 'capacity-building' in order to avoid scrutiny by UN human rights bodies, as will be explored in Chapter 8 with regard to Sudan.

Another major reform proposal resulted in the Office of the High Commissioner for Human Rights being created. The 1993 World Conference in Vienna appointed a UN High Commissioner for Human Rights. Secretary-General Boutros Boutros-Ghali reminded the conference of the desperate need for a concerted response to various, but poorly coordinated, UN procedures. Appointment of the UNHCHR led to reform of the Department for Human Rights (now called OHCHR).

Citing the Capacity Study,[15] Smithers argues that piecemeal reform, due to a lack of general reform, tends to do an international organisation more

11　T.J. Farer and F.D. Gaer, 'The UN and Human Rights: At the End of the Beginning', in A. Roberts and B. Kingsbury (eds.), *United Nations, Divided World*, 2nd edn., Oxford: Oxford University Press, 1993, p. 274.

12　Mary Robinson, 'Human Rights: Challenges for the 21st Century', *First Annual Dag Hammarskjöld Lecture*, Uppsala, Sweden, 1 October 1998.

13　United Nations Development Programme, 'Capacity Development Practice Note', May 2008, 4–5, (Online). Available HTTP: <http://www.undp.org/oslocentre/docs08/sofia/CD%20PN%20May%202008.pdf> (accessed 22 July 2012).

14　cf. D. Eade, *Capacity-Building: An Approach to People-centred Development*, Oxford: Oxfam UK & Ireland, 1997.

15　R.G.A. Jackson, *A Study of the Capacity of the United Nations Development System*, (2 volumes), Geneva: United Nations, 1969.

damage than good.[16] Commission reforms occurred in a haphazard manner, reflecting the body's many tensions, not least due to growth in UN membership. Reforms occurred in response to UN and international political change, rather than as part of a coherent framework. Rahmani-Ocora comments that the Commission debated a range of reform proposals but did not implement reforms that could effectively impact upon the body's work.[17] That failure led to the Secretary-General's suggestion that the Commission be disbanded and replaced by a new UN human rights body.

2.1.2 *Inclusion of Commission in general UN reform proposals*

Reforming the UN was an oft-raised issue between 1996 and 2006. Schrijver notes that reforming the Commission became part of those general UN reform discussions.[18] Reforming the Commission was discussed although, as Gutter notes, the objective was not to replace the body.[19] Debate focused on the need to depoliticise the Commission's work in order to allow better fulfilment of the body's mandate. Commission politicisation and its use by members to advance national political agendas had become a recognised problem. Despite a lack of coherent reform strategies for the Commission, Steiner *et al.* note that support for the Commission was limited to a very small number of states and NGOs.[20] As a result, the Commission's 'death knell soon started to be heard'.[21] Lack of support for the Commission indicated that reform proposals were insufficient, and that attention should focus on Commission abolition and creation of a new body.

Secretary-General Kofi Annan gave a speech to the General Assembly in September 2003 in which he recognised need for reforms on the UN collective security mandate.[22] Annan identified that collective security was inherently linked with, amongst others, 'development and poverty eradication [and] the struggle for human rights, democracy and good governance'.[23] In order to implement UN reforms, Annan established a High Level Panel on Threats, Challenges and Change in 2003. He insisted that the Panel was needed to

---

16 (Sir) P. Smithers, 'Towards Greater Coherence Among Intergovernmental Organizations Through Governmental Control', in B. Andemicael (ed.), *Regionalism and the United Nations*, Dobbs Ferry, NY: Oceana Publications Ltd, 1979, p. 32.

17 L. Rahmani-Ocora, 'Giving the Emperor Real Clothes: The UN Human Rights Council', *Global Governance*, Vol. 12 (1), 2006, 16.

18 N. Schrijver, 'The UN Human Rights Council: A New "Society of the Committed" or Just Old Wine in New Bottles', *Leiden Journal of International Law*, Vol. 20 (4), 2007, 812.

19 J. Gutter, *Thematic Procedures of the United Nations Commission on Human Rights and International Law: In Search of a Sense of Community*, Antwerp: Intersentia, 2006, pp. 93–4.

20 Steiner *et al.*, *International Human Rights*, p. 814.

21 *Ibid.*

22 The Secretary-General Address to the General Assembly, New York, 23 September 2003, UN Doc. A/58/PV.7, (Online). Available HTTP: <http://www.un.org/webcast/ga/58/statements/sg2eng030923.htm> (accessed 22 July 2012).

23 *Ibid.*, 2.

'assess current threats to international peace and security; to evaluate how our existing policies and institutions have done in addressing those threats; and to make recommendations for strengthening the United Nations'.[24] After the 2001 attacks on the World Trade Centre in New York City, in a political atmosphere dominated by terrorism issues, global security had become an area with wide-reaching consequences for human rights. The High Level Panel was an appropriate place to discuss human rights due to its relationship with security issues at that time. 'Collective security for all' refers as much to human rights violations as to war and terrorism. Discussions reflected the change in UN focus from interstate war, after the Second World War, to recognition of other global issues, such as human rights, that impacted upon states' collective security.

The idea for the Commission's replacement with the Human Rights Council was originally a Swiss initiative that began to be developed after the Commission's 59th Session. The Swiss government asked the Bern Institute of Public Law to produce reform proposals regarding the UN human rights body.[25] Walter Kälin and Cecilia Jimenez produced a draft proposal which contained the idea of creating a Human Rights Council to replace the Commission.[26] A proposal to that effect was put forward by Swiss Ambassador Calmy-Rey at the body's 60th Session.[27]

The Swiss initiative was discussed by the High Level Panel but was reported not to have been unanimously accepted by states or non-state actors.[28] Scannella and Splinter assert that some states viewed it as an opportunity to strengthen and improve the UN human rights machinery.[29] Others viewed the proposal as a potential risk to the UN's principal human rights body which had continuously developed throughout the UN's existence.

In 2004 the Panel published its report 'A More Secure World: Our Shared Responsibility'.[30] Although the Panel did not formally recommend the Commission's abolition, Ghanea traces the Council's creation to that report, arguing that it signalled the end of the Commission.[31] The report stated that the

24 Report of the High Level Panel on Threats, Challenges and Change, 'A More Secure World: Our Shared Responsibility', Note by the Secretary-General, 2 December 2004, UN Doc. A/59/565, para. 3.
25 W.A. Brülhart, 'From a Swiss Initiative to a United Nations Proposal (from 2003 until 2005)', in L. Müller (ed.), *The First 365 Days of the United Nations Human Rights Council*, Switzerland: Baden, 2007, p. 16.
26 *Ibid.*
27 Oral Statement of Swiss Ambassador Calmy-Rey, 'Commission on Human Rights Sixtieth Session: Summary Record of the 4th Meeting', 17 March 2004, UN Doc. E/CN.4/2004/SR.4.
28 P. Scannella and P. Splinter, 'The United Nations Human Rights Council: A Promise to be Fulfilled', *Human Rights Law Review*, Vol. 7 (1), 2007, 68–9.
29 *Ibid.*
30 Report of the High Level Panel on Threats, Challenges and Change, UN Doc. A/59/565.
31 Ghanea, 'From UN Commission on Human Rights to UN Human Rights Council', 698.

Commission had lost credibility and professionalism[32] and noted that 'in recent years States have sought membership of the Commission not to strengthen human rights but to protect themselves against criticism or to criticize others'.[33] However, rather than recommending its abolition, the report called for reform of the Commission.[34] In particular, it recommended expansion of the Commission to universal membership[35] in order to deal with the various criticisms regarding that body's membership. Moreover, it further proposed that all Commission members 'designate prominent and experienced human rights figures as the heads of their delegations',[36] which directly addressed criticisms regarding state delegates. Gutter notes that various recommendations were put forward on which no consensus could be found.[37] Alston comments that the High Level Panel chose not to set membership criteria despite the many issues raised regarding the Commission's membership.[38] The High Level Panel determined that membership criteria would not solve these issues, and they regarded setting membership criteria as risking further politicisation.

The High Level Panel, having noted the Commission's decreasing credibility, accused the body of failing to fulfil its mandate. Owing to the integral problems at the Commission, including its double standards and lack of professionalism, the Panel discussed its abolition and replacement.[39] Crucially, the report did not recommend the Commission's abolition and replacement with a Human Rights Council, but instead simply encouraged states to, in the longer term, 'consider upgrading the Commission to become a "Human Rights Council" that is no longer subsidiary to the Economic and Social Council but a Charter body'.[40]

Reforming the Commission was an attractive option to those states that had used the Commission to shelter from scrutiny. Proposals for a substantially different body, where politicisation and regionalism would be marginalised, threatened to undermine those states' position within the UN human rights framework. Non-democratic and known abuser states felt threatened by the proposals, and instead advocated reforming the old body. Other states argued that the Commission was an effective body in need of reform rather than replacement. Those positions were not adopted by the majority of states, nor

32 Report of the High Level Panel on Threats, Challenges and Change, UN Doc. A/59/565, para. 283.
33 *Ibid.*, para. 283.
34 *Ibid.*, paras 284–91.
35 *Ibid.*, para. 285.
36 *Ibid.*, para. 286.
37 J. Gutter, 'Special Procedures and the Human Rights Council: Achievements and Challenges Ahead', *Human Rights Law Review*, Vol. 7 (1), 2007, 94–5.
38 Alston, 'Reconceiving the UN Human Rights Regime', 197.
39 Ghanea, 'From UN Commission on Human Rights to UN Human Rights Council', 698.
40 Report of the High Level Panel on Threats, Challenges and Change, UN Doc. A/59/565, para. 291.

indeed by the UN Secretary-General for whom creation of the Council became a priority. Despite the lack of consensus, and the Panel's failure to recommend such action in its final report, the Swiss delegation again proposed creating a Human Rights Council at the Commission's 61st Session.[41]

2.1.3 Specific proposals

At the Commission's 61st Session, Swiss Ambassador Calmy-Rey reiterated the idea of replacing the Commission with a Human Rights Council. Five days later, Kofi Annan dealt with that same topic in the 2005 report 'In Larger Freedom: Towards Security, Development and Human Rights for All'.[42] The Secretary-General argued that human rights could not become secondary to security or development issues, and must be at the fore of all UN activities. Annan emphasised the importance of human rights by reiterating its position as the third pillar of the United Nations.[43] Annan underlined the interdependence of security, development and human rights, insisting that none could be achieved without the others.[44] The report recognised the expansion of human rights within the UN system, emphasising that new and old mechanisms, such as technical support or institution building, would not succeed 'where the basic principle of protection is being actively violated'.[45] Despite dealing with various aspects of the UN human rights machinery, the strongest reform proposals were directed towards the Commission. Annan acknowledged this in a speech to the Commission the following month, saying that these were the report's 'most dramatic' proposals.[46]

Criticising the Commission's lack of credibility, Annan argued that it 'casts a shadow on the reputation of the United Nations system as a whole'.[47] The Secretary-General proposed replacing the Commission with a smaller body, a proposal in stark contrast with the High Level Panel's reform proposals for the Commission's membership to become universal. In his explanatory note[48] Annan explained that a smaller body would allow 'more focused debate and

41 Oral Statement of Swiss Ambassador Calmy-Rey, 'Commission on Human Rights Sixty-First Session: Summary Record of the 3rd Meeting', 14 March 2005, UN Doc. E/CN.4/2005/SR.3.

42 General Assembly, 'In Larger Freedom: Towards Development, Security and Human Rights for All', *Report of the Secretary-General*, 21 March 2005, UN Doc. A/59/2005.

43 *Ibid.*, para. 183.

44 *Ibid.*, para. 17.

45 *Ibid.*, para. 143.

46 Speech of Secretary-General Kofi Annan to the Commission on Human Rights, 'Reforming UN Human Rights Machinery', 7 April 2005, UN Press Release SG/SM/9808 HR/CN/1108.

47 Report of the High Level Panel on Threats, Challenges and Change, UN Doc. A/59/565, para. 182.

48 General Assembly, Addendum to 'In Larger Freedom: Towards Development, Security and Human Rights for All', *Report of the Secretary-General*, 21 March 2005, UN Doc. A/59/2005/Add.1.

discussions'.[49] It was recommended that the body be either a primary organ, equal to the Security Council and ECOSOC, or a subsidiary organ of the General Assembly. Creating a primary organ would have elevated the status of human rights within the UN, but would have presented practical difficulties, as it would have required amendments to the UN Charter.

On 20 June 2005, the Commission held informal consultations[50] with states and the High Commissioner for Human Rights[51] on the recommendations from 'In Larger Freedom' and the explanatory note. While many states supported the Commission's replacement, and the elevation of the Council to a standing body,[52] several delegations were sceptical about whether those steps would overcome the Commission's shortcomings.[53] Moreover, the view was expressed that reform of the Commission was more appropriate than its abolition.[54] Issues discussed included, amongst others, the role and functions of the proposed new body, possible new mechanisms, and the body's status and composition. Divergence of opinion was common throughout the discussions, with states frequently expressing opposed views on key issues. Those differences continued throughout negotiations on the Resolution establishing the Council, and were manifested in the body's early sessions through contrasting approaches to the Council's mandate, work and proceedings.

In 2005, the General Assembly held its 60th Session during which a High Level Plenary meeting took place. The 2005 World Summit of Heads of State and Government brought together world leaders and agreed on fundamental changes and pledges relating to the UN's mandate. The Secretary-General's explanatory note had identified key issues regarding the Council to be discussed by states and non-state actors before the 2005 World Summit.[55] Those issues included the Council's mandate and function, composition, size and whether it would be a principal or subsidiary body.

The World Summit sought to address issues within the UN human rights machinery by creating a new Human Rights Council to address 'violations of human rights, including gross and systemic violations, and make recommendations thereon'.[56] Schoenbaum insists that 'regretfully this tepid idea does not address the real problems: the hypocrisies of the U.N. Human Rights Commission'.[57]

---

49 *Ibid.*, para. 4.
50 GA; ECOSOC, 'Summary of the open-ended informal consultations held by the Commission on Human Rights pursuant to Economic and Social Council Decision 2005/217, prepared by the Chairperson of the sixty-first session of the Commission', 21 June 2005, UN Doc. A/59/847; E/2005/73.
51 *Ibid.*, para. 4.
52 *Ibid.*, para. 12.
53 *Ibid.*, para. 13.
54 *Ibid.*
55 General Assembly, Addendum to 'In Larger Freedom', paras 9–14.
56 GA Draft Res, '2005 World Summit Outcome', 20 September 2005, UN Doc. A/60/L.1, para. 159.
57 T.J. Schoenbaum, *International Relations – The Path Not Taken: Using International Law to Promote World Peace and Security*, Cambridge: Cambridge University Press, 2006, p. 277.

Indeed, little was mentioned as to the Commission's failings, nor how they would be overcome at a new body. The Human Rights Council was briefly mentioned in the World Summit's Outcome Document,[58] saying generally that its mandate would include promoting and protecting human rights and addressing situations of gross violations. The World Summit requested that the GA conduct negotiations to establish the HRC's practicalities and to create the body.[59]

Recommendations on three key areas will be examined from the years leading to the Council's creation. The three main proposal areas reflect the most severe criticisms of the Commission: membership and election, mechanisms and proceedings, and universal periodic review.

2.1.3.1 *Membership and election*

Membership issues, as already discussed, were a serious concern that undermined the Commission's credibility. It comes as no surprise, then, that a major area for reform focused on membership and elections to the new body. Alston observes that debates on the number of members, criteria, if any, for membership, and election processes, dominated the reform discussions.[60] The emphasis placed on these issues reflected the gravity of concerns of almost all states and regional groups.

One significant issue was the number of Council members. The Commission, as previously explained, had expanded from 18 to 53 states, reflecting increased UN membership. The High Level Panel recommended universal membership[61] in order to 'get rid of the politicization' and 'underscore universal commitment to the Charter'.[62] It aimed to remove attention from national political agendas and refocus it on human rights issues. Kofi Annan took the opposite approach, proposing that the Council be composed of 15 states as compared with the Commission's 53.[63] This proposal was Annan's only real dissent from the Panel's recommendations. A smaller body reflected prioritising fulfilment of mandate over power struggles and advancing national objectives. Fewer members would result in fewer national policies being represented at the body. Decreasing membership would eliminate some of the power struggles affecting the body's work. Although politics could not entirely be divorced from the body without changing its composition, the impact of national agendas could have been minimised by limiting membership to a few states. Annan's recommendation demonstrates his desire that the Council focus more on fulfilling its mandate and less on politics.

58 GA Res. 'World Summit Outcome', 24 October 2005, UN Doc. A/Res/60/1.
59 *Ibid.*, paras 158–60.
60 Alston, 'Reconceiving the UN Human Rights Regime', 189.
61 Report of the High Level Panel on Threats, Challenges and Change, 'A More Secure World: Our Shared Responsibility', Note by the Secretary-General, UN Doc. A/59/565, para. 285.
62 Ghanea, 'From UN Commission on Human Rights to UN Human Rights Council', 699–700.
63 General Assembly, 'In Larger Freedom', UN Doc. A/59/2005, para. 183.

Most states involved in the Commission's informal consultations on the creation of the Council recommended a larger membership for reasons of transparency and inclusion of developing nations.[64] However, some states supported Annan's proposals, citing issues of efficiency and effectiveness and reduction of politicisation.[65] Membership numbers were discussed by Kälin and Jimenez.[66] They noted that while a smaller body would work more efficiently, the underlying political tensions would remain. Kälin and Jimenez adopted a realist approach; disagreements would always occur between states at such a body owing to its role and functions.[67] Without legally binding powers – which was not formally recommended by anyone involved in the reform proposals – the body would remain a political arena, at times used by states to advance national aims. They recommended that membership numbers should not be altered, as they argued that a smaller membership would not produce any changes to the politicisation of the new body.

Another discussion focused on membership criteria. The High Level Panel's 2004 proposals had rejected membership criteria 'because it believed it would risk politicizing the Commission yet further'.[68] Representatives from post-colonial states or developing nations would argue that membership criteria favours one particular political system, negating the body's credibility as an international organisation. The majority of states were not in favour of election criteria,[69] or proposed that soft criteria, such as voluntary pledges and commitments, would be preferable.[70] Rahmani-Ocora argued that it would be impossible to have membership criteria as there is no single universal view of human rights, and all states could be shown to violate the UDHR in some manner.

In 2004 the US proposed that only 'real democracies' should be granted membership.[71] That proposal reflected the idea that democratic values underpin much of the field of human rights. Indeed, that view is supported by both

64 GA; ECOSOC, 'Summary of the open-ended informal consultations held by the Commission on Human Rights pursuant to Economic and Social Council Decision 2005/217, prepared by the Chairperson of the sixty-first session of the Commission', UN Doc. A/59/847; E/2005/73, paras 29–30.

65 *Ibid.*

66 W. Kälin and C. Jimenez, 'Reform of the UN Commission on Human Rights', Study Commissioned by the Swiss Ministry of Foreign Affairs (Political Division IV), Geneva: University of Bern, 30 August 2003, pp. 6–7.

67 *Ibid.*

68 Ghanea, 'From UN Commission on Human Rights to UN Human Rights Council', 699–700.

69 Rahmani-Ocora, 'Giving the Emperor Real Clothes', 17.

70 GA; ECOSOC, 'Summary of the open-ended informal consultations held by the Commission on Human Rights pursuant to Economic and Social Council Decision 2005/217', UN Doc. A/59/847; E/2005/73, para. 33.

71 Ambassador Richard Williams, US Representative to the United Nations for Special Political Affairs, US Government Delegation to the 60th Commission on Human Rights, discussion on 'Item 4: Report of the United Nations High Commissioner for Human Rights and Follow-Up to the World Conference on Human Rights' (2004).

the Commission and the General Assembly having adopted a number of resolutions reaffirming that democracy is important for the protection of other rights.[72] One main problem with the US proposal is that it would not have gained sufficient support, as most states would not meet this criterion. Other proposals built on the US proposal, or at least called for membership criteria along similar lines. Human Rights Watch (2003) initially asserted – although they later amended these proposals in 2006 when it became clear that they would not be adopted – that membership criteria should include ratification of core human rights treaties, compliance with reporting obligations, and lack of recent condemnation by the Commission, amongst others. Rahmani-Ocora suggested that excluding certain states from membership, such as countries with recent human rights resolutions passed about them, would increase the body's credibility.[73]

Alston noted the difficulty with only including states with good human rights records or democratic countries.[74] He argues that excluding known abusers was both impractical and undesirable, politically and diplomatically, as it would instead create an exclusive and homogenous regime, consisting primarily of Western states, imposing international human rights law. From the point of view of developing nations, exclusionary membership criteria would result in a body with homogenous membership, thus undermining its credibility.

Protecting and promoting universal human rights standards requires a representative membership for the body to have legitimacy in the eyes of all states. Excluding certain political systems or groups of states reinforces arguments that human rights are used to oppress developing or non-democratic countries. A non-representative human rights body would serve to strengthen the position that human rights are a preserve of Western and developed UN member states. Moreover, excluding countries from standing for election is fundamentally at odds with the key UN Charter principle of sovereign equality of member states. That crucial principle is the basis for the UN's legitimacy as a universal organisation, and the notion of its principal human rights body overriding that principle directly contradicts the Charter itself. Moreover, exclusionary tactics would similarly contravene the need to balance the legitimacy of UN bodies with member states. A main mechanism for legitimacy rests on membership of UN bodies, particularly principal ones, being open to all states to seek membership.

An alternative proposal regarding membership focused on positive criteria rather than exclusionary ones. Kälin and Jimenez give examples, including ratifying UN human rights treaties and having national human rights

72 U. Khaliq, *Ethical Dimensions of the Foreign Policy of the European Union: A Legal Appraisal*, Cambridge: Cambridge University Press, 2008, pp. 72–4.

73 Rahmani-Ocora, 'Giving the Emperor Real Clothes', 17.

74 P. Alston, 'Richard Lillich Memorial Lecture: Promoting the Accountability of Members of the New UN Human Rights Council', *Journal of Transnational Law and Policy*, Vol. 15, 2005–2006, 58–9.

institutions.[75] They argue that agreement amongst the majority of states is necessary in order to protect and promote human rights, and that excluding states from the debate undermines the ability to achieve that consensus.

Membership criteria would potentially allow powerful states to ensure that only their allies are granted membership, and that their positions are supported. One way of ensuring that powerful states could not control membership was distributing seats in a geographically proportionate manner. Rahmani-Ocora observes that proportionate geographic representation would stop any one region from dominating proceedings, thus maintaining the body's credibility.[76]

Reforms to the electoral process were proposed as another method for improving credibility and work of the UN human rights body. The Secretary-General insisted that the Human Rights Council 'must be a society of the committed'.[77] Such language was used to emphasise the need for elections to focus on states' commitment to human rights. Kofi Annan argued that, in order to be more accountable and representative than the Commission, 'those elected [to the HRC] should have a solid record of commitment to the highest human rights standards'. He proposed that election by a two-thirds majority of the General Assembly would make the body more accountable and representative.[78] Requiring a large majority would stop the practice of electing members based on political alliances, and instead focus attention on positive criteria for membership. That would result in stronger international support for, and greater legitimacy of, the UN human rights body.

Annan's proposals were supported by other stakeholders who also emphasised that electoral rules would ensure better human rights credentials of member states. Amnesty International, for example, called for electoral rules that would encourage members' commitment to human rights protection and promotion. The NGO repeated Annan's suggestion that each state's election require a two-thirds majority of the General Assembly.[79] Rahmani-Ocora suggested that the OHCHR should publish reports on the human rights records of all potential members in order to assist in the election process.[80] Publication of such reports would be used to encourage other states not to elect members that the OHCHR classified as having a dubious record.

2.1.3.2 *Mechanisms and proceedings*

Another area requiring reform was the body's mechanisms and proceedings. Rahmani-Ocora, amongst others, suggested that the Council could overcome

75 Kälin and Jimenez, 'Reform of the UN Commission on Human Rights', 6–7.
76 Rahmani-Ocora, 'Giving the Emperor Real Clothes', 17.
77 Speech of Secretary-General Kofi Annan to the Commission on Human Rights, 'Reforming UN Human Rights Machinery', 7 April 2005, UN Press Release SG/SM/9808 HR/CN/1108.
78 *Ibid.*
79 Amnesty International, 'Meeting the Challenge: Transforming the Commission on Human Rights into a Human Rights Council', 12 April 2005, AI Index IOR 40/008/2005.
80 Rahmani-Ocora, 'Giving the Emperor Real Clothes', 17.

the Commission's flaws by being a principal organ of the UN.[81] Indeed, in May 2005 the Secretary-General commented that the Council ought to be a principal UN organ in order to 'raise human rights to the priority accorded to it in the Charter'.[82] As a principal organ, the Council would have independence, resources and powers not available to the Commission. As mentioned, however, that shift would have required changes to the UN Charter, a matter not easily undertaken. The Secretary-General emphasised the need for the new Council to be a standing body, with a permanent meeting place and specific resources entirely devoted to it.[83] In the 'In Larger Freedom' report, Annan recommended that the HRC become a standing body through being either a UN principal organ or a General Assembly subsidiary body.[84] The Secretary-General asserted that, if the UN is 'to meet the expectations of men and women everywhere' and is 'to take the cause of human rights as seriously as those of security and development', the Council must be a standing body.

Emphasis on the HRC being created as a standing body stemmed from the need for the Council to hold regular meetings dealing with an ongoing agenda and to be able to reconvene at short notice to deal with crisis situations. The ability to respond to crises, according to Rahmani-Ocora, would make the Council better equipped than the Commission to protect human rights.[85] The emphasis on the body's ability to do more than simply 'fight fires' reflected an ongoing impetus that the Council's mandate be extended to include both human rights protection and promotion. That shift to a dual mandate will be explored later in detail. The Commission's informal consultations highlighted the need to increase the body's capacities for standard-setting, assistance and other forms of human rights promotion.[86] Moreover, regular meetings would allow the Council to investigate grave and crisis situations, increasing its capacity in relation to human rights protection.

Proposals for a standing body meeting regularly would, however, emphasise the difference in resources between powerful and weak states. Economically less developed countries would not be able to afford permanent delegations, or at least those of the size and expertise of richer countries. The difference in member states' resources and personnel, and their ability to engage with the Council and its work, mirrored the already apparent power struggles present at the body. The EU proposed between four and six annual sessions

81 *Ibid.*
82 Human Rights Council, 'Explanatory Note by the Secretary-General', 23 May 2005, UN Doc. 59/2005/Add.1, para. 1.
83 Ghanea, 'From UN Commission on Human Rights to UN Human Rights Council', 701–702.
84 General Assembly, 'In Larger Freedom', UN Doc. A/59/2005.
85 Rahmani-Ocora, 'Giving the Emperor Real Clothes', 19.
86 GA; ECOSOC, 'Summary of the open-ended informal consultations held by the Commission on Human Rights pursuant to Economic and Social Council Decision 2005/217', UN Doc. A/59/847; E/2005/73, para. 19.

lasting a minimum of 12 weeks in total. As a group of powerful and rich nations, the EU was less concerned with state resources than many of those opposing longer and more frequent sessions. Other states proposed fewer sessions with less minimum weeks, although almost all agreed on the necessity of regular sessions and the ability to convene special sessions at the request of the Council.

Proposals on special sessions were mainly focused on how they should be convened. The body had to be able to respond to grave crises without allowing the sessions to become a political tool used to further national objectives. A balance was needed to determine how many members should call for a session to ensure that it was not used as a tool for politicisation. It was important to ensure that small minorities of states could not seek to further political aims either by convening or blocking sessions.

2.1.3.3 *Peer review of states' human rights*

Perhaps the most innovative reform proposals focused on peer review of all states' human rights records. Universal review was proposed to combat criticisms of selectivity and bias levelled at the Commission's members and at its monitoring work. Underlying this mechanism were the principle of universal standards and the practical approach of ensuring compliance with such norms. State and non-state actors repeatedly expressed the need for cooperation and consent of the states being reviewed, emphasising the need for an inclusive and interactive approach.[87] Needless to say, any such criterion of sovereign consent effectively authorises the worst abusers to eschew scrutiny.

Compliance with human rights monitoring, let alone standards, was sorely lacking amongst some Commission members. Ramcharan notes that some states were 'strongly opposed' to the Commission's monitoring work.[88] States would refuse entry to experts and mandate holders, or even ignore their requests, where monitoring conflicted with national aims. Rahmani-Ocora observes that states' attitudes towards human rights monitoring had to change in order for the Council to overcome the Commission's failings.[89] Peer review was the main proposal for changing attitudes towards human rights evaluation.

The Secretary-General introduced the concept of 'universal peer review' as part of his proposal to disband the Commission and create a replacement body. The High Commissioner for Human Rights, Louise Arbour, emphasised the importance of peer review in her speech at the Commission's final session.[90]

---

87 See, for example, GA; ECOSOC, 'Summary of the open-ended informal consultations held by the Commission on Human Rights pursuant to Economic and Social Council Decision 2005/217', UN Doc. A/59/847; E/2005/73, paras 20–21.

88 B.G. Ramcharan, *The UN Human Rights Council*, London: Routledge, 2011, p. 27.

89 Rahmani-Ocora, 'Giving the Emperor Real Clothes', 17.

90 Speech of the High Commissioner for Human Rights, CHR 61st Session, 14 March 2005.

Arbour acknowledged that no intergovernmental human rights body could, or even should, be devoid of national politics. Arbour insisted that peer review, alongside other reforms, would combat politicisation, allowing the new body to deal with human rights in a non-selective and credible manner.[91] It was perhaps naïve to suggest that even a perfect peer review system could combat politicisation. Selectivity and bias had occurred not only due to known abusers being members of the Commission, but also through regionalism and power politics. Whilst peer review might discourage abusers from seeking election, owing to states no longer being able to use membership as a method for avoiding scrutiny, that only deals with part of the politicisation issue. Arbour, and indeed other peer review proponents, also failed to confront the possibility that the review mechanism itself would be subject to selectivity.[92]

Annan recommended that peer review be truly universal, with all UN member states being reviewed regarding all human rights obligations.[93] Emphasis was placed on the voluntary involvement of states in discussions and cooperation with the reviewers. Although great support was expressed, states disagreed on the standards by which countries' human rights records were judged. Proposals ranged from judging states against their own human rights commitments to holding all states accountable against a proscribed international standard. Ensuring impartiality and transparency was hoped to minimise politicisation issues. However, without concrete proposals on how the review mechanism would work in practice, peer review remained conceptual. Creation of the Council provided the opportunity for this and other proposals to be discussed as practical, rather than theoretical, matters.

91 Rahmani-Ocora, 'Giving the Emperor Real Clothes', 20.
92 See Chapter 9 for concrete examples of selectivity in the UPR process.
93 Speech of Secretary-General Kofi Annan to the Commission on Human Rights, 'Reforming UN Human Rights Machinery', UN Press Release SG/SM/9808 HR/CN/1108.

3 Creation and mandate

The Council's mandate is set out in its constituent instrument, UN General Assembly Resolution 60/251. In order to explore the mandate, the main provisions of Resolution 60/251 need to be analysed to ascertain whether they have significantly addressed the Commission's failings. The leading changes found in Resolution 60/251 are the HRC's founding principles, membership and election issues, procedures and mechanisms, and the universal periodic review mechanism. Those changes reflect some of the most serious criticisms levelled at the Commission before and during reform negotiations. In particular what needs to be explored is whether Resolution 60/251 addressed the Commission's flaws whilst retaining its positive attributes, or whether it did not go far enough adequately to overcome criticisms of that body. It is only once that analysis has been made that the Council's mandate under Resolution 60/251 can then be scrutinised. The Resolution sets out what the Council is mandated to do; the manner in which it is mandated to achieve those ends; the mechanisms it is mandated to use or create; and the powers afforded to the Council, including exploration of which powers it has not been given.

3.1. Background to GA Resolution 60/251

Negotiations on the new Human Rights Council took place between 2005 and 2006. Discussions focused on the body's composition, procedures, and functions, and on which aspects of the Commission should be retained, removed or reformed at the new body. The result was Resolution 60/251, creating the Council. Alston maintains that there was general agreement on the Commission's failure, the need to establish a new body, and the requirement to strengthen the UN human rights machinery.[1] However, he observes that there were serious disagreements about why the Commission failed and what the Council should do to overcome these flaws. Alston argues that the final resolution only gave broad guidelines regarding the Council's procedural and institutional arrangements because of this failure to agree on what had previously gone wrong with the human rights body.[2]

1 P. Alston, 'Reconceiving the UN Human Rights Regime: Challenges Confronting the New UN Human Rights Council', *Melbourne Journal of International Law*, Vol. 7, 2006, 186.
2 *Ibid.*

Compromise was key to negotiations on the final text of Resolution 60/251. Controversial issues included the suspension clause, membership and election, and the Universal Periodic Review (UPR). However, the compromise agreement satisfied most, if not all, states. The US voted against the Council's creation. Crook[3] commented that, despite the US strongly advocating replacing the Commission, it did not believe Resolution 60/251 sufficiently safeguarded against states with poor human right records becoming members of the HRC.[4] The US had supported the Secretary-General's proposal that for states to be elected they must secure a two-thirds majority of the General Assembly (GA). The US also proposed excluding known gross and systemic human rights abusers from membership. Neither of those proposals appeared in the final text of the Resolution. Ambassador John Bolton commented that the US 'did not have sufficient confidence [. . .] to be able to say that the HRC would be better than its predecessor'.[5] Despite voting against the Resolution, the United States did not seek to introduce proposed changes to the draft resolution, a tactic that would have derailed the entire process.[6] As the US did not withdraw funds from the Council, despite voting against its creation, observers have argued that the US position was, in fact, a 'soft no'.[7]

On 15 March 2006 the GA passed Resolution 60/251, establishing the Council. Resolution 60/251 is a constituent document that creates the Council as a subsidiary organ of the GA. Article 22 of the UN Charter gives the GA the power to 'establish such subsidiary organs as it deems necessary for the performance of its functions'. If subsidiary organs assist the GA in carrying out its tasks,[8] then the Council assists the Assembly in fulfilling its mandate on human rights through providing a body solely focusing on human rights issues.

There are various types of GA subsidiary organs,[9] but all are subordinate to the Assembly. Subordination is a legal characteristic of these subsidiary organs,[10] with the GA retaining organisational power and control over the bodies' structure and activities. For example, the GA votes to elect the Council's members; has the power to suspend a Council member; may dictate which

3 J.R. Crook, 'United States Votes Against New UN Human Rights Council', *American Journal of International Law*, Vol. 100, 2006, 697–9.

4 Ambassador John R. Bolton, 'Explanation of Vote by U.S. Permanent Representative John R. Bolton on the Human Rights Council Draft Resolution', 15 March 2006, USUN Press Release No. 51(06).

5 *Ibid.*

6 P. Maurer, 'About the Negotiation Process in New York (from 2005 until 2006): Of Ants, Caterpillars and Butterflies', in Lars Müller (ed.), *The First 365 Days of the United Nations Human Rights Council*, Switzerland: Baden, 2007, p. 35.

7 *Ibid.*

8 L.M. Goodrich, E. Hambro and A.P. Simons, *Charter of the United Nations: Commentary and Documents*, New York: Columbia University Press, 1969, p. 186.

9 B. Simma (ed.), *The Charter of the United Nations: A Commentary*, Oxford: Oxford University Press, 1995, pp. 423–6.

10 *Ibid.*, pp. 430–31.

situations the body must address; and receives an annual report from the Council. However, according to Simma, the GA has 'loosened its institutional relationship with the semi-autonomous organs', allowing them a wide degree of autonomy.[11] Indeed, they are given similar powers to specialised agencies.[12] Regardless of that autonomy, the Council does directly report back to, and rely on, the GA. The Council's lack of autonomy can be compared with, for example the Human Rights Committee – a treaty-based body of independent experts that monitors implementation of the ICCPR by states party to that treaty – which retains a degree of autonomous decision-making not found within a subsidiary body.[13]

3.2. GA Resolution 60/251

GA resolutions establishing the operations and framework of subsidiary organs have 'far-reaching legal and practical effects for States'.[14] In order to explore Resolution 60/251, and its impact on states and the Council, rules of interpretation of international instruments must be used. The general rule for interpretation is set out in Article 31 of the Vienna Convention on the Law of Treaties (1969), which achieves a compromise between the two competing approaches – literal interpretation and the contextual approach.[15] It states that 'A treaty shall be interpreted in good faith in accordance with the ordinary meaning to be given to the terms of the treaty in their context and in the light of its object and purpose' (Article 31(1)). Klabbers stresses the central importance of this rule despite interpretation being 'as much art as it is science'.[16]

GA Resolution 60/251 creates the Council and establishes its modalities. It also reiterates the central importance of human rights within the UN system. Referring to human rights as the UN's third pillar demonstrates the link between that field and those of development and security. 'Strong and uniting'[17] language is used to emphasise the message that human rights work requires dialogue, cooperation, and understanding between states, cultures

---

11 *Ibid.*

12 *Ibid.*, pp. 431–2.

13 D. McGoldrick, *The UN Human Rights Committee: Its Role in the Development of the International Covenant on Civil and Political Rights*, Oxford: Oxford University Press, 1994, pp. 52–3.

14 B. Sloan, 'General Assembly Resolutions Revisited, (Forty Years After)', *British Yearbook of International Law*, Vol. 58, 1987, 113–14.

15 cf. A. Aust, *Modern Treaty Law and Practice*, Cambridge: Cambridge University Press, 2000, pp. 184–211; M.N. Shaw, *International Law*, 6th edn., Cambridge: Cambridge University Press, 2008, pp. 932–8.

16 J. Klabbers, *Introduction to International Institutional Law*, Cambridge: Cambridge University Press, 2002, p. 96.

17 GA President Jan Eliasson, introductory statement delivered at the occasion of the adoption of the resolution establishing the Human Rights Council, GA 60th session, 15 March 2006.

and religions. Countries are entreated to work together to achieve fundamental freedoms and rights for all people. Moreover, the need for universality, objectivity, impartiality and non-selectivity in human rights work is repeated throughout, reflecting criticisms that the Commission was used for biased and politicised aims.

The preamble reflects key concerns raised during discussions and negotiations on the Council's creation. It begins by emphasising relevant UN Charter principles and purposes, particularly the sovereign equality of all states, the fundamental nature of rights and freedoms for all peoples, and the importance of international cooperation (preamb. para. 1).[18] The foundations of the UN human rights system (preamb. para. 2), the equality of all rights, and their universal application, (preamb. para. 3) are reaffirmed, as is the need for all states to respect all rights of all peoples (preamb. para. 5) regardless of cultural, or other, differences (preamb. para. 4). Human rights is identified as the UN's third pillar (preamb. para. 6), with the text acknowledging the role of both state and non-state actors in the human rights field (preamb. paras 7 and 11). Although the preamble notes the Commission's work (preamb. para. 8), it also recognises that body's main failings (preamb. para. 9) and emphasises the need for cooperation, dialogue, and capacity-building (preamb. para. 10) in order to overcome these flaws and effectively protect and promote (preamb. para. 10) all human rights (preamb. para. 12).

The Resolution's operative paragraphs are divided into sections dealing with different topics. The sections deal with: general paragraphs on the Council's creation; the Council's mandate, roles and functions; the body's interaction with wider UN human rights machinery; membership and election; sessions and special sessions; rules of procedure and working methods; timeline and method for creation and review. Common themes throughout include: underlying principles upon which work is based; dual mandate of protection and promotion of human rights; elimination of key Commission failings; importance and applicability of universal human rights; state consent and cooperation; types of rights, including the right to development; capacity-building; the Council's assumption of some aspects of the Commission. Key passages from Resolution 60/251 will now be highlighted, in turn, with explanations of important paragraphs and overall themes.

3.2.1 The Council's creation

Paragraph 1 of Resolution 60/251 establishes the Council, to replace the Commission, as a subsidiary organ of the GA. As the Council is a standing body, permanent resources were made available to it, including meeting rooms and administrative staff, all of which could be used for long-term projects or at short notice. Such resources improved on those available to the

---

18 GA Res. 60/251, 'Human Rights Council', 15 March 2006, UN Doc. A/RES/60/251.

Commission, ensuring that the Council could overcome its predecessor's failure to devote adequate time and resources to long-term and short-term human rights problems.

3.2.2 *Overview of the mandate*

Paragraphs 2, 3 and 4 of Resolution 60/251 introduce the body's two broad mandates and its underlying principles. Those paragraphs are explained and elaborated upon throughout the resolution. Paragraph 2 sets out the Council's first mandate, to be 'responsible for promoting universal respect for the protection of all human rights'. The requirement to promote human rights recognises that states, particularly those from the Global South, require technical assistance, capacity-building, and practical help to develop national human rights capabilities. Emphasis is placed on the promotion mandate being conducted 'without distinction of any kind and in a fair and equal manner' (para. 2). That language reflects some states' concerns that economic, social and cultural rights should be treated in the same way as civil and political rights, which can be traced back to Cold War politics.[19] That passage also reiterates the importance of devoting equal time and resources to both non-controversial and controversial rights, stemming from criticisms that the Commission disproportionately focused attention and resources on some rights to the exclusion of others. Moreover, emphasis on fairness and equality addresses the problem of the Commission's selectivity by mandating that all rights and freedoms of all peoples should be equally protected. This can be read as a general instruction not to single out countries, regions or peoples for unfair attention, nor to ignore others nor shield them from scrutiny.

Paragraph 3 outlines the second part of the Council's mandate, which requires the body to protect human rights. The body is directed that it 'should address situations of violations of human rights, including gross and systematic violations, and make recommendations thereon' (para. 3). The word 'should' creates an affirmative duty to address those situations. The Council's mandate to deal with human rights situations is imperative for the body to protect individuals from abuses. Although the Council must specifically address 'gross and systemic violations', that provision is illustrative not exhaustive. The word 'including' suggests that it is one example, and that this type of situation was deemed particularly important during negotiations. Singling out gross and systemic violations reflects criticisms that the Commission failed to address such situations. Alongside addressing them, the Council is mandated to make recommendations on those situations. Recommendations are one of the main powers by which the Council can protect human rights. Although the body's powers are laid out throughout Resolution

---

19 See Chapter 1, Section 1.1.3.

60/251, it is important to note that recommendations are the sole power enunciated in the opening, general paragraphs. Recommendations, as will be discussed, provide a practical and political tool for encouraging and assisting states to comply with human rights obligations.

Paragraph 3 sets out another element of the Council's mandate which spans both protection and promotion of human rights. The Council 'should also promote the effective coordination and the mainstreaming of human rights within the United Nations system' (para. 3). The requirement ('should') to work as part of the wider UN machinery aims to ensure that human rights are not dealt with in a vacuum. Again, reform proposals and negotiations are crucial for understanding why this passage was included as part of the opening paragraphs. States were not only concerned that the Council should not duplicate the work of other bodies, but were also keen to ensure that the body continue to set standards and share information, and improve on the Commission's interaction with the UN human rights machinery. The Council's mandate to raise human rights' profile and strengthen interactions with other UN concerns, such as development and security, further stems from calls for the body to be a UN principal organ and the proposals for the status of human rights as the UN's third pillar to be more rigorously acknowledged.

Paragraph 4 directs that the Council 'shall be guided by the principles of universality, impartiality, objectivity and non-selectivity, constructive international dialogue and cooperation'. The founding principles are crucial for assessing the new body.[20] They underscore that the Council must fulfil its mandate in a fair manner across all UN member states. Enunciation of universality reminds the body to protect and promote all rights within the UDHR and to ensure that they are upheld within all countries. Universality reiterates that all states must comply with their human rights obligations, and that the body must strive to hold any state accountable for non-compliance. Emphasis on impartiality, objectivity and non-selectivity seeks to ensure that the Council will overcome the Commission's main failings. These underlying principles directly deal with many key criticisms of the Commission. Aspirations for the Council, particularly from the Global North, include: promoting and protecting human rights in a universal manner; being impartial when doing so; taking an objective approach; not selecting which countries to focus on based on political factors extraneous to the human rights mandate.

The founding principles also include the need for dialogue and cooperation. This reflects the Global South's concerns that human rights are an issue of exclusive domestic jurisdiction, and that international human rights are often used as a neo-colonial tool of oppression against states with limited human rights capacities or capabilities. Ensuring states' consent and cooperation is an integral feature of the Council's work and proceedings. It is based on the

20 See Section 3.5.

idea, promoted by the Global South, that such cooperation is required to ensure that states can, and indeed will, comply with human rights obligations.

Paragraph 4 further reiterates that the body's work should be aimed at 'enhancing the promotion and protection of all human rights, civil, political, economic, social and cultural rights, including the right to development'. All categories of rights, as well as the right to development, are afforded equal treatment. That provision deals with positions taken by the Global South and former socialist states that economic, social and cultural rights should be afforded equal weight as civil and political rights. Economically weaker and decolonised states were particularly concerned that the right to development should be emphasised in order to take into account states' capacities for human rights. Human rights and development are interlinked; without national capabilities to protect and promote human rights states cannot fulfil their obligations. Recognition of this right underscored the body's duty to assist states with building national human rights infrastructure.

3.2.3 *Functions and powers*

Resolution 60/251 next sets out the Council's functions and powers. Paragraph 5 identifies the roles and functions that the Council 'shall' undertake. Each subsection provides a non-exhaustive list of the Council's roles and functions, with the imperative 'shall' mandating the body to carry out the enumerated tasks. The paragraph is divided into promotion, protection and the Council's interactions with the wider human rights machinery.

Subsection (a) sets out ways in which the Council must promote human rights within individual states: 'Promote human rights education and learning as well as advisory services, technical assistance and capacity-building' (para. 5 (a)). Those functions aim to assist states in complying with human rights obligations within their territories. The four mandated methods are intended as 'forward-thinking' subheadings by which the Council may determine the most appropriate methods of human rights promotion. The subsection directs that the promotion of rights 'be provided in consultation with and with the consent of Member States concerned' (para. 5 (a)). As human rights remain predominantly a national matter, the themes of consent and cooperation are of particular importance for the promotion mandate, which focuses on building, amongst others, the knowledge, understanding, capabilities and institutions of individual states.

Subsection (b) requires the new body to 'serve as a forum for dialogue on thematic issues on all human rights' (para. 5 (b)). The word 'serve' implies that the body should facilitate dialogue between state and non-state actors, as opposed to directing the dialogue itself. Subsection (b) again stresses the recurrent theme that no one right, nor class of right, should be given disproportionate time or resources. The express requirement, however, provides that the body be a forum for dialogue on thematic issues. Although the Council is not precluded from being a forum for dialogue on country-specific matters, the lack of requirement to do so is crucial. Thematic human rights issues tend to be less controversial and less susceptible to politicisation than country-specific matters. Thematic discussions are, therefore, more likely than country-specific debates to be constructive and less likely to be sidelined by national or regional political agendas, thus better enabling the body to fulfil its mandate.

Subsection (c) sets out one of the Council's key powers, to 'make recommendations to the General Assembly for the further development of international law in the field of human rights' (para. 5 (c)). As previously noted, subsidiary organs assist the GA in carrying out its roles and functions; the Council does not exist in a vacuum. Its work promoting human rights, particularly standard-setting and development of human rights law, is specifically noted in subsection (c). The Council must provide recommendations for the GA to utilise when undertaking human rights work. Recommendations are the Council's main power. As will be explored below, they are a 'soft' power, which, although not legally binding, are useful for drawing the GA's attention to important matters and information.

In addition to standard-setting, the Council must 'promote the full implementation of human rights obligations undertaken by States and follow-up to the goals and commitments related to the promotion and protection of human rights emanating from United Nations conferences and summits' (para. 5 (d)). 'Obligations' refers to universal rights that all UN members must uphold, whereas 'commitments' are voluntary undertakings, for example through treaties. This paragraph underlines that all of a state's human rights duties are treated equally by the Council. Promoting human rights includes monitoring states' compliance with the wider UN human rights machinery, underscoring that the body's work does not exist in a vacuum. One mechanism for such monitoring is the UPR, as set out in subsection (e). That mechanism was created as a direct response to concerns that the Commission was selective in terms of which countries it monitored, and that Commission membership was sought by known abusers to shield themselves or allies from scrutiny. The UPR was an innovative mechanism designed to improve member states' accountability. As in subsection (d), the Council is mandated to use this mechanism to monitor every UN states' human rights obligations and commitments.

Subsection (e) sets out the UPR's aims and objectives. It must be 'based on objective and reliable information, of the fulfilment by each State of its human rights obligations and commitments in a manner which ensures universality of coverage and equal treatment with respect to all States' (para. 5 (e)). Again, emphasis is placed on the body's underlying principles, reaffirming the importance of universal application and equal treatment. Paragraph 5 (e) repeats ongoing themes of cooperation, consent and capacity-building. The UPR is mandated ('shall') to be 'a cooperative mechanism, based on an interactive dialogue, with the full involvement of the country concerned and with consideration given to its capacity-building needs'.

The UPR seeks both to protect and to promote human rights. Promotion occurs through monitoring states' compliance with obligations and commitments, as well as through providing assistance following the initial review. Rahmani-Ocora argues that equal, regular and public human rights monitoring of all states, if it occurs in practice, will encourage countries to change their attitudes towards the UN human rights machinery.[21] The Resolution only gives a broad outline of the methods to be used in undertaking the review. It does not, however, set out the UPR's modalities. Instead, a clear timeframe is given for that process to occur: 'the Council shall develop the modalities and necessary time allocation for the universal periodic review mechanism within one year'. Proposals were made for stricter standards to be applied in the review process than those finally adopted.[22]

The UPR's relationship with the wider UN human rights machinery was of particular concern to certain states during the negotiating process. Subsection (e) takes into account criticisms that the Commission duplicated work of other bodies. In particular, the Council is required to ensure that the UPR 'shall complement and not duplicate the work of treaty bodies'.

The UPR is aimed primarily at promoting human rights, whereas subsection (f) sets out functions associated with the protection mandate. The body is required to 'contribute, through dialogue and cooperation, towards the prevention of human rights violations and respond promptly to human rights emergencies' (para. 5 (f)). Preventing human rights violations and responding to crisis situations are bound together in this subsection. Protection occurs through prompt responses and through prevention of violations, which are both direct responses to human rights abuses. Promoting human rights, on the other hand, aims to prevent those violations from occurring in the first place. The word 'contribute' clearly demonstrates that the Council cannot, and must not, work in a vacuum. Human rights protection must, therefore, occur in tandem with other parts of the UN human rights machinery and, perhaps, with other organisations, states and non-state actors. The central themes of dialogue and cooperation are again reiterated, reflecting concerns during negotiations that the Council should not be given the power to take unwanted or intrusive action in national jurisdictions.

The following two subsections in Paragraph 5 relate to the Council's relationship with specific organisations and actors. Subsection (g) mandates the Council to 'assume' the Commission's relationship with the OHCHR under GA Resolution 48/141. The OHCHR was created to assist with promoting and protecting human rights. Retention of this aspect of the Commission's work demonstrates the importance of the OHCHR's work. Subsection (h) requires the Council to 'work in close cooperation [. . .] with Governments, regional organizations, national human rights institutions and civil society'.

21 L. Rahmani-Ocora, 'Giving the Emperor Real Clothes: The UN Human Rights Council', *Global Governance*, Vol. 12 (1), 2006, 16.
22 See Chapter 9.

Emphasis on interactions with other actors and the need for cooperative working methods reflects key concerns throughout the negotiations. This, arguably, non-exhaustive list mentions key human rights actors with which the Council must work in fulfilling both aspects of its mandate.

Lastly, Paragraph 5 sets out two key methods by which the Council must fulfil its mandate. The Council must 'make recommendations with regard to the promotion and protection of human rights' (para. 5 (i)). Making recommendations, rather than being able to take direct action, is the Council's main power. The reasons for this, and its impact on the body, will be explored in detail below.[23] Subsection (i), as with other sections in the Resolution, identifies recommendations as key to both the protection and promotion mandates. Submitting 'an annual report to the General Assembly' (para. 5 (j)) is the other power which the Council is required to use to discharge its mandate. As a subsidiary organ of the GA, the Council assists that body with carrying out its human rights responsibilities. Annual reports allow the Council to identify key human rights issues for the Assembly to discuss and act upon. The report is heard by all UN members who can then participate in debates, offering an opportunity for non-members of the Council to play an active role on its work. Moreover, through this power, the Council is able to protect and promote human rights using wider UN machinery.

Paragraph 6 deals with the Council's assumption of certain Commission functions. The Council must 'assume, review and, where necessary, improve and rationalize all [Commission] mandates, mechanisms, functions and re-sponsibilities' (para. 6) within its first year. This enables the body to 'maintain a system of special procedures, expert advice and a complaint procedure' (para. 6). Those mechanisms were crucial to the Commission's work, and most negotiating states had sought to ensure they were retained in some form. The Special Procedures system developed by the Commission consists of independent experts who operate within the broader UN system. Gutter comments that there was considerable tension regarding whether to keep, modify or scrap special procedures, complaints mechanisms, and other working methods.[24] A compromise was reached whereby Special Procedures mechanisms were retained for the body's first year in order to conduct a review, rationalisation and improvement process on individual mandates (para. 6).

The Council's creation was guided by the need to preserve the Commis-sion's achievements and fix its failings,[25] as expressed in the resolution's preamble.[26] Procedures that had been heavily criticised were modified and some,

---

23 See Section 3.4.
24 J. Gutter, 'Special Procedures and the Human Rights Council: Achievements and Challenges Ahead', *Human Rights Law Review*, Vol. 7 (1), 93–107.
25 P. Scannella and P. Splinter, 'The United Nations Human Rights Council: A Promise to be Fulfilled', *Human Rights Law Review*, Vol. 7 (1), 2007, 68–9.
26 '*Recognizing* the work undertaken by the Commission on Human Rights and the need to preserve and build on its achievements and to redress its shortcomings'.

which were inherently flawed, were abolished altogether.[27] The controversial 'no-action' motion, for example, does not appear in Resolution 60/251. On the other hand, procedures commonly recognised as positive were maintained without the review and rationalisation stipulation that was placed on the Special Procedures system. Consultative status of NGOs, for example, was acknowledged in the preamble[28] and insisted upon in Paragraph 11.

3.2.4 *Membership and election*

Membership and election are discussed in Paragraphs 7, 8 and 9. Increasingly, problems with the Commission's membership and election undermined that body's credibility. Despite wide-ranging reform proposals, there is little fundamental change to the Council's composition, albeit with steps taken towards accountability of member states. The process by which states are elected to the Council is an improvement on its predecessor.

Council membership was determined to 'consist of 47 Member States' (para. 7), as compared with the Commission's 53. Weiss insists that this small reduction in size was disappointing as it retained the status quo rather than taking up the radical reform proposals for either a far smaller body or, conversely, universal membership.[29] Alston argues that the Council's size reflects a great number of states' desire to participate in proceedings, which would not have occurred had membership been restricted to the US proposal of 20 states.[30]

Paragraph 7 dictates that membership be 'based on equitable geographical distribution'. The African Group holds 13 seats, East European countries received 6 seats, GRULAC 8, Asia 13, and Western Europe and Others 7. Schrijver compares the percentage proportion of Commission seats with those allocated to the Council for each regional group.[31] The African Group's percentage share (28%) remained the same, the Asian Group (28%) gained an extra five per cent and Eastern Europe (13%) gained four per cent. Latin American states (17%) lost four per cent, as did Western Europe and Others (15%). African and Asian states hold the majority of Council seats, giving these groups significant power. Maurer comments that the impression was given that 'certain EU members realised only relatively late what the loss in terms of geographic distribution would mean for the group of Western states in a smaller Council'.[32] The Global South controls the Council, with Western states marginalised despite close ties with countries, such as Japan, from

27 Rahmani-Ocora, 'Giving the Emperor Real Clothes', 19.
28 '*Acknowledging* that non-governmental organizations play an important role at the national, regional and international levels, in the promotion and protection of human rights'.
29 T.G. Weiss, *What's Wrong with the United Nations and How to Fix It*, Cambridge: Polity Press, 2008, pp. 146–7.
30 Alston, 'Reconceiving the UN Human Rights Regime', 198.
31 N. Schrijver, 'The UN Human Rights Council: A New "Society of the Committed" or Just Old Wine in New Bottles', *Leiden Journal of International Law*, Vol. 20 (4), 2007.
32 Maurer, 'About the Negotiation Process in New York', 35.

other regional groups. The Council's composition does not take into account cross-regional blocs, such as the Organisation of the Islamic Conference (OIC) and the Non-Aligned Movement (NAM). Boyle[33] notes the many political alliances within the Council, and Hampson argues that states will continue to work in these blocs at the new body.[34]

Members are 'elected directly and individually' (para. 7), providing a more open process than at the Commission. The Commission allowed regional groups to nominate members, with ECOSOC usually rubber-stamping these nominations.[35] Regional groups could present 'closed slates', with only the same number of nominated states as regional seats, resulting in inability to challenge inappropriate states' nominations.[36] Electing states individually *supposedly* allows a candidate to be rejected by the GA. This provision sought to end the practice of closed slates, whereby unsuitable candidates could become members owing to no other options being available. In theory, collective action can no longer occur through using closed slates, however regional groups frequently ensure that only one state is nominated for each of their allocated seats. States are, effectively, forced to re-open nominations in order to reject a candidate in such circumstances. It remains unlikely, however, that this will occur in practice.

The Resolution also sets out that election occurs 'by secret ballot' (para. 7). Votes are cast by writing the state's name in the appropriate box and anonymously posting the ballot paper. The result is that, even with the new variation of a closed slate, an inappropriate state may be rejected through abstentions by the majority of states. Individual states require a majority of the GA to vote for them, which means that a state may be rejected even if that means a seat is left vacant and new nominations have to be made. This is a significant improvement on the Commission, where the inability to prevent known abusers from gaining membership undermined the body's credibility. Secret ballots also allow states to vote without fear of repercussions from the country concerned, its regional group or allies.

Despite reform proposals requiring a higher majority, the Resolution sets out that states are elected 'by the majority of the members of the General Assembly' (para. 7). Observers criticised the choice of simple majority instead of the proposed two-thirds requirement.[37] However, the lower threshold arguably had little practical effect on whether known human rights abusers

33   K. Boyle, 'The United Nations Human Rights Council: Power, Politics and Human Rights', *Northern Ireland Law Quarterly*, Vol. 60 (2), 2009, 129.

34   F.J. Hampson, 'An Overview of the Reform of the UN Human Rights Machinery', *Human Rights Law Review*, Vol. 7 (1), 2007, 14–15.

35   cf. Boyle, 'The United Nations Human Rights Council: Power, Politics and Human Rights', 126.

36   L.C. Moss, 'Will the Human Rights Council have Better Membership than the Commission on Human Rights?', *Human Rights Brief*, Vol. 13 (3), 2006.

37   Y. Terlinghen, 'The UN Human Rights Council: A New Era in UN Human Rights Work?', *Ethics & International Affairs*, Vol. 21 (2), 2007, 167–78.

gained membership. Cuba, China, Russia and Libya all have poor human rights records, but each received more than two-thirds of the vote[38] despite only needing to secure a simple majority. Czech Republic and Poland, on the other hand, secured far fewer than two-thirds of the vote[39] despite having better human rights records than other candidates. It is clear, therefore, that political rather than human rights considerations were used during elections, and that the higher threshold would have had little impact on known abusers being elected to the body. The elections did, however, result in some known abusers failing to gain membership. Iran withdrew its candidacy once it became clear that it would not gain even a simple majority, while Belarus was defeated during the vote. Those states' failure to be elected could arguably be based on their human rights records but, bearing in mind the known abusers which did gain membership, it is more likely attributable to political factors.

State members are elected 'for a period of three years and shall not be eligible for immediate re-election after two consecutive terms' (para. 7). This ensures that no state has *de facto* permanent membership, which the five permanent Security Council members ended up having at the Commission. Blocking dominant states will reduce some of the power struggles that plagued the Commission. A two-term limit also encourages more states to engage with the Council as members, allowing smaller states and different forms of political systems to be represented.

Although all states can seek Council membership (para. 6), Paragraph 8 outlines criteria that must ('shall') be taken into account during elections. Those criteria are 'the contribution of candidates to the promotion and protection of human rights and their voluntary pledges and commitments made thereto' (para. 8). The requirement that states should have regard to voluntary pledges and commitments provides 'soft' criteria for membership. Although this requirement achieves a compromise between the views of various stakeholders,[40] it does not adequately deal with the issues that beset the Commission's membership. Redondo argues that the criteria have greater importance because these commitments and pledges are included in the UPR process, whereby states' human rights records are examined by the Council.[41] Regardless of the degree of strength given to these criteria, they are a far cry from some of the stronger exclusionary proposals set out in Chapter 2. Alston comments that formal membership criteria were abandoned because they were viewed as unworkable and ineffective in practice.[42] Voluntary, or 'soft',

38 UN Department of Public Information, 'General Assembly Elects 47 Members of New Human Rights Council', 9 May 2006, UN Doc. GA/10459.

39 *Ibid.*

40 See Chapter 2 for reform proposals on membership criteria.

41 E.D. Redondo, 'The Universal Periodic Review of the UN Human Rights Council: An Assessment of the First Session', *Chinese Journal of International Law*, Vol. 7 (3), 2008, 727.

42 P. Alston, 'Richard Lillich Memorial Lecture: Promoting the Accountability of Members of the New UN Human Rights Council', *Journal of Transnational Law and Policy*, Vol. 15, 2005–2006, 67.

commitments were urged, and indeed reflected in the Resolution, although no enforcement mechanisms were provided. Encouraging state pledges on human rights to be taken into account is still an improvement on the Commission, which lacked any membership criteria.

Arguably, certain countries did not run for election owing to these criteria. Membership no longer protects human rights abusers, as the criteria results in membership providing 'less cover than in the past'.[43] Weiss notes that Sudan, Libya, Syria, Nepal, Egypt, Zimbabwe, Uzbekistan, North Korea, and Belarus,[44] all former Commission members, did not place their hats in the ring. However, Gaer insists that membership of states such as China, Cuba, and Saudi Arabia undermined the Council's claim regarding improved membership.[45]

Paragraph 8 gives the GA power 'by a two-thirds majority' to suspend any 'member of the Council that commits gross and systematic violations of human rights'. Although this provision signals that grave violations may be dealt with through suspension, it is unlikely to be used as often as warranted, owing to political and diplomatic reasons as well as the difficulty in gaining a two-thirds majority of the GA. Alston nevertheless insists that the clause 'is an important symbolic component in the sense that it would allow for any country that is widely condemned for its human rights record to be suspended from membership'.[46] It may be symbolic, but the high threshold for suspension discourages its use for power politics.[47]

In 2011 Libya became the first state to have its membership of the Council suspended. While some might argue that this suspension demonstrates both that the mechanism works and is useful, the question must be asked as to why it took five years for this, or indeed any, suspension. Libya, arguably, should have been denied membership of the Council in the first instance, owing to its human rights record. Even once it had gained membership, the ongoing violations within that state could have triggered the suspension mechanism at any time. It took widespread condemnation, by the Security Council, NATO, the Arab League, the OIC and the media, of Libya's crimes against humanity for the GA to suspend that state from the Council. Moreover, far from testifying to the utility of that mechanism, Libya's suspension arguably raises questions as to the GA's previous and continued inaction on violations within that country and other similar states.

43 Weiss, *What's Wrong with the United Nations*, pp. 146–7.
44 Altogether, 64 countries ran for 47 seats on the HRC in its first year.
45 F.D. Gaer, 'A Voice Not an Echo: Universal Periodic Review and the UN Treaty Body System', *Human Rights Law Review*, Vol. 7 (1), 2007, 135.
46 Alston, 'Reconceiving the UN Human Rights Regime', 202.
47 Article 7 TEU provides a similar clause allowing suspension of certain rights of an EU Member State where there is an expectation of human rights violations. That deterrent signals the organisation's commitment to protecting human rights, although some scholars have argued against its usefulness in practice.

Paragraph 9 reiterates that Council members 'shall uphold the highest standards in the promotion and protection of human rights'. It then gives a formal mechanism for assessing whether states are complying with this requirement: all Council members 'shall [. . .] be reviewed under the universal periodic review mechanism during their term of membership' (para. 9). That is a crucial difference from the Commission, where membership was often sought by states as protection from scrutiny of their human rights records.

The 'soft' criteria in Paragraph 8 regarding 'the contribution of candidates to the promotion and protection of human rights and their voluntary pledges and commitments' should be read alongside further accountability provisions in Paragraph 9 that members 'shall uphold the highest standards in the promotion and protection of human rights'. Alston observes that one of the HRC's major challenges regarding member accountability is the best method to encourage states to elect members based on human rights records.[48] He insists that educating states about human rights will be key to ensuring that this occurs.

Moss asserts that it was innovative for the Resolution to state expressly that the UN's principal human rights body should consist of states with good human rights records.[49] The new provisions seek to set standards for HRC membership, indicating the importance of members' national human rights compliance. Moss insists that these paragraphs demonstrate the hope that members will be elected according to human rights criteria rather than political motivations.[50] I shall examine, throughout the book, whether these hopes were fulfilled in practice.

3.2.5 *Modalities and working methods*

The Council was mandated to meet more regularly than the Commission and for longer periods. Despite the EU's proposal for between four and six sessions over a minimum 12-week period, Paragraph 10 sets out that the HRC would meet 'no fewer than three' times per year 'for a total duration of no less than ten weeks'. This can be compared with the Commission's single annual session lasting six weeks. It was hoped that regular meetings would allow adequate time to deal with agenda items. The Resolution also sets out that the body 'shall be able to hold special sessions when needed' (para. 10). The Council is given the ability to convene such sessions, rather than being mandated to hold them.

Moreover, the Resolution does not specify when Special Sessions should be held, but rather it leaves this mechanism open for the Council to interpret and utilise as it sees fit. Special Sessions can be held at the request of one member, but only if one-third of Council members support holding the

---

48 Alston, 'Reconceiving the UN Human Rights Regime', 69.
49 Moss, 'Will the Human Rights Council have Better Membership'.
50 *Ibid.*

session. It was hoped that the latter requirement would discourage the use of Special Sessions as a political tool, whilst still allowing them to be convened quickly and efficiently where required. Creation of special sessions dealing with crisis or grave human rights situations was a direct response to the criticism that the Commission lacked the mechanisms to deal effectively with such situations.

The Council must maintain the involvement of state and non-state actors, as had occurred at the Commission. The Resolution directs the body to ensure 'the participation of and consultation with observers, including States that are not members of the Council, the specialized agencies, other intergovernmental organizations and national human rights institutions, as well as non-governmental organizations' (para. 11). Under Paragraph 11, the body is required to ensure 'the most effective contribution of these entities'. This ensures that the body can utilise expertise from other actors. Wide participation also aims at ensuring legitimacy amongst non-members and civil society. That aim is repeated in Paragraph 12, which requires the Council to have 'transparent, fair and impartial' working methods. That paragraph deals with the criticism that much of the Commission's work was opaque and done behind closed doors, precluding non-state actors from participating.

The Council's working methods 'shall enable genuine dialogue, be results oriented, allow for subsequent follow-up discussions to recommendations and their implementation and also allow for substantive interaction with special procedures and mechanisms' (para. 12). Those requirements are linked to the promotion mandate, and underscore the need for the body to ensure effective follow-through, at the national level, on its work.

3.3. The Council's mandate

Resolution 60/251 sets out the Council's mandate, but the text is open to interpretation. Kälin *et al.* argue that the Council has three separate but interlinked mandates: promotion, protection and prevention.[51] Arguably, 'prevention' is subsumed under the protection mandate. Prevention of violations occurs during grave, crisis, or other situations,[52] to protect individuals from human rights abuses. Prevention, although in some ways similar to human rights promotion, occurs as part of the protection mandate. The Council's interaction with the wider UN human rights machinery and other human rights actors can also be seen as a separate mandate. That aspect of the Council's work, nevertheless, reasonably falls under both the protection and promotion mandates. Engagement with human rights actors enables the Council to

51 W. Kälin, C. Jimenez, J. Künzli and M. Baldegger, 'The Human Rights Council and Country Situations: Framework, Challenges and Models', Study commissioned by the Swiss Ministry of Foreign Affairs, Geneva: Institute of Public Law, University of Bern, 2006, pp. 15–16.

52 *Ibid.*

promote human rights compliance; similarly, protection is enhanced through wider involvement with other UN bodies, which may act upon or support the Council's work. I shall therefore treat the Council's mandate as divided into two broad categories: promoting human rights and protecting human rights. Those mandates are expressly and tacitly set out in Resolution 60/251. The Council's roles, functions and powers broadly fall under either or both of those categories.

Promotion Mandate. The Council has been tasked with promoting human rights within all UN member states. Again, Paragraph 2 states that: 'the Council shall be responsible for promoting universal respect for the protection of all human rights and fundamental freedoms for all'. Paragraph 4 requires the Council's work to be undertaken 'with a view to enhancing the promotion and protection of all human rights, without distinction of any kind and in a fair and equal manner'. The Resolution lists some activities that the Council must undertake to promote human rights. The list should be deemed non-exhaustive, serving only to illustrate the types of activities that are necessary to fulfil the mandate.

'Promotion' is defined by the *Oxford English Dictionary* as 'the action of helping forward; furtherance; advancement'. The Council's promotion activities include those that help, support or enable states to implement their human rights obligations and commitments.[53] The promotion mandate requires the Council to identify gaps in states' human rights compliance or to respond to information from non-state actors, other UN bodies or the country concerned. Promotion activities, therefore, can respond to individual states' needs and provide specific assistance with particular problems.

Resolution 60/251 lists certain functions and activities that the body must undertake to fulfil its promotion mandate. Those functions seek to assist states with fulfilling their human rights obligations and commitments. Paragraph 5 (a), for example, requires the Council to promote human rights education. Knowledge and understanding of human rights is crucial for implementing those rights at a national level. Moreover, education is key for civil society actors to advocate and promote rights and for individuals' awareness of their rights. The Council must provide human rights advisory services and technical assistance, which may include assistance and expertise from UN staff, other states, and human rights experts.

The Council, crucially, is required to support and enable national human rights capacity-building. During negotiations on the Council's creation, states from the Global South called for assistance with national human rights implementation, arguing that the Commission's atmosphere of 'shaming and blaming' failed to assist underdeveloped human rights systems particularly within decolonised states. Many of those states raised concerns that capacity-building and technical assistance were needed for post-colonial and developing

53 *Ibid.*, p. 15.

states adequately to fulfil human rights obligations and commitments to the same standards as Western nations. Capacity-building activities promote human rights by providing states with tools for universal adherence to human rights norms. States nevertheless do, at times, request capacity-building as a way to avoid scrutiny of human rights abuses, relying on weaknesses of national capabilities as an excuse for failing to comply with human rights.[54]

Resolution 60/251 mandates the Council to promote human rights by enabling dialogue on thematic issues (para. 5 (b)). Such dialogue occurs throughout Council sessions. Discussions facilitate interactions between states, human rights experts, NGOs and other non-state actors. Dialogue promotes human rights by providing a forum for advice, assistance and support. That function continues beyond Council sessions, with UN staff and human rights experts providing further opportunities for dialogue, for example through country visits.[55] The focus on thematic issues reflects the greater need to promote thematic rights, as opposed to country-specific matters where human rights tend, instead, to need protection. Thematic issues are frequently non-contentious, thus often requiring dialogue and other non-intrusive methods to promote compliance.

The Council's interactions with the wider UN human rights machinery requires the body to promote state implementation of goals, commitments and obligations 'emanating from United Nations conferences and summits' (para. 5 (d)). That function is key for the Council to support and further UN human rights work. Moreover, it is central to the Council's role as the UN's principal human rights body that it takes responsibility for supporting, advising and monitoring implementation of broader UN human rights work.

Again, a new and central mechanism for promoting rights is the UPR. Resolution 60/251 does not set out the UPR's modalities, but rather provides a broad overview of the mechanism and its aims. The Council must review all UN member states in order to monitor compliance with their obligations under various human rights instruments. Emphasis is placed on state co-operation to enable effective promotion of rights. The Council is required, in particular, to address capacity-building needs. The promotion mandate includes preventing human rights abuses; the very act of preventing abuses will also promote rights. Prevention goes further than identifying gaps in states' fulfilment of obligations. It implies the need to promote human rights where the potential for violations has been identified. Kälin *et al.* argue that prevention is 'aimed at ensuring that human rights violations do not occur or re-occur'.[56]

The Council's promotion mandate extends beyond monitoring, supporting and enabling states' compliance with human rights norms. The Council must contribute to the 'development of international law in the field of human rights'

---

54 See, for example, Chapter 8 and the discussion on Sudan.
55 As will be explored, throughout, in relation to the Special Procedures system.
56 Kälin *et al.*, 'The Human Rights Council and Country Situations', p. 15.

(para. 5 (c)). That mandate involves making recommendations to the GA (para. 5 (c)). Promotion in this regard occurs by increasing and developing legal aspects of human rights, and by identifying areas needing further attention.

Protection Mandate. The protection mandate requires the Council to protect individuals from abuses. It is primarily aimed at situations or ongoing violations within a particular state. Ongoing or systemic abuses are often committed, or tolerated, by governments. Protecting human rights within a state's national jurisdiction is more contentious than promoting rights, and often leads to tensions with the country concerned. Protection ideally includes a swift, strong, and short-term response to violations. Promotion, conversely, identifies long-term problems that do not always require immediate or strong action. The Council's protection activities are typically unlikely to be invited, or indeed cooperated with, by the country concerned.

'Protection' is defined by the *Oxford English Dictionary* as 'the act of protecting; defence from harm, danger or evil'. The Council must respond to human rights violations. The Resolution's language implies that the Council must protect the victims, in contrast with the promotion mandate which focuses on the rights. Again, Paragraph 4 emphasises that the Council must address situations that include, but are not limited to, 'gross and systemic violations'. Inclusion of 'other situations of violations of human rights' indicates that any situation of human rights abuses may be addressed under this mandate. Power is thus given to the Council to respond to violations whenever and however they occur.

The Council is required to 'address situations of human rights violations' (para. 3). Addressing those situations is a broad mandate, but the body is required to 'make recommendations thereon' (para. 3). Kälin *et al.* argue that this provision allows the body to adopt country-specific resolutions outside of the UPR.[57] Those recommendations are not limited to being solely condemnatory, as had occurred at the Commission, but can incorporate all aspects of the body's protection and promotion mandates. Recommendations on such situations can, and arguably should, for example, include 'emphasis on encouraging it and addressing its capacity-building needs' alongside condemning violations.[58]

Another key protection mechanism is convening Special Sessions to discuss grave or crisis situations. Special Sessions is an innovative mechanism that enables the Council to respond to human rights situations. A main failing of the Commission was that its annual session allowed neither the time nor the swiftness of response to deal with crisis situations or crises within ongoing situations. Special Sessions are separate sessions and because of this, convening Special Sessions enables a quick and focused response to grave situations without using time and resources that had been allocated for other human rights matters.

57 *Ibid.*, p. 16.
58 *Ibid.*

The protection mandate will undoubtedly be more difficult to discharge than the promotion mandate, not least owing to the contentious nature of acting on human rights violations. Other UN bodies have the power to intervene in, or to protect human rights during grave or crisis situations. Those bodies are not, however, principally concerned with human rights. The protection mandate requires the Council to fulfil a role not undertaken elsewhere. It is, therefore, crucial that the Council discharges its duties.

General Requirements. Resolution 60/251 also includes more general requirements that advance both the promotion and protection mandates. Those requirements relate to the Council's role in the wider field of human rights. The Council, for example, is mandated to work closely and maintain a relationship with other human rights bodies, organisations, and state and non-state actors.[59] Interaction with the wider field is of particular importance for the promotion mandate because it enables greater information sharing as well as support and advisory services. Requirements for the Council to make human rights recommendations (para. 5 (i)) and submit an annual report to the GA (para. 5 (j)) ensure that the body's work is wide-reaching, and that it enables protection and promotion by other actors.

Resolution 60/251 mandates the Council to work with the Special Procedures system to protect and promote human rights (paras 6 and 12). Special Procedures mandates are either thematic or country-specific. Thematic mandates focus more on promotion whereas country-specific mandates are more involved with protection. All mandate holders promote human rights through fact-finding and work with all actors to identify gaps in national human rights systems. Similarly, all mandate holders protect rights by identifying and reporting on violations. The Special Procedures system operates independently, within the UN as a whole, which poses difficulties despite that system's importance to the Council fulfilling its mandate. This issue will be explored in Chapter 5.

Although both protection and promotion are key to the body's work, I shall focus more on the protection mandate when assessing the Council. Promotion of human rights is undertaken by various organisations, bodies, and non-state actors, and is crucial for long-term compliance with human rights norms. Protection, on the other hand, is often solely undertaken by the Council. Promoting rights is relatively non-contentious. Protecting human rights is a more difficult mandate to achieve in practice, and difficulties often arise. It will take some time before the impact of promotion activities can be assessed, whereas protection, or the failure to do so, can be assessed relatively swiftly. Protection is crucial for the Council to achieve its aims.

---

59 GA Res. 60/251, 'Human Rights Council', 15 March 2006, UN Doc. A/RES/60/251, para. 5 (h).

3.4. The Council's powers

There are four types of international instruments: binding (law-making); administrative (applying the law); household (relating to the internal functioning of the organisation); and non-binding.[60] International organisations are generally limited in their abilities to undertake institutional acts which bind their members outside of the organisation.[61] It is widely accepted that a body can only adopt binding acts if its constituent document expressly gives such powers.[62] Although most bodies do not have binding powers,[63] many are able to 'make recommendations to members of the organisation within their field of competence, in order to promote or help to achieve the organisation's objectives'.[64]

The Council has only non-binding powers. Despite some calls for it to be a principal UN organ, the Council is a subsidiary organ of the GA. Maurer comments that, during negotiations on the Council's creation, some states sought to limit further the Council's powers.[65] China and Russia, for example, were adamant that the body should not be allowed to submit recommendations directly to any principal UN organs other than the GA. Attempts to limit the Council's powers resulted in Resolution 60/251 allowing the body to adopt only non-binding acts. However, non-binding acts can have both legal effects and political implications.[66] Non-binding acts seek 'to influence behaviour, but without creating law',[67] but frequently form the basis for 'soft law'.[68] Such acts include recommendations, declarations, codes of conduct or other generally non-binding resolutions.[69] These instruments require state cooperation and consent for implementation.

Non-binding instruments provide international organisations with a pragmatic compromise for decision-making.[70] Unanimous decision-making results in greater legitimacy, but binding decisions will be almost impossible to reach. Majoritarian decision-making threatens states 'that have something to lose'.[71] Tammes asserts that non-binding acts provide a method for taking

---

60 cf. Klabbers, *Introduction to International Institutional Law*, pp. 200–201.
61 P. Sands and P. Klein, *Bowett's Law of International Institutions*, London: Sweet & Maxwell, 2001, pp. 261–2.
62 *Ibid.*, p. 280.
63 *Ibid.*, p. 280.
64 *Ibid.*, pp. 285–6.
65 Maurer, 'About the Negotiation Process in New York', 36.
66 Sands and Klein, *Bowett's Law of International Institutions*, pp. 261–2.
67 Klabbers, *Introduction to International Institutional Law*, p. 201.
68 cf. M.N. Shaw, *International Law*, 5th edn., Cambridge: Cambridge University Press, 2003, pp. 110–12.
69 Klabbers, *Introduction to International Institutional Law*, p. 201.
70 A.J.P. Tammes, 'Decisions of International Organs as a Source of International Law', *Recueil des Cours*, Vol. 94, 1958-II, p. 304.
71 *Ibid.*

action by majority decision because the acts create no legal obligations and therefore are less threatening to states which do not fully agree to them.[72] Klabbers notes that, despite their non-binding nature, such instruments 'may be as effective (or ineffective) as legally binding ones'.[73] When the Council gains consensus, or at least wide agreement, on its acts, the nominally non-binding powers are expected to be adopted across most, if not all, states owing to the countries' participation in and agreement to the decision-making. Moreover, consensus ensures that greater and more unified political pressure may be asserted regarding state implementation.

The Council has various powers that assist fulfilment of its mandate. Klabbers notes that it only 'makes sense' to create an international organisation if it is capable of performing acts rather than merely being an arena for discussions.[74] However, it is not always clear what powers a body holds, particularly as constituent documents may be ambiguous as to which acts may be undertaken.[75] Resolution 60/251 sets out certain powers that the Council must exercise. As with the body's mandate, the Resolution is rather general and broad regarding the Council's powers. Therefore, some uncertainty exists regarding which powers the Council are, and are not, granted. The Council's four main powers are: recommendations, standard-setting, compliance powers, and technical powers.

3.4.1 Recommendations

The Council's main power, or at least the one most often mentioned in Resolution 60/251 (paras 3, 5 (c), 5 (i), 12), is making recommendations. As a general matter, recommendations, whilst being important for politics,[76] are not binding on member states outside of the organisation.[77] Organisations may, however, use recommendations to state the current or suggested law.[78] Recommendations may even have some legal effects, for example requiring members to implement and monitor the suggested measures.[79] Implementation and follow-up is common practice at UN specialised agencies.[80]

---

72 *Ibid.*

73 Klabbers, *Introduction to International Institutional Law*, p. 201; See, for example, B. Kingsbury, 'The Concept of Compliance as a Function of Competing Conceptions of International Law', in E.B. Weiss (ed.), *International Compliance with Nonbinding Accords*, Washington: American Society of International Law, 1997.

74 Klabbers, *Introduction to International Institutional Law*, p. 97.

75 *Ibid.*, p. 197.

76 On the political weight of recommendations, see H.G. Schermers and N.M. Blokkers, *International Institutional Law*, 3rd edn., Dordrecht: Martinus Nijhoff, 1995, para. 1226.

77 I. Detter, 'The Effect of Resolutions of International Organizations', in J. Makarczyk (ed.), *Theory of International Law at the Threshold of the 21st Century: Essays in Honour of K. Skubiszewski*, London: Kluwer Law, 1996, pp. 389–90.

78 Sands and Klein, *Bowett's Law of International Institutions*, pp. 286–7.

79 *Ibid.*

80 *Ibid.*

The Council may make recommendations on a broad range of areas, including thematic human rights, country-specific situations, and gross and systemic violations. Recommendations may be used in relation to the Council's promotion and protection mandates. Kälin *et al.* assert that the general language of Paragraph 5 (i), giving the Council the power to make recommendations, requires the body to use that power to protect and promote rights across both thematic and country-specific issues.[81] Recommendations seeking to promote rights are generally less contentious than those made under the Council's protection mandate.[82] States are more likely to achieve consensus, or near unanimity, on promoting rights. Protection focuses on more politically sensitive issues, thus requiring greater efforts to achieve state cooperation with creating and implementing recommendations. Generally, recommendations aimed at protection do condemn violators. However, Kälin *et al.* insist that recommendations on country-specific situations should not solely condemn violators.[83] Instead, those recommendations should also promote state compliance with human rights obligations. Country-specific recommendations could, or perhaps should, include focus on assisting the cessation of abuses and supporting prevention of recurrences.

3.4.2 *Standard-setting*

Standard-setting is another key power set out in Resolution 60/251. Sands and Klein note that the power to adopt norms is common among international organisations.[84] Standard-setting, particularly through adopting norms, is often central to those bodies' mandates.[85] A key aspect of the Commission's work had been to set human rights standards which, as previously discussed, constituted much of the body's early work.

The Council is mandated to assume the Commission's standard-setting role. The power to adopt norms extends to various aspects of the Council's mandate. The Council's standard-setting may produce acts which bind all UN members because the 'norms enunciated [. . .] may be linked to one or another "classical" source of international law'.[86] For example, the Council's contributions to the development of international law (para. 5 (c)) may include recommending that the GA adopt human rights norms which are already legally binding under international customary law.

3.4.3 *Compliance powers*

The Council is given the power to undertake certain supervisory roles, such as monitoring state compliance with human rights. Sands and Klein note

81 Kälin *et al.*, 'The Human Rights Council and Country Situations', p. 15.
82 *Ibid.*
83 *Ibid.*, p. 16.
84 Sands and Klein, *Bowett's Law of International Institutions*, p. 262.
85 *Ibid.*, p. 261.
86 *Ibid.*, pp. 287–8.

that states in breach of their obligations may face diplomatic or political pressure, including 'protest and censure by the organisation, the postponement or cancellation of visits and meetings, and the reduction of diplomatic representation. More far reaching, however, are [. . .] the suspension of rights relating the organisation.'[87] The Council may suspend member states under Paragraph 8. That power is a direct response to criticism that known abusers held Commission membership. As the example of the aforementioned suspension of Libya suggests, however, that tactic has thus far been used only to limited effect. The Council also has powers to deal with states that do not cooperate with the body's recommendations or monitoring. Such measures include recommending visits from Special Rapporteurs, appointing a country-specific mandate holder, or calling on the GA or Security Council to look into the situation.[88]

3.4.4 *Technical powers*

Another Council function is information sharing. This is an expansive power as it involves various actors, including states, UN bodies and staff, and NGOs. The Council is mandated to work within the wider UN system, and with civil society actors, to protect and promote human rights. The body has the power[89] to share information with, and receive information from, those actors. Its implied powers extend to capacity-building, a recurrent theme throughout Resolution 60/251. The Council has powers, then, to assist with capacity-building, despite those powers not being set out in the Resolution. The same can be said for other Council functions, including providing advisory services and technical assistance, and other roles, including being a forum for dialogue between various stakeholders.

3.5. Founding principles

The Council's founding principles impose legal requirements. They reflect the criticisms levelled at the Commission, and stem from interstate negotiations on the Council's creation. The Council's founding principles divide into two broad categories: principles that guide its work on human rights, and principles that guide its relationship to individual states. The principles concerning human rights work seek to ensure that the work is even-handed and non-selective. The principles aimed at the Council's relationship with states seek to ensure effective fulfilment of its mandate.

The principles include non-selectivity, universality, objectivity, cooperation, and dialogue. Repetition of these principles throughout the Resolution (e.g.

---

87 *Ibid.*, pp. 330–31.

88 See, for example, Kälin, *et al.*, 'The Human Rights Council and Country Situations', p. 18.

89 On whether such powers need to be express or can be implied see Sands and Klein, *Bowett's Law of International Institutions*, pp. 319–20.

paras 2, 4, 5 (e), 12) underscores that they apply to all aspects of the body's mechanisms, proceedings and work.[90]

The founding principles are first set out in Preambular Paragraph 9, which stresses 'the importance of ensuring universality, objectivity and non-selectivity [. . .] and the elimination of double standards and politicization'. Universality is integral to the UN human rights system. The UDHR first enshrined the notion of universal rights; that human rights apply across the world to all people. All states are required, in theory, to protect and promote all rights within their own and other countries' jurisdictions. The UN has adopted the universality approach despite some states, regional groups or political blocs viewing human rights from other theoretical perspectives.[91]

Despite emphasising universality, Resolution 60/251 is silent on the concept of even-handedness when universally applying human rights. Although some countries may be judged against each other's standards, this is not always the case, because states often have different capabilities for implementing human rights. States' capacity for upholding human rights is dependent on factors such as development, resources, and national institutions. Sweden, for example, cannot be compared with Somalia. Despite not formally being recognised as a central principle, various actors have emphasised the importance of adopting an even-handed approach to human rights. For example, the former High Commissioner for Human Rights, Louise Arbour insisted that human rights 'must be discussed in context: simply comparing one situation to another is arguably less useful than assessing each on its own terms'.[92]

The second founding principle calls for objectivity within the Council's work. An objective approach requires the Council to adopt a neutral approach to human rights, particularly country-specific situations. It seeks to ensure that the body's work is guided by human rights rather than by states or groups' agendas.

Bias and selectivity, as previously discussed, were two main Commission failings. The principle of non-selectivity seeks to address these flaws. Non-selectivity requires the Council to protect and promote human rights in an even-handed manner, allocating proportionate time and resources dependent on an individual state's needs, without the Commission's culture of blame. Repeated focus on a state's human rights record, or the singling out of a state for constant resolutions, to the detriment of examining other similar or worse abusers, would violate this principle. Non-selectivity requires the body to avoid both overt politicisation and politicisation through an ostensible 'success story', whereby the focus on one country means ignoring other known

90 Kälin, *et al.*, 'The Human Rights Council and Country Situations', p. 16.
91 cf. A, Gewirth, *Human Rights: Essays on Justification and Applications*, London: University of Chicago Press, 1982; J. Griffin, *On Human Rights*, Oxford: Oxford University Press, 2008, p. 33.
92 Speech of the High Commissioner for Human Rights, CHR 61st Session, 14 March 2005.

abusers.[93] The Council is required to eliminate politicisation and double standards. These principles reflect negotiating positions that the Council should move away from the Commission's confrontational 'shaming and blaming', which was widely viewed as ineffective and had been criticised by many states, particularly countries from the Global South. The HRC is expected to adopt a more constructive approach to human rights protection and promotion through cooperation and dialogue. Cooperation and dialogue arguably combat that 'shaming and blaming' culture, in theory providing a more effective way to protect and promote human rights. In practice, however, and as will be demonstrated throughout Part 3, cooperation and dialogue have frequently provided states with an easy shield from scrutiny.

State cooperation enables countries being discussed at the body to be involved with the Council's work. That principle acknowledges that human rights are a domestic concern and that working with individual states may provide an effective method for implementing human rights standards and norms. The Council's lack of binding powers requires, and indeed reflects the need for, the body to work with states in order to achieve its aims. Effective implementation of human rights requires a culture of cooperation as well as assistance for states which need, for example, capacity-building. Dialogue is key for this cooperative approach, reflected in its emphasis as a founding principle. Inter-state dialogue, and the inclusion of non-state actors, provides human rights expertise and assistance as well as affording states an opportunity to engage with the process of protecting and promoting human rights. Cooperative methods, while important in theory, provide the Council with little practical assistance with protecting or promoting human rights; instead they afford states an opportunity to avoid taking responsibility for non-compliance.

The founding principles emphasise the Council's primary function to promote and protect all human rights across UN member states. Although they deal with many key criticisms of the Commission, the principles' central aim is to ensure the Council fulfils its mandate. Scannella and Splinter remain sceptical about the body's ability to adhere to these principles, despite the Resolution's assurances that politicisation would not dominate the Council.[94] They argue that, as the Council remains a political body, the achievement of the founding principles in eliminating politicisation should not be judged until they are put into practice, or otherwise.[95] Furthermore, until governments accept and apply these principles, nothing will change at the UN human rights body.[96]

Scannella and Splinter note that the founding principles 'are valuable reminders of how the promotion and protection of human rights should be approached in the United Nations'.[97] Assessing the Council's adherence to

---

93 See Chapter 6, Section 6.3.
94 Scannella and Splinter, 'The United Nations Human Rights Council', pp. 68–9.
95 *Ibid.*
96 *Ibid.*
97 *Ibid.*, pp. 50–51.

these principles poses certain difficulties. The principles are open-ended and somewhat ethereal, indicating that they are guidelines rather than precise requirements. Neither the body nor other actors have interpreted their meanings. No method has been created to determine whether the body has complied with these principles. I shall adopt a simple methodology throughout Part 3 to identify instances where striking non-adherence has occurred. Selectivity can be measured through disproportionate focus on a state for political aims, or indeed shielding known abusers for similarly political motivations. Partiality impacts upon the body's work and proceedings when certain states or thematic rights are favoured over others. Lack of universality results in a lack of even-handedness and proportionality when dealing with country-specific situations and thematic rights.

3.6. The Institution Building Package

The Institution Building Package (IBP) adds details to areas left broad or undefined in Resolution 60/251. The IBP was finalised at the Council's Fifth Session, after months of consultations, and was adopted on 18 June 2007. The Chairperson sought to achieve consensus on the IBP,[98] but areas of disagreement remained even during the final negotiations. Schrijver notes that the final text was only agreed upon 'during the very final days and hours' of the Fifth Session.[99] In contrast to Resolution 60/251, which broadly sets out the Council's mandate functions, the IBP details the modalities of the Council's mechanisms and instruments, as well as the general agenda for future sessions. The IBP elaborates upon the founding principles,[100] detailing additional powers and functions, and gives guidelines for the Council's work, for example, rules for the new UPR mechanism and details of the revised complaints procedure.

The IBP sets out the Council's permanent agenda to be followed at each regular session.[101] The permanent agenda aims to ensure that the Council can overcome its predecessor's failure to deal adequately with all human rights matters. Agenda Items 3 and 4 provide broad banners under which member

---

98 'We must try to finish our work by Thursday 15 June. If we have a constructive spirit, we will be able to do this. In the talks over the last few days, the biggest question I have been asked is whether I consider if we have been making a true contribution, or simply a Least Common Denominator. I say no, and that real progress has been made. Although the text does need improvement, it does have a high degree of agreement. We have been working largely in consensus.' Oral intervention of Council Chairman, Informal meeting, 5th Session, 8 June 2007.

99 Schrijver, 'A New "Society of the Committed"', 818.

100 HRC Res 5/1, 'Institution Building of the United Nations Human Rights Council', 18 June 2007, UN Doc. A/HRC/RES/5/1, Chapter V 'Agenda and Framework for the Programme of Work' Section A 'Principles'.

101 On the role of mandate holders, see HRC Res 5/1, 'Institution Building of the United Nations Human Rights Council', 18 June 2007, UN Doc. A/HRC/RES/5/1, Item B.

states may raise any issues relating to protection or promotion of thematic human rights (Item 3) or country-specific human rights (Item 4). Agenda Item 3 allows states to raise protection and promotion issues pertaining to all human rights, and sets out broad categories – 'civil, political, economic, social and cultural rights' – under which matters may be raised. Item 3 does, however, emphasise one individual right; 'the right to development'. That right appears as a result of the Global South's concerns that the Council should recognise the link between human rights and development, and also that the body should not allow human rights to be used as a tool of neo-colonial oppression.

Alongside providing a broad basis for discussions, the agenda focuses Council attention on specific human rights areas which directly correlate to various aspects of Resolution 60/251. Item 10 reflects the body's duty to promote human rights through technical assistance and capacity-building. This item allows states time to raise concerns about, or enter into dialogues on, those aspects of the Council's work, and emphasises their importance for promoting human rights. Agenda Items 2, 5 and 8 reflect the body's duties to interact with the wider UN human rights machinery and non-state actors. Item 6 solely focuses on the UPR.

Two agenda items, however, directly contradict the Council's founding principles of non-selectivity and universality. One country-specific situation, as previously discussed, is singled out, under Agenda Item 7, to be discussed at every regular Council session. To focus permanent attention solely on the human rights situation in 'Palestine and other occupied Arab territories' is clearly selective, particularly given the persistence of other long-standing crisis regions or situations, many of which have claimed far greater numbers of victims. Moreover, one thematic right is also singled out and placed on the permanent agenda. Item 9 mandates the Council to discuss 'racism, racial discrimination, xenophobia and related forms of intolerance' at every regular session. Both of these agenda items were proposed and supported by Organisation of the Islamic Conference (OIC) members and their allies. That bloc's dominance at the Council enabled it to secure items clearly related to its political objectives despite the obvious violation of the body's founding principles.

The IBP includes additional powers. Paragraph 118,[102] for example, encompasses 'recommendations, conclusions, summaries of discussions and President's Statement'. The text indicates that those powers have 'different legal implications [which] should supplement and not replace resolutions and decisions'. Paragraph 118, therefore, provides further mechanisms for fulfilling both aspects of the mandate. The IBP also provides greater detail of how the Council's mechanisms will work. Paragraph 128, for example, expands on Special Sessions, stating that they 'should allow participatory

---

102 *Ibid.*, Item C.

debate, be results oriented and geared to achieving practical outcomes, the implementation of which can be monitored and reported on'. Although primarily concerned with protecting rights, the IBP requires Special Sessions to focus on promoting rights through providing long-term goals which are to be implemented during and after the sessions. The IBP generally seeks to ensure that both the protection and promotion mandates are fulfilled across all of the Council's work.

3.7. Summary

GA Resolution 60/251 sets out two distinct, yet interwoven mandates – protection and promotion of human rights. The Council is tasked with addressing short-term human rights situations where victims need to be protected from abuses. Various tools are available for the body to fulfil this mandate: convening Special Sessions, making recommendations, passing decisions and resolutions, and instigating fact-finding and investigations. The Council is also required to promote longer-term human rights compliance through capacity-building, advisory services, fact-finding, dialogue with states and non-state actors, and providing technical and other assistance. The Council's mandate can only be understood in light of the background to the body's creation, particularly its predecessor's failure and the proposed reforms. Assessing the body will require greater focus on the protection mandate than the promotion mandate, not least because the former is more contentious and harder to discharge. Protecting human rights is, in many respects, easier to assess over the Council's relatively short existence. The short-term results, or lack thereof, from the protection mandate can more easily be quantified than the longer-term promotion mandate.

The constituent instrument sets out the powers and mechanisms by which the Council can discharge its mandate. Those powers are not legally binding, which reflects a general focus on cooperation, inclusiveness and dialogue between states, non-state actors and the body itself. The Commission's atmosphere had increasingly become one of naming, shaming and blaming states, a culture that the drafters of Resolution 60/251 clearly sought to avoid. The Resolution emphasises inclusiveness through constant repetition of the need for cooperation and dialogue. However, the Council's lack of binding powers results in it relying on state cooperation for its mandate to be discharged through national implementation. That cooperation may occur through the body's own channels and relationships with countries, or through political pressure from other member and non-member states.

The Commission's failure can largely be attributed to various forms of increasing politicisation during its final years. Politicisation occurred through, amongst others, regionalism, power struggles, and misuse of procedural mechanisms. Although politicisation was widely identified as the Commission's main failing, the former UN High Commissioner for Human Rights did say that such criticisms have been equivalent to 'fish criticising one another for being wet'.[103] Some radical reform proposals aimed to eliminate politicisation from the new human rights body. Most of them were not implemented, or were diluted, largely owing to fears that radical reforms would fundamentally affect the Council's legitimacy. A main example of those fears was that greatly reducing the number of member states, or indeed limiting membership to countries with greater capacity for human rights, would undermine the legitimacy that stems from proportionate geographic representation. Instead, the new body, with its particular focus on member states' accountability, aimed to eradicate politicisation as far as possible whilst retaining a geographically representative membership. The founding principles provide broad guidelines for eliminating politicisation, but are of little practical value. Observers and some states, such as the US, expressed reservations about whether, without radical reforms being implemented, the theoretical hope of eliminating politicisation could be achieved in practice. Rahmani-Ocora asserts: '[a] fresh start may be just what the international human rights machinery needs; however, with the same players in entrenched positions, the old political game is likely to be repeated.'[104]

Lack of radical reform resulted in many similarities between the bodies, both in terms of their form and their mandates. The Council has barely a handful fewer members than the Commission, despite calls for a smaller, more streamlined body which would be less affected by politicisation and regionalism. Delegates at the Council remain governmental rather than being independent experts. These factors, combined with the adoption of 'soft' membership criteria, results in the Council resembling the Commission in terms of its members and their representatives. The Council's size and its inclusiveness regarding eligibility for membership are key for granting the body legitimacy at the UN and amongst its member states. Negotiations on the new body underscored the central importance of that legitimacy.

In the following chapters the methodology alluded to above, along with theories on international relations set out in Part 2, will be applied to the Council. It will be shown how, despite the desire to move away from the Commission's failures and to inject credibility into the human rights body, the Council is at times undermined, and arguably delegitimised, by politicisation.

---

103 Sergio Vieira De Mello, Statement of the High Commissioner for Human Rights to the closing meeting of the 59th Session of the Commission on Human Rights, 25 April 2003.
104 Rahmani-Ocora, 'Giving the Emperor Real Clothes', 16.

Part 2

Criteria for assessing the Council

4   International relations theories

4.0. Introduction to part

No intergovernmental body can be assessed without reference to theories of international organisations. Owing to the political nature of intergovernmental bodies, theories of international relations as applied to international organisations must be utilised to understand the work and proceedings of any such body. Five main theories will be explored here – realism, idealism, social constructivism, institutionalism, and Marxism[1] – and then applied to the Council's mandate, roles and functions, work and proceedings. Each of the five theories provides a 'map' of the international system, which Slaughter deems essential for approaching international relations from either a political or legal position.[2] The theories engage with the practical realities occurring within the Council, providing a method of assessment that moves beyond the legal language of the body's documents. None of the theories is an exact fit. All have some merits, as will be shown through application and analysis of the Council in relation to each theory. Weaknesses will be dealt with, in turn, in order to demonstrate that no single approach suffices when examining HRC proceedings.

Scholars of international law and of international relations maintained a distance from one another for many years, despite recognising each other's work. Simmons explores the reasons for this separation, identifying relatively few instances of collaboration between international law and international relations scholars.[3] Henkin notes that compliance with international commitments is a fundamental component of international relations.[4] Slaughter

---

1 The preceding chapters, and the chapters that follow, demonstrate that it is impossible to discuss the Commission and the Council without considering post-colonial discourses. Much of that discourse stems from Marxism and post-Marxist theories.

2 A.-M. Slaughter, 'International Law and International Relations', *Hague Academy of International Law*, Vol. 285, 2001, 27.

3 B.A. Simmons, 'International Law and International Relations: Scholarship at the Intersection of Principles and Politics', *American Society of International Proceedings*, Vol. 95, 2001, 274–8.

4 L. Henkin, *How Nations Behave: Law and Foreign Policy*, New York: F.A. Praeger, 1968, pp. 256–7.

comments that international law cannot be separated from its political context.[5] Whilst law plays a role in governing almost every area of international relations and international relations impacts upon the creation of and compliance with international law, scepticism about the overlapping roles has historically resulted in little scholarship combining these two fields.[6]

Current scholars, such as Goldstein and Keohane, recognise the intrinsically bound nature of international law and politics. They argue that international law cannot be separated from international politics, as law is interwoven with and affected by the machinery and interests of international politics.[7] Slaughter goes further, noting the difficulty in determining whether international law is more than a mere manifestation of states' political will.[8] I adopt an innovative approach that focuses on the intersection of international law and politics. International law is used to understand the Council's mechanisms, whereas international relations theory assists with understanding the body's actual work, proceedings, and the manner in which it undertakes its mandate.

4.1. Realism

Realist writers on international relations can trace their origins to the 1930s.[9] Realist theory in relation to international organisations was a reaction to the failure of the League of Nations to prevent invasions, for example, of Abyssinia and Manchuria, and the spread of fascism across Europe. Some realists challenged the relevance of international law to state behaviour,[10] while others[11] questioned the creation of the League of Nations for international governance when Germany was re-arming and preparing for a second world war.[12] The Second World War, followed by the Cold War, gave credibility to the realist view that a lack of common authority over states results in international anarchy.[13] Neo-realism developed from the early 1980s. Although it adopts much of classical realism's premises, it develops different conclusions.[14]

5   Slaughter, 'International Law and International Relations', 21.

6   Simmons, 'International Law and International Relations', 271–9.

7   J. Goldstein, M. Kahler, R.O. Keohane and A.-M. Slaughter, 'Legalization and World Politics', *International Organization*, Vol. 54 (3), 2000, 387.

8   Slaughter, 'International Law and International Relations', 22.

9   C. Archer, *International Organizations*, London: George Allen & Unwin, 1983, p. 75.

10   R.E. Osgood and R.W. Tucker, *Force, Order and Justice*, Baltimore, MD: Johns Hopkins University Press, 1967, pp. 269–70.

11   E.H. Carr, *The Twenty Years' Crisis, 1919–1939: An Introduction to the Study of International Relations*, [1939], New York: St Martin's Press, 1964, p. vii.

12   Slaughter, 'International Law and International Relations', 22.

13   *Ibid.*, 33.

14   See, for example, J. Mearsheimer, 'The False Promise of International Institutions', *International Security*, Vol. 19 (3), 1995, 10–14.

International relations realists have traditionally proposed a state-centric view of the world, regarding international organisations as part of institutionalised relationships that exist between states and their governments. Classical realist theory views states, unified and self-contained entities, as the decisive actors in international politics.[15] States are continually seeking power, much as national political parties are always striving to have and retain power.[16] The struggle for power is the focal point of all international relations.[17] International organisations are used by powerful states to implement power politics and to pursue their own self-interest.[18] International law and institutions only work if they reflect the most powerful states' interests.[19]

Disillusioned by the failure of the League of Nations, Carr argued that, to be successful, the international system must take into account the realities of existing power relationships between states.[20] One of the main problems that he identified was discrimination in the international community between the different treatments afforded to cases regarding different countries.[21] Carr illustrated that discrimination with reference to the different international reactions to the invasions of Greece (1940) and Abyssinia (1935).[22] The international community, and in particular Britain and France, harbouring their own imperial ambitions, all but ignored the Italian invasion of Abyssinia, merely deeming it regrettable. Italy's invasion of Greece five years later resulted in support for the invaded country from both Britain and France, with Italy's actions being deemed unacceptable.

Morgenthau's body of work constantly referred to three key elements of international relations: that states are the most important actors; there is a clear distinction between national and international politics; and international relations are predominantly about the struggle for power.[23] As such, Morgenthau viewed international organisations simply as instruments used by states in their search for power. Morgenthau described the UN as 'the new setting for the old techniques of diplomacy' explaining that even this international organisation was mainly a forum for intergovernmental discourse.[24] The HRC, with various states and regional groups vying for power, is a good example of the use of an international organisation in this manner.

15 See, for example, Carr, *The Twenty Years' Crisis*.
16 M.J. Smith, *Realist Thought from Weber to Kissinger*, Baton Rouge, LA: Louisiana State University Press, 1986, p. 13.
17 See, for example, H.J. Morgenthau, *Politics Among Nations: The Struggle for Power and Peace*, New York: McGraw-Hill, 1993.
18 See, for example, A. Roberts and B. Kingsbury (eds.), *United Nations, Divided World*, 2nd edn., Oxford: Oxford University Press, 1993.
19 Slaughter, 'International Law and International Relations', 31.
20 E.H. Carr, *Nationalism and After*, London: Macmillan, 1946.
21 *Ibid.*, p. 166.
22 *Ibid.*
23 J.A. Vasquez, 'Colouring it Morgenthau: New Evidence for an Old Thesis on Quantitative International Politics', *British Journal of International Studies*, Vol. 5 (3), 1979, 211.
24 Morgenthau, *Politics Among Nations: The Struggle for Power and Peace*, p. 497.

Comparisons can be drawn between international organisations where power politics prevail, and, for example, the Universal Postal Union, where power struggles between states play no role.[25]

Realist theorists maintain that states' primary objective is asserting and ensuring their own interests. Where states exist within an anarchic world, they prioritise that primary objective during all interstate relations. International relations becomes a game whereby states seek sufficient power in order to be protected from other countries.[26] Blocs of states, in the form of regional or like-minded groups, are one way in which states can amass and maintain power and influence at international organisations. Weaker states allied with each other can, at times, exert more influence than powerful states on their own. One of the Commission's main failings was the power struggle between groups of states.

Morgenthau criticises those who define international organisations as anything other than political arenas.[27] He includes in this analysis 'functional organisations', i.e. those relating to practical and technical matters, for example the World Health Organisation, as opposed to more intergovernmental political arenas such as the General Assembly. Morgenthau, sceptical that even the most 'functionalist' agencies could be anything other than political arenas, comments that ultimately interstate conflicts overshadow any positive contributions made by international organisations to individual countries or the international community as a whole.[28] Steinberg similarly argues that international law is nothing more than states furthering their national interests.[29] NGOs, the media and scholars have criticised, from the outset, the HRC for being used by states for political objectives. Such furtherance of national interests is displayed in the debates and discussions focusing on a few states, and the systematic failure to scrutinise of some of the most egregious violators, which also undermined the body's credibility.

A lack of action on situations involving grave violations, either through silence or blocking of meaningful action, results in a body where political conflicts take precedence over fulfilment of its mandate. As a subsidiary body of the General Assembly, the HRC is not solely a 'functional' agency, although it does provide some practical and technical assistance for the protection and promotion of human rights. The Council's main role is to deal with human rights issues as opposed to undertaking low-level functional tasks. Despite such differences between subsidiary bodies and specialised agencies, Morgenthau's

25 T.G. Weiss, *What's Wrong with the United Nations and How to Fix It*, Cambridge: Polity Press, 2008, p. 49.
26 Slaughter, 'International Law and International Relations', 32.
27 H.J. Morgenthau, *Politics Among Nations*, New York: Alfred A. Knopf, 1960.
28 Morgenthau, *Politics Among Nations*, p. 528.
29 R.H. Steinberg, *The Greening of Trade Law? International Trade Organizations and Environmental Issues*, Lanham, MD: Rowman & Littlefield Publishers Inc., 2002.

criticism applies to the HRC, as the body influences the work of specialised agencies whose work overlaps with human rights.[30] Political conflicts that overshadow the body's work thus have a strong impact upon the contributions of the UN functional agencies in the field of human rights.

Realists view international organisations as ineffective mechanisms for effective regulation of state behaviour. The democratic voting rules mean that groups of weaker states, whose domestic regimes are often undemocratic, can exert more influence at the Council than individually powerful countries. Downs *et al.* rather implausibly call for enforcement mechanisms to back up all international legal arrangements in order to combat such ineffectiveness, without which they argue that the arrangements are obsolete, as governments will continue to act as they would have done in the absence of a legal commitment.[31] Council decisions, being only hortatory, that is of an advisory or persuasive nature, remain political. Indeed, states can choose to ignore the Council's work. However, international organisations that pass binding rules effectively force weaker members to submit to the will of stronger ones.[32] The HRC cannot pass legally binding resolutions, nor does it have its own enforcement mechanisms. Human rights issues can only be legally enforced through such bodies with legally binding powers or enforcement mechanisms, such as the UN Security Council, which occurs very rarely. Moreover, decisions at such bodies to legally enforce human rights are made according to the political strength of individual members.

The United States under the Bush administration, for reasons examined in detail in Chapter 7, declined to stand for election for the HRC's first three years, from 2006–2009. It did so knowing that the body was unable to impact on its sovereignty. At the HRC, powerful states often choose to take a back seat, with certain powerful states and groups particularly notable for abstaining during controversial resolutions or for taking neutral stances in debates.[33]

4.2. Idealism

Former United States President Woodrow Wilson was a prominent proponent of idealism. The League of Nations was founded on the expectation that societies would always prefer peace, thus preventing individual states from going to war. Idealism regards actors as being directed by values and norms that are generally shared, if not universal. That notion has been a subject of controversy, particularly from a post-colonial perspective which rejects the stance that all Western human rights norms are universal. States therefore

30 Morgenthau, *Politics Among Nations*.
31 G. Downs, D. Rocke and P. Barsoom, 'Is the Good News About Compliance Good News About Cooperation', *International Organization*, Vol. 50 (3), 1996, 379–406.
32 Goldstein *et al.*, 'Legalization and World Politics', 391.
33 See, generally, Part 3, in particular on the EU's role at the Council.

behave in a manner guided by what is appropriate according to values rather than being driven by what consequences may be expected. Normative ideal-ists therefore oppose realism, arguing that people, not states, are the central actors in international relations.[34] According to idealists, people are moral actors guided by ideals, values and norms, and states act in accordance with those values. Realists, however, would argue that states do not necessarily represent societal values, especially within non-democratic countries where governments do not represent the people. Falk asserts that the rapid rise of human rights 'to a position of prominence', nationally and internationally, was both unprecedented and unexpected.[35] Idealists explain the rapid rise as being due to increased emphasis on human rights within societies and societal groups. Falk further argues that '[t]his rise cuts across the grain of both the structure of world order and the "realist" outlook of most political leaders acting on behalf of sovereign states'.[36]

Idealism plays a different role in international human rights issues than in, for example, the law of the sea or civil aviation. If human rights were not centred around what are, or should be, common ideals between states, then they might as well only be dealt with by national legal systems. The core of international human rights reflects idealist theories. Idealism is encom-passed in the Universal Declaration of Human Rights, with the preamble describing all people as 'members of the human family'.[37] Resolution 60/251, in a similar vein, is couched in idealist language. The preamble reiterates general aims of the UN such as: 'developing friendly relations among nations' (preamb. para. 1) and 'promoting and encouraging respect for human rights and fundamental freedoms for all' (preamb. para. 1). That language stresses the values that should guide states' actions. States are encouraged to 'respect human rights and fundamental freedoms for all, without distinction of any kind as to race, colour, sex, language or religion, political or other opinion, national or social origin, property, birth or other status' (preamb. para. 5). That passage illustrates an idealist vision which raises complex issues of universality and relativism that go beyond the scope of this assessment. Although idealism is not uncommon in international human rights docu-ments, the preamble's repetition of idealist aims raises realist questions about feasible expectations.

The Council's founding principles also use idealist language, for example underlining the need for universality applying values and norms to all states. However, the principles arguably take a realist approach towards human rights by requiring cooperation, dialogue and inclusiveness. Those

34 W. Wilson, *President Wilson's Great Speeches and Other History Making Documents*, Chicago, IL: Stanton and Van Vilet, 1917/18.

35 R. Falk, 'Foreword', in R. Normand and S. Zaidi (eds.), *Human Rights at the UN: The Political History of Universal Justice*, Bloomington: Indiana University Press, 2008, p. xv.

36 *Ibid.*

37 GA Res. 217A (III), 'Universal Declaration of Human Rights', (1948) UN Doc. A/810, 71.

requirements recognise the reality that a state's involvement with the Council's work will more likely result in subsequent recommendations being implemented or assistance being accepted.

Idealism assists with understanding the theory behind the HRC, but its practical application is of more limited use. Different societies may have competing values and norms, yet idealists hold that common ground can always be found. An international organisation stabilises the common ideals and values of its member states. A major problem with the HRC is that different states, and indeed regional groups, voice fundamentally different positions regarding human rights. Although the norms contained in the UDHR may once have represented shared values, such idealist hopes arguably are no longer realistic. Invocations of competing values obstruct Council efforts. That difficulty reflects the broader problem of universality of human rights and cultural relativism. Lack of action even in the face of grave violations, for example in terms of women's rights in Islamic states, can be explained due to the competing values and norms articulated by member states.

HRC proceedings demonstrate that where there are common norms and values, for example on the relatively non-contentious rights to adequate housing or sanitation, its effectiveness exceeds that of its work in contentious areas. The problem with normative idealism is that too high an expectation is placed on common ground prevailing. Insufficient attention is paid to problems arising where states argue that there are competing values, particularly as there are usually political, as opposed to sincere, motivations for such arguments.

4.3. Social constructivism

Social constructivism, whilst technically identified as a branch of idealism, bridges the gap between realism and normative idealism, demonstrating that the divide between these two theories is more prevalent in theory rather than in practice. Indeed, Slaughter comments that in practice '[i]t is unclear that the supposed divide between Realists and Idealists serves anything other than polemical purposes'.[38] She asserts that the dichotomy between the two theories is not 'a distinction worth dwelling on'.[39] Social constructivists adopt a position that is not merely a 'compromise' between realism and idealism, but rather a distinct theory of state conduct which adopts elements of both approaches.

Social constructivists stress that social actors behave in accordance both with selfish interests and in response to shared values and norms. International organisations emerge, according to Risse, where the values they represent are widely shared by participating states.[40] Problems occur where societies stake

38 Slaughter, 'International Law and International Relations', 23.
39 *Ibid.*, 24.
40 T. Risse, 'Lets Argue! Communicative Action in World Politics', *International Organization*, Vol. 54 (1), 2000, 1–39.

out different positions on issues, hampering the success and effectiveness of the organisation. According to idealists, human rights represent common interests among people, even if rights are perceived differently within different regions and cultures. Realists, however, argue that governments, particularly non-democratic ones, do not necessarily represent their peoples' interests in human rights.

Universal membership of the UN is widely deemed to be represented at the HRC through membership being apportioned according to geographic boundaries,[41] resulting in a broad range of interests and strategies regarding the issues at hand. Problems arise where conflicts occur, for example, the right to freedom of expression in conflict with defamation of religion. The Danish cartoons depicting the Prophet Mohammad[42] resulted in ongoing debates regarding freedom of speech and defamation of religion, with various states continuously arguing that both issues should be afforded the same level of protection. That controversy arose at the Council, which facilitated a number of debates and resolutions aimed at striking a balance that would solve 'the problem'.[43] Western states underlined the fundamental right to freedom of expression whereas other states, predominantly OIC members, called for defamation of religion to be granted the same status. Haas comments that effective organisations are only likely to occur where states hold a common position regarding how to solve 'the problem'.[44] A lack of uniform opinion on 'solutions' to human rights 'problems' impeded the Commission's work, and continues to do so at the Council.

Another facet of social constructivism is a focus on social groups that lobby for specific norms within their area of interest. Collectively, these groups are a mechanism for expressing shared or societal values. NGOs, regional groups, and other social groups, use the mechanisms of international organisations to encourage states' behaviour to comply with the norms of those institutions. Various social groups use the HRC to encourage changes in states' behaviour, particularly focusing on national implementation of human rights norms. Moreover, the Council is mandated to provide a platform for such groups to raise concerns, share information and provide expertise.

Reports on rights relating to food, housing and poverty, for example, have provided tools for states to implement changes with the help of social groups. International organisations promote their own norms which support the work of the social groups, leading to individual states changing their behaviour and interests. A primary aim of the HRC is to affect such change, and the

---

41   GA Res. 60/251, 'Human Rights Council', 15 March 2006, UN Doc. A/RES/60/251, para. 7.

42   See, for example, N. Nathwani, 'Religious Cartoons and Human Rights', *European Human Rights Law Review*, Vol. 4, 2008, 488–507.

43   See, for example, HRC Res. 1/107, 'Incitement to Racial and Religious Hatred and the Promotion of Tolerance', 30 June 2006, UN Doc. A/HRC/1/107; 'Combating Defamation of Religions', 30 March 2007, UN Doc. A/HRC/4/9.

44   P.M. Haas, 'Introduction: Epistemic Communities and International Policy Coordination', *International Organization*, Vol. 46 (1), 1992, 1–35.

innovative Universal Periodic Review mechanism was set up in order to achieve that purpose. The review aims to afford states an opportunity to provide advice and assistance for the country concerned in an environment of co-operation and support.

Social constructivism provides a useful theory for the HRC, because it encompasses idealist and realist positions whilst focusing on the fundamental interest that all states ought to have in human rights. The Council's provision of technical assistance and advisory services underlines the social constructivist approach that organisations should enable changes in states' behaviour. However, social constructivists fail to address the problem of effectiveness, where competing positions on norms and values exist within an international organisation, as occurs at the Council. Although, in theory, states ought to have a fundamental interest in human rights, politicisation of the Council, and indeed its predecessor, shows that this is not always achievable in practice.

4.4. Institutionalism

Institutionalism, like social constructivism, offers a separate theory of state behaviour that includes some realist and idealist assumptions. Indeed, social constructivists use language which relies heavily on institutionalism. After the Second World War, international relations theorists moved away from a mainly state-centred approach. Increase in the numbers and importance of international organisations, coupled with growing influence of non-state actors, resulted in revised approaches to international relations. Institutionalists offer an alternative to realism by giving credence to international rules, norms, principles, and decision-making procedures.[45] Institutionalists argue that these mechanisms enable states to pursue common aims.[46] There are a range of theories that fall under the umbrella term 'institutionalism'. These include: federalism, functionalism, transactionalism, interdependence, and neo-institutionalism.

Federalism is the oldest school of thought within institutionalism. Federalists view a common order being established through mass support within states for countries to join together whilst maintaining individual identities.[47] Federalists advocate the constructive transfer of sovereignty with the aim of integration and institutionalisation. A distinction must be drawn between federalism in the US, where states altogether abandoned sovereign powers, and that of the EU, where states retain sovereignty. The United Nations seeks neither to produce a 'world government' nor, as emphasised in the UN Charter,[48] for its members to sacrifice sovereignty.

45 S.D. Krasner, *International Regimes*, Ithaca, NY: Cornell University Press, 1983, p. 2.

46 Slaughter, 'International Law and International Relations', 35–6.

47 See, for example, C.J. Friedrich, *Trends of Federalists in Theory and Practice*, New York: Praeger, 1968.

48 United Nations Charter, (1945), Article 2(1).

Institutionalist 'functionalism' (as distinct from Morgenthau's usage of the term) rejects any such federalist unions as illusory, arguing that international organisations exist to enable states to overcome common problems or in the pursuit of common goals.[49] Functions are delegated from states to the organisations, increasing the importance of international organisations and decreasing the states' political roles. Functionalism focuses on economic rather than political integration, and provides an alternative to realism and to federalism by aiming for transnational administrative networks.

Institutionalism developed throughout the 1970s and 1980s, focusing on the emerging European Union as a model. 'Transactionalism' advocates integration through regional, continental and inter-continental organisations, as opposed to aiming for a world federation or the abandonment of states' sovereignty. Transactionalist theory emerged as a result of increasing numbers of security communities, such as NATO. Deutsch argued that increased transaction flow and communication between states would lead to greater integration and better understanding between people.[50]

The dominant institutionalist theories throughout the past two decades are 'interdependence' and 'neo-institutionalism'. Interdependence theorists challenge the realist emphasis on states as the primary entity in international relations. They stress the role of NGOs, multinational corporations, and other non-state actors. Neo-institutionalists build on traditional institutionalist theories by incorporating aspects of the interdependence approach. I shall explore institutionalism's application to international organisations by focusing on those two branches of theory.

Institutionalists argue that states' interests are neither mutually exclusive nor harmoniously in agreement. International relations results in outcomes that involve joint gains or losses for states on any given 'problem'. A common interest between states, even where their political agendas may differ, is the avoidance of such joint losses or the acquisition of such joint gains. States are united by the pursuit of that which they cannot achieve on their own, and thus international organisations are more than the sum of their parts. Even the most powerful states depend upon weaker ones, depending either on formal voting rules or on actual geo-political circumstances. Complex interdependence in a variety of areas will result in a state's goals varying according to the different matters under consideration. Those factors do not, however, mean, as realists maintain, that states pursue only their immediate self-interest. International organisations allow a state to deal with each issue separately, thus affording a country an opportunity to pursue goals without constant reference to its overall power. Instead, a state's strength in relation to an individual 'problem' becomes more important than its overall strength.

49 See, for example, D. Mitrany, *A Working Peace System*, Chicago, IL: Quadrangle, 1966.
50 K.W. Deutsch, *The Analysis of International Relations*, Englewood Cliffs, NJ: Prentice-Hall of India, 1989, p. 212.

Lijnzaad explores the problems with applying the law of treaties as a framework for human rights.[51] Models based so strongly on bargaining, and on individual gain for states, depart from the ideals behind human rights law, which fundamentally rejects the *do ut des* framework upon which many treaties have, traditionally, been based. Lijnzaad argues that human rights treaties deal with matters where compromise and bargaining should not exist owing to the fundamental nature of each right.[52] 'Problems' with human rights are often solved through state reservations, which Lijnzaad insists are fundamentally at odds with the purpose of such treaties.[53] Although reservations enable states to implement some human rights norms and allows them to engage with the wider human rights machinery, the use of bargaining and compromise undermines the system of human rights.

Keohane sets out an institutionalist position which does acknowledge that states are primary actors.[54] Certainly, in the absence of institutions states pursue power despite their underlying interests not necessarily conflicting. That is precisely why institutions allow state cooperation. International organisations allow all states to pursue their goals in an area, rather than submitting to the will of strong states on every issue. Links from other issues, as well as the power distribution within a particular area, will affect the agenda. Weaker states have more power through collaboration and bargaining than in international organisations which only focus on a few issues. The more issues dealt with, the greater the opportunity for collaboration with like-minded states, whether on one or many matters, or for bargaining power across different areas.

The interdependence approach developed in the US during the 1970s.[55] It adopts aspects of transactionalism, placing emphasis on societal transactions between various entities. Rejecting realism, it regards the increase in controversial situations as resulting from ever more complex interdependence between states owing to increasing globalisation and transnational interactions. Its exponents argue that the importance of international organisations increases in order to deal with those situations. Neo-institutionalism acknowledges this increasing interdependence, using it to build on traditional institutionalist theory.

Keohane demonstrates the link between increasingly interdependent relationships of states and the creation and increased importance of international organisations.[56] Smithers argues that an increasingly globalised world presents

51 L. Lijnzaad, *Reservations to UN-Human Rights Treaties: Ratify and Ruin?*, Dordrecht, Boston and London: Martinus Nijhoff Publishers, 1995.

52 *Ibid.*, pp. 3–5.

53 *Ibid.*, pp. 4–5.

54 R.O. Keohane, *International Institutions and State Power*, Boulder, CO: Westview Press, 1989, p. 11.

55 See, for example, R.O. Keohane and J.S. Nye, *Power and Independence*, 3rd edn., New York: Longman.

56 R.O. Keohane, *After Hegemony: Cooperation and Discord in the World Political Economy*, Princeton, NJ: Princeton University Press, 1984.

a range of interconnected problems, presenting international organisations with ever more complex problems.[57] One reason for the growth of human rights as an area of international concern is the emergence of an interdependent world. Globalisation, albeit only a factor in this growth, has impacted upon the awareness of human rights issues.[58] Unlike idealism, which focuses on shared values regarding human rights, neo-institutionalism highlights the increase in states' common problems arising from human rights abuses. Grave violations of human rights[59] impact upon more states than those where such abuses occur, and repercussions of human rights situations occur in neighbouring countries and beyond. For example, grave violations of human rights result in refugees fleeing into neighbouring states. Human rights abuses impact upon state relations with known abusers, and violations do occur against persons with links to other countries. Human rights situations are not confined to the state where they occur, and transnational impact increases the global importance of this issue.

Focus on human rights situations has grown owing, in part, to the increasing ability to report on such situations, and the wider public's response has generally been to call for more action to be taken to prevent such violations. The HRC consists of member states proportionately representing the geographic make-up of the UN. Attitudes towards human rights generally, and especially individual rights, vary greatly across regions. During the Cold War there was increasing disparity between Western and non-Western notions of human rights ideals. Schoenbaum comments that one approach requires human rights to be subject to cultural and religious traditions.[60] Kausikan examines the increasing impact of cultural sensitivities on human rights.[61] The 1993 Vienna World Conference on Human Rights acknowledged '[t]he significance of national and regional particularities and various historical, cultural and religious backgrounds must be borne in mind.'[62] An example of different attitudes towards human rights can be seen in various approaches towards women and human rights. Twenty-four Muslim countries have made reservations to the 1979 Convention on the Elimination of Discrimination

57 (Sir) P. Smithers, 'Towards Greater Coherence Among Intergovernmental Organizations Through Governmental Control', in B. Andemicael (ed.), *Regionalism and the United Nations*, Dobbs Ferry, NY: Oceana Publications Ltd, 1979, pp. 13–14.

58 See, for example, R. McCorquodale and R. Fairbrother, 'Globalization and Human Rights', *Human Rights Quarterly*, Vol. 21 (3), 1999, 735–66; M. Monshipouri, 'The Search for International Human Rights and Justice: Coming to Terms with the New Global Realities', *Human Rights Quarterly*, Vol. 23 (2), 2001, 370–401.

59 Expanded upon by W. Kälin and J. Künzli, *The Law of International Human Rights Protection*, Oxford: Oxford University Press, 2009, p. 149.

60 T.J. Schoenbaum, *International Relations – The Path Not Taken: Using International Law to Promote World Peace and Security*, Cambridge: Cambridge University Press, 2006, p. 254.

61 B. Kausikan, 'Asia's Different Standards', *Foreign Policy*, Vol. 92, 1993, 24–41.

62 GA World Conference on Human Rights, 'Vienna Declaration and Programme of Action', 25 June 1993, UN Doc. A/CONF.157/23, para. 5.

against Women[63] on the basis of conflicting Sharia law regarding marriage and family.[64] Moreover, various African states still allow female genital mutilation[65] to take place under the guise of 'cultural identity'[66] or 'religious practice'.[67]

Government policies do not always reflect different cultural or societal attitudes towards human rights, although, as previously discussed, these differences are often used as a justification for states' non-compliance with human rights norms.[68] According to Normand and Zaidi, there is a gap between values espoused and rights implemented due to a lack of adequate mechanisms for implementing human rights, as compared with, for example, international economic law.[69] Human rights are 'both a source of universal values and an arena of ideological warfare'.[70]

Interdependence theories use the notion of 'common interest' to explain international organisations. The preamble to Resolution 60/251 emphasises the need for a common interest in order to ensure that the Council overcomes the Commission's failure to uphold universally human rights norms and standards. The passage: 'all human rights are universal, indivisible, inter-related, interdependent and mutually reinforcing' (preamb. para. 3) reflects language used at the Vienna World Conference on Human Rights (1993). However, the idealised common interest of states in ensuring human rights compliance is complicated by different states having varying degrees of interest in upholding human rights. Realists would argue that states recognise self-interest above any common interest. Totalitarian or dictatorial states indeed have a particular interest in non-compliance with human rights in order to repress dissent.[71]

---

63 GA Res. 34/180, 'Convention on the Elimination of All Forms of Discrimination against Women', 18 December 1979, UN Doc. A/34/46.

64 See, for example. A.G. Hamid and A.I. Kulliyyah, 'Reservations to CEDAW and the Implementation of Islamic Family Law: Issues and Challenges', *Asian Journal of International Law*, Vol. 1 (3), 2006, 121–55.

65 See, for example. CEDAW, 'Concluding Observations of the Committee on the Elimination of Discrimination Against Women, Kenya', UN Doc. A/58/38 (Part I), para. 213; CEDAW, 'Concluding Observations of the Committee on the Elimination of Discrimination Against Women, Ghana', UN Doc. CEDAW/C/GHA/CO/5 (2006), para. 21; CEDAW, 'Conclusions and Recommendations of the Committee on the Elimination of All Forms of Discrimination against Women, Cameroon', UN Doc. CEDAW/C/CMR/CO/3 (2009), paras 28–29.

66 See, also, 'While noting the entrenched cultural underpinning of female genital mutilation [. . .]', CEDAW, 'Concluding Observations of the Committee on the Elimination of Discrimination Against Women', Eritrea, UN Doc. CEDAW/C/ERI/CO/3 (2006), para. 18.

67 See, for example, Schoenbaum, *International Relations – The Path Not Taken*, p. 254.

68 See Chapter 1, Section 1.1.1.

69 R. Normand and S. Zaidi, *Human Rights at the UN: The Political History of Universal Justice*, Bloomington: Indiana University Press, 2008.

70 *Ibid.*, p. 2.

71 cf. E. Heinze, 'Truth and Myth in Critical Race Theory and LatCrit: Human Rights and the Ethnocentrism of Anti-Ethnocentrism', *National Black Law Journal*, Vol. 20 (2), 2007, 107–62.

Within international human rights bodies, compromise agreements become increasingly important to fulfil their mandates. Compromise agreements at the HRC involve members or blocs bargaining over wording of resolutions, or indeed taking action on a human rights situation. States seeking the common interest of human rights compliance are, problematically, forced to compromise on some aspects of human rights in order to achieve the broader aim of protecting or promoting other rights. Whilst the HRC itself cannot take action regarding human rights violations, its work is of great importance in the reporting of, and recommendations about, such situations.

Neo-institutionalism regards international organisations as helpful in enabling states to cooperate successfully in pursuit of common interests. States holding common interests are able to raise such issues at the HRC through a collective voice, not only with each other, but with states who may join the alliance due to other common interests. Common interests in practice are not always the pursuit of human rights ideals. States may assert common positions that result in the majority being able to steamroll over the minority, even where it allows non-compliance with international human rights standards. Neo-institutionalists hold that the success of an international organisation requires alignment of common interests, or at least that interests are not mutually exclusive. Some common interests at the HRC, for example the right to safe drinking water, are less politically contentious than others. The right to freedom of expression is thought in some national contexts to conflict with defamation of religion, resulting in interests that are diametrically opposed.[72] Neo-institutionalism is perhaps too idealistic to apply to the HRC. At that body, discussions regarding safe drinking water will result in close cooperation between states to protect and promote that right for all people. Discussions regarding the freedom of expression, where the right conflicts with a value held by many member states, result in ineffective decision-making.

Slaughter asserts that institutionalism requires states to hold common interests across the board.[73] She insists that power politics, either between states or groups, will prevail unless states hold shared aims. Impact of common interests depends on the degree of commonality and the lack of opposing state self-interests, which relies heavily on idealist theories. As with idealism, institutionalism is more applicable to bodies which deal with less controversial subjects. Proportionate geographic representation at the Council allows weaker states, particularly from the African Group and the OIC, to promote common goals, as will be shown from both the HRC's agenda and work. Weaker states may have an impact upon the HRC, but, as realism reminds us, the incentive for any state, especially powerful ones, to defect from joint

---

72 See, for example, S. Parmar, 'The Challenge of "Defamation of Religions" to Freedom of Expression and the International Human Rights', *European Human Rights Law Review*, Vol. 3, 2009, 353–75.

73 Slaughter, 'International Law and International Relations', 38.

cooperation will always exist where it is in the state's interest to do so. Powerful but isolated states may be especially tempted to defect from the Council owing to the impact of regionalism at the body, thereby allowing weaker states jointly to pursue common goals. Refusal of the US to stand for election to the HRC has been argued to have occurred due to its reticence to have its own human rights record scrutinised or to be subjected to regular attacks at sessions by other member states.[74]

Institutionalism applies to the HRC in terms of the collaboration of states to achieve political goals. However, emphasis on interdependence between states disregards the overall dominance of powerful states. Focus on weaker states' ability to pursue their own goals through bargaining power and collaboration fails to deal either with the issue of powerful states withdrawing from an international organisation, or with the impact of powerful states' general dominance over weaker countries.

4.5. Marxist and Post-Marxist theories

Marxism, as applied to international organisations, does not hold states or non-state actors as being of primary importance. It does, however, recognise the need to acknowledge states as part of a 'stage' in world history. Although Marx lived in a 19th-century world dominated by nationalism, he saw divisions as being based on economic class rather than state borders. He argued that 'working men have no country'.[75] Marx saw the nation state, and particularly nationalism, as one of a number of mechanisms by which the proletariat were suppressed.

State governments combining to reach global decisions would be anathema to Marx's theories. He envisaged solutions being found across national boundaries. Marx argued that true internationalism had no national interests because all distinctions between states must ultimately disappear, and the common interests of the proletariat would be pursued regardless of territory. Marx predicted that '[t]he supremacy of the proletariat will cause [national differences] to vanish still faster.'[76] Marx did not incorporate any concept of international organisations of states, as he expected the state to 'wither away'[77] after successful socialist revolutionary activity. There was no place, in his model, for the pursuit of national (or regional) interests within an intra-national framework.

Subsequent Marxist treatment of international organisations was influenced by the post-revolutionary Soviet Union's approach. The Soviet Union, for example, promoted international labour organisations, while remaining

74 See Chapter 7.
75 K. Marx and F. Engels, *The Communist Manifesto*, Oxford: Oxford University Press, [1888] 2008, p. 23.
76 *Ibid.*
77 F. Engels, *Anti-Duhring*, London: Lawrence & Wishart Ltd, 1955, p. 333.

isolationist in many areas of foreign policy. The First World War prompted Lenin's writings, which previously focused on Russian affairs, to deal with the problem of imperialism. Lenin considered Russia's place in the world amongst 'imperialist' states, and its duty to encourage the socialist revolution in other countries. Stalin wrote that 'Leninism is Marxism in the epoch of imperialism and the proletarian revolution',[78] implying that Lenin's revisions to Marxism occurred because of the evolution of European capitalism and colonialism.

Soviet links with developing countries, prior to decolonisation, advanced after the Second World War and throughout the Cold War, with the Soviet Union's insistence on the right to national self-determination. International relations were to focus on the relationship between developed and developing nations, and the need for solidarity with states oppressed by imperialist nations.[79] Many post-colonial states continue to deploy post-Marxist discourses. Pashukanis, a Soviet legal scholar, accepted that international legal mechanisms, for example, treaties and custom, provide the outline for international relationships.[80] He advocated the requirement for socialist states to fill in the outline with socialist content.[81] Soviet policy later stressed the difference between relations with developing nations and like-minded states, comparing them with a necessary, peaceful co-existence with capitalist countries despite ideological differences.[82]

Co-existence with capitalist countries was reflected through the Soviet Union's membership of international organisations. Although socialist and capitalist ideals were fundamentally incompatible, mixed organisations (consisting of socialist, capitalist, developing and other nations) were viewed as part of this system of peaceful co-existence.[83] Traditional Soviet thinking, applied to international organisations, focused on those bodies' founding instruments as determinative of their legal personality which, if present, conferred similar international legal standing to that of a sovereign state.[84] Tunkin, a post-Stalin Soviet scholar, emphasised the need for wide representation of all classes – or, in this instance, types of states – before an international organisation was to be generally recognised as having international

---

78 J.V. Stalin, 'The Foundations of Leninism' (1993), in *Problems of Leninism*, Peking: Foreign Languages Press, 1976, pp. 8–9.

79 A.G. Meyer, *Leninism*, Cambridge, MA: Harvard University Press, 1957, p. 270.

80 E.B. Pashukanis, quoted in P. Beirne and R. Sharlet (eds.), *Pashukanis: Selected Writings on Marxism and Law*, London: London Academic Press, 1980.

81 *Ibid.*, p. 168.

82 Khrushchev began to promote peaceful co-existence between the Soviet Union and the West in 1953, arguing that war was not necessary for communism to triumph over capitalism. See, generally, R.H. McNeal, *Lenin, Stalin, Khrushchev: Voices of Bolshevism*, Englewood Cliffs, NJ: Prentice Hall, 1963, p. 150.

83 C. Osakwe, *The Participation of the Soviet Union in Universal International Organizations*, Leiden: A.W. Sijthoff International Publishing Company, 1972, p. 35.

84 *Ibid.*, p. 30.

legal personality.[85] That view betokens the emerging link between Marxist and post-colonialist theory during the period of decolonisation.

Various more recent critiques have built on these ideas. Theories which have adopted a post-Marxist discourse include some schools of cultural relativism and Third World theories,[86] both of which seek to challenge imperialism and Western hegemony. According to post-Marxists, cultural relativism does have a 'good side',[87] providing a counterbalance to the universalism promoted by Western states to advance their own objectives without reference to weaker states' norms, cultures or positions. Third World theorists challenge the use of international organisations by powerful states seeking to impose Western aims and to continue neo-colonial impositions and oppression.[88] These two approaches have played a significant role in states' and groups' positions and agendas at the UN Human Rights Council. Indeed, such post-colonial discourses on human rights are frequently utilised by states, groups and blocs at the Council.

Other post-Marxist theories have also played a role at the Council. World systems theory emphasises capitalism's role in shaping a world order divided into powerful core states and weaker peripheral states.[89] That theory examines the fusion between state and class power, and the common interest between core and peripheral states, in maintaining an unequal and exploitative *status quo*. The neo-Gramscian approach argues that inequality stems from the ideologies of the powerful states, for example neo-liberalism.[90] International law, according to that theory, reflects the ideologies and interests of the global elite rather than acting as a neutral force in international politics.

HRC membership is apportioned according to geographic boundaries, as opposed to political systems. Proportional geographic representation has ensured membership of states with a wide range of political systems. Marxist and post-Marxist theories have influenced the structure, proceedings and work of the Council. States from the Global South, in particular decolonised

85 G.I. Tunkin, *Theory of International Law*, Cambridge, MA: Harvard University Press, 1974, pp. 21–49.

86 M.-B. Dembour, 'Critiques', in D. Moeckli, S. Shah and S. Sivakumaran (eds.), *International Human Rights Law*, Oxford: Oxford University Press, 2010, pp. 72–85.

87 E. Hatch, 'The Good Side of Cultural Relativism', *Journal of Anthropological Research*, Vol. 59, 1997, 371.

88 See, for example, E. Said, *Orientalism*, London: Routledge, 1978; H. Bhabha, *The Location of Culture*, London: Routledge, 1994; A. Anghie, *Imperialism, Sovereignty and the Making of International Law*, Cambridge: Cambridge University Press, 2004; R.L. Doty, *Imperial Encounters: The Politics of Repression in North–South Relations*, Minneapolis, MN: Minnesota Press, 1962; T.M. Franck, *Human Rights in Third World Perspective*, Dobbs Ferry, NY: Oceana Publications Inc, 1982.

89 See, for example, I. Wallerstein, *The Modern-World System*, New York: Academic Press, 1974; J. Hobson, *The State and International Relation*, Cambridge: Cambridge University Press, 2000.

90 See, for example, S. Gill, *American Hegemony and the Trilateral Commission*, Cambridge: Cambridge University Press, 1992.

states, alongside countries such as China, Venezuela and Cuba, have deployed post-Marxist discourses at the body. Moreover, weaker states have frequently acted across national borders in pursuit of common interests, utilising bloc tactics in order to assert collective power over typically more dominant states or groups.

4.6. Summary

The failure of the League of Nations led to changing theories of international organisations during, and immediately after, the Second World War. The effectiveness of theories such as normative idealism, upon which the League of Nations had been built, and state-centric realism, had been undermined by the Second World War. Although the UN reflected emerging theories, incorporating institutionalism and social constructivism, amongst others, states were wary of ceding too much control over domestic affairs to the organisation.

Constituent documents, and indeed UN resolutions, decisions and other documents, tend to reflect idealist theory on international organisations. The preamble to such documents regularly repeat idealist aims set out in the UN Charter. Idealism is nevertheless counterbalanced by the realist approach states take towards the organisation and the proceedings within its bodies. The Council is not an exception to this juxtaposition between idealist theory and realist practice. However, when assessing the body from a legal perspective, the realities of international relations cannot supersede the legal documents upon which the body has been built.

According to Klabbers, theoretical idealists often assert that, in practice, they are realists.[91] International lawyers perhaps do accept that, in practice, a realist approach ought to be taken towards international organisations. That acceptance is based, in no small part, on state behaviour, in particular the use of those bodies as political arenas as well as weaker states' use of regional groups and political blocs to influence work and proceedings. However, when taking a theoretical approach, international lawyers often follow, and seek to uphold, the idealist approach. International lawyers focus on an organisation's constituent document and other relevant legal instruments, expecting the body to adhere to those texts. Such an approach is, essentially, idealism; expecting a body to fulfil the legal basis upon which it was created. Moreover, the substance of those documents often contains idealist aims, which scholars of international law then expect the body to uphold. The Council's constituent document and its Institution Building Package include many idealist principles. That, then, skews legal assessments towards focusing heavily, or indeed solely, on idealism.

---

91 J. Klabbers, *Introduction to International Institutional Law*, Cambridge: Cambridge University Press, 2002, p. 30.

The divide between realism and idealism provides too blunt an instrument for assessing the HRC. Institutionalism is useful for understanding the centrality of interstate collaboration at the Council. Bargaining and compromise are key working methods at the HRC, although that is problematic in terms of human rights. Institutionalism incorporates aspects of realism and idealism, but in so doing it fails adequately to address the weaknesses of either theory; institutionalists do not explain how isolated, powerful states can be encouraged to remain within a body, nor how to construct shared aims particularly where conflicting values already exists.

Social constructivism provides the most useful method for understanding the Council both in theory and in practice. Social constructivists stress that human rights are a fundamental interest for all states, but admit that this position is not accepted by every country. Theorists therefore focus on how to change states' behaviour in order to ensure compliance with human rights norms. Affecting changes forms a significant part of the Council's mandate, work and proceedings, through promotion of human rights, technical assistance, advisory services, and support. Moreover, social constructivists recognise the importance of actors other than states, which is reflected in the Council's interactions with NGOs, social groups, human rights experts, and UN administrative staff.

Social constructivism is the most appropriate theory for understanding the Council, whereas Marxism and post-Marxist discourses are useful for exploring state and group behaviour at the body. The HRC is dominated by decolonised and developing states. Those countries typically adopt post-Marxist discourses on human rights. African states, in particular, emphasise a lack of national capabilities for human rights, often seeking the body's assistance with capacity-building, and drawing upon Third World theories to underscore Western states' duties to support such efforts. Indeed, states have regularly referred to human rights as a 'neo-colonial tool of repression'. Many states hide behind capacity-building in order to excuse non-compliance, using post-Marxist discourses as a shield to avoid scrutiny. Similarly, cultural relativism, which draws upon some Marxist ideas, is frequently deployed to justify non-compliance. OIC members and African states are particularly prone to using that discourse despite it being fundamentally at odds with the concept of human rights.

5 Roles and functions of international organisations

Resolution 60/251 requires the Council to fulfil certain roles and functions in order to protect and promote human rights. The body's roles and functions are intrinsically linked to, and dependent on, the UN, wider human rights machinery, NGOs, states and non-state actors.

5.1. Roles of international organisations

General theories on the relationship between international organisations and states may assist understanding of international organisations' roles.[1] International organisations are presented as playing various roles, of which three main theories will be examined: arenas, instruments and actors.

Conor Cruise O'Brien, one-time Special Representative to the UN Secretary-General, described the UN as 'stages set for a continuous dramatisation of world history'.[2] This metaphorical view is perhaps better explained by Archer: the UN is often seen as solely an 'arena' in which member states can advance their own viewpoints and suggestions in a public and open forum.[3] Member states, observers and NGOs use regular HRC sessions as an 'arena' to voice opinions and to set forth their agendas. State and non-state entities use HRC mechanisms to air their opinions. Informal meetings, the complaints procedure, and Special Sessions, are examples of such mechanisms. As an 'arena', the HRC is privy to vast amounts of information from states and specialised entities. This enables the Council to examine many human rights issues at each of its regular sessions. Despite the body's clear emphasis on its role as an 'arena', and the importance of this function for its work, the HRC aims to be more than merely a forum for discussion. The Council is able to act through, for example, undertaking fact-finding missions, reporting on human rights issues, and passing decisions and resolutions.[4] Powers for the body to be proactive in protecting and promoting human rights, even though those

---

1 cf. D. Kennedy, 'The Move to Institutions', *Cardozo Law Review*, Vol. 8, 1987, 841–988.
2 C.C. O'Brien and F. Topolski, *The UN – Sacred Drama*, London: Hutchinson, 1968, p. 9.
3 C. Archer, *International Organizations*, London: George Allen & Unwin, 1983, p. 136.
4 GA Res. 60/251, 'Human Rights Council', 15 March 2006, UN Doc. A/RES/60/251.

powers are non-binding, indicates that the Council was intended to be more than simply an 'arena' for interstate discussions.

'Perhaps the most usual image of the role of international organisations is that of an instrument being used by its members for particular ends'.[5] International organisations as instruments go beyond an 'arena' by doing more than staging debates. Instruments, as the regular use of the word indicates, are used to achieve results. A main hope at the HRC's inception was that it would actively protect and promote human rights issues. Nobel Laureate Karl Gunnar Myrdal[6] stated that 'international organisations are nothing else than instruments for the policies of individual governments', implying that actions of an international organisation result directly from one or more member states' national policies.[7] That assertion is supported by McCormick and Kihl's study of international organisations, which concluded that international organisations 'are used by nations primarily as selective instruments for gaining foreign policy objectives'.[8] Despite political agendas dominating the Commission's final years and significantly contributing to its demise, the Council has failed adequately to address and overcome this problem.

Claude, re-stating the institutionalist position, explained that 'an international organisation is most clearly an actor when it is most distinctly an "it", an entity distinguishable from its member states'.[9] One fundamental way to distinguish an organisation from its members is through an ability of the former to regulate the latter's behaviour. International organisations employ different methods of decision-making, but in order for the organisation to achieve 'actor-capacity', resolutions, recommendations or orders must compel member states to behave differently than they would have otherwise done.[10]

The theories of arenas, instruments and actors do not address the nature of the powers that an organisation holds. The fewer binding powers an international organisation has, the more likely it will be used for political aims. Countries are reluctant to relinquish autonomy to international organisations holding legally binding powers. Kahler asserts that the higher the degree of obligation under an agreement, the more credibility is given to a government commitment.[11] Similarly, he argues that where an agreement is strengthened by enforcement mechanisms and the ability to adjudicate on

5 Archer, *International Organizations*, p. 130.

6 Former Executive-Secretary of UN Economic Commission for Europe.

7 Karl Gunnar Myrdal, 'Realities and Illusions in Regard to Inter-Governmental Organizations', in *Hobhouse Memorial Lecture*, Oxford: Oxford University Press, 1955, pp. 4–5.

8 J.M. McCormick and Y.W. Kihl, 'Intergovernmental Organizations and Foreign Policy Behaviour: Some Empirical Findings', *American Political Science Review*, Vol. 73 (2), 1979, 502.

9 I.L. Claude, *Swords into Ploughshares*, 4th edn., New York: Random House, 1971, p. 13.

10 A. Wolfers, 'The Actors in International Politics', in A. Wolfers (ed.), *Discord and Collaboration: Essays on International Politics*, Baltimore, MD: Johns Hopkins Press, 1962, p. 22.

11 M. Kahler, 'The Causes and Consequences of Legalization', *International Organization*, Vol. 54 (3), 2000, 663.

issues of non-compliance, the credibility of a government commitment is also increased.[12]

5.2. Functions of international organisations

Three main functions are: inputs, outputs and the conversion process. International organisations can be understood as political systems that convert inputs into outputs.[13] Demands and support from the organisation's environment are transformed into that institution's policies. Many of the demands and support for international organisations stem from its member states or expert bodies. The power position of a state, and its control over relevant resources, is of great importance. Power is manifested through specific control over resources in an area, or through overall control of issue-transcending resources.[14] States may use control of important resources in other issue areas to exert influence in areas where they lack relevant power.

5.2.1 *Inputs*

The Council's inputs demonstrate that the body is fulfilling the requirements, under Resolution 60/251, that it operate within the UN human rights machinery and work with wider society and non-state actors. Input sources include a variety of actors, which create ties between the Council and the wider human rights field. Three main input sources are specifically mentioned in Resolution 60/251. Input from all three forms part of the Council's legal mandate.

Administrative Staff. Input sources include the administrative staff of an international organisation. Administrative staff can exert considerable influence on the input aspect of policy making. Creation of the HRC, and the many reform proposals regarding its predecessor, can be attributed to Secretary-General Kofi Annan's 2005 'In Larger Freedom' report.[15] Speeches of the High Commissioner for Human Rights at HRC sessions demonstrate administrative staff's ability to influence the agenda. The Secretary-General, although his words are not always adhered to, often calls for the Council to deal with particular thematic or country-specific issues. States have, at times, attempted to discredit information provided by administrative staff.[16]

Special Procedures. Communities of experts are another main source of input at the HRC. Institutionalists, such as Keohane, regard expert advice

12 Kahler, 'The Causes and Consequences of Legalization', 663.
13 On international law as an operating system, see P.F. Diehl and C. Du, *The Dynamics of International Law*, Cambridge: Cambridge University Press, 2010.
14 R.O. Keohane and J.S. Nye, *Power and Independence*, Boulder, CO: Westview Press, 2001, pp. 3–47.
15 General Assembly, 'In Larger Freedom: Towards Development, Security and Human Rights for All', *Report of the Secretary-General*, 21 March 2005, UN Doc. A/59/2005.
16 See Chapters 7 and 8.

as being of growing importance due to the increasingly complex problems being dealt with by organisations. UN bodies make frequent use of individual experts and committees of experts, selected according to the usual geographic criteria. Expertise is provided which may be lacking among administrative staff and member states. Effect on policy-making is inevitable. Unanimity amongst experts, as is often the case at the HRC either through joint fact-finding missions or where experts provide similar recommendations to countries, lends greater credibility to the advice. However, states do ignore or attack experts' reports at the Council, particularly on politically sensitive or contentious issues. Experts are frequently used to undertake HRC fact-finding missions, provide reports, or indeed are appointed as mandate holders regarding specific human rights issues.

The Special Procedures system plays a role within every aspect of the Council's work. However, assessing the system itself goes beyond the scope of this work.[17] A general understanding of Special Procedures will be necessary in order to assess the Council. Special Procedures were described, by former UN Secretary-General Kofi Annan, as 'the crown jewel of the [UN human rights] system'.[18] The system assisted human rights protection and promotion, primarily by investigating and reporting on human rights violations, and making recommendations. The Commission on Human Rights' Special Procedures system[19] was adopted by the Council under General Assembly Resolution 60/251 Paragraph 6. Special Procedures were established to assist the Commission's human rights monitoring and allow investigation of specific human rights situations within individual countries or of general, global human rights issues. Special Procedures mechanisms are universal, reflecting the UDHR's universality. Human rights protection and promotion thus applies across all UN member states, unlike at treaty bodies which only deal with states party to the relevant treaty.

The legal basis for mandates derives directly from the Commission's powers to submit proposals, recommendations and reports concerning all questions of human rights.[20] Special Procedures involve a range of activities, including:

17 On Special Procedures and the HRC see, for example, S.P. Subedi, S. Wheatley, A. Mukherjee and S. Ngane, 'Special Issue: The Role of the Special Rapporteurs of the United Nations Human Rights Council in the Development and Promotion of International Human Rights Norms', *The International Journal of Human Rights*, Vol. 15 (2), 2011, 155–61.
18 Secretary-General Kofi Annan, 'Secretary-General urges human rights activists to "fill leadership vacuum", hold world leaders to account, in address to international day event', Time Warner Centre (US), 8 December 2006, SG/SM/10788 HR/4909 OBV/601, (Online). Available HTTP: <http://www.un.org/News/ossg/sg/stories/statments_full.asp?statID=39> (accessed 22 July 2012).
19 See, for example, I. Nifosi, *The UN Special Procedures in the Field of Human Rights*, Antwerp: Intersentia, 2005.
20 ECOSOC Res 5(I), 'Commission on Human Rights', 16 February 1946, UN Doc. E/Res/5(I), as amended on 18 February 1946 ESCOR 1946, Verbatim and Summary Records, Annex 8, 163, para. 1; ESC Res 9(II), UN ESCOR, 2nd session, Annex 14, 21 June 1946, UN Doc. E/RES/9(II), p. 400, para. 1.

fact-finding missions; meeting local authorities, NGOs, human rights defenders, and individuals; and visiting relevant facilities. Information gathered is used for reports and recommendations. Special Procedures mandate holders communicate with concerned governments about alleged violations, requesting responses and corrective actions. Clarification is sought on alleged violations, and governments are encouraged to fulfil human rights duties. Special Procedures issue public statements on human rights situations to draw wider attention to violations. The main function for mandate holders is submitting annual reports to the Council, and sometimes to the General Assembly, and making recommendations. Mandate holders are almost always active participants in an interactive dialogue on their reports.

Special Procedures impact on states' national jurisdiction through investigating country-specific or thematic human rights issues and issuing reports and recommendations on the findings. Fact-finding and other aspects of Special Procedures allows information sharing, which can damage states' national interests. Certain countries, in particular those from the Global South, sought to restrict Special Procedures at the new body. Those states were most affected by, or most fearful of, the system's impact on domestic jurisdiction.

Special Procedures' functions are key for protecting and promoting human rights, and are utilised by the entire UN human rights machinery. Farer and Gaer argue that, at the Commission, mandate holders fulfilled their duties to a high level, and gave 'recommendations that push beyond traditional thinking and practice at the UN'.[21] It is therefore imperative that the system be maintained, not only for the new body but for the UN as a whole. However, although mandate holders provide useful information and encouraged protection and promotion of human rights, Special Procedures were criticised at the Commission for lacking practical impact. Hampson criticises the Commission's failure to devote sufficient time to consider Special Procedures' reports or for follow-up to such reports.[22] She argues that failure to listen to or act upon expert advice was a main failing of the Commission. Farer and Gaer similarly comment on a lack of systematic follow-up to reports given by thematic mandate holders.[23] They argue that reports were not discussed at the Commission in any systematic way, which limited their exposure and efficacy.

Resolution 60/251 requires the Council to 'maintain a system of special procedures, expert advice and a complaint procedure'.[24] The Council was not mandated to adopt the Commission's system in its entirety, but instead was given the ability to adapt and change aspects of Special Procedures so long

21 T.J. Farer and F.D. Gaer, 'The UN and Human Rights: At the End of the Beginning', in A. Roberts and B. Kingsbury (eds.), *United Nations, Divided World*, 2nd edn., Oxford: Oxford University Press, 1993, pp. 287–8.

22 F.J. Hampson, 'An Overview of the Reform of the UN Human Rights Machinery', *Human Rights Law Review*, Vol. 7 (1), 2007, 19.

23 Farer and Gaer, 'At the End of the Beginning', p. 288.

24 GA Res. 60/251, 'Human Rights Council', UN Doc. A/RES/60/251, para. 6.

as a system was maintained. Schrijver notes that, prior to the Council's creation, tensions arose regarding modifying the system.[25] The compromise was to retain the system for the Council's first year, and undertake a review as to whether to keep, and where necessary rationalise or improve, individual mandates. Prior to the review taking place, Scannella and Splinter argued that the Council should strengthen rather than preserve the system.[26] They advocated focusing on gaps in coverage and creating a comprehensive system. The review occurred throughout early sessions, culminating in the Institution Building Package's adoption. Part II of the text establishes Special Procedures' modalities and mechanisms and the review process for individual mandates.

The Special Procedures system operates independently of the Council. Although there is much overlap, its existence as a concurrent system allows mandate holders to retain independence of the Council and, indeed, any UN body. That independence is crucial for the Special Procedures system. However, respecting that independence does raise questions regarding, for example, adherence to the Council's founding principles, fulfilment of its mandate, and the impact of politicisation.

Each mandate is allocated a mandate holder. Mandate holders occupy unique positions as independent experts with wide investigative and reporting powers. They are expected to be independent, are unpaid by the UN, and serve in a personal capacity for a maximum of six years.[27] Farer and Gaer comment that mandate holders, by virtue of their expertise, 'have in general seemed insulated from the sort of political pressure that cripples effective and impartial inquiry'.[28] Perhaps, as experts, such persons have been afforded sufficient respect by delegations to ensure they are not targeted for political aims. However, at times, politicisation has occurred.[29]

Almost all mandate holders are human rights experts, either Special Rapporteurs of the Commission, Special Representatives of the Secretary-General[30] or Independent Experts.[31] Despite little practical difference between

---

25 N. Schrijver, 'The UN Human Rights Council: A New "Society of the Committed" or Just Old Wine in New Bottles', *Leiden Journal of International Law*, Vol. 20 (4), 2007, 812–14.

26 P. Scannella and P. Splinter, 'The United Nations Human Rights Council: A Promise to be Fulfilled', *Human Rights Law Review*, Vol. 7 (1), 2007, 60.

27 Two terms of three years for thematic mandates, and six one-year terms for country mandates.

28 Farer and Gaer, 'At the End of the Beginning', pp. 287–8.

29 See Chapter 7.

30 In reality, there is very little difference in the ways in which these different types of Special Procedure operate. One exception is that Special Representatives tend to be appointed by the Secretary-General, whereas the others are appointed by the Chairperson of the Commission (now the President of the Council).

31 See, for example, OHCHR, Human Rights Fact Sheet No.27, *Seventeen frequently asked questions about the United Nations special rapporteurs*, (Online). Available HTTP: <http://www.ohchr.org/Documents/Publications/FactSheet27en.pdf>

these forms of mandate holders, Farer and Gaer comment that a hierarchy emerged at the Commission with Special Rapporteurs being favoured over Special Representatives or Independent Experts.[32] It was rarer for the Commission to appoint Working Groups as mandate holders. Working Groups are composed of five human rights experts, one from each of the geographic regions. That format is considered more suitable when a collegiate body is required, either to promote wider discussions or to render opinions on cases with participation of experts from different legal backgrounds. The Working Group model is also favoured by some because of representation from all five regional groups. Hampson notes the confusion between different forms of Special Procedures.[33] Her opinion is that Working Groups should only be used where each individual's legal knowledge of his/her region is required in order for the mandate to be fulfilled, for example on arbitrary detention.

NGOs. Interest groups are another HRC input. NGOs have consultative status[34] at the body and are a source of specialised quality input through formal and informal channels. International organisations need access to the information and expertise held by NGOs. One innovative reform to the UN human rights body enabled the HRC to be one of very few international organisations that allow NGOs to participate directly in the body's proceedings. These input sources directly implement Resolution 60/251, which mandates the body to provide a forum for information sharing and for dialogue between state and non-state actors. NGOs are also an input source for the Special Procedures system. NGOs provide specialised input through formal and informal channels Scannella and Splinter comment that NGO participation was widely accepted by states, and that they engaged with the substance of NGO concerns rather than the legitimacy of NGO involvement.[35] Rudolf comments that Special Procedures provide an 'independent intermediary' between NGOs and states.[36] NGOs or other human rights activists may provide information to mandate holders, which then forms part of the overall report and recommendations. Although NGOs are given the opportunity to participate in the Special Procedures system, their role during Council discussions on individual mandates is not afforded sufficient weight. NGOs are given the opportunity to speak after states during the interactive dialogue with mandate holders. However, the list of NGO speakers is often limited due to time constraints. State delegates leave the

32 Farer and Gaer, 'At the End of the Beginning', p. 284.
33 Hampson, 'An Overview of the Reform of the UN Human Rights Machinery', p. 19.
34 ECOSOC Res 1993/31, 'Consultative Relationship between the United Nations and Non-Governmental Organizations', 25 July 1996, UN Doc. E/1996/96.
35 Scannella and Splinter, 'The United Nations Human Rights Council: A Promise to be Fulfilled', 57.
36 B. Rudolf, 'The Thematic Rapporteurs and Working Groups of the United Nations Commission on Human Rights', *Max Planck Yearbook of United Nations Law*, Vol. 4, 2000, 291.

room or stand at the back of the chamber talking and using phones during NGO interventions. Such behaviour is not unusual at the Council, but occurs far more frequently during NGO, rather than country, statements. Observers at Council sessions, this author included, frequently witness such behaviour. Many observers, however, do not include descriptive details in their reports or scholarship, despite it being of critical importance for understanding the Council.

5.2.2 *Conversion process*

The conversion process takes place in Council sessions and through informal meetings, Working Groups and negotiations. Special Procedures play a role in the conversion process through mandate holders presenting reports during Council sessions, followed by interactive dialogues with states, observers and NGOs. Discussions provide the opportunity for mandate holders to explain their findings, as well as for states to express any concerns. Conversion is intended to create suitable outcomes, usually in the form of resolutions or decisions.

Conversion of inputs into outputs at the HRC occurs in two main ways. Intergovernmental negotiations are a common mechanism for decisions to be taken within international organisations. Negotiations occur between the most powerful actors representing divergent interests.[37] Decisions require either a package deal or a compromise; an agreement on the lowest common denominator of all parties. Intergovernmental negotiations result in the most powerful states, groups or blocs controlling the decision-making. Informal meetings occur throughout regular HRC sessions, either between member states, involving entire regional groups, or with various states from like-minded groups in attendance. Draft resolutions and decisions are created through informal meetings, as well as internal decisions taken regarding states' approaches to agenda items.

Majority voting, the other method of conversion most often used at the HRC, is decision-making characterised by formation of a majority through coalition building. Decisions represent the interests of the majority rather than of powerful states. International organisations become executors of shifting coalitions of member states. HRC membership is ever-changing, as states serve three-year terms with one-third of the body changing annually. Coalitions are often formed within regional groups or through alliances between these groups, as will be discussed. Majority voting is easier for member states to accept where the decisions taken are legally non-binding. Majority voting thus suffices at the HRC for most states regarding most issues. However, political sensitivities regarding the hortatory power of the Council's decisions and resolutions often results in a high level of informal and formal inter-governmental negotiation before the majority voting takes place.

---

37 J.Q. Wilson and J.J. DiIulio, *American Government: Institutions and Policies*, 7th edn., Boston, MA: Houghton Mifflin Harcourt, 1997.

Resolution 60/251 does not expressly state the need for unanimity consensus in decision-making. At the Commission, where unanimity was required, each state effectively had a veto. However, it had been generally understood that consensus should be reached. The Chairperson usually seeks, and stresses the importance of, consensus but this has generally meant very little in practice. One key example was the, somewhat controversial, lack of consensus on the IBP. Much of the body's work is arguably undermined by failure to reach unanimous decisions.

The Council Chairperson seeks to ensure consensus, rather than calling for a vote, as this gives significant weight to the decision or resolution. Achieving consensus sends a strong message about the decision reached. It has been observed that consensus is often reached through the lowest common denominator, both within and between groups.[38] At the Fifth Session, Council Chairman de Alba, discussing negotiations on the IBP, noted this issue but stressed the importance of achieving consensus:

> [i]n the talks over the last few days, the biggest question I have been asked is whether I consider if we have been making a true contribution, or simply a lowest common denominator. I say no, and that real progress has been made. Although the text does need improvement, it does have a high degree of agreement; we have been working largely in consensus.[39]

Despite the emphasis placed on reaching decisions by consensus, Scannella and Splinter comment that, at the Council's First Session, members of the Organisation of the Islamic Conference undermined attempts to ensure that all decisions were adopted by consensus.[40] The OIC is the strongest bloc at the Council, with members and allies from across all of the regional groups. Rather than engaging with intergovernmental negotiations on its draft resolutions, the OIC and its allies often vote as a bloc at the Council in order to further the group's political agendas.

The majority of Council decisions are reached by consensus. However, where consensus cannot be reached and a vote is called, member states often express disappointment. Votes tend only to be called where a decision or resolution is on a particularly sensitive subject matter, often on a country-specific situation or regarding a contentious human rights issue.[41] At times, non-achievement of consensus angered state delegates who sought to underscore politically sensitive decisions or resolutions.

38 T.G. Weiss, *What's Wrong with the United Nations and How to Fix It*, Cambridge: Polity Press, 2008, p. 53.
39 Ambassador Luis Alfonso de Alba (Mexico), Informal meeting, 5th Session, 8 June 2007.
40 Scannella and Splinter, 'The United Nations Human Rights Council: A Promise to be Fulfilled', 68–9.
41 Author's own observations from attending Human Rights Council sessions.

5.2.3 *Outputs*

International organisations create outputs in the form of, amongst others, policy programmes, operational activities and information activities. Most of the HRC's work takes one of those three forms. Policy programmes aim to direct states' behaviour by setting normative standards. General rules prescribe or proscribe certain behaviour in certain circumstances, acting as guidelines for states. Programme decisions impact directly on states' autonomy by providing norms and rules directing states' behaviour. States wish to dominate this type of decision-making process. Programme decisions affecting states' autonomy are unlikely to be allowed unless the states are directly involved in the process. Morgenthau notes that even when rules are violated they are not always enforced, and that even when enforcement takes place it is not always effective.[42] From a realist perspective, HRC policy programmes are merely political recommendations, owing to a lack of enforcement mechanisms within that body. Although the Human Rights Council at times calls for other bodies to enforce its recommendations,[43] such calls are generally not heeded.

Norms and rules of policy programmes generally require implementation, typically occurring through national governments. International organisations usually assist member states to implement norms and rules, as opposed to implementing them directly.[44] This occurs at the HRC through assisting states to implement policy programmes at a national level. Monitoring of implementation, by the international organisation, is required. As previously discussed, Resolution 60/251 mandates the body to provide, amongst others, advisory services, technical assistance, and capacity-building (para. 5 (a)). Assistance with implementation of policy programmes, when they occur in practice, fulfils these aspects of the mandate.

Fact-finding missions and reports given to the Council are examples of monitoring by this body. Fact-finding primarily occurs through the Special Procedures system, either through pre-existing mandate holders or through Working Groups set up by the Council to investigate specific human rights situations. Although the Special Procedures system operates independently of the Council, its role in fact-finding is crucial for the Council to fulfil its mandate. Steiner *et al.* comment that the concept of fact-finding, that is of international monitoring of a situation to verify 'facts' given by a sovereign government, would have been inconceivable 'not many years ago'.[45] However, today, fact-finding is a commonplace task which, when carried out fairly, is

---

42 Archer, *International Organizations*, p. 79.
43 For example, 'Report of the United Nations Fact Finding Mission on the Gaza Conflict', 15 September 2009, UN Doc. A/HRC/12/48, paras 1765–1767 – giving recommendations for the Council to refer to the Security Council and International Criminal Court for implementation.
44 Direct implementation occurs, for example, through UN peacekeeping missions.
45 H.J. Steiner, P. Alston and R. Goodman, *International Human Rights in Context*, 3rd edn., Oxford: Oxford University Press, 2008, p. 747.

widely accepted by all parties.[46] Fact-finding enables the Council to identify where and when human rights protection and promotion is required, and to monitor implementation of previous outputs in that regard.

Reporting requirements are another method for monitoring human rights standards and implementation. Sands and Klein note that many international organisations have reporting requirements, with some expressly including them in the constituent instrument.[47] The Council arguably included a reporting requirement through the mandate for the UPR to be carried out on all member states during their term of Council membership. Although reporting requirements in the human rights field have been criticised, not least due to the backlog and delays within many treaty bodies,[48] the UPR arguably is a stringent requirement owing to its review of all UN member states within a four-year cycle, resulting in all states complying with the requirement on a regular, and indeed perhaps frequent, basis.

Some international organisations may also adjudicate on issues of compliance, although the HRC does not hold this power. If a member state insists that it has implemented a programme but other states disagree, the international organisation may be asked to intervene to determine compliance. HRC discussions often centre on disputes regarding human rights, whether between states and experts or between states themselves. Members, observers and NGOs will discuss reports on specific issues, and the Council may pass resolutions on the findings. Member states may raise issues of violations within other countries, which the HRC will debate and pass resolutions where required. Special sessions are convened to deal with urgent human rights situations.

Compliance with HRC decisions will largely depend on political factors. Abbott *et al.* commented that the less legally binding a resolution is, the greater the influence of politics on compliance:

> On the whole [we have reached] the rejection of a rigid dichotomy between 'legalization'[49] and 'world politics'. Law and politics are intertwined at all levels of legalization. One result of this interrelationship [. . .] is the considerable difficulty in identifying the causal effects of legalization. Compliance with rules occurs for many reasons other than their legal status. Concerns about reciprocity, reputation, and damage to valuable state institutions, as well as other normative and material considerations, all play a role. Yet it is reasonable to assume that most of the time, legal and political considerations combine to influence behaviour.[50]

46 *Ibid.*
47 P. Sands and P. Klein, *Bowett's Law of International Institutions*, London: Sweet & Maxwell, 2001, pp. 316–17.
48 See, for example, Sands and Klein, *Bowett's Law of International Institutions*, pp. 317–18.
49 Abbott uses the term 'legalization' to mean subsuming into legal discourse, as opposed to the more general use of the term to mean making something legal.
50 K.W. Abbott, R.O. Keohane, A. Moravcsik, A.-M. Slaughter and D. Snidal, 'The Concept of Legalization', *International Organization*, Vol. 54 (3), 2000, 419.

Information activities include collecting and publishing information relating to the international organisation's mission. Reports influence the organisation's own decision-makers, as well as states and other actors. Information activities are an important factor in the social construction of reality, and can influence political positions of actors within member states.[51] Experts' reports and fact-finding missions often gather information that is difficult to access. This may be disseminated through the HRC to a wide audience of states, NGOs and the public. The impact of human rights information activities cannot be underestimated. Very often the information is used further in a wide range of settings at national, regional and global levels. Information activities are particularly influential when transnational groups of experts make similar assessments to each other.[52] International organisations facilitate the exchange of information between member states, and also between member states and NGOs. Furthermore, allowing NGO participation at Council sessions results in information sharing from those organisations with specialist knowledge that would not otherwise be available to the Council.

51 M.N. Barnett and M. Finnemore, *Rules for the World: International Organization in Global Politics*, Ithaca, NY: Cornell University Press, 2004.
52 J. Goldstein and R.O. Keohane (eds.), *Ideas and Foreign Policy: Beliefs, Institutions and Political Change*, Ithaca, NY: Cornell University Press, 1993, pp. 3–30.

6 Politicisation of international organisations

6.1. The concept of politicisation

Politicisation will always occur to some degree within international organisations, owing to the nature of interstate relations. Non-conflict within international organisations only occurs when member states have similar legal and social structures. One example is the Nordic Council, where states have similar legal systems and cooperation is more easily achieved than in other organisations. However, some divergence, and thus some degree of politicisation, still occurs.

While politicisation affects all intergovernmental bodies, its impact must still be identified and analysed. Politicisation plays a key role in a body's work and proceedings, and ultimately the fulfilment of its mandate. Acceptance that domestic agendas are always present is different to tolerating political conflicts subsuming a body. Problems arise where an organisation ceases to fulfil its mandate because of politicisation overshadowing, or preventing, work from being successfully undertaken.

Whether politicisation occurs is often in the eye of the beholder. Brown asserts that 'politicization seems to be something that states are quite willing to accuse each other of doing but that they never seem to admit to doing themselves'.[1] States with common political aims will not view those aims being furthered as politicisation, while countries with opposing interests will immediately cry foul in those circumstances. The United States, for example, criticised Arab states for politicising the International Labour Organisation (ILO) June Conference in 1991 when they accused Israel of labour injustices,[2] whereas the Arab states viewed their behaviour as a legitimate use of that body. The furthering of political aims is inevitable at any political body, and states may often differ as to whether 'politicisation' has occurred. Therefore,

---

1 B.S. Brown, *The United States and the Politicization of the World Bank: Issues of International Law and Policy*, Publication of the Graduate Institute on International Studies, New York; London: Kegan Paul International, 1992, p. 22.
2 J.S. Gibson, *International Organizations, Constitutional Law and Human Rights*, New York: Praeger Publishers, 1991, p. 107.

I shall assess the Council by reference to forms of gross politicisation which render the body unfit for purpose.

Lyons *et al.* examine politicisation's origins, explaining that, from the early 1950s, UN economic and social activities began to be viewed as non-political.[3] That 'myth' developed, with the US delegations, in particular, arguing that political issues should be confined to the General Assembly (GA) and Security Council, resulting in the expectation that UN specialised agencies should not be politicised.[4] Mitrany argues that specialised agencies should be given the authority to deal with transnational technical matters, leaving other international bodies to deal with more politically sensitive areas.[5] A lack of conflict within such agencies was expected to encourage more general inter-governmental cooperation.

Mitrany, in an institutionalist vein, envisaged a world where everyday functions are undertaken across regional, continental or universal frontiers, overseen by international organisations.[6] The UN's specialised agencies do undertake cooperative tasks, but problems remain. Archer notes that, often unrelated, political disputes affect all levels of international activities, usually with no positive impact on the activity involved.[7] Politicisation at the HRC exemplifies this analysis.

The view that specialised agencies are solely technical fails to acknowledge politics' role in international affairs.[8] Sewell argues that functionalists, by disparaging the impact of politics and failing to discuss its role at international organisations, view the 'political' as being completely removed from the 'functional' aspect of such bodies.[9] Functionalists hoped that international political agendas would be confined to certain organisations whilst allowing specialised agencies to deal with functional – that is technical and practical – issues. Lyons *et al.* insist that '[e]ven if "depoliticization" were possible in an "objective" sense, it is [. . .] irrelevant to countries, especially those in the third world, for which these agencies are a major forum for mobilizing their combined forces to argue for systemic changes.'[10] Therefore, no matter what steps are taken to depoliticise an intergovernmental body, it is not possible to depoliticise the member states and their delegates.

Surprisingly, weaker states have thus far politicised the HRC more frequently than stronger states. Weaker states, predominantly from the Global

3 G.M. Lyons, D.A. Baldwin and D.W. McNemar, 'The "Politicization" Issue in the UN Specialized Agencies', *Proceedings of the Academy of Political Science*, Vol. 32 (4), 1977, 83.
4 *Ibid.*, 83–4.
5 D. Mitrany, *A Working Peace System*, Chicago, IL: Quadrangle, 1966.
6 D. Mitrany, *The Functional Theory of Politics*, London: St Martin's Press, 1976.
7 C. Archer, *International Organizations*, London: George Allen & Unwin, 1983, pp. 85–6.
8 P. Sands and P. Klein, *Bowett's Law of International Institutions*, London: Sweet & Maxwell, 2001, p. 79.
9 J.P. Sewell, *Functionalism and World Politics*, Princeton, NJ: Princeton University Press, 1966, pp. 43–4.
10 Lyons *et al.*, 'The "Politicization" Issue in the UN Specialized Agencies', 83.

South, form alliances and use group tactics, such as bloc voting, to further common agendas. Some of the more powerful states, including Japan, Brazil, Germany and India, rarely speak out during Council proceedings. In contrast, other powerful states, including the US, Canada and the UK, have more actively called for added serious focus on grave violations. However, in view of the one-state one-vote structure, these powerful states lack the collective strength to overcome the politicisation that has dominated Council proceedings. Weaker states bring political aims and conflicts into the arena as a mechanism for voicing issues in a forum where more powerful states will be forced to listen, as will be explored throughout Part 3.

'"Politicization"', according to Lyons *et al.*, 'can be viewed as an organizational defect to be corrected, an indicator to be understood, or a bargaining tactic to be dealt with.'[11] In a realist vein, many scholars argue that it is naïve to view politicisation as an organisational defect. They assert that international organisations cannot be divorced from the political agendas of their members. Humphrey comments that human rights in particular cannot be divorced from politics, saying that '[I]n a sense nothing could be more political; and it would have been quite unreal had the great international debate on human rights not reflected the deep differences which divide nations and groups.'[12] Recognition that political agendas will always exist at interstate organisations results in an acceptance, or tolerance, of some degree of politicisation as a natural consequence, rather than an organisational defect, of international organisations. If politicisation is not a defect, then it cannot readily be 'corrected'.

Politicisation as an indicator emphasises that the advancement of objectives within an international organisation reflects trends in the international system. Politicisation directly mirrors current political, military, economic or cultural conflicts between states, groups and blocs. Elimination of highly sensitive conflicts would not deal with the underlying reasons for politicisation of international organisations. International political tensions, rather than individual situations, would have to be resolved before politicisation could cease within an international organisation. Politicisation of the HRC is indicative of schisms within the international community that must be dealt with in order to eliminate, or at least to reduce, the manifestation of those inherent problems. Using politicisation as an indicator of international politics allows for some politicisation to occur within international organisations. A high degree of politicisation would nevertheless result in the Council's credibility being undermined.

Politicisation may also be used as a form of protest. HRC proceedings demonstrate that weaker states engage in politicisation of proceedings in order to ensure their protest is registered. Weaker states may also politicise

11 *Ibid.*, 86.
12 J.P. Humphrey, *Human Rights and the United Nations: A Great Adventure*, New York: Transnational Publishers Inc., 1984, p. 25.

a body in order to improve their bargaining power elsewhere. International organisations become arenas where, sometimes unrelated or controversial, issues are raised in order for weaker states to have their policy aims heard by more powerful countries.

6.2. Regionalism

Politicisation can occur in many ways. The most important kind of politicisation, needing particular explanation, is regionalism. Regionalism is useful for understanding HRC proceedings in relation to groups' power and influence[13] at that body. Geographic regional groups are not the only form of alliances at the UN. Social sciences define regions not just by geographic characteristics but also on economic, social and cultural grounds.[14] Russett focused on five aspects, which he identified as key to understanding alliances: social and cultural homogeneity; similar attitudes or external behaviour; political interdependence; economic interdependence; and geographic proximity.[15] Russett's study demonstrated that examining all five factors allowed a number of groups to emerge with almost the same boundaries for each criterion. None of these groups was in fact a subsystem of international law, and none had the same inclusions and exclusions for all of the criteria. However, Russett's 1967 study highlighted four major areas with much in common under the five criteria. The groups consisted of a core number of states, with other peripheral 'hangers-on' dependent on the individual criterion being examined. The four main groups identified were: Eastern Europe,[16] Latin America,[17] Western community, and Asia (including some Arab and African states). The Middle East also emerged from the study as one cluster of less homogeneous, but still intrinsically linked, states. Despite the study being undertaken 40 years prior to the Council's creation, many of those groups play a central role at the body.

Various factors gave rise to the regional alliances at the UN, including Cold War politics, decolonisation, nuclear proliferation and issues of collective security, and perceptions of global interdependence.[18] Political coalitions have, over time, become as influential as the geographically linked groups.[19] Developing nations have formed subgroups, within or across regional groups,

---

13 See, for example, C.B. Smith, *Politics and Process and the United Nations: The Global Dance*, Boulder, CO: Lynne Rienner, 2006.
14 Archer, *International Organizations*, p. 44.
15 B.M. Russett, *International Regions and the International System: A Study in Political Ecology*, Chicago, IL: Rand-McNally, 1967, pp. 2–7.
16 USSR, Poland, Czechoslovakia, Romania, Bulgaria, and Hungary.
17 Although from the 1960s Cuba moved towards Eastern Europe group.
18 D. Nicol, 'Interregional Co-ordination Within the United Nations: The Role of the Commonwealth', in B. Andemicael (ed.), *Regionalism and the United Nations*, Dobbs Ferry, NY: Oceana Publications Ltd, 1979, p. 100.
19 *Ibid.*, p. 102.

asserting collective strength to pursue collective aims. Weiss comments that 'the various roles on the international stage and in the global theater are played by actors from the two major troupes, North and South'.[20] Quoting Black's view that 'axis descriptors – developing/developed, non-industrialized/industrialized, rich/poor – are crude and value-laden',[21] Weiss argues that membership of the South/North has nothing to do with geographic location but is rather about economic, social and other similar factors.[22]

The UN's main political groups give strength to Weiss' argument. Political groups form alliances between either developed or developing states. Furthermore, developing states have formed stronger political alliances, such as the Non-Aligned Movement (NAM), Group of 77 (G-77) and the Organisation of the Islamic Conference (OIC), than developed nations, owing to their greater need for collective strength. The UN was designed by colonial powers and strong states. With increasing independence of former colonies, political alliances were needed for new states' interests to be collectively represented at the body. Strong alliances between developing countries allowed them to challenge the world economic order as set out by industrialised nations,[23] and to secure methods for trade, development, and economic growth. Initially, two groups were formed to represent developing nations' interests: the NAM and the G-77. Those groups, although formed for economic motivations, also enabled developing states to use collective strength on political matters.

The Non-Aligned Movement's name indicates that its membership was comprised of states not immediately involved in the Cold War – that is not aligned to either the US or the Soviet Union. Of course,[24] despite their claims, 'most nationalist movements and Third World regimes had diplomatic, economic, and military relations with one or both of the superpowers'.[25] Weiss comments that 'amateur lexicographers might have problems in finding a commonsensical dictionary entry for "non-aligned" that included such Soviet lackeys as Fidel Castro's Cuba and such American ones as Mobutu Sese Seko's Zaire'.[26] NAM developed from the Asian-African Conference, a political

20 T.G. Weiss, *What's Wrong with the United Nations and How to Fix It*, Cambridge: Polity Press, 2008, pp. 50–51.
21 M. Black, *The No-Nonsense Guide to International Development*, 2nd edn., Oxford: New Internationalist, 2007, p. 16.
22 Weiss, *What's Wrong with the United Nations*, p. 50.
23 J.S. Nye, 'UNCTAD: Poor Nations' Pressure Group', in Robert W. Cox and Harold K. Jacobson (eds.), *The Anatomy of Influence: Decision Making in International Organization*, New Haven and London: Yale University Press, 1973, pp. 334–70.
24 See, for example, G. Lundestad, *East, West, North, South: Major Developments on International Politics Since 1945*, Oxford: Oxford University Press, 1999; P. Worsley, *The Third World*, London: Weidenfeld and Nicolson, 1964.
25 M.T. Berger, 'After the Third World? History, Destiny and the Fate of Third Worldism', *Third World Quarterly*, Vol. 25 (1), 2004, 13.
26 Weiss, *What's Wrong with the United Nations*, pp. 51–2.

gathering held in Bandung, Indonesia, in April 1955.[27] The conference was convened in part due to frustration by many newly independent countries unable to secure UN membership due to Cold War politics. The two then-superpowers refused to admit states seen as belonging to the other camp. Indeed no new members were admitted between 1950 and 1954.[28] G-77 was named at its creation in 1964, when 77 states[29] jointly prepared for the UN Conference on Trade and Development. It worked in parallel with NAM, focusing on economic issues. Weiss comments that 'on many key areas of UN concern [. . .] the NAM and G-77 remain the only way to organize international debates and negotiations between industrialized and developing states'.[30]

The OIC was established in 1969 to unite Muslim countries after the 1967 War, in which Israel established control of Jerusalem. The OIC, with 57 member states, is the largest alliance of states within the UN.[31] Many of its members are influential within other groups or alliances. As such, the OIC has far-reaching political power. For example, in 2006, 17 of the 47 Council member states were OIC members. Three OIC members, Algeria, Saudi Arabia and Azerbaijan, chaired the regional groups for Africa, Asia, and Eastern Europe.

Traditionally the OIC has agreed collective group positions that advance regional aims, in the interests of the governing regimes. The 'Arab Spring' of 2011, beginning with the national uprising in Tunisia, may affect the OIC's future role. A main strength of that political bloc has been regional unity of political agendas. However, national discontent within individual regimes indicates that OIC states will need to engage more seriously in discussions on national issues, which may lead to less cohesion within the group on international political affairs. National governments may move away from their political allies within the OIC, with dictators and ruling elites making way for a range of different forms of governing powers, including perhaps military rule, secular governments, or Islamist movements.

Western regionalism has played an important role at the UN. During the Cold War, Western states were united through affiliation to the US. NATO was the epitome of a Western political alliance in the period immediately following the Second World War. NATO was created[32] as an alliance of like-minded,

---

27 Key Third World leaders at the Conference included Indian Prime Minister Jawaharlal Nehru, Egyptian president Gamal Abdel Nasser, and Zhou Enlai, foreign minister and prime minister of the People's Republic of China.
28 Weiss, *What's Wrong with the United Nations*, p. 51.
29 There are currently 130 members.
30 Weiss, *What's Wrong with the United Nations*, p. 49.
31 21 Sub-Saharan African, 12 Asian, 18 Middle Eastern and North African States, 3 Eastern European and Caucasian, 2 South American, and 1 Permanent Observer Mission. See Organisation of the Islamic Conference; Permanent Missions of OIC Member States to the United Nations in New York (website). (Online). Available HTTP: <http://www.oicun.org/categories/Mission/Members/> (accessed 16 October 2012).
32 'The North Atlantic Treaty', Washington, DC, 4 April 1949, 34 U.N.T.S. 243.

Western states who sought to defend its members' territories and also their common interests and values.[33] That alliance was primarily founded to provide a defence and security outside of the UN system, one 'that would not be subject to Soviet interference'.[34] The Cold War also saw the emergence of what would become the European Union, which began in 1950 with economic and political ties through, for example, the creation of the European Coal and Steel Community.[35] The EU's actions as a political bloc set a precedent for the rise of regionalism at international bodies, including at the Commission.[36]

The Treaty of Lisbon[37] requires EU member states to seek and advance common foreign policies.[38] Article 34(1) TEU (ex. Article 19 (1)) provides that EU members 'shall coordinate their action in international organisations and [. . .] shall uphold the common positions in such forums'. EU member states were, from 1993,[39] required to speak with one voice on foreign policy matters, which occurs by negotiating and compromising to find common ground between member states. This requirement is particularly difficult regarding foreign policy, as member states have different interests, allegiances, priorities, and preferences. Khaliq comments that the process is rarely straightforward.[40] The common position's often fragile nature greatly affects EU states' ability to negotiate with other states or groups, owing to the difficulties of renegotiating or deviating from the common position.

Weiss argues that, even after the Cold War has ended, groups and alliances are still obstructing the UN's work, with the North–South divide impeding a 'sensible regrouping of the majority of voices, which should change from issue to issue'.[41] Regional alliances do allow a larger number of states' views to be represented through collective voices, as opposed to powerful states dominating Council proceedings. Abebe, a delegate to the Council from Ethiopia, argues that such subgroups are necessary because human rights

---

33 See, for example, A. Wenger, C. Nuenlist and A. Locher, *Transforming NATO in the Cold War: Challenges Beyond Deterrence in the 1960s*, London: Taylor & Francis, 2007, pp. 3–4.

34 L.S. Kaplan, *NATO Divided, NATO United: The Evolution of an Alliance*, Westport, CT: Greenwood Publishing Group, 2004, p. 2.

35 Treaty Establishing the European Coal and Steel Community, Paris, 18 April 1951, 261 U.N.T.S. 140.

36 cf. P.D. Lombaerde and M. Schulz (eds.), *The EU and World Regionalism: The Makeability of Regions in the 21st Century*, Aldershot: Ashgate Publishing Ltd, 2009.

37 European Union, 'Treaty of Lisbon Amending the Treaty on European Union and the Treaty Establishing the European Community', 13 December 2007, 2007/C 306/01.

38 European Union, 'Consolidation Version of the Treaty on European Union', *reproduced* 30 March 2012, 2010/C83/01. Title V, in particular Articles 24–35.

39 The common position requirement was first adopted in European Union, 'Treaty on European Union (Consolidated Version), Treaty of Maastricht', 7 February 1992, Official Journal of the European Communities C 325/5, *entered into force* 1 November 1993.

40 U. Khaliq, *Ethical Dimensions of the Foreign Policy of the European Union: A Legal Appraisal*, Cambridge: Cambridge University Press, 2008, p. 88.

41 Weiss, *What's Wrong with the United Nations*, p. 51.

discourse and practice are skewed towards Western experiences, resulting in developing states requiring subgroups to represent their views and allow participation in human rights bodies.[42]

However, these alliances had a generally negative effect on the Council's proceedings. Ultimately, such groups have served to undermine much of the body's work in its early years. UN alliances are represented at the Council despite many states from each group not holding membership at that body. Council alliances arise out of membership allotments and represent the interests of HRC members and non-members from those general UN groups. States often hold membership of more than one regional or political alliance. For example, Egypt[43] is a member of both the African Group and the OIC. Slovakia[44] is a member of the Eastern European Group and the European Union. States holding membership of more than one group, especially those with large membership, may have more allies. Alliances between groups remain, as occurred at the Commission, which often results in what Schrijver identifies as 'the Rest against the West'.[45]

The Council's composition contributes to its politicisation. Developing states have strong representation at the HRC. African and Asian states hold thirteen seats each, while Latin American and Caribbean states (GRULAC) hold eight seats. States forge alliances through groups, ensuring power as a collective despite being individually weak. The OIC is the dominant group at the Council. The OIC is comprised of developing or weaker nations as members, and it has a large number of allies from other political alliances such as the NAM and G-77. The North–South divide, expounded upon by Weiss, is particularly apparent at the HRC owing to its large number of developing nations and the natural alliances formed between such states.[46] The OIC exerts great power and influence over Council proceedings, ensuring that the political agendas of its members and allies remain at the fore within the HRC. Politicisation has been apparent through advancement of political objectives, groups shielding their allies from Council scrutiny, and politically motivated attacks on certain states which have obstructed the HRC from taking action in other, needed, areas.[47]

Groups and alliances fundamentally structure Council discussions. Talks following expert reports, as well as general debates on agenda items, tend to begin with representatives of the main alliances stating a general position that is universal or predominant among its members. Those general positions are followed by pronouncements by individual state members, expressly or

---

42 A.M. Abebe, 'Of Shaming and Bargaining: African States and the Universal Periodic Review of the United Nations Human Rights Council', *Human Rights Law Review*, Vol. 9 (1), 2009, 2.

43 Membership 2007–2010.

44 Membership 2008–2011.

45 N. Schrijver, 'The UN Human Rights Council: A New "Society of the Committed" or Just Old Wine in New Bottles', *Leiden Journal of International Law*, Vol. 20 (4), 2007, 812.

46 Weiss, *What's Wrong with the United Nations*.

47 As will be explored throughout Part 3.

tacitly referring back to the broader positions of one or more of the allied blocs. That tactic allows weight to be added to groups' positions, through repetition of pronouncements on particular issues. The intensity of the repetition varies across the regional groups and political blocs. Western states tend only to make statements that introduce new information or take different positions than already mentioned by other countries during a discussion. By contrast, African states and OIC members most frequently simply repeat their groups' position rather than adding anything new to the discussion. Concerned countries, non-member states, and observers are afforded the opportunity to make statements where appropriate, which often follow the trend of repeating positions taken by their regional groups or political allies.

6.3. Forms of politicisation

Three main forms of politicisation at the UN are: politicisation through ideological discourse, overt politicisation, and politicisation through an ostensible 'success story'. Politicisation of human rights through ideological discourse occurred throughout the Cold War, for example in the tension between discussing civil and political rights and economic and social ones. Those discussions centred around ideologies, which underscored the political divisions between the Socialist bloc and Western states.[48] Politicisation through ideological discourse continues to exist at the HRC, with developing states emphasising promotion of human rights, capacity-building, and technical assistance, in contrast with Western states primarily focusing on protecting victims and preventing gross and systemic violations. The tension between those groups demonstrates a deeper political and ideological divide on the role of human rights bodies and the responsibilities of individual states.

Bosch insists that the two situations which have caused the most problems within the UN are the Israel–Palestine conflict and South African *apartheid*.[49] That assertion relates to the manner in which Israel and *apartheid* South Africa have been dealt with at the UN, rather than comparing the actual situations. There are similarities between the violations in South Africa and those in Israel and the Occupied Palestinian Territories (OPT). Such similarities may also be found in other countries where gross and systemic violations occur. Comparisons between Israel and South Africa[50] are controversial and

---

48 See Chapter 1, Section 1.1.3.
49 M.M. Bosch, *Votes in the UN General Assembly*, The Hague: Kluwer Law International, 1998, p. 42.
50 See, for example, A.M. Badran, *Zionist Israel and Apartheid South Africa: Civil Society and Peace Building in Ethnic-National States*, London: Routledge, 2009; M. Bishara, *Palestine/ Israel: Peace or Apartheid: Occupation, Terrorism and the Future*, London: Zed Books, 2002; U. Davis, *Israel, an Apartheid State*, London: Zed Books, 1987; Y. Laor, 'Israel's Apartheid is Worse than South Africa's', *Haaretz*, 1 November 2008; C. McGreal, 'Worlds Apart', *The Guardian*, 6 February 2006; I. Pappe, *Peoples Apart: Israel, South Africa and the Apartheid Question*, London: I.B. Tauris, 2011.

frequently fail to acknowledge the many fundamental differences between those situations. Exploring the weaknesses within those comparisons goes beyond the scope of this work but nevertheless must be acknowledged.[51] Bosch nonetheless stresses the 'negative influence' that both situations have had on the UN.[52] In particular, they 'polarized' the GA, undermining its work and 'producing the most heated debates and the most drawn out procedural discussions, and were the object of repeated (and repetitive) resolutions'.[53] Israel and South Africa respectively provide perhaps the clearest examples of overt politicisation and politicisation through an ostensible success story at the UN.

6.3.1 Overt politicisation: Israel

Overt politicisation occurs where groups or blocs of states seek to further a common political aim through the use of group tactics within a UN body or organ. Overt politicisation can only occur where a sufficient number of member states either hold a common aim or support allied states in the furtherance of their political aim. Where groups or blocs ally together to form a majority within a body, they are able to dominate proceedings and overtly politicise the body by voting *en masse* for political resolutions often unrelated to, or going beyond, the body's mandate.

The GA, with universal membership where each state has equal rights and voting powers, provides a forum where overt politicisation occurs. By contrast, the Security Council has a small membership, including five permanent members holding veto rights, which allows for a very different form of politicisation whereby those states are able unilaterally to advance political objectives by blocking action. The HRC, although with limited membership, is an arena similar to the GA, whereby weaker states are afforded the same opportunity to exert influence as states that are economically, militarily or politically more powerful. Political agendas of groups or blocs gain more attention at bodies such as the HRC, where member states enjoy sovereign equality and geographic groups are proportionately represented. The Council is particularly vulnerable to overt politicisation in this regard due to the strength and dominance of the African Group and the OIC. As observed in Chapter 8, both rely heavily on tactics such as group voting, repetition of statements, and shielding allies.

Many UN bodies and organs have been politicised regarding Israel. The GA, in particular, has been overtly politicised in its targeting and treatment of Israel. As will become apparent, that situation requires special attention,

---

51 cf. A. Dershowitz, *The Case Against Israel's Enemies: Exposing Jimmy Carter and Others Who Stand in the Way of Peace*, Hoboken, NJ: John Wiley, 2009; J. Lelyveld, 'Jimmy Carter and Apartheid', *The New York Review of Books*, 29 March 2007.

52 Bosch, *Votes in the UN General Assembly*, p. 42.

53 *Ibid.*

as it directly correlates to politicisation in the HRC. A case in point is the passing of the 1975 GA Resolution 3379, entitled 'Zionism Is Racism',[54] and its later repeal in 1991.[55] Resolution 3379 reflected international politics and diplomatic relations at that time. Arab countries, supported and encouraged by the Soviet Union and its allies within the Socialist bloc, had gained significant strength and influence, which Bosch asserts was primarily due to 'the oil weapon'.[56] Many Arab states had participated in or supported the wars against Israel in 1948, 1967 and 1973. They increasingly used the GA to focus attention on the Palestinian cause. The Arab states sought to denounce Israeli treatment of the Palestinians, but instead 'submitted a text that said something altogether different'.[57] Resolution 3379, which equated Zionism with racism, challenged the state of Israel *as such*. According to Jacoby it sought 'to annul the UN resolutions which brought into being the creation of Israel'.[58]

Resolution 3379 was passed in its grossly politicised form because of widespread support for the Arab states' aims. To be sure, the Palestinians' predicament raised grave questions about human rights and about people's rights to self-determination. Yet dictatorial regimes in both the Arab and Soviet blocs raised equally serious questions about whether human rights, or indeed any serious form of self-determination through political participation exercised directly by the people, existed in most of the states that supported the resolution. Only decades later, first with the fall of the Soviet bloc, then with the Arab Spring of 2011, would some sense of people asserting real rights of self-determination through open participation begin to emerge within the states that had so long opposed Israel. Before those seismic shifts had occurred, global action against Israel served more to deflect attention from such states' own human rights abuses than to manifest any serious concern for the rights of Palestinians. Indeed, with the advent of democracy, most Eastern European states reversed their earlier positions, voting in 1991 to repeal Resolution 3379.[59] Whilst many Western states might have supported more candid criticism of Israel within the context of broader, even-handed scrutiny of human rights throughout the whole of the Middle East, the obstinate singling out of Israel, which would recur in a host of institutional contexts well into the 21st century, became symptomatic of the sheer manipulation of human rights for power political ends.

54 GA Res. 3379 (XXX), 'Elimination of All Forms of Racial Discrimination', 10 November 1975, UN Doc. A/RES/3379 (XXX).
55 GA Res. 46/86, 'Elimination of Racism and Racial Discrimination', 16 December 1991, UN Doc. A/RES/46/86.
56 Bosch, *Votes in the UN General Assembly*, pp. 41–2.
57 *Ibid.*, p. 41.
58 T.A. Jacoby, *Bridging the Barrier: Israeli Unilateral Disengagement*, Aldershot: Ashgate Publishing Ltd., 2007, p. 87.
59 See, generally, Heinze commenting on states' voting records (E. Heinze, 'Even-handedness and the Politics of Human Rights', *Harvard Human Rights Journal*, Vol. 21 (7), 2008, 7–46).

Bosch notes that, by 1975, a large part of the international community had grown impatient with Israel.[60] The USSR supported the Arab states for various reasons. Israel had once been viewed as a potentially socialist state, but was increasingly allied with the US. Decolonised states lent their support, perhaps due to alliances with the USSR, or perhaps on anti-imperialist grounds, particularly striking in view of the Soviet Union's own domination of many subordinated national minorities.[61] The draft resolution was proposed by Cuba, Libya and Somalia, on behalf of the non-aligned states. Virtually the entire Soviet bloc supported the Resolution, alongside all Arab states and most African countries. 139 of the UN's then 145 member states took part in the vote: 71 in favour, 35 against and 33 abstentions.[62] The Resolution was supported by almost half of the UN membership, and by more than two-thirds of those 'present and voting'.

The 1991 repeal of Resolution 3379 further demonstrates its originally political motives. Although international opinion on Israel's treatment of Palestinians had not changed fundamentally in 1991, there was widespread agreement that Resolution 3379 had been aimed not at the occupation, but merely at delegitimising the State of Israel. International relations changed from the mid-1980s, with the eventual dissolution of the USSR and the end of the Cold War politics that had dominated the UN. Dominance of political blocs, such as the Socialist bloc, NAM and G-77, receded during the nineties, enabling regional groups and political blocs to advance more of their own interests rather than participating in the ideological warfare between the US and the USSR. The shifting international climate enabled other blocs to gain power, albeit not to the same extent that had previously occurred. That climate enabled the US, particularly under the administration of President George Bush, Sr., to garner support for repealing the Resolution.[63]

The international climate in 1991 resulted in only 25 states, out of the UN's then 166 members, voting against repealing Resolution 3379.[64] All of those countries were either OIC members, or were closely allied with that bloc. Of the 71 countries that had supported the Resolution in 1975, 13 absented themselves in 1991, five abstained, two had merged with other states, 29 did a complete about-face, and only 22 opposed its repeal (the other three opponents of the repeal were not member states when Resolution 3379 was passed).

60 Bosch, *Votes in the UN General Assembly*, p. 41.
61 cf. E. Heinze, 'Truth and Myth in Critical Race Theory and LatCrit: Human Rights and the Ethnocentrism of Anti-Ethnocentrism', *National Black Law Journal*, Vol. 20 (2), 2007, 107–62.
62 United Nations Department of Public Information (New York), *Yearbook of the United Nations 1991, Vol. 45*, Dordrecht: Martinus Nijhoff Publishers, 1992, p. 537.
63 cf. B.A. Gilman, *The Treatment of Israel by the United Nations: Hearing Before the Committee on International Relations, U.S. House of Representations*, Darby, PA: Diane Pub. Co. 1999, pp. 74–9.
64 149 of the then 166 member states participated in the decision: 111 in favour, 25 against and 13 abstentions.

The Council has demonstrated, from the outset, some members' eagerness to continue the excessive focus on Israel. Throughout the Council's early sessions, various states, the High Commissioner for Human Rights, and indeed the Secretary-General, called on the Council to devote attention and resources to grave situations other than the OPT. These calls were a response to the Council's repeated focus on Israel to the detriment of other serious situations in, for example, the DPRK (North Korea), the DRC (Congo), Myanmar (Burma), Sri Lanka, and Zimbabwe, amongst others. Observers, and indeed states themselves, drew comparisons between the ways in which the Commission[65] and the Council treated Israel.[66]

Despite warnings about selectivity, bias, double standards, and loss of credibility, from the outset Council discussions were dominated by states seeking to vilify Israel and to retain focus on that region. A large number of OIC states were able to express, and use their votes to achieve, collective positions. The OIC sought to retain focus on the OPT as part of national and regional foreign policies. OIC agendas included political, religious, cultural and regional ties with the Palestinians and with affected neighbouring states. OIC states also used the situation to divert attention away from other gross and systemic violations within the Middle East or within influential OIC Council members such as Pakistan, Algeria, and Egypt.

A further political motivation, particularly for states allied with but not members of the OIC, was Israel's ties with the US. Israel is seen as the US foothold in the Middle East. Realists and institutionalists would argue, for different reasons, that this relationship encouraged anti-US states, such as Cuba, China, Venezuela, and Russia, to use the situation in the OPT to attack US hegemony and interference. From a realist perspective, this group of states allied themselves with the OIC to attack a more powerful country through attacking its allies. Institutionalists might counter the realist position by arguing, instead, that this is an example of a group of states seeking to further a common interest, with the interest here being the OPT. However, that highlights the problem with institutionalism being applied to human rights – as explored in Chapter 4 – because it appears that the 'common interest' need not be human rights orientated.

Israel is also viewed by some as a remnant of colonialism, particularly in terms of its treatment of the Palestinians. Neo-Marxists or Third World theorists perhaps view Israel as a remnant of colonialism because it occupies Palestinian lands and is widely seen to have racist and discriminatory practices towards the indigenous people. Developing states identified with the Palestinian cause, seeking to use the Council to eliminate similar violations as had been perpetrated in colonial countries.

---

65 As explored in Chapter 1, Section 1.2.3.
66 F.J. Hampson, 'An Overview of the Reform of the UN Human Rights Machinery', *Human Rights Law Review*, Vol. 7 (1), 2007, 7–27; P. Scannella and P. Splinter, 'The United Nations Human Rights Council: A Promise to be Fulfilled', *Human Rights Law Review*, Vol. 7 (1), 2007, 41–72.

Scannella and Splinter argue that bias, selectivity and politicisation have 'been most evident in the Council's handling of situations involving Israel'.[67] The situation in Israel and the OPT is one of gross and systemic human rights violations. The Council's attention ought to be drawn to that situation, and indeed Israeli violations in Lebanon and the Occupied Syrian Golan. However, the Council's excessive focus on Israel, which frequently results in other gross and systemic situations being ignored altogether, occurs owing to the gross politicisation of the Council. Indeed, politicisation of the body's mechanisms and proceedings are often exemplified by the Council's treatment of Israel. The Council, as will be explored in Part 3, has excessively focused on Israel during related and unrelated discussions, during Special Sessions, and through reports by various thematic mandate holders.

To illustrate the overt and excessive politicisation of the HRC regarding Israel, I shall briefly explore Council discussions about the country-specific mandate on Israel and the OPT. The Council, having adopted its predecessor's Special Procedures system, utilises both thematic and country-specific mandates. States critical of country resolutions at the Commission remained committed to that position at the Council. Those states tended to be decolonised states, members of NAM, and OIC members. Despite vehemently opposing country-specific mandates in general, the states and groups which called for their end constantly gave the caveat that the mandate on the OPT must be retained. Justification for that position was the constantly repeated argument that the OPT mandate dealt with foreign occupation, rendering it thematic rather than country-specific.[68] Conversely, Israel was the sole country-specific mandate not to be supported by Western and other developing nations, despite their general support for country-specific mandates. In particular, those states criticised the body's selective, bias and partial treatment of Israel.

Steiner *et al.* note that the Council does not examine human rights violations in Israel, but rather violations committed by Israel in the OPT.[69] That supports the argument that the OPT is a thematic mandate. However, thematic mandates do not solely focus on one country, which clearly the OPT mandate does. For the OPT mandate to be thematic, it should arguably encompass other issues of foreign occupation in, for example, Northern Cyprus

---

67 *Ibid.*, 61.

68 These calls were led, notably, by China on behalf of the Like-Minded Group, who provided the initial caveat that the OPT mandate could not be regarded as country-specific because it dealt with the thematic issue of foreign occupation (Oral statement of the Chinese delegate, 2nd Session, 3 October 2006). China's comments about the thematic issue of foreign occupation is interesting given its position regarding its occupation of Tibet and its frequent use of the 'no-action motion' to block Commission discussions and action on Tibet. The 'no-action' motion was used from 1992–1996 to block all draft resolutions that mentioned Tibet.

69 H.J. Steiner, P. Alston and R. Goodman, *International Human Rights in Context*, 3rd edn., Oxford: Oxford University Press, 2008, p. 814.

and Tibet. States arguing that the OPT is a thematic mandate were silent on other issues of foreign occupation within any other region. That silence suggests the argument was based on political, rather than technical, motives. Ultimately, country-specific mandates were not abolished. However, states' tactics resulted in Israel being singled out in every discussion on country-specific mandates, thus keeping the spotlight on Israel to the detriment of other country-specific situations.

The Commission's loss of credibility has been attributed to a number of factors, a main one being the body's treatment of Israel. One significant manifestation of these problems was the placing of Israel on the Commission's permanent agenda.[70] Israel, a democratic state, does commit violations against Palestinians and Israeli Arabs. Israel does also allow protection and promotion of human rights through granting wide access to human rights organisations and NGOs, providing legal recourse for human rights violations through domestic and international courts and tribunals, and through its formal commitment to international human rights law obligations. Yet, of all the human rights situations across the globe, including those states under despotic rulers and those which provide almost no access to the outside world to ascertain severity of the situation,[71] the only country-specific mandate to be placed on the Council's permanent agenda is Israel and the OPT.[72] Moreover, while all other country-specific mandates exist for one year and must be renewed annually, the mandate on Israel and the OPT is open-ended and will last until the end of the occupation.

Some degree of politicisation may be expected at intergovernmental organisations, and the Council is no exception. Anything that is 'overt', however, goes beyond the realm of what may be tolerated within a political body. Overt politicisation tips the balance and becomes harmful to the Council's functioning. As the focus on Israel has shown, overt politicisation runs the risk of undermining the Council's founding principles of universality, impartiality and non-selectivity.

6.3.2 Ostensible 'success story': South Africa

The UN's approach to *apartheid* in South Africa is perhaps the clearest example of politicisation through an ostensible 'success story'. Politicisation through an ostensible 'success story' occurs where failures are masked behind a success story that is used to deflect attention away from inaction elsewhere. UN action, alongside diplomatic and political pressure, was indeed key to

---

70 The Commission established a mandate valid until the end of the occupation, see CHR Res. 1993/2, 'Question of the Violation of Human Rights in the Occupied Arab Territories, Including Palestine', 19 February 1993, UN Doc. E/CN.4/RES/1993/2.

71 For example, Myanmar (Burma), or DPRK (North Korea).

72 HRC Res. 5/1, 'Institution Building of the United Nations Human Rights Council', 18 June 2007, UN Doc. A/HRC/RES/5/1, Chapter IIV Part C, Item 7.

South Africa ending its policy of *apartheid* in the 1990s. The UN was able to focus on South Africa because both the Western and Soviet blocs agreed, or tacitly accepted, that action be taken on that situation. Western states, many of whom were former imperial powers, tended to take a back seat during discussions on South Africa. Soviet states, by contrast, were more actively involved in pushing for action to be taken against that state.[73] That position reflects the USSR's anti-imperialist stance and support for decolonisation across Africa.[74]

Developing states, as a result of the Western and Soviet attitudes to South Africa, did not have to choose sides between the US and the USSR. This allowed them to promote their own national and regional political objectives. Many decolonised states sought to highlight ongoing imperialist practices which flagrantly violated human rights in a similar vein to recent historical abuses, using South Africa 'to channel emotional anti-Western feelings into lasting political gains'.[75] Moskowitz points out that 'the vast majority of those who called for freedom, human rights and racial equality in South Africa hardly conceded them to their own peoples'.[76] He argues that many abuser states denounced South Africa in order to deflect attention away from their own human rights records.[77]

The UN's ability to deal with abuses in South Africa indicates that such action did not contravene the political aims of either the Western or Soviet bloc. That was not the case for many other human rights situations. The UN was unable to take action on other egregious violations because of a lack of agreement by one or both groups owing to political objectives that often were unrelated to human rights. The Western and Soviet blocs frequently shielded allied states from scrutiny, even where violations were gross and systemic.[78] Indeed, many other grave violations occurring elsewhere at that time resulted from similar policies adopted by other states to discriminate against indigenous populations.

China occupied Tibet in 1949, and since then China has committed egregious violations in that territory.[79] Discrimination and abuses in Tibet have

73 cf. D. Birmingham, *The De-colonization of Africa*, London: Routledge, 1995, pp. 51–61; R.H. Shultz, *The Soviet Union and Revolutionary Warfare: Principles Practices, and Regional Comparisons*, Stanford University, US: Hoover Press, 1988, pp. 115–47.

74 cf. Birmingham, *The De-colonization of Africa*, pp. 9, 28–39.

75 M. Moskowitz, *The Roots and Reaches of United Nations Actions and Decisions*, Alphen aan den Rijn, the Netherlands: Sijthoff & Noordhoff, 1980, p. 49.

76 *Ibid.*

77 *Ibid.*

78 D. Matas, *No More: The Battle Against Human Rights Violations*, Toronto: Dundum Press Ltd, 1994, p. 211.

79 cf. R. McCorquodale and N. Orosz, *Tibet, The Position in International Law: Report of the Conference of International Lawyers on Issues Relating to Self-Determination and Independence for Tibet, London 6–10 January 1993*, Chicago, IL: Serindia Publications Inc., 1994; D. Lal, *Indo-Tibet–China Conflict*, New Delhi: Gyan Publishing House, 2008, pp. 131–5; Asia Watch, *Human Rights in Tibet*, Asia Watch Committee, 1988.

been described as 'apartheid' policies.[80] Chitkara goes further, insisting that 'even the worst form of apartheid enforced in South Africa pales into insignificance when compared to the atrocities which the Chinese have committed and are continuing to commit in Tibet'.[81] China, owing to its powerful position at the UN, its leadership of political alliances between developing states, and its links to the USSR, was able effectively to ensure little scrutiny of those abuses. Similarly, the USSR was shielded from scrutiny of its discriminatory human rights abuses despite, as Heinze notes, the Soviet Union having 'crushed vast numbers of minority and ethnic groups'.[82] Heinze names the 'Chechens, Ingush, Balkars, Baltic peoples, Roma, Jews, Muslims, Romanian ethnic Hungarians, Tibetans or Uighurs' as just a few of the groups that were repressed by the Soviet Union's policies.[83] The USSR's strength at the UN, owing more broadly to Cold War politics, enabled it to avoid scrutiny of almost all such human rights situations. The US also committed discriminatory human rights violations against its indigenous population, which the GA altogether failed to address during the time that focus was on South Africa. It is clear from these examples that international relations and political objectives dictated which *apartheid*-type situations were and were not discussed. The UN's 'success' in taking action on South Africa resulted from a lack of overt politicisation from the US and USSR, which both masked a common underlying aim of deflecting attention away from other gross and systemic violations, and underlined the many instances where politicisation directed the organisation's work.

The GA produced more resolutions on *apartheid* than any other single item between 1952 (when it first appeared on the GA agenda) and 1994 (when the policy was ended). *Apartheid* in South Africa provided a unifying issue on which developing countries spoke with one voice in much the same way as decolonisation and self-determination had done previously. The sheer number of decolonised and developing states seeking action against South Africa, and the many Soviet and Western states who supported them, ensured ample backing for any tabled resolutions. That support resulted in a disproportionate number of resolutions on South Africa as compared with other similar, gross and systemic violations. Other situations attracted little attention or, more often, were ignored altogether.

Between 1946 and 1992 the GA adopted by recorded vote 234 resolutions on *apartheid*, 111 on Namibia, and 224 on other issues regarding Southern Africa. Those 569 resolutions totalled approximately one-fifth of the total

---

80 See, for example, Dalai Lama, *The Spirit of Tibet, Universal Heritage: Selected Speeches and Writings of HH the Dalai Lama XIV*, New Delhi: Allied Publishers, 1995, p. 161; B.N. Mullik, *The Chinese Betrayal: My Years with Nehru*, Bombay and New York: Allied Publishers, 1971, p. 603.

81 M.G. Chitkara, *Toxic Tibet Under Nuclear China*, New Delhi: APH Publishing, 1996, p. 110.

82 Heinze, 'Truth and Myth in Critical Race Theory and LatCrit', 22.

83 *Ibid.*, p. 23.

recorded votes. On average, the GA passed between five and ten resolutions annually on *apartheid* policies. Some sessions saw almost double that number of resolutions focusing specifically on South Africa.[84] Mertus notes that each year approximately 20 per cent of GA resolutions relate to human rights, which underlines the disproportionate attention given to Southern Africa.[85] By contrast, during that time the GA passed five resolutions regarding gross and systemic violations by China against indigenous peoples: three on Tibet[86] and two on Burma.[87] Similarly, only four resolutions were passed regarding grave abuses committed by the USSR: one general resolution[88] and three concerning violations in Hungary.[89] Moreover, violations against Native Americans were ignored altogether, as were similar practices and policies against the Aborigines in Australia, the Maoris in New Zealand, and other such situations.

From 1965, states regularly challenged South Africa's credentials at the GA. Usually verification of a delegation's credentials was aimed at resolving situations where competing governments within a state sent different delegations to the GA and each one claimed to represent that country.[90] The challenge to South Africa's credentials instead sought to delegitimise that state's delegation, leaving the country without any representation at the GA, a clearly political act. The challenge raised objections to the credentials of South Africa's delegation at the GA on the basis that they were sent by a non-representative and illegitimate government.[91] States, particularly decolonised ones, insisted that the exclusively white government represented less than 20 per cent of the population, and therefore could not be viewed as legitimate.

84 For example, 18 Resolutions on South Africa were passed at the 33rd Session, with 15 of those focusing specifically on aspects or effects of *apartheid* policies.

85 J. Mertus, *The United Nations and Human Rights: A Guide for a New Era*, Abingdon: Taylor & Francis, 2009, p. 40.

86 GA Res. 1353, 'Question of Tibet', 21 October 1959, 14th Session, UN Doc. A/RES/1353 (XIV); GA Res. 1723, 'Question of Tibet', 20 December 1961, 16th Session, UN Doc. A/RES/1723 (XVI); GA Res. 2079, 'Question of Tibet', 18 December 1965, 20th Session, UN Doc. A/RES/2079 (XX).

87 GA Res. 717, 'Complaint by the Union of Burma Regarding Aggression Against it by the Government of the Republic of China', 8 December 1953, 8th Session, UN Doc. A/RES/717 (VIII); GA Res. 815, 'Complaint by the Union of Burma Regarding Aggression Against it by the Government of the Republic of China', 29 October 1954, 9th Session, UN Doc. A/RES/815 (IX).

88 GA Res. 285, 'Violation by the Union of Soviet Socialist Republics of Fundamental Human Rights, Traditional Diplomatic Practices and Other Principles of the Charter', 25 April 1949, 4th Session, UN Doc. A/RES/285 (III).

89 GA Res. 1312, 'The Situation in Hungary', 12 December 1958, 13th Session, UN Doc. A/RES/1312 (XIII); GA Res. 1454, 'Question of Hungary', 9 December 1959, 14th Session, UN Doc. A/RES/1454 (XIV); GA Res. 1741, 'Question of Hungary', 20 December 1961, 16th Session, UN Doc. A/RES/1741 (XVI).

90 C.F. Amerasinghe, *Principles of the Institutional Law of International Organizations*, Cambridge Studies in International and Comparative Law, Cambridge: Cambridge University Press, 2005, p. 130.

91 cf. Moskowitz, *The Roots and Reaches of United Nations Actions and Decisions*, pp. 65–8.

Resolution 2636 A (XXV) 1970 approved the Credentials Committee's Report 'except as regards the credentials of the representatives of South Africa'. That rejection was repeated in 1971, 1972 and 1973. Up until that point, a successful challenge to a state's credentials had political rather than practical consequences. That changed in 1974 when the Assembly voted to interpret this annual rejection as a repudiation of South Africa's participation at the GA, which effectively expelled that country from the Assembly. Resolution 3207 (XXIX) 30 September 1974 called on the Security Council to review the relationship between South Africa and the UN. The GA had been urged to expel South Africa[92] in accordance with Article 6 of the Charter which permits expulsion 'upon the recommendation of the Security Council'. France, the UK and the US used their veto powers at the Security Council. As a result of the triple veto, 'the General Assembly intensified its condemnation of South Africa' and focused excessive and repetitive criticism of those three Western states during discussions on South Africa.[93]

The UN's focus on South Africa was 'successful'; South Africa eventually withdrew from Namibia, ended the *apartheid* policy, and ceased to be a pariah state. Success in the campaign against South Africa's racist and discriminatory policies provided an opportunity for decolonised states to engage with UN bodies and to interact with other, more established, blocs. In particular, it provided a bridge connecting decolonised countries and the Soviet bloc. Beyond the success story and, indeed, the opportunity for weaker and newer states to use a collective voice, South Africa afforded protection for other abuser states by deflecting attention away from ongoing gross and systemic violations elsewhere. A clear parallel can be drawn between oppression of non-Russian, indigenous peoples within the USSR,[94] and the *apartheid* policy which oppressed the non-white peoples in South Africa. The USSR, however, received scant attention for those practices, with millions of victims being ignored, whereas South Africa was focused upon throughout the UN.

Politicisation through an ostensible 'success story' is the opposite of overt politicisation. Where overt politicisation is an open display of irrelevant political discussion, success stories allow other states to shy away from the HRC's scrutiny. Although initially less noticeable, its results are visible. As the sheer numbers of resolutions suggests, the focus on South Africa left many gross and systemic violations virtually untouched. This type of politicisation would breach the Council's principles of universality, partiality and non-selectivity, and also undermine the body's fulfilment of its mandate, namely to protect and promote human rights across all UN member states.

---

92 GA Draft Res. 'Relationship Between the UN and South Africa', 30 October 1974, UN Doc. S/11543.
93 Bosch, *Votes in the UN General Assembly*, p. 45.
94 cf. Heinze, 'Truth and Myth in Critical Race Theory and LatCrit'.

6.4. Politicisation of UN bodies

UN organs and bodies have been politicised, to varying degrees, from the organisation's outset. The UN's first decade saw the US and the Soviet Union use the organisation to achieve their diplomatic and foreign policy aims.[95] Cold War politics resulted in both the US and the USSR, and their respective allies, politicising UN bodies. Cold War political agendas were introduced into specialised agencies throughout the 1950s and 1960s.

The US opposed Communist China joining the ILO, and withheld contributions following the appointment of a Soviet Assistant-Director-General in 1970. The World Bank has always had an American president, with one exception,[96] and a voting system reflecting US financial importance, leading to criticisms of it being politicised and a pawn of US policy. Some might question whether such stances can merely be dismissed as 'political', since the Cold War involved questions of fundamental principles about the very nature of rights, law and citizenship in any society. For example, those who fervently believed in liberal democracy, in opposition to totalitarianism, would not call their opposition to Soviet or Chinese influence merely 'playing politics'. They saw it as a defence of core human values. Meanwhile, others criticised liberal democracies for preaching human rights whilst pursuing neo-imperial or neo-colonial practices. Whilst it lies beyond the scope of this study to rehearse the rights and wrongs of Cold War politics, the fact remains that such polarisation constantly shaped international diplomacy, on the broadest range of issues.

In 1974 the US withheld payments to UNESCO until anti-Israel resolutions were changed. In particular, on 7 November 1974, UNESCO voted 'to withhold assistance from Israel in the fields of education, science and culture because of Israel's persistent alteration of the historic features of Jerusalem'.[97] US pressure resulted in alterations to that resolution. Another political resolution, on 20 November 1974, denied Israel membership of the European group, leaving it the only state not assigned a regional group.[98] This amounted to a *de facto* expulsion of Israel from UNESCO[99] and, owing to Western pressure, was reversed in 1976. The US withdrew from UNESCO in 1984, in protest at its anti-Western bias, rejoining only in 2003.[100] The US asserted that UNESCO was being used to discuss political matters,

---

95 Archer, *International Organizations*, p. 181.

96 James Wolfensohn (Australia) 1995–2005.

97 Resolution 3.427, 'Implementation of the General Conference and decisions of the Executive Board concerning the protection of cultural property in Jerusalem', in *Records of the General Conference, 18th Session*, Paris, 1974, Vol. 1, pp. 59–60.

98 *Ibid.*

99 Y. Abdulqawi, *Standard-setting in UNESCO*, Leiden and Boston: Martinus Nijhoff Publishers, 2007, pp. 380–81.

100 cf. A. McDermott, *The New Politics of Financing the UN*, Basingstoke and New York: Palgrave Macmillan, 2000, pp. 97–8.

including peace and security, which fell outside its mandate, and which should have been left to appropriate organs, such as the GA and SC. The American response to UNESCO's politicisation made use of its powerful position, financially and politically. Withdrawal from UN agencies as an 'ultimate sanction' developed as a US multilateral policy in the 1970s,[101] and continues to be used as a method for that state to demonstrate its displeasure with a body's work. Indeed, as I shall explore in Chapter 7, the US pulled out of the Council within two years of the body's creation.

The Soviet Union also used the UN for political aims. Parsons notes that the USSR used the UN to ally non-aligned states to the Soviet bloc by supporting their causes, particularly decolonisation, in order globally to isolate the US and Europe.[102] The USSR did not support self-determination for all peoples, particularly those nations living within the USSR. It did, however, adopt an anti-imperialist discourse regarding decolonisation in order to support peoples fighting against Western imperialism and to ally those emerging states with the Soviet bloc.

Decolonisation led to UN membership expanding, making the superpowers less able to dominate proceedings. That change was notable within the GA, and in agencies comprising proportionate geographic representation. From the 1960s onwards, the emergence of developing nations shifted the balance of power.[103] Lyons *et al.* recognised this shift in the 1970s, commenting that developing nations began to dominate UN bodies through collective voting, which was used to further common objectives.[104]

Weiss argues that developing nations protect each other through regional and political alliances.[105] Weiss cites South African support for Mugabe's regime in Zimbabwe as a 'contemporary example of misplaced Southern solidarity'.[106] Mugabe's regime commits gross and systemic human rights violations, including: widespread arbitrary detention and torture of prisoners; curtailment of the right to freedom of association and assembly; attacks on human rights defenders; and violations of rights to food, sanitation, adequate housing and safe drinking water.[107] However, despite US and EU targeted sanctions and political pressure, Mugabe's retention of power, particularly after the 2008 elections, demonstrates the strength of support from regional and political allies within the UN and the African Union. Mugabe, building

---

101 W. Preston, E.S. Herman and H.I. Schiller, *Hope and Folly: The United Nations and UNESCO*, Minneapolis, MN: University of Minnesota Press, 1989, p. 137.

102 A. Parsons, 'The UN and National Interests of States', in A. Roberts and B. Kingsbury (eds.), *United Nations, Divided World*, 2nd edn., Oxford: Oxford University Press, p. 113.

103 L. Ziring, R.E. Riggs and J.C. Plano, *The United Nations International Organization and World Politics*, 2nd edn., Belmont, CA: Wadsworth, 1994, p. 99.

104 Lyons *et al.*, 'The "Politicization" Issue in the UN Specialized Agencies', pp. 81–2.

105 Weiss, *What's Wrong with the United Nations*, p. 61.

106 *Ibid.*

107 cf. Amnesty International, *Annual Report 2007*, London: Amnesty International, 2008, pp. 333–6.

on that support, has constantly attacked the West, particularly the UK, for imperialism and hegemony. Weiss argues that Southern support for Mugabe exists 'presumably to maintain solidarity with one of the storied examples of anti-colonial and anti-imperial struggle'.[108]

Politicisation can be found throughout the UN. Acknowledging that politicisation will occur is, however, markedly different to accepting politicisation overshadowing a body's work and the ultimate fulfilment of its mandate. The GA, which has universal membership and is tasked with considering political matters, is regularly politicised by states, groups and blocs seeking to further political objectives. Much of the politicisation has been attributed to international political situations such as the Cold War, unity of decolonised states, the emergence of the European Union, or the more recent increase in strength of the Islamic bloc. Politicisation at the GA can be measured by examining statements made, resolutions tabled or, perhaps most pertinently, voting records.[109]

Although some technical bodies are politicised to a far lesser extent than political bodies, none are completely divorced from members' political agendas. Even bodies responsible for non-political matters are affected by state and regional considerations. The International Whaling Commission (IWC) arguably should not be politicised owing to it being a single-issue body focused highly on one subject, unlike the UN Charter-based human rights body which has a broad jurisdiction owing to everything invariably being connected to human rights. Prima facie, the IWC is so specific that it might be expected to be solely a technical body that keeps any politics under control. Yet this ostensibly manageable body is steeped in politics. The IWC has been identified as a 'dysfunctional organ'[110] which 'requires normalising'.[111] The IWC has 88 state parties, the majority of which are not whaling nations, and yet are able to influence the Commission's policy,[112] even where that policy undermines the body's fulfilment of its mandate.[113] Modern whaling has been driven by economic factors as much as cultural ones,[114] resulting in divergent factors, including economic considerations, rights of indigenous people, and state sovereignty.

The Human Rights Council is distinct from other UN bodies, regardless of their levels of politicisation in two main ways. The Council's composition as a body of limited membership with proportionate geographic representation

---

108 Weiss, *What's Wrong with the United Nations*, p. 62.

109 cf. Bosch, *Votes in the UN General Assembly*, pp. 117–62.

110 M. Fitzmaurice, 'Indigenous Whaling, Protection of the Environment, Intergenerational Rights and Environmental Ethics', *Yearbook of Polar Law*, Vol. 2, 2010, 255.

111 International Whaling Commission Res. 2006-1, 'St Kitts and Nevis Declaration', 18 June 2006, UN Doc. IWC/58/16/Res/2006-1.

112 Fitzmaurice, 'Indigenous Whaling, Protection of the Environment, Intergenerational Rights and Environmental Ethics', 254–5.

113 International Whaling Commission Res. 2006-1, UN Doc. IWC/58/16/Res/2006-1.

114 cf. C. Epstein, *The Power of Words in International Relations: Birth of an Anti-Whaling Discourse*, Cambridge, MA: Massachusetts Institute of Technology, 2008, pp. 27–53.

allows for a range of political objectives to be advanced by various government delegates, regional groups and political blocs. Furthermore, as the Council's work is so inherently political, owing to the breadth of universal human rights, a greater degree of politicisation must be expected than at many other bodies.

6.5. Politicisation of human rights bodies

Politicisation at the Commission occurred in three distinct ways during three separate phases. At the Commission's outset, the body was used by Western states seeking to advance human rights whilst simultaneously retaining colonial practices. With increasing UN membership due to decolonisation, politicisation of the Commission increasingly mirrored Cold War politics. Following the dissolution of the USSR and the Socialist bloc, with which many decolonised states were allied, the Commission became politicised through disproportionate focus on a few, politically isolated states – Israel, as we have seen, standing out as a conspicuous example – whilst shielding grave abusers.

The kind of politicisation that occurred during the Commission's final years is found in much international human rights activity. Failure to treat states in an even-handed manner is a main way in which the field of human rights becomes politicised. Alongside human rights bodies, such politicisation can occur within, for example, NGOs[115] and the media.[116] Heinze notes that the concept of even-handedness has not adequately been explored.[117] He provides a three-part test to identify lack of even-handedness.[118] Under the third prong of his test, selection of human rights violators becomes illegitimate when motivated by a 'political, social or cultural conflict' unrelated to the content of the human rights at issue.[119] The ongoing, overwhelmingly disproportionate focus on a state such as Israel, in both the Commission and the Council, often as a pretext for sidelining violations claiming far greater numbers of victims than the Israel–Palestine conflict has done (as I shall further examine in Chapter 8), raises serious questions about the Council's adherence to its mandate. Even-handedness does not require equal attention to be devoted to all states, but rather that the level of condemnation should be 'roughly proportionate to actual levels of abuse'.[120]

---

115 cf. Heinze, 'Even-handedness and the Politics of Human Rights'.

116 cf. E. Heinze and R. Freedman, 'Public Awareness of Human Rights: Distortions in the Mass Media', *International Journal of Human Rights*, Vol. 14 (4), 2010, 491–523; E. Heinze, 'The Reality and Hyperreality of Human Rights: Public Consciousness and the Mass Media', in R. Dickenson, E. Katselli, C. Murray and O.W. Pedersen (eds.), *Examining Critical Perspectives on Human Rights: The End of an Era?*, Cambridge: Cambridge University Press, 2011.

117 Heinze, 'Even-handedness and the Politics of Human Rights', 8.

118 *Ibid.*, 8–9.

119 *Ibid.*, 31.

120 Heinze and Freedman, 'Public Awareness of Human Rights', 498.

Politicisation of human rights bodies, particularly the phenomenon of excessive politicisation, arguably results from the interlinked nature of human rights and politics. Gearty criticises what he terms the false dichotomy between these fields in which politics becomes subordinate to law.[121] Instead, he deems it crucial to view human rights as part of, rather than superior to, politics. That claim does, however, contradict the Universal Declaration of Human Rights and subsequent human rights instruments. The UN sought to prioritise human rights as separate and superior to politics, giving them a higher-order status to competing political interests. It is that superiority to politics which dictates that human rights should be upheld universally. Gearty's assertion focuses on the everyday practice, rather than the fundamental significance, of human rights. Human rights compliance frequently relies on politics and, conversely, violations are often able to occur because of political factors. Tyagi recalls that the legal formulations of human rights are themselves products of political, and politicised, processes.[122] Even after such processes, regional or political groupings often take different, sometimes competing, stances on human rights, based on cultural norms and political agendas. Politics plays an integral role in human rights, with the two fields not easily divorced from one another.

The UN treaty-based human rights committees are frequently held out as examples of bodies where politicisation is sufficiently minimised so as to allow focus to remain solely on the task at hand – an important achievement, since those bodies handle many of the same controversial matters as the Charter-based bodies. That discrepancy can be explained by those bodies' mandates to monitor implementation of treaties in contracting state parties, which allows relatively little contention as compared with the Council's broad mandate.

The Human Rights Committee, for example, consists of independent experts and it is their independence from governmental or institutional influences that 'at least gives it the potential to be effective'.[123] Independent experts at the Committee are not required to have personal independence from their governments, and members include former ambassadors, government ministers, and members of parliament.[124] These experts' involvement at the highest level of politics ensures delegates have the expertise to engage with the political aspects of international human rights. The success of that body lies, predominantly, in the delegates' independence from their state

121 C. Gearty, *Can Human Rights Survive?*, Cambridge: Cambridge University Press, 2006, pp. 60–98.
122 Y. Tyagi, *The UN Human Rights Committee: Practice and Procedure*, Cambridge: Cambridge University Press, 2011, p. 6.
123 D. McGoldrick, *The UN Human Rights Committee: Its Role in the Development of the International Covenant on Civil and Political Rights*, Oxford: Oxford University Press, 1994, p. 44.
124 *Ibid.*

governments.[125] Another reason for the committees avoiding politicisation is the concerted efforts made by those independent experts to proceed on the basis of consensus in order to avoid confrontation and politicisation.[126] The committees have sought to create environments of dialogue and to avoid 'relating closely to the [UN's] political control bodies and policy organs'.[127]

The Human Rights Committee is, informally, regarded as *'primus inter pares'*.[128] There are, however, other UN human rights committees which, despite efforts to avoid confrontation, have somewhat greater degrees of politicisation. When many states make reservations to a treaty, for example the Convention on the Elimination of Discrimination against Women (CEDAW),[129] it indicates that countries are likely to have differing political objectives viz those human rights. The Committee on the Elimination of Discrimination against Women is highly politicised and is, arguably, as complex and difficult as the HRC.[130] CEDAW has mainly experienced problems in relation to OIC states which have sought to maintain discriminatory practices against women,[131] requiring the body to manoeuvre between state parties' conflicting interests in order to achieve the necessary balance. The HRC similarly experiences problems with states claiming 'cultural sensitivities' as the basis for non-compliance with human rights norms. OIC members, in particular, have politicised the Council in this manner. The difficulties and complexities at CEDAW, as at the Council, require the body to take a 'soft' approach towards compliance that primarily focuses on diplomatic pressure and ongoing discussions.

Despite the similarities between CEDAW and the HRC, when assessing the Council, I shall focus on the Human Rights Committee as a comparator because the Committee provides a model of best, indeed 'exemplary', practice.[132] Tyagi claims that the Human Rights Committee has, on the whole, avoided the 'East–West' and 'North–South' divides.[133] The Committee, with relatively less politicisation than other bodies, provides a benchmark against which the Council may be assessed. However, its nature as a body consisting of independent experts is fundamentally different to the Council which

125 *Ibid.*, pp. 44–5.
126 See, for example, Th.C. van Boven and F. Coomans, *Human Rights From Exclusion to Inclusion: Principles and Practice*, The Hague: Martinus Nijhoff Publishers, 2000, p. 72.
127 *Ibid.*
128 Tyagi, *The UN Human Rights Committee*, p. 792.
129 See text accompanying notes 8, 9 and 10, Chapter 4.
130 cf. S. Goonesekera, 'CEDAW: Reflections on the Framework', in M. Shivdas and S. Coleman (eds.), *Without Prejudice: CEDAW and the Determination of Women's Rights in a Legal and Cultural Context*, Commonwealth Secretariat, 2010, pp. 191–2.
131 cf. M. Shivdas and S. Coleman (eds.), *Without Prejudice: CEDAW and the Determination of Women's Rights in a Legal and Cultural Context*, Commonwealth Secretariat, 2010.
132 Tyagi, *The UN Human Rights Committee*, p. 311.
133 *Ibid.*

consists of state representatives; although it should not be forgotten that one of the radical – and rejected – reform proposals was to change from state delegates to experts. Despite the lack of scholarship assessing the practical impact of various types of delegates, it is clear that this difference is fundamental. Using the Committee as a benchmark for assessing the Council's politicisation will, therefore, require constant reference to this intrinsic difference and its impact on the Council's work and proceedings.

Regional human rights institutions are another type of body where politicisation may be minimised, or at least does not fundamentally undermine the bodies' work. Politicisation is minimised at the European Court of Human Rights (ECtHR) due to that body being unable to select the cases it hears, despite a constantly increasing workload. The doctrine of margin of appreciation which is crucial in relation to issues of morality is, arguably, one main reason for the high level of compliance with the Court's rulings. The UN system also uses similar kinds of proportionality criteria[134] where political tensions may exist between various states. One area where national political agendas do come into play is the selection of judges to sit at the Court. The selection process was criticised by, amongst others, Interrights,[135] which noted the possibilities for governmental interference with judicial candidates and sitting judges.[136] Such interference resulted in greater potential for politicisation of the Court. Despite that weakness, the ECtHR has been held out as a model of best practice for an intergovernmental human rights institution. Gibson, recognising the success of European institutions, argues that regional functionalism occurs as a result of the common politics and goals of those states which 'is not necessarily transferable either to other regions or to states on a universal scale'.[137]

The Human Rights Committee and the ECtHR are both concerned with a limited number of rights as well as particular groups of states. The Committee was created to supervise the compliance of state parties to the ICCPR with their obligations under that treaty.[138] The European Court supervises EU member states' compliance with obligations under the European Convention on Human Rights. States parties to these conventions agreed to be supervised by those bodies.[139] As a result of states placing themselves under these regimes, and due to the limited nature of the rights governed by those bodies, states are less able to use the body as a forum for changing the

---

134 Steiner *et al.*, *International Human Rights in Context*, pp. 964–5.

135 International Centre for the Legal Protection of Human Rights.

136 J. Limbach, *Judicial Independence: Law and Practice of Appointments to the European Court of Human Rights*, London: Interrights, 2003, p. 9.

137 Gibson, *International Organizations, Constitutional Law and Human Rights*, p. 107.

138 GA Res. 2200A (XXI), 'International Covenant on Civil and Political Rights', 16 December 1966, UN Doc. A/6316 (1966), *entered into force* 23 March 1976, Article 28.

139 Although there is some discussion as to whether those EU members which joined the Union before the Convention can be said to have voluntarily placed themselves under the Court's jurisdiction.

interpretation or application of the rights themselves. Other bodies, such as CEDAW, are used to advance cultural norms or political agendas regarding that convention's rights through states' use of reservations to that treaty. The Council, which is concerned with rights of universal application rather than conventions, is frequently politicised by states seeking to advance cultural or political aims through changing the interpretation or application of the rights.

The Council is a universal body consisting of members from across all UN regional and political groups. As such, many political views on human rights are represented. Moreover, being comprised of government delegates, the very nature of the body's membership is political. Political appointees have little concept of 'functionalism' because their responsibility and accountability is to their national governments rather than to the UN.[140] Oberleitner remarks that it is unsurprising, and somewhat inevitable, that an intergovernmental body comprised of state representatives acts along political lines.[141] Owing to the unavoidable low-level politicisation that will occur as a result of its membership, assessment of the body will focus on instances of gross politicisation and the extent to which they have undermined the Council.

Despite the problems caused by politicisation, human rights bodies remain key for protecting and promoting rights. As will be explored, human rights bodies undertake crucial roles and functions, including fact-finding, information sharing, and reporting on human rights situations. Although politicisation can undermine the work of such bodies, many victims of human rights violations would be in a far worse position were those bodies to cease to exist. Assessment of the Council will, necessarily, examine the extent to which politicisation is undermining the body's fulfilment of its mandate. Criticisms of the Council in this regard will not negate the body's positive achievements, but rather seek to identify areas for improvement.

I shall explore the impact of politicisation in undermining the Council's ability to pursue and achieve its mandate. There are no set criteria for identifying politicisation. Therefore, throughout Part 3, I shall assess politicisation of the Council using the forms and methods set out in this chapter. The use of group tactics to advance political agendas, and the impact of regional and political aims on the Council's work and proceedings, are key to assessing the body. Moreover, the Council must be examined in light of states' use of politicisation to direct the body's work and proceedings, to introduce unrelated issues into discussions, and either to shield states from scrutiny or to ensure disproportionate focus on states for political motives.

140 Gibson, *International Organizations, Constitutional Law and Human Rights*, p. 107.
141 G. Oberleitner, *Global Human Rights Institutions*, Cambridge: Polity Press, 2007, p. 47.

Part 3

Assessment of the Council

7 The United States and the Human Rights Council

7.0. Introduction to part

> The worst fear of any of us is that we fail to navigate an effective way between the Scylla of being seen as a cat's paw of the sole superpower, and the Charybdis of being seen as so unhelpful to the sole superpower that they disregard the value of the United Nations.[1]

Using the relationship between the US and the Council as a case study, I shall examine the body's fulfilment of its protection mandate and adherence to its underlying principles, assessing to what extent it has overcome the Commission's failings. The relationship between the US and the Council provides a broad canvas from which to draw regarding problems such as politicisation, even-handedness, selectivity and bias across the Council's work and proceedings. Applying the theories set out in Chapter 4 to the relationship between the US and the Council enables an understanding of how international relations affect the body's work and proceedings. The US, despite not gaining membership of the Council until 2009,[2] played an active role in the body's proceedings from the outset. Exploring US involvement with, and opinions on, the body will enable assessment of the Council's early years. The body's treatment of the US highlights many of the criticisms already levelled at the body during the Council's formative years. Similarly, US positions taken at the Council highlight a variety of issues with the HRC's proceedings and work.

Despite countries including China, India, and Brazil becoming increasingly more powerful, the US has maintained significant influence in many spheres of the UN system. Resentments towards that country are manifested through regular power struggles against the US from other states. States use international organisations to voice criticisms of American actions. Furthermore, US unilateralism and exceptionalism has affected its relations with

---

1 S. Tharoor (UN Under-Secretary General) quoted in F. Barringer, 'U.N. Senses It Must Change, Fast, or Fade Away', *New York Times*, 19 September 2003, A.5.
2 See, UN Department of Public Information Press Release, 'United States Elected to Human Rights Council for First Time, with Belgium, Hungary, Kyrgyzstan, Norway, as 18 Seats Filled in Single Round of Voting', 12 May 2009, UN Doc. GA/10826.

international organisations.[3] The US attempted to exert its strength and influence over the Council before, during and after the body's creation. Failure to impose its will on the Council at its creation resulted in the US relationship with the new body being problematic from the outset. Realists might point to the US approach as demonstrating that it, too, was willing to use power politics in order to further its own interests. However, unlike many other states, the US pursued aims regarding the Council itself rather than using the body for domestic political objectives or for unrelated power struggles against other countries.

US election to the HRC in 2009 displayed a shift in US foreign policy under President Barack Obama. The Obama administration's decision to engage with the Council by seeking membership, for the first time since the Council's creation, reversed the approach taken under George W. Bush. During General Assembly discussions aimed at establishing the Council, the Bush administration had objected to key provisions. The US had argued that the proposed Council would fail to overcome the shortcomings of its predecessor, the Human Rights Commission.[4] When the Council was established in 2006, the US did not stand for election to one of the body's 47 seats,[5] registering its protest about failure to adopt more radical reforms.[6] It instead opted for permanent observer status, which entitles a state to participate in all sessions. In 2008, the US withdrew its mission, disenchanted with the tone and progress of Council proceedings. The withdrawal was a pivotal moment in US policy towards the UN. Analysis of events leading up to the 2008 withdrawal will shed light on the overall performance of the Council since its creation.

Two broad factors are relevant to the US withdrawal. Although US policy at that time had done much to inflame international relations, countries used proceedings to attack America on issues related and unrelated to agenda items. Perhaps more importantly for the relationship between the US and the HRC, the Council's Special Procedures mandate holders[7] did focus,

---

3 cf. M. Ignatieff, *American Exceptionalism and Human Rights*, Princeton, NJ: Princeton University Press, 2005, pp. 304–38.

4 UN Department of Public Information Press Release, 'General Assembly Establishes New Human Rights Council by Vote of 170 in Favour', 15 March 2006, UN Doc. GA/10449.

5 The Council's membership of 47 states consists of the following number of countries per regional group: 13 African States, 13 Asian States, 6 Eastern European States, 8 Latin American and Caribbean States, 7 Western European and Other States. See GA Res. 60/251, 'Human Rights Council', 15 March 2006, UN Doc. A/RES/60/251.

6 See Chapter 2.

7 On the role of mandate holders, see HRC Res. 5/1, 'Institution Building of the United Nations Human Rights Council', 18 June 2007, UN Doc. A/HRC/RES/5/1. See generally, 'Special Procedures of the Human Rights Council', OHCHR (Website). (Online). Available HTTP: <http://www2.ohchr.org/english/bodies/chr/special/index.htm> (accessed 16 October 2012). See, also, HRC Res. 5/1, 'Institution Building of the United Nations Human Rights Council', 18 June 2007, UN Doc. A/HRC/RES/5/1, Item B; S.P. Subedi, S. Wheatley, A. Mukherjee and S. Ngane, 'Special Issue: The Role of the Special Rapporteurs of the United Nations Human Rights Council in the Development and Promotion of International Human Rights Norms', *The International Journal of Human Rights*, Vol. 15 (2), 2011, 155–61.

sometimes unwarranted, attention on the US, often to the neglect of far more serious human rights situations elsewhere in the world. For example, the Special Rapporteur on Extrajudicial, Summary or Arbitrary Executions, Philip Alston, visited the US in 2008, despite having visited that country a decade earlier, and despite not having visited other countries which committed at least as grave abuses of this right including, for example, Kenya, Bangladesh, or Iraq.[8] As mandate holders have independence to determine which states to visit, such selectivity cannot be attributed directly to the Council. I shall, however, explore the argument that mandate holders do give disproportionate or unnecessary attention to the US at the Council and, indeed, other UN bodies. Use of Council time to discuss and take action on such reports results in less time and fewer resources to devote to fulfilling its mandate by protecting human rights within other states or regions.

Selectivity did occur from member states and the Council itself. Treatment of the US by Council staff, members, and participants during the body's proceedings show the trend for politicisation, not least through the form of double standards, inherent throughout the Council. Selectivity was often a manifestation of power struggles against the US. As such, it is an indicator of international trends and the international political atmosphere at that time. Selectivity directed towards the US was used by states as a mechanism for promotion of national policies, as well as a method used by weaker countries to gain bargaining power. National political agendas and conflicts, according to realist theories, will always dictate state behaviour at UN bodies. The Council has proved to be no exception. Treatment of the US demonstrates member states' disregard for the Council's underlying principles of non-selectivity and impartiality. Attacks on the United States have, so far, been stronger and more constant than against any other country except Israel. States' positions regarding the US demonstrate some of the main politicisation issues at the Council from the outset.

7.1. US exceptionalism and unilateralism

In order to explore the relationship between the US and the Human Rights Council, that state's general approach to international organisations and international human rights must be examined. After the end of the Cold War, the US emerged as the main, if not sole, superpower. Therefore, having spent decades leading Western states, it viewed itself as having greater responsibilities for world order than any other country. The US approach of unilateralism and exceptionalism continued, arguably increasing as a result of the change in global politics.

8 For a list of visits see, OHCHR (website). (Online). Available HTTP: <http://www2.ohchr. org/english/issues/executions/visits.htm> (accessed 25 June 2012); it is important to note that the Special Rapporteur did request visits to, for example, Iran, China, Pakistan and Saudi Arabia, but was not invited to visit those states.

Schoenbaum argues that, despite its early involvement, the United States no longer plays a leading role in the protection and promotion of human rights.[9] He insists that by the time of the Council's creation the US had 'largely abandoned the field to others [. . .] and retreated into exceptionalism and unilateralism'.[10] He comments that the US role since the end of the Cold War has been at best that of a passive bystander and has at worst undermined the international human rights system. The US long advocated human rights, to a greater extent than other powerful states, yet has sought to defend its own sovereignty and power by failing proportionately to implement the human rights standards which it advocates that other states must adopt. Schoenbaum's observations illustrate the changing relationship between the US and UN human rights machinery, particularly leading up to its non-election to the Commission in 2001 and its decision not to stand for election to the Council in 2006.[11] Much of this change can be attributed to the general US approach to international organisations.

US exceptionalism and unilateralism can be seen particularly clearly in its approach to international treaties.[12] Despite being the first country to ratify the UN Charter,[13] within the UN's first decade the US demonstrated its unilateralist position. In 1953, the Eisenhower Administration announced a new policy towards UN human rights: 'while we shall not withhold our counsel from those who seek to draft a treaty or covenant on human rights',[14] the US would not ratify any human rights treaty,[15] largely to appease southern conservatives who feared that international human rights would be used to promote racial equality, amongst others.[16] The US only ratified its first UN human rights treaty, the International Covenant on Civil and Political Rights, in 1992. Despite being a signatory to a number of UN human rights treaties, the US has ratified very few.[17] Schoenbaum notes that the US

9 T.J. Schoenbaum, *International Relations – The Path Not Taken: Using International Law to Promote World Peace and Security*, Cambridge: Cambridge University Press, 2006, p. 251.
10 *Ibid.*
11 *Ibid.*
12 See, for example, L. Henkin, 'U.S. Ratification of Human Rights Conventions: The Ghost of Senator Bricker', *The American Journal of International Law*, Vol. 89 (2), 1995, 341–45.
13 T.G. Weiss, *What's Wrong with the United Nations and How to Fix It*, Cambridge: Polity Press, 2008, p. 130.
14 Statement by Secretary of State John Foster Dulles before the US Senate Judiciary Committee, 6 April 1953, reproduced in 'Review of the United Nations Charter, A Collection of Documents, 83rd Congress, 2nd Session', Senate Doc. No.87, 1954, pp. 295–6.
15 P. Alston, 'Reconceiving the UN Human Rights Regime: Challenges Confronting the New UN Human Rights Council', *Melbourne Journal of International Law*, Vol. 7, 2006, 208.
16 Ignatieff, *American Exceptionalism and Human Rights*, p. 19.
17 Including: Convention on the Elimination of All Forms of Racial Discrimination (ratified in 1994), the two Optional Protocols to the Convention on the Rights of the Child (ratified in 1999 and 2002) and the Convention against Torture and Other Cruel, Inhuman or Degrading Treatment or Punishment (ratified in 1994).

reservation that both treaties be non-self-executing results in them having no impact on US domestic law.[18] The Human Rights Committee has criticised the US for its:

> failure to take fully into consideration its obligation under the Covenant not only to respect, but also to ensure the rights prescribed by the Covenant; and [. . .] its restrictive approach to some substantive provisions of the Covenant, which is not in conformity with the interpretation made by the Committee before and after the State party's ratification of the Covenant.[19]

The US approach towards other international bodies can be used to understand its relationship with the Human Rights Council. A recent example is the US position on the International Criminal Court (ICC). Initially, the US favoured the ICC as it represented that state's values regarding law, justice and human rights.[20] McGoldrick[21] insists that US eventual opposition to the ICC was political rather than ideological,[22] as the US was concerned about the potential impact on its military personnel.[23] Such opposition placed it 'in the company of "despotic" states such as Cuba, Iran, Iraq, North Korea and Sudan'.[24] One of the key problems with the American approach to international organisations is that the state is often placed alongside countries that the US itself regularly condemns. US positions towards international organisations are at least partly based on the belief that such bodies take an anti-American and anti-Israeli stance.[25] McGoldrick argues, somewhat sympathetically, that the US doubts the legitimacy of such organisations, especially where there are such credibility issues regarding membership as had occurred at the Commission.[26] The US approach towards the Council reflects its general stance, as the membership of that body constantly includes known human rights abusers, as well as many totalitarian and other non-democratic regimes. US preference to share a platform with other democratic states rather than totalitarian ones is, according to Khaliq, understandable.[27]

18 Schoenbaum, *International Relations*, p. 271.
19 UN Human Rights Committee, 'Concluding Observations of the Human Rights Committee, United States of America', UN Doc. CCPR/C/USA/CO/3 (2006), para. 10.
20 D. McGoldrick, 'Political and Legal Responses to the ICC', in D. McGoldrick, P. Rowe and E. Donnelly (eds.), *Permanent International Criminal Court*, Oxford: Hart, 2004, p. 400.
21 *Ibid.*, p. 442.
22 cf. P. Sands, 'After Pinochet: The Role of National Courts', in P. Sands (ed.), *From Nuremberg to The Hague*, Cambridge: Cambridge University Press, 2003, pp. 76–7.
23 See, for example, C. Patten, 'Globalization and the Law', *European Human Rights Law Review*, Vol. 6, 2004. 6–13.
24 McGoldrick, *Permanent International Criminal Court*, p. 442.
25 *Ibid.*
26 *Ibid.*
27 U. Khaliq, *Ethical Dimensions of the Foreign Policy of the European Union: A Legal Appraisal*, Cambridge: Cambridge University Press, 2008, p. 75.

However, the US position has often resulted in it choosing not to enter an arena where it disapproves of other actors.

Former US Secretary of State Henry Kissinger commented that the US position towards international organisations and institutions is based on strategic interests as to how they will affect the 'many Americans engaged in global responsibilities'.[28] This approach underscores a main idea behind American exceptionalism, that the US has a special position owing to its global responsibilities and that it ought to be treated differently because it takes a different role to all other states.[29]

McGoldrick insists that the high level of US involvement in international affairs, particularly through its military, is used by some 'to explain American exceptionalism, non-compliance with international agreements, non-ratification of signed treaties, rights narcissism, and its distinctive rights culture'.[30] Byrnes and Charleworth disapprovingly argue that the US, because of its military strength, believes it has the right to act unilaterally in order to defend the world order.[31]

It is unsurprising that the US has had an uneasy relationship with the HRC. It is difficult for a hortatory, intergovernmental organisation to tolerate a state's exceptionalism and unilateralism. Institutionalists might identify that the US and the UN share a common desire for human rights. However, the methods by which they seek to achieve those common aims generate practical unworkability that undermines their relationship.

7.2. The US vote against establishment of the Council

News that the US had withdrawn its observer mission was first reported in *Human Rights Tribune* in June 2008, between the Seventh and Eighth Sessions.[32] That move effectively ended US involvement with the Council, ceasing its input into the body's discussions and activities. Confirmation came through the US announcement at its daily State Department briefing that it would only participate in Council discussions where 'absolutely necessary'.[33] The Bush administration pursued no further involvement since the Seventh Session, which ended in 2008. Withdrawal, from a realist perspective, was a demonstration of US power within the wider UN sphere. Unable to exert sufficient influence at the Council to avoid what the US deemed as unfair levels of scrutiny, it instead withdrew altogether, knowing the impact that this would have on the new body. Arguably, however, from an idealist

---

28 H. Kissinger, 'NATO At The Crossroads; NATO's Uncertain Future In A Troubled Alliance', *San Diego Union-Tribune*, 1 December 2002.
29 McGoldrick, *Permanent International Criminal Court*, p. 443.
30 *Ibid.*
31 A. Byrnes and H. Charleworth, 'Action Urged on Statute', *The Canberra Times*, 22 May 2002.
32 C. Doole, 'US Quits Human Rights Council?', *Human Rights Tribune*, 6 June 2008.
33 *Ibid.*

perspective, US withdrawal displayed its frustration with the Council's failure to fulfil its mandate adequately and frequent selectivity, bias and inaction on human rights situations. As with the Commission in 2001, when the US failed to secure re-election, US withdrawal was viewed as a blow to the Council's credibility. Disengagement of the most powerful and influential state challenged the Council's legitimacy and highlighted some major issues very early in its existence.

The Obama administration announced its decision to stand for election to the Council early in Obama's Presidency.[34] In order to secure US membership, New Zealand withdrew its candidacy, thus using the new version of a 'closed slate' to allow the US to gain an unopposed seat in the Western European and Other States group,[35] removing the possibility of it failing to gain re-election, as had occurred once before near the end of the Commission.

Those are only recent chapters of a turbulent history. In the original discussions the United States had focused on membership issues in objections to the draft resolution establishing the Council. The Secretary-General at that time, Kofi Annan, had proposed that the Council be elected by a two-thirds majority of the General Assembly.[36] The US pushed for additional criteria in order to ensure that 'gross and systemic' violators could not be elected.[37] Annan had deemed the Commission's decreasing credibility to be crucial to its demise,[38] emphasising the number and prominence of members with poor human rights records.[39] Worried that the Council's membership would, like the Commission, include states with different positions on human rights, the US sought to advance its own national ideals by pushing for liberal democratic membership criteria that reflected its own positions on human rights issues. Despite some states' support for these aspirations, the final resolution simply required human rights records to be taken into account during elections.[40] The US Ambassador, John Bolton, insisted that the resolution should go further in excluding countries with the worst

---

34 US Department of State, 'Announcement on U.S. Seat on U.N. Human Rights Council', statement of Gordon Duguid, acting deputy spokesman, 1 April 2009, (Online). Available HTTP:<http://www.america.gov/st/texttrans-english/2009/April/20090401120727eaifas4.264468e-02.html> (accessed 16 October 2012).

35 See, for example, V. Havel, 'A Table for Tyrants', *New York Times*, 10 May 2008.

36 UN Department of Public Information Press Release, 'General Assembly Establishes New Human Rights Council by Vote of 170 in Favour', 15 March 2006, UN Doc. GA/10449.

37 *Ibid.*

38 General Assembly, 'In Larger Freedom: Towards Development, Security and Human Rights for All', *Report of the Secretary-General*, 21 March 2005, UN Doc. A/59/2005. On problems of credibility of inter-governmental and non-governmental organisations, see E. Heinze, 'Even-handedness and the Politics of Human Rights', *Harvard Human Rights Journal*, Vol. 21 (7), 2008, 7–46.

39 For example, in its later years states such as Sudan and Saudi Arabia held membership. Another example was Libya's election as chair of the Commission in 2003.

40 See GA Res. 60/251, 'Human Rights Council', UN Doc. A/RES/60/251.

human rights records from gaining membership.[41] The lack of assurance of a credible membership would, he argued, result in the Council being no better than the Commission.[42] The test would be whether countries such as 'Cuba, the Sudan, Zimbabwe, Iran, Belarus and Burma' acquired membership.[43] Those states, with different forms of non-democratic regimes, were each, for different reasons, ones which the US held national political reasons for seeking to exclude from the Council and, more generally, criticise within the international sphere.

Unsurprisingly, Bolton's views won little sympathy from member states he had previously criticised. In 1994, Bolton had claimed, 'There is no such thing as the United Nations. There is only the international community, which can only be led by the only remaining superpower, which is the United States'.[44] He famously declared, 'If the UN Secretariat building in New York lost ten storeys, it wouldn't make a bit of difference'.[45] Bolton has regularly criticised the UN's existence, even criticising President Clinton for engaging with the organisation rather than pursuing unilateralist policies.[46] Bolton's opinions, even those views which are valid, are, therefore, frequently rejected by diplomats and administrative staff at the UN. Bolton's opinions on Council membership carried little weight among the countries increasingly suspicious of the Bush administration, in view of such high profile US foreign policy failures, such as Guantanamo Bay, invading Iraq and the war in Afghanistan. Although Bolton made serious points about the Council, his standing at the UN, and the standing of the Bush administration generally, guaranteed that his opinions would garner little support. Bolton's backing for the invasion of Iraq further undermined his ability to steer the UN on human rights. Politicisation can be seen to have had an impact even prior to the Council's creation. Valid criticisms and proposals were ignored during the Council's creation, largely owing to the international political atmosphere against the US.

Struggles for influence, both by and against the US, at times overshadowed states' legitimate efforts to protect and promote human rights. It is frequently difficult to distinguish between real claims to protect and promote human rights and instances where such claims sought instead to advance underlying power struggles. In those instances where a state's position in fact undermined

41 Oral intervention of US Ambassador John Bolton, GA debate on the HRC establishment, 15 March 2006.
42 *Ibid.*
43 *Ibid.*
44 R. Watson, 'Bush Deploys Hawk as New UN Envoy', *The Times*, 8 March 2005. Reporting comments made by Bolton twelve years earlier at the 1994 Global Structures Convocation.
45 *Ibid.*
46 cf. J.R. Bolton, 'The Creation, Fall, Rise and Fall of the United Nations', in T.G. Carpenter (ed.), *Delusions of Grandeur: United Nations and Global Intervention*, Washington, DC: Cato Institute, 1997, pp. 45–59.

rather than advanced interests of human rights, gross politicisation is clearly apparent. Less clear, however, are the statements which do genuinely advance human rights interests but simultaneously further a state's political aims which are in direct conflict with other states or groups. Many of Bolton's assertions were, indeed, right. Yet it is apparent that the US positions sought to promote liberal, democratic approaches to human rights to the exclusion of other ideological discourses. Although the US did seek to promote its own political aims, proceedings were politicised by the outright rejection of its suggestions for motives other than in the interests of human rights.

Bolton advised the General Assembly never to 'settle for good enough, for a compromise' in the promotion and protection of human rights.[47] GA Resolution 60/251 nevertheless passed with 170 states in favour, 4 against,[48] and 3 abstentions.[49] The vote was called by the US, to the chagrin of those who had hoped that the text would pass unanimously (a vote is only called for when there are countries that oppose the draft resolution in question). Before the vote, Cuba accused the US of taking a 'punitive and sanctioning' approach.[50] Accusing the US of power politics, the Cubans alleged that America and its allies had exerted 'strong pressure and resorted to their traditional blackmail' in pursuing its preferred outcome.[51] That statement altogether ignored that the US had committed to, and indeed did, finance the Council irrespective of it voting against the body's creation. Had the US sought to use underhand tactics to undermine the new body, it could simply have refused to provide financial support, which would have seriously hampered efforts to create the Council. The US vote against the Council's creation arguably registered its displeasure about the new body's form rather than seeking to undermine its existence. Cuba's allegations, even at this early stage, demonstrate the power struggles already occurring around the HRC, with long-standing foes using the discussions as an opportunity to vilify the US, attacking it under the guise of human rights while, somewhat transparently, pursing unrelated political objectives. That Cuba's position was a sheer attack is evidenced by its silence towards the abstainers, which included two of its key allies, Iran and Venezuela, despite the abstentions also negating the Assembly recording a unanimous vote.

After the vote, Bolton reminded the General Assembly that the US had counted, historically, among the strongest voices for the global protection and promotion of human rights, since the founding of the UN. That claim

---

47 Oral intervention of US Ambassador John Bolton, GA debate on the HRC establishment, UN Doc. GA/10449.

48 Israel, Marshall Islands, Palau, United States.

49 Belarus, Iran, Venezuela.

50 Oral intervention of Cuban Ambassador Rodrigo Malmierca Diaz, GA debate on the HRC establishment, 15 March 2006, UN Department of Public Information Press Release, 'General Assembly Establishes New Human Rights Council by Vote of 170 in Favour', 15 March 2006, UN Doc. GA/10449.

51 *Ibid*.

underscored America's failure to acknowledge US politicisation of human rights bodies and its one-dimensional approach to human rights. He pointed out that the UN 'can, and should, do more. We had an historic opportunity to create a primary human rights organ in the United Nations, poised to help those most in need.'[52] Although expressing disappointment, he nevertheless went on to pledge US assistance in strengthening the Council. The US declined to stand for membership, leaving its status formally peripheral, in comparison to its earlier, full-fledged membership of the Commission. By not fully engaging with the new body, the US emphasised its reservations about the Council from the outset. Perhaps, noting the strength of feeling against the US, it chose not to stand rather than to face the indignity of not being elected as had occurred at the Commission in 2001.

Nevertheless, the American delegation energetically participated in Council sessions and activities as a permanent observer until the end of the Seventh Session. The Council retained the Commission's rules regarding observer states and bodies.[53] Observer status entitled the US to be present at all Council sessions, and to participate in all discussions. The US vigorously exercised that prerogative, exerting its influence on Council proceedings, as we shall now see from the many and varied discussions in which it participated.

7.3. US views on the Council's activities

US views on Council activities scarcely changed during the seven sessions in which it participated. Its initial fears that the Council would be biased and opaque, continuing the politicisation prevalent at the Commission, were repeated in its comments on working methods. The Council's inaction on grave human rights situations was a source of US consternation, echoing its initial fears that the Council would not go far enough in discharging its mandate.

The US expressed strong opinions about the Council's working methods, and further frustration in its appeals for more constructive methods. From the outset, the US stressed the need for dialogue, as opposed to confrontation, and the importance of involving NGOs, national observers, and all other stakeholders.[54] The US emphasised the Council's underlying, idealist principles, including 'the need to have clarity and transparency', arguing that the Council 'must follow clear and predictable guidelines'.[55] The US seemed particularly concerned that the Council should avoid the Commission's

---

52 Oral intervention of US Ambassador John Bolton, GA debate on the HRC establishment, UN Doc. GA/10449.

53 HRC Res. 5/1, 'Institution Building of the United Nations Human Rights Council', 18 June 2007, UN Doc. A/HRC/RES/5/1.

54 American delegate, 3rd Session, 30 November 2006, during discussions on Methods of Work, Agenda, and Rules of Procedure.

55 *Ibid.*

earlier opacity, by preferring open, formal procedures over closed, informal and unreported meetings. While the US may be criticised for its own secrecy on the Security Council, a feature shared by permanent members, such insistence on transparency at the Council is not necessarily hypocritical, as security issues often require different approaches than human rights. The protection and promotion of human rights are rarely placed at risk by transparent procedures, particularly outside declared states of emergency.[56] Unfortunately, thus far, those calls have gone unheeded at the Council. Major decisions are still being taken within closed, informal, unreported meetings. The Council does hold open, informal meetings which, whilst not available via webcast, are open to observers including NGOs, academics, practitioners, and individuals who secure UN accreditation. However, throughout Council sessions there are constant closed informal meetings held by regional groups or other alliances, as well as intergovernmental negotiations behind closed doors. Most of the work on draft resolutions takes places in these meetings, as do negotiations regarding votes and voting tactics. That method of work shrouds the Council in secrecy for observers, the secretariat, non-member states, and states not affiliated with the powerful groups.

The US repeated the need for transparency in discussions on Universal Periodic Review (UPR). The US emphasised that UPR success would 'lie in its openness'.[57] The Americans stressed that UPR, and other working methods, should not supplant certain established procedures. For example, they stressed that the Council should be able to continue to consider country-specific situations on its own initiative and at any time.[58] The US also recalled its earlier fears about politicisation, reminding the Council, for example, that there should be 'no double standards'[59] when using UPR.

The theme of impartiality and non-politicisation in the Council's working methods continued in the US comments about country-specific mandates. Whilst the US advocated the continuation of such mandates as a strong tool for keeping 'the spotlight on human rights abuse',[60] it expressed reservations

---

56 For example, ICCPR states: 'In time of public emergency which threatens the life of the nation and the existence of which is officially proclaimed, the States Parties to the present Covenant may take measures derogating from their obligations under the present Covenant to the extent strictly required by the exigencies of the situation, provided that such measures are not inconsistent with their other obligations under international law and do not involve discrimination solely on the ground of race, colour, sex, language, religion or social origin.' GA Res. 2200A (XXI), 'International Covenant on Civil and Political Rights', 16 December 1966, UN Doc. A/6316 (1966), *entered into force* 23 March 1976.

57 American delegate, 2nd Session, 2 October 2006, during debate on UPR with the Working Group Facilitator, Moroccan Ambassador, Mohammed Loulichki.

58 American delegate, 3rd Session, 4 December 2006, in response to UPR Working Group Facilitator, Ambassador Loulichki.

59 American delegate, 2nd Session, 2 October 2006, during debate on UPR with the Working Group Facilitator, Moroccan Ambassador, Mohammed Loulichki.

60 American delegate, 4th Session, 23 March 2007, during discussion on country-specific mandates.

about the singling out of Israel and the Occupied Territories by the Council under the guise of these mandates.[61] The US asserted that such focus 'makes the system politicised and non-universal',[62] and advocated that the Occupied Palestinian Territories' mandate 'be subject to modification in the normal procedure'.[63]

The US repeated its general positions on Council working methods during both formal and informal debates. It regularly used discussions on working methods to air concerns about the Council's effectiveness, reminding the body of the need for 'independent, impartial experts in order to maintain credibility'.[64] It also insistently reminded the Council of the need to implement its resolutions.[65] American delegates repeatedly recalled the need to improve human rights mechanisms at the UN, reminding the Council of the Secretary-General's report,[66] especially the strong criticisms contained therein, that had acted as a catalyst for the body's creation.

Despite the US insistence at the Council's formation that it would not become a member of the body, it sought to play an active role in shaping the HRC from the outset. Realists would reason that the US was keen to advance its own national policies on human rights, seeking to implement liberal, democratic norms, despite its lack of official involvement with the body. The US has frequently sought to ensure that the Western approach to human rights remains at the fore at international bodies. Others might argue that the US sought to protect and promote all forms of human rights for their own sake even though it disagreed with many aspects of the new body. Regardless of its motives, the US constantly insisted that the Council adhere to its own idealistic founding principles.

The Council's primary objective of protecting and promoting human rights was frequently repeated by the US during both general discussions and those regarding specific activities. The US also criticised the Council's inaction on specific situations. It singled out serious and ongoing violations in DPRK,[67] Myanmar,[68] Sudan[69] and Zimbabwe[70] as requiring immediate attention and

---

61 *Ibid.*

62 *Ibid.*

63 *Ibid.*

64 American delegate, 3rd Session, 5 December 2006, in response to the Review of Mandates Facilitator, Czech Ambassador Tomas Husak.

65 American delegate, 3rd Session, 7 December 2006, informal session with the Experts Advice Facilitator, Jordanian Ambassador Burayzat.

66 General Assembly, 'In Larger Freedom: Towards Development, Security and Human Rights for All', *Report of the Secretary-General*, 21 March 2005, UN Doc. A/59/2005.

67 See, for example, American delegate, 4th Session, 23 March 2007, in response to SR on DPRK, Vitit Muntarbhorn.

68 See, for example, American delegate, 4th Session, 15 March 2007, during interactive dialogue with UNHCHR, Louise Arbour.

69 See, for example, American delegate, 2nd Session, 18 September 2006, during interactive dialogue with UNHCHR, Louise Arbour.

70 American delegate, 4th Session, 15 March 2007, during interactive dialogue with UNHCHR, Louise Arbour.

action. It urged the Council to act on a number of occasions, mentioning the ongoing atrocities, and urging immediate action. Emphasis on gross and systemic violations in these states, rather than in those countries with which the US had other ties, mirrors behaviour at the Commission for which it was criticised. Although the US raised valid issues regarding those countries, its silence about countries such as Sri Lanka and Pakistan, states with which it had important security ties, demonstrated the US again advancing its national policies with the UN human rights body. Despite widely participating in Council discussions, the US maintained a somewhat conspicuous silence when both of those countries were raised at the body. Although mere silence does not amount to obstructionism, the US arguably applied double standards in terms of its allies.

The US stressed its support for, amongst others, the Special Session on Darfur,[71] extra resources for the Office of the High Commissioner for Human Rights on the ground in these aforementioned regions,[72] and the continuation of reports and recommendations from mandate holders.[73] The US again condemned politicisation of the Council, criticising the incessant focus on Israel as compared with states committing equal or worse levels of abuse.[74] The lack of even-handedness regarding Israel, with grossly disproportionate scrutiny of that state diverting time and resources away from other abusers, was a source of constant US frustration. The Council, as with the Commission, increasingly targeted Israel at the expense of other gross and systemic situations.

7.4. US objections to the Council's work

Throughout the first seven sessions, the US voiced strong objections to the work undertaken by the Council, as expressed both in (a) country-specific and (b) thematic debates. Whereas country-specific debates focus on many rights within one state, thematic debates examine one right across several states. US objections can be viewed from different perspectives, again including idealist advancement of human rights standards or motivated by national policies such as promoting liberal, democratic human rights principles to the exclusion of other categories of human rights.

Country-specific debates. The US commented on a number of the country-specific situations brought to the Council's attention during its first two years. The situations discussed were either ongoing or dire, requiring country-specific mandate holders to report on them. The raising of specific situations depended

---

71 American delegate, 3rd Session, 29 November 2006, during interactive dialogue with UNHCHR, Louise Arbour.
72 American delegate, 2nd Session, 18 September 2006, during interactive dialogue with UNHCHR, Louise Arbour.
73 American delegate, 5th Session, 11 June 2006, in response to SR on Independence of Judges and Lawyers, Leando Despouy.
74 American delegate, 7th Session, 27 March 2008, during the informal meeting.

on considerations such as the gravity of the crisis as well as political motives of Council members. The impact of regional ties was particularly strong. Organisation of the Islamic Conference members, for political reasons, ensured that the Council's attention remained on Israel whilst the body ignored situations in, for example, Libya, Syria and Saudi Arabia, and made sure that action on Darfur was blocked. Regionalism in this context resulted in the Council not focusing solely on the gravest situations, but also on those countries that fell foul of prominent groups of member states.

During the first seven sessions, Israel was brought to the Council's attention on numerous occasions. There were reports on various aspects of the human rights situations pertaining to the Occupied Territories, the conflict between Israel and the Occupied Palestinian Territories, and the situation following the Lebanese war in the summer of 2006. Notably, the US did not defend Israeli violations; it did, however, note abuses committed on the Palestinian[75] and Lebanese[76] sides. The US approach emphasised the need for balance and impartiality, a position not taken by any country other than Canada.[77] During discussions on Israel, the US highlighted the human rights abuses on both sides, and called for the Council to act to ensure that all sides cease violations.[78] The US statements in these discussions were strongly contrary to popular and media representations of US 'blind' or one-sided support for Israel. The US reminded the Council of the underlying principles that established the body,[79] stating that 'the unbalanced focus on Israel'[80] was inconsistent with them:

> The Council must be more balanced [. . .] The Human Rights Council can express concern about Israel's human rights violations, but it should be equally concerned with Palestinian terrorism and other human rights violations in the world.[81]

75 For example, 'Palestinian rocket attacks must stop, and terrorist attacks that target civilians must stop', American delegate, 7th Session, 6 March 2008, in response to the UNHCHR report on resolutions concerning the Israel/Palestine conflict.

76 For example, the American delegate condemned the Hezbollah attack on Israel and the kidnapping of two Israeli soldiers which directly preceded the war, 2nd Session, 4 October 2006, in response to UN Doc. A/HRC/2/7 (2006).

77 Canada is the only member of the Human Rights Council to have voted against every resolution critical of Israel, where a vote was called.

78 'Israel must dismantle those settlements built since March 2001, and the Palestinians must prevent terrorist activities. We [. . .] call on parties to fulfil their obligations [. . .] We call on Israel to take into account the humanitarian impact [. . .] [of the] wall and avoid action that could prejudice issues that should be determined by negotiations. We urge everyone not to consider this situation as a one-sided context', American delegate, 2nd Session, 29 September 2006, in response to SR on the Occupied Palestinian Territories, John Dugard.

79 '[. . .] the work of the Council shall be guided by the principles of universality, impartiality, objectivity and non-selectivity, constructive international dialogue and cooperation [. . .]', GA Res. 60/251.

80 American delegate, 2nd Session, 29 September 2006, in response to SR on the Occupied Palestinian Territories, John Dugard.

81 *Ibid.*

At the same session, the US spoke of 'the human suffering on both sides' during the Israel–Lebanon war in 2006. In another intervention, the US called for 'Israel to take into account the humanitarian impact' of the security wall.[82]

The US regularly repeated its commitment to a two-state solution.[83] That, seemingly even-handed statement, contrasted with US unequivocal support for Israel under the Bush administration, particularly within the General Assembly and through the use of its veto at the Security Council. Within the HRC, where the US had far less power or influence than at other organs, the US sought to play the role of mediator between Israel and its OIC-led detractors. Unsurprisingly, other states were frequently distrustful of US efforts in this regard.

American delegates attempted to steer Council discussions towards addressing solutions, contrary to the frequent criticism levelled against Israel through decisions, resolutions,[84] and the calling of Special Sessions (Israel was the subject of four of the seven Special Sessions convened during the Council's first two years). At the Sixth Session,[85] the US again insisted that 'addressing the Israel–Palestine conflict requires a balanced and forward-looking approach', asserting that 'the Arab states should stop the incitement of hatred in the media and should cease their refusal to recognize the existence of Israel'.[86] Arguably, the Arab press is predominantly a tool of national governments, promoting national and regional interests as exemplified by the quantity and quality of its reporting on Israel.[87] Indeed, Rugh argues that Arab governments use the conflict with Israel, or the need to confront Israeli policies, as justification for their influence over the media.[88] Arab media provides continuous coverage of Israel as a news story.[89] As occurs at the Council, vilification of, and constant focus on, Israel enables Arab countries to avoid national scrutiny of their own human rights violations, as well as providing a central unifying policy for all regional media outlets.[90]

The US repeatedly berated the Council's anti-Israel bias, but such concerns were largely dismissed because of the close relationship between these two

---

82 American delegate, 2nd Session, 26 September 2006, in response to SR on OPT, John Dugard.

83 See, for example, American delegate: 2nd Session, 26 September 2006; 4th Session, 20 September 2007; 7th Session, 6 March 2008.

84 19 resolutions critical of Israel were passed between 2006 and 2008.

85 6th Session, 10–28 September 2006, resumed 10–14 December 2006.

86 American delegate, 6th Session, 20 September 2007, during discussions pursuant to HRC resolutions requiring UNHCHR to report to the HRC on the implementation of Res. 1/1 adopted by HRC at 1st special session dispatching a SR to Israel.

87 cf. M. Fandy, *Arab Media: Tools of the Government, Tools for the People?*, Darby, PA: Diane Publishing, 2008.

88 W.A. Rugh, *Arab Mass Media: Newspaper, radio and television in Arab politics*, Westport, CT: Praeger Publishers, 2004, p. 7.

89 N. Sakr, *Arab Media and Political Renewal: Community, Legitimacy and Public Life*, London: I.B. Tauris, 2007, p. 126.

90 cf. Rugh, *Arab Mass Media*.

countries. Rubenberg claims that unconditional US support for Israel 'goes beyond any traditional relationship between states in the international system'.[91] Unsurprisingly, that relationship affects perception of US comments about Israel, even when those positions are valid. Frum and Perle suggest that unconditional US support for Israel is always in the US national interest.[92] This is a questionable thesis, as US foreign relations suffer as a direct result of that relationship. However, many states agree with Frum and Perle's opinion, thus further undermining comments made by the US on the Council's treatment of Israel. The only state that generally supported the US position was Canada. Other Western and democratic states, with the occasional exception of Australia and Japan, perhaps fearing the same impact of regional alliances as dominated Commission proceedings, took neutral positions during most of these discussions. The EU regularly abstained during votes and made neutral comments during discussions regarding Israel. The EU's reluctance to take sides could be due to that bloc's need to internally negotiate a collective position, and the varied stances of its members on the Israel–Palestine situation. The EU and its dominant state members also tended to seek a mediating role. The EU's neutrality is, however, more likely to have resulted from the power and influence held by the large bloc of OIC member states sitting at the Council. The size and geographical diversity of its membership gave the OIC significant weight in the Council, and that influence was often deployed to ostracise those countries that disagreed with the OIC's collective stance. The EU's recognition of the OIC's influence at the Council can be contrasted with wider perceptions, particularly within the media, that the US is always dominant at the UN. The UN is often, falsely, assumed to replicate the Security Council's power structure, with scant understanding of the composition of various organs and bodies. The repercussions for a state taking a stand against the OIC can be seen in the reactions of that bloc, its allies, and the African Group.[93] That deterrent undoubtedly played a role in the weakening of the Council's resolutions and decisions. This demonstrates a weakness in the conversion process insofar as states, groups and blocs are able to use power politics to manipulate the vote on a resolution or decision.

The US, as the most powerful state and due to its already poor relations with many OIC members and allies in the aftermath of the Iraq war, had less to lose by criticising the Council's targeting of Israel. It was able to push for more balanced and less selective discussions without fear of reprisals at the body from regional groups, due both to its strength as well as its position as an observer rather than Council member.

Sudan is of particular interest throughout the period of the Bush administration. The US in general, and particularly under the Bush administration,

91 C. Rubenberg, *Israel and the American National Interest: A Critical Examination*, Urbana, IL: University of Illinois, 1986, p. 330.
92 D. Frum and R. Perle, *An End to Evil: How To Win The War On Terror*, New York: Random House, 2003, p. 181.
93 See Chapter 8, Section 8.3.4.

has repeatedly spoken out against the genocide in Darfur, and was often alone in calling for, and taking, constant action to improve the situation.[94] The Bush administration, as with many of its recent predecessors, was influenced by the Congressional Black Caucus, which was founded in 1971 to represent black Congressmen. The caucus has had significant influence on domestic and foreign affairs, although little scholarship exists on the caucus' impact on foreign policy.[95] Eager claims that the caucus, alongside other US actors, promotes and influences legislation salient to Africa.[96] Of all African and Caribbean states, Sudan features as the one which found most common ground between the Bush administration and the Congressional Black Caucus owing, in no small part, to widespread bipartisan condemnation of the worsening situation in Darfur during Bush's presidential terms.[97] Sudan was frequently discussed, and indeed the subject of US national legislation, throughout Bush's presidency. The US behaved in a similar manner at the Council, despite the seeming indifference of many members towards the escalating crisis. Constant US statements about human rights abuses in Sudan could be seen as promoting human rights for their own sake. However, US national political focus on Sudan indicates that promoting the situation in Sudan to the Council over other similarly gross and systemic violations was due, at least in part, to domestic concerns.

Although the US, amongst others, constantly brought Sudan to the Council's attention, the body took no meaningful action on the situation in Darfur. Reports on Sudan were presented by the Special Rapporteur and the Group of Experts, as well as by the High Commissioner and others. These reports provided the basis for Council discussions on Sudan. Throughout the discussions, the US maintained its strong condemnation of the escalating humanitarian crisis, calling for steps to be taken to ensure a resolution to the conflict. At the Second Session the US asked the Special Rapporteur on Sudan[98] to provide further information on human rights violations occurring in Sudan[99] due to the gravity of the situation. As the situation escalated, the US insisted that 'the Council cannot ignore the ongoing crisis in Sudan',[100] repeating 'that in the Darfur region there are gross violations of human rights'.[101]

---

94 See, for example, A. Bohm, 'Sie sind schwarz? Tut uns leid!', *Die Zeit* (Germany), 19 October 2006, p. 23.

95 cf. R.W. Copson, *The Congressional Black Caucus and Foreign Policy*, New York: Novinka Books, 2003.

96 P.W. Eager, 'The Voice of the Congressional Black Caucus in American Foreign Policy', in G.A. Persons (ed.), *Expanding Boundaries of Black Politics*, New Brunswick, NJ: Transaction Publishers, 2007, p. 273.

97 *Ibid.*, p. 282.

98 Sima Samar, UN-appointed SR on Sudan.

99 American delegate, 2nd Session, 27 September 2006, in response to SR on Sudan, Sima Samar.

100 American delegate, 6th Session, 14 December 2007, discussion on renewal of mandate on Sudan.

101 American delegate, 7th Session, 17 March 2007, in response to SR on Sudan, Sima Samar.

The US maintained that the reports given to the Council left 'no further doubt that action is demanded'.[102] Throughout these Sessions, the US claimed that the 'Council has yet to adequately address the human rights violations in Sudan',[103] repeating that it 'remain[ed] very concerned' and was 'call[ing] on the government to end its destructive behaviour'.[104] The US spoke about possible methods, including sanctions, to encourage a resolution of the conflict.[105] American delegates asked why the Council was so slow to take action. Having secured sanctions against Sudan in the Security Council, the US encouraged the HRC and member states to take decisive action. The Americans encouraged the Council to act swiftly rather than spend months or years awaiting reports from mandate holders and fact-finding missions, or passing somewhat neutral resolutions calling for change without condemning the parties responsible for atrocities. However, other Council members stressed the need to follow the Council's procedures in decision-making regarding this, and other, human rights situations. The US desire to 'rip up the rule book' and take swift, decisive action where necessary in crisis situations such as Darfur, lacked credibility, they declared, due to the US having taken similar steps before the invasion of Iraq, and the subsequent international condemnation of that action. However, the delaying tactics of other states, under the guise of following legitimate procedures, increasingly lacked credibility in much the same way as the US desire to ignore those procedures altogether.

The US raised concerns not only about the impact of regionalism through OIC tactics of blocking action on humanitarian crises occurring within OIC member states such as Sudan, but also about the Council's disregard for other situations across the world. Various factors affected the Council's inaction regarding such states, notably the lack of will to interfere with repressive regimes that afforded little access to the international community, or the lack of interest in those states that afforded no political gains for individual members of the Council. For example, the US expressed concern about Myanmar throughout discussions on what it termed 'one of the most repressive regimes'.[106] The US highlighted the 'lack of inclusive and genuine dialogue with all stakeholders'[107] as being a fundamental obstacle to the protection of human rights through national reconciliation. Despite the lack of access to, or information from, Myanmar, the US set out the ongoing human rights violations, including the large numbers of refugees,[108] detention of

---

102 American delegate, 4th Session, 16 March 2007, in response to Jody Williams, Mission to Sudan.

103 American delegate, 5th Session, 13 June 2007, in response to SR on Sudan, Sima Samar.

104 American delegate, 7th Session, 17 March 2007, in response to SR on Sudan, Sima Samar.

105 American delegate, 5th Session, 13 June 2007, in response to SR on Sudan, Sima Samar.

106 American delegate, 4th Session, 23 March 2007, in response to SR on Myanmar, Paulo Sergio Pinheiro.

107 American delegate, 2nd Session, 27 September 2006, in response to SR on Myanmar, Paulo Sergio Pinheiro.

108 '[. . .] hundreds of thousands of refugees [. . .]', American delegate, 2nd Session, *Ibid.*

political prisoners,[109] police brutality,[110] and restrictions on the activities of NGOs and other such parties.[111] The crux of the US position on Myanmar was to 'urge this Council, the international community, and Myanmar to protect those Burmese persons whose rights are being violated'.[112] In order for this to occur, 'continued international attention [requiring] sustained commitment'[113] was called for in order to ensure the cooperation of the government in the implementation of Human Rights Council recommendations. The US condemnation of the regime was echoed by other Western states, and was repeated throughout all sessions. However, the situation was of little interest domestically for many of the Council members, as opposed to, for example, the situation in Israel. Therefore, the Council failed to discharge its mandate to protect human rights. As had occurred at the Commission, Council attention was given to the Israel–Palestine conflict at the expense of the victims in Myanmar.

The US raised other similar country-specific situations such as Belarus,[114] Burundi,[115] Cambodia,[116] Cuba,[117] Liberia,[118] North Korea[119] and Somalia,[120] amongst others. The US focus on these repressive regimes and their ongoing

---

109 'How can we support the release of political prisoners?', American delegate, 2nd Session, *Ibid.*; 'Pro-democracy advocates continue to be arrested', American delegate, 7th Session, 13 March 2007, in response to SR on Myanmar, Paulo Sergio Pinheiro.

110 'The excessive force against civilians during peaceful demonstration led to the numerous killings, detention, and injuries', American delegate, 6th Session, 12 December 2007, in response to SR on Myanmar, Paulo Sergio Pinheiro.

111 'The Red Cross has had to halt its activities [. . .]', American delegate, 4th Session, 23 March 2007, in response to SR on Myanmar, Paulo Sergio Pinheiro.

112 American delegate, 7th Session, 13 March 2007, in response to SR on Myanmar, Paulo Sergio Pinheiro.

113 American delegate, 7th Session, 17 March 2007, in response to SR on Myanmar, Paulo Sergio Pinheiro.

114 See, for example, American delegate, 2nd Session, 27 September 2006, in response to SR on Belarus, Adrian Severin.

115 See, for example, American delegate, 2nd Session, 27 September 2006, in response to SR on Burundi, Akich Okola; American delegate, 4th Session, 23 March 2007, in response to SR on Burundi, Akich Okola.

116 See, for example, American delegate, 2nd Session, 26 September 2006, in response to SR on Cambodia, Yash Ghai; American delegate, 7th Session, 19 March 2007, discussions on renewal of mandate on Cambodia.

117 See, for example, American delegate, 2nd Session, 26 September 2006, in response to SR on Cuba, Christine Chanet; American delegate, 5th Session, 12 June 2007, in response to SR on Cuba, Christine Chanet.

118 See, for example, 2nd Session, 29 September 2006, in response to SR on Liberia, Charlotte Abaka; American delegate, 4th Session, 23 March 2007, in response to SR on Liberia, Charlotte Abaka.

119 See, for example, American delegate, 2nd Session, 27 September 2006, in response to SR on DPRK, Vitit Muntarbhorn; American delegate, 4th Session, 23 March 2007, in response to SR on DPRK, Vitit Muntarbhorn; American delegate, 7th Session, 13 March 2007, in response to SR on DPRK, Vitit Muntarbhorn.

120 See, for example, American delegate, 2nd Session, 26 September 2006, in response to SR on Somalia, Ghanim Alnajjar; American delegate, 5th Session, 12 June 2007, in response to SR on Somalia, Ghanim Alnajjar.

human rights abuses followed the same pattern regardless of the countries involved. It condemned regimes for not cooperating with the Council or other UN bodies, it called for increased international action to ensure protection and promotion of human rights, and commended and supported the efforts of UN mandate holders in these regions. Unlike the OIC, whose political objectives drove its responses to human rights abuses, the US consistently denounced humanitarian situations even within closely allied states such as Israel or Pakistan, albeit that its criticism of those countries' governments was somewhat muted. The contrast between the positions taken by the US and the OIC demonstrates the difference between low-level and overt politicisation; muted criticism of allies is altogether different to ignoring, or blocking scrutiny of, human rights abuses committed within allied states.

The belief that international aid and intervention could most appropriately assist such areas was emphasised by US calls for such action to be taken. The US demanded action and expressed frustration that the Council was dragging its heels when dealing with crisis situations. The US initial fears that the Council would become biased and politicized can be seen to have been realised in respect of the focus on certain human rights situations and the body's inaction on others. Although some may assert that the US used the Council to further its own national aims, any politicisation on its part was of the low-level expected, and to some degree tolerated, within an intergovernmental body. Moreover, that level of politicisation is overshadowed by the gross politicisation from OIC and African states. Politicisation had already come to dominate the fledgling body, with regional groups able to steer discussions towards or away from their choice of situations. The frustration that this caused was evident from the American interventions during all of the seven sessions in which it participated before its withdrawal.

Thematic debates. The US frequently reiterated the importance of international support in order for Council mandates to be fulfilled, usually those promoting liberal human rights standards that reflected US national positions. It singled out topics such as protection of women and children from violence and trafficking, freedoms of religion and expression,[121] and the protection of human rights defenders, as being of particular concern. For example, the position that 'violence against women is indefensible'[122] was repeated in the context of abuses against women and children, including the trafficking of people in both groups as well as sex-tourism.[123] The US identified Sudan

---

121 'There is often an overlap between freedom of religion and freedom of expression', American delegate, 2nd Session, 22 September 2006, in response to SR on Freedom of Religion, Asma Jahangir.

122 American delegate, 4th Session, 21 March 2007, in response to SR on Violence Against Women, Yakin Ertuk.

123 See, for example, American delegate, 2nd Session, 25 September 2006, in response to SR on the sale of children and child pornography, Juan Miguel Petit; American delegate, 2nd Session, 20 September 2006, in response to SR on Violence Against Women, Yakin Ertuk.

and Myanmar as the two countries where it believed these groups were particularly vulnerable, arguing that such 'human rights abuses [were being] used to terrorise people'[124] due to government involvement in human rights violations.

The US discussed the need to promote freedom of religion,[125] calling for all countries to 'ensure that freedom of religion is respected for all religions [. . .] [and] the freedom to not affiliate with any religion at all, or to change religion must also be respected',[126] due to the central importance of this right for people across the world.[127] When discussing freedom of expression, the US stressed that 'the right is a cornerstone in the protection of human rights',[128] arguing that ongoing support of 'the mandate is urgently needed'.[129] The strength of the US support for these two freedoms was not solely based on its traditional domestic regard for these rights,[130] but also on the juxtaposition between freedoms of religion and expression and the OIC demand that defamation of religion be afforded equal protection. The US interventions on certain rights and freedoms showed its desire to promote those typically Western values that underpinned the UDHR, thus ensuring that they remained prevalent within the human rights system. That showdown of cultural values echoed the old US–Soviet controversies that once politicised the Commission and other human rights work at the UN. Despite hopes that the Council would protect and promote all human rights, differences couched in language of cultural sensitivities reflected similar problems at the Commission.

During discussions of various reports given by the Secretary-General's Special Representative on Human Rights Defenders,[131] the Council was strongly reminded of the absolute imperative of protecting human rights defenders. The US noted that 'some governments feel restricted by [human rights defenders] and attempt to restrict them',[132] and criticised this 'obviously political' motivation.[133] The US was disturbed by the violations perpetrated

124 American delegate, 4th Session, 21 March 2007, in response to SR on Violence Against Women, Yakin Ertuk.
125 American delegate, 2nd Session, 21 September 2006, in response to SR on Freedom of Religion, Asma Jahangir, and Special Rapporteur on Freedom of Expression, Ambeyi Ligabo.
126 American delegate, 2nd Session, 22 September 2006, in response to SR on Freedom of Religion, Asma Jahangir.
127 *Ibid.*
128 American delegate, 7th Session, 14 March 2008, in response to SR on Freedom of Expression, Ambeyi Ligabo.
129 *Ibid.*
130 The Constitution of the United States, Amendment 1.
131 Hina Jilani.
132 American delegate, 2nd Session, 22 September 2006, in response to SR on Human Rights Defenders, Hina Jilani.
133 *Ibid.*

against many of these people, particularly the harassment, detention, and attacks on human rights defenders.[134] It called for the Council to join it in 'standing with courageous defenders' and to 'call into account those governments that seek to undermine their liberties'.[135] The US wished to ensure that 'individuals and groups [. . .] be able to fight for human rights'[136] and asked for support in this regard. The support that the US expressed for human rights defenders could also have been a way of criticising those regimes that do not allow open and easy access to such people. Many of those states that attacked the US at the Council could be accused of repressive laws and actions against human rights defenders, especially members of the OIC. The strenuous positions taken by the US in related discussions reflected its deteriorating relations with such countries.

Throughout the Council sessions, the US spoke out against regimes committing the worst human rights abuses. General debates were used to flag the atrocities in specific states such as Zimbabwe,[137] China[138] and Uzbekistan.[139] The US noted violations of specific rights, as well as the general culture of violations prevalent within these countries. The US also used general discussions to encourage the Council to focus on 'implementation of human rights, and on providing "relevant and practical advice"' without politicisation.[140] This tied in with its initial fears that the Council would be selective and bias in terms of which rights it chose to protect and promote. The realisation of these fears was apparent in the vociferousness of US interventions and calls for the body to discharge its mandate. The body's failure to listen to the US positions was arguably a main reason for its temporary disengagement from the body.

7.5. The US human rights record

Towards the end of the Commission, the body increasingly shielded its members from scrutiny. As already discussed, a number of states became members in order to avoid scrutiny, allowing abuses to continue within their

---

134 American delegate, 4th Session, 28 March 2007, in response to SR on Human Rights Defenders, Hina Jilani.

135 *Ibid.*

136 American delegate, 7th Session, 14 March 2008, in response to SR on Human Rights Defenders, Hina Jilani.

137 American delegate, 4th Session, 29 March 2007, during 'related debate'.

138 American delegate, 7th Session, 25 March 2007, during discussions on Agenda Item 8 'Tibet'.

139 American delegate, 6th Session, 24 September 2007, during general debate on Agenda Item 4.

140 American delegate, 2nd Session, 27 September 2006, in response to Sub-Commission on Promotion and Protection of Human Rights Representative, Marc Bossuyt.

own borders.[141] The Council adopted a number of safeguards to combat its predecessor's reputation, particularly in relation to member states' human rights commitments and scrutiny of their records.[142] In contrast to the view that the US under George W. Bush's administration decided not to stand for election because of dissatisfaction, some have argued that it feared its own record would be scrutinised more harshly as a member than as an observer.[143] The desire to deflect attention from its human rights record may be traced to the repeated criticisms, often heard at the UN, of the Bush administration's anti-terrorism tactics after the 2001 attacks on the World Trade Centre. Another view, however, is that the US decision not to stand for election resulted from its fear of an embarrassing defeat similar to the one suffered in its 2001 bid for re-election. That view is supported by the US reform proposal, rejected by the majority of states, under which the permanent members of the Security Council would also be 'permanent members' of the Council. Had that proposal been adopted, the US would have been guaranteed a seat, thus avoiding the need for election. The US would have been granted a powerful position of being able to assert influence at the Council without fear of reprisals during elections. Power would have allowed the US to pursue its human rights objectives, regardless of its reasons for particular stances or positions.

The US domestic human rights record. The US domestic human rights record was raised at the Council by various mandate holders, which led to the question of whether the US was being unfairly singled out. The US concern that it was being treated disproportionately more harshly than other states was reflected in its responses to being the only Western state repeatedly raised in reports to the Council. The US reaction must be examined not only with respect to the possibly disproportionate focus on it, but also with respect to legitimate concerns about US domestic human rights.

Various methods were used to ensure that the Council focused on the US. Mandate holders, in particular, were able to ensure that discussions took place examining US violations. Mandates are established and defined by the resolution creating them, but the mandate holders work independently of any UN body. Mandate holders receive information on human rights abuses,

141 See, for example, 'Yet the Commission's capacity to perform its tasks has been increasingly undermined by its declining credibility and professionalism. In particular, States have sought membership of the Commission not to strengthen human rights but to protect themselves against criticism or to criticise others. As a result, a credibility deficit has developed, which casts a shadow on the reputation of the United Nations system as a whole', General Assembly, 'In Larger Freedom: Towards Development, Security and Human Rights for All' *Report of the Secretary-General*, 21 March 2005, UN Doc. A/59/2005, para.182.

142 See Chapter 3.

143 H. Harris, 'The Politics of Depoliticization: International Perspectives on the Human Rights Council', *Human Rights Brief*, Vol. 13 (3), 2006. 8–9.

and they determine based on that, and other information, which countries to visit and report on, and which countries to include in their annual reports. States, at the request of a mandate holder, determine whether to extend an invitation for a country visit. Many states do extend standing invitations, which allow visits. Each mandate holder may visit two countries each year. As independent experts, thematic mandate holders determine which states to visit. The Council has little control over which states will be visited, beyond providing mandate holders with visit requests or information on human rights violations.

The Council heard, and subsequently discussed, issues relating to domestic US human rights from mandate holders who included the US in annual reports or who undertook a country visit to the US. Such mandates included contemporary forms of racism[144] and extreme poverty. The latter mandate, on extreme poverty, provides a useful example of the way in which the US domestic human rights record was examined. The US officially welcomed visits and recommendations by mandate holders. In response, however, it questioned what was being done to improve far worse situations in other countries. Whilst this stance can be argued to have missed the point of the reports, the US position was legitimate. The inclusion of the US in these reports resulted in other states not being discussed at the Council, despite there being ongoing, dire situations across the world. This was not an issue that went unnoticed by other states at the Council, for example, during discussions on extreme poverty. Despite Arjun Sengupta, the Special Rapporteur on Extreme Poverty, saying that 'most of the problems I saw in the United States need to go a long way before there is a solution',[145] a number of developing countries expressed disappointment that the US had been the sole focus of the report. Mali questioned why the Special Rapporteur visited 'one of the richest countries in the world' rather than 'a poor country', stating that 'the living conditions in Africa cannot be the same as in the US'.[146] Statements made by developing countries underscored the power given to mandate holders to determine which states to visit, and the sometimes arbitrary results. Sengupta's decision to visit the US highlighted the potential for politicisation or abuse of the process by which country visits are chosen.

Mandate holders are given the freedom and independence to determine which country visits to undertake. Some guidance, however, is provided by the mandate itself. The resolution establishing the mandate on extreme poverty stressed the need to promote human rights for people living in such

144 'Report of the Special Rapporteur on contemporary forms of racism, racial discrimination, xenophobia and related intolerance', 27 March 2007, UN Doc. A/HRC/4/19; Oral intervention of SR on Contemporary Forms of Racism, Doudou Diène, 4th Session, 28 March 2007.

145 Oral statement of SR on Extreme Poverty, Arjun Sengupta, 2nd Session, 27 September 2006.

146 Mali delegate, 2nd Session, 27 September 2006, in response to SR on Extreme Poverty, Arjun Sengupta.

circumstances.[147] Sengupta expressly recognised this need,[148] and indeed provided some individual examples of the link between poverty and denial of rights.[149] However, his report focused almost exclusively on the poverty itself rather than any general trends or links between extreme poverty and other human rights violations such as discrimination against women, modern forms of slavery, or denial of sanitation, safe drinking water or adequate housing. Sengupta's decision to spend time and resources on scrutinising the US human rights record at the expense of other states impacted most upon those countries which expressly requested to utilise mandate holders' expertise to improve the rights within their own, or neighbouring, territory.

Although mandate holders used their reports to provide neutral and facilitative advice to almost all states concerned, the manner in which the US was dealt with was somewhat different. For example, despite the mandate holder being required to 'make recommendations and, as appropriate, proposals in the sphere of technical assistance',[150] the Special Rapporteur on Extreme Poverty's report on the US at the Second Session did not include any constructive recommendations that could be applied to the US or to other countries. Instead, the Special Rapporteur's conclusions repeatedly emphasised the US position as 'the wealthiest country in the world' before noting various problems and criticising various practices without providing alternatives or solutions.[151] Sengupta failed to fulfil a key element of his mandate,[152] and, as a result, a number of states, including Brazil, Cameroon, Philippines, and Senegal, asked the Special Rapporteur for concrete proposals, or a list of best practices, for states dealing with extreme poverty. That report and subsequent discussion can be contrasted with the useful and facilitative country report on Ecuador given by the Special Rapporteur on Extreme Poverty at the Eleventh Session, Magdalena Sepúlveda Carmona.[153] That report gave strong guidance and advice, in particular on the 'cash transfer programme' and the relationship between social spending, human rights and extreme poverty, which was useful for many other countries, especially states within the same region as Ecuador. Contrasting Sengupta and Carmona's reports raises questions about the competence of individual mandate holders, which the Council has no power in terms of selection. This is a key concern in terms of the Council's relationship with the Special Procedures system which, necessarily, must remain wholly independent of any UN body.

---

147 CHR Res. 1998/25, 'Human rights and extreme poverty', 17 April 1998, UN Doc. E/CN.4/1998/24, para. 8(a).
148 'Mission to the United States of America', 27 March 2006, UN Doc. E/CN.4/2006/43/Add.1, para. 9.
149 *Ibid.*, paras 59–73.
150 *Ibid.*, para. 8(c).
151 *Ibid.*
152 *Ibid.*
153 'Report of the independent expert on the question of human rights and extreme poverty, 19 May 2009, UN Doc. A/HRC/11/9/Add.1.

It is interesting to note that Sengupta no longer held the mandate for Extreme Poverty at the Eleventh Session. However, he did give an annual report at the Fifth Session[154] which can be contrasted, in terms of its utility and applicability, with his earlier country report on the US. Although an annual report is aimed at providing guidance and advice for many states and regions, the contrast between this and the US country report is stark enough to demonstrate the politicisation of that mandate in relation to the US country visit. The annual report dedicated separate chapters outlining neutral and constructive proposals for dealing with extreme poverty across Africa, Asia and even, to some extent, the European Union. The manner in which the US was dealt with in terms of extreme poverty was clearly politically motivated rather than being a constructive exercise in facilitating human rights.

The inclusion of the US as the sole Western state, and sometimes even the sole country, in mandate holders' reports on various topics indicated that it was being disproportionately singled out. Its inclusion in reports alongside grave abusers indicated selectivity by mandate holders. One might suspect that mandate holders, relying on the high levels of politicisation at the Council, assumed that they could ensure support for their reports and recommendations by singling out and criticising the US. This was apparent from the response to the Special Rapporteur on Extreme Poverty from countries such as China, Cuba, Ecuador, Indonesia, Morocco, and Saudi Arabia. All of these countries, as well as other states who had tense relations with the US, congratulated the Special Rapporteur for focusing on the US, although their reasons for doing so were not always apparent.

Some mandate holders argued that the US was widely reported on in order to uphold the principles of impartiality and non-bias, thus ensuring that all states be subjected to scrutiny rather than focusing solely on poor or developing nations.[155] For example, Sengupta expressed this position by saying:

> The reason that I chose the United States is not because I do not think that developing countries have no problems. I wanted to point out that it is not a problem of per capita income, but a problem of society, so I chose the richest country in the world. I wanted to focus on basic problems of people in US with the intention to show that human rights are a basic issue of empowerment and dignity, which is not accepted by all the countries.[156]

154 'Report of the independent expert on the question of human rights and extreme poverty', 11 June 2007, UN Doc. A/HRC/5/3; see, also, Oral statement of SR on Extreme Poverty, Arjun Sengupta, 2nd Session, 27 September 2006. (n. 108)

155 See, for example, 'Mission to the United States of America', para. 3.

156 Oral statement of SR on Extreme Poverty, Arjun Sengupta, 2nd Session, 27 September 2006.

Despite that and other similar explanations, it appears that the US was used as an example in certain thematic reports where, to better fulfil the Council's mandate, time should have been devoted to grave situations in other countries. The failure of many member states to question, and indeed the decision by some to laud, the mandate holder for choosing to visit the US suggests that political objectives and power politics, rather than the body's mandate, were at the fore.

The US was prepared to accept some of the sharper focus that its standing in the world entailed. However, as will be shown, it is clear from the US response to mandate holders on human rights issues relating to counter-terrorism that it viewed the attention on these issues as grossly disproportionate and lacking in even-handedness. The US regarded states and mandate holders focusing on its human rights record as seeking to exert influence and gain power. However, despite that disproportionate attention, there were instances where, as will be explored, focus on the US was required to fulfil the Council's protection mandate.

Mandate holders discussed the US in relation to issues of counter-terrorism, torture, enforced disappearances and rights of detainees. The debates primarily focused on Guantanamo Bay and the US tactics employed in the 'war on terror'. Despite its support for many Council mandates, one notable exception that the US disagreed with was the Special Rapporteur on Protection and Promotion of Human Rights While Countering Terrorism, Martin Scheinin.[157] Scheinin was mandated to:

> gather, request, receive and exchange information and communications from and with all relevant sources, including Governments, the individuals concerned, their families, their representatives and their organizations [. . .] on alleged violations of human rights and fundamental freedoms while countering terrorism.[158]

The mandate holder was required to make recommendations,[159] identify and promote best practices,[160] and to work with other relevant mandate holders and UN bodies[161] to ensure the protection and promotion of human rights and fundamental freedoms while countering terrorism.

---

157 Scheinin (Finland) was appointed in April 2005 by the CHR as SR on the promotion and protection of human rights and fundamental freedoms while countering terrorism. The HRC assumed this mandate, extending it for one year. In December 2007 the Council extended the mandate for three years. See 'Special Rapporteur on the promotion and protection of human rights while countering terrorism', (Online). Available HTTP: <http://www2. ohchr.org/english/issues/terrorism/rapporteur/srchr.htm> (accessed 16 October 2012).

158 CHR Res. 2005/80, 'Protection of Human Rights and Fundamental Freedoms while Countering Terrorism', 21 April 2005, UN Doc. E/CN.4/RES/2005/80, para. 14(b).

159 *Ibid.*, para. 14(a).

160 *Ibid.*, para. 14(c).

161 *Ibid.*, para. 14(d).

At the Second Session, Scheinin signalled his intention to look at various state and institutional trends in this area, in order to set out best practices regarding issues such as racial profiling, secret detentions and extraordinary renditions. Despite having omitted specific mention of the US in his report, Scheinin was nonetheless criticised by that country. The US questioned 'whether certain areas of the Special Rapporteur's work are sufficiently necessary and effective'.[162] The US, which regularly queried the mandate's necessity, has frequently asserted that counter-terrorism is exclusively a matter of domestic concern. At the Second Session, Scheinin accused unspecified countries of abusing the notion of terrorism, although he clearly alluded to the US and its allies in the 'war on terror'.[163] He spoke of a 'trend of states to stigmatise movements and ethnic groups they simply do not like and fight against terrorism while not defining the term "terrorism"'.[164] That and similar comments were arguably understood to be aimed at states including the US and UK, as well as countries such as Russia. The US rejected Scheinin's calls for research aimed at developing a single definition of terrorism, stressing that there had already been 'thousands' of such debates, and questioning the utility of such an exercise.[165] While the UN had discussed this issue on a number of recent occasions, this intervention missed the point of the mandate. The Special Rapporteur was concerned with defining terrorism in order to combat human rights violations, as opposed to the ongoing debates as to whether terrorism should be defined as an act of war. The US obtuseness in this regard was arguably motivated by its sensitivity to having any of its anti-terrorism tactics scrutinised by the mandate holder or indeed the Council. This hostility arguably resulted from the US insistence that counter-terrorism solely fell within national jurisdiction and therefore should not be defined by an international body.

The Special Rapporteur not only discussed the US in his reports[166] but also undertook a country visit to that state during the Council's first year, which was reported on at the Sixth Session. The mission's report repeatedly identified the US role as a world leader and its subsequent responsibility to protect and promote human rights while being at the fore of countering terrorism.[167] That position reflects a more general approach that the US should be held to higher standards than other states. While an even-handed

---

162 American delegate, 2nd Session, 25 September 2006, in response to SR on Protection and Promotion of Human Rights While Countering Terrorism, Martin Scheinin.

163 Oral intervention of SR on Protection and Promotion of Human Rights While Countering Terrorism, Martin Scheinin.

164 *Ibid.*

165 American delegate, 2nd Session, 25 September 2006, in response to SR on Protection and Promotion of Human Rights While Countering Terrorism, Martin Scheinin.

166 See, for example, 'Report of the Special Rapporteur on the promotion and protection of human rights and fundamental freedoms while countering terrorism', 29 January 2007, UN Doc. A/HRC/4/26.

167 'Mission to the United States of America', UN Doc. A/HRC/6/17/Add.3.

approach requires factors such as wealth, national human rights institutions, and capacity to be taken into account, 'world leadership' is not one of those criteria. However, mandate holders and, indeed, states did use this factor as a justification for holding the US to proportionately greater scrutiny than any other country.

Scheinin expressed grave concerns regarding detainees at Guantanamo Bay and other prisoners suspected of terrorism, as well as interrogation techniques, extraordinary renditions, and degrading treatment by the CIA. The US was 'disappointed by the report' due to its 'unfair and oversimplified criticisms'.[168] For example, the report alleged that detainees were denied the right to a fair trial[169] and criticised various administrative processes. The US criticised the Special Rapporteur, alleging that he had not acknowledged the situation's complexity, especially with regard to his rejection of the status of detainees as 'unlawful enemy combatants'.[170] The US argued that the classification of the detainees was fundamental in terms of the rights they were afforded under international law. According to the US, the Special Rapporteur's insistence that the detainees be treated as prisoners of war or as criminal suspects failed to address arguments raised by the US that a war was, in fact, occurring. The US alleged that selectivity and politicisation was apparent not only in what was reported, but also that the report was prefaced with remarks such as, 'the USA is a world leader, and has a responsibility to ensure respect for human rights and international humanitarian law'.[171] The US clearly objected to its world position being used to justify disproportionate scrutiny when other states were committing similar, and worse, abuses, for example Russia's ongoing violations against Chechen separatists.

Scheinin's mandate required him to investigate US human rights abuses while countering terrorism and, indeed, he explained throughout the reports and oral statements why he held that state to higher standards. He primarily focused on America's duty, as a world leader and powerful state, to set an example for other countries. Although these reasons do raise serious concerns about the criteria for proportionate scrutiny, other mandate holders have been less convincing, or even silent, as to any reasons for excessively focusing on the US. The aforementioned stance that the US should be held to a higher standard than less-developed countries was explicitly or implicitly repeated in the reports of other mandate holders regarding issues relating to the 'war on terror'. The position was especially apparent in reports where the US was the sole Western state raised alongside countries known to commit grave

---

168 American delegate, 6th Session, 12 December 2007, in response to Martin Scheinin, Special Rapporteur on Protection and Promotion of Human Rights While Countering Terrorism.

169 'Mission to the United States of America', UN Doc. A/HRC/6/17/Add.3., para. 12.

170 *Ibid.*, para. 11.

171 Oral statement of SR on Protection and Promotion of Human Rights While Countering Terrorism, Martin Scheinin, 6th Session, 12 December 2007.

and systematic abuses. Whilst such remarks could be argued to be non-controversial in terms of the standards that other Western nations were held to by mandate holders, the repeated focus on the US alone (aside from Israel), despite other countries such as the UK being accused of similar abuses, indicated a lack of even-handedness in the way that the US was treated at the Council. The US desire not to have its human rights record scrutinised was arguably a factor in its response to various mandate holders' reports but, as will be demonstrated, the selectivity and bias apparent through disproportionate attention devoted to the US gave weight to its reaction.

The mandate on Enforced Disappearances also, perhaps dubiously, focused on the US. The Working Group on Enforced Disappearances[172] was the Commission's first thematic mandate, and was created as a result of Argentina's resistance to having a country-specific mandate to deal with the human rights violations occurring as a result of enforced disappearances within that state. Throughout the history of that thematic mandate, the focus has largely been on Central and South America[173] and no country visits have been undertaken to Western states.

The report on enforced disappearances[174] at the Second Session discussed countries such as Guinea, Burundi, and Colombia, before identifying the US as being one of the four main countries of concern regarding its 'anti-terrorist activities [which] are used as an excuse for not applying international obligations'.[175] Extraordinary rendition is essentially an issue of torture. The inclusion of extraordinary rendition within the report on 'enforced disappearances' seemed somewhat tenuous as that mandate has always focused on, national political disappearances rather than transnational renditions, torture or terrorism. The Human Rights Committee, in contrast, criticised the US practice of secret detention,[176] but in no way linked this to an issue of enforced disappearances. The Working Group's report was discussed during the Council's first year when the body simultaneously was reviewing all Special Procedures mandates. Inclusion of the US in this report arguably was a ploy to attract attention and support for the mandate from US detractors at the Council. US inclusion in that report was perhaps selective and bias for what appears to be political reasons.

The Working Group gave constructive and neutral advice to countries that had been visited, including Sri Lanka and Colombia, but solely criticised the US rather than providing any other comments. Although that discrepancy alone does not necessarily imply selectivity, it does demonstrate that, once again, the US was treated differently to other states. During the subsequent

---

172 CHR Res. 20 (XXXVI), 29 February 1980, UN Doc. E/CN.4/1435.

173 With almost half of all country visits to that region.

174 Oral statement of the President of the Working Group on Enforced Disappearances, Stephen Toope, 2nd Session, 19 September 2006.

175 *Ibid.*

176 UN Human Rights Committee, 'Concluding Observations of the Human Rights Committee, United States of America', para. 12.

discussion, a number of countries requested further advice, such as a list of best practices, from the Working Groups on issues as disparate as enforced disappearances of political opponents or hostage-taking by non-state actors.[177] Other than the US response, no other states discussed extraordinary rendition during the debate, arguably due to its anomalous and unrelated inclusion within this report. The US expressed respect for its international obligations. It recognised 'that the international community has not always agreed with US positions' but that, with respect to extraordinary rendition, 'to bring suspects to other countries is not inherently unlawful'.[178] However, its comments during subsequent discussions on domestic human rights issues, at this and other sessions, indicated a waning patience with being singled out for criticism whilst known abusers and critical situations were seemingly ignored by mandate holders and the Council itself.

Mandate holders continued to identify the US alongside states known as human rights abusers during general reports on issues pertaining to the treatment of detainees. The US not only disagreed with assertions made in a number of reports,[179] but further accused some of misrepresenting facts.[180] Further struggles occurred between the US and the Council-appointed mandate holders. For example, the US criticised the independent experts that made up the Working Group on the Situation of Detainees at Guantanamo Bay[181] for not accepting its open invitation to visit Guantanamo Bay, which subsequently led to their report being based on 'second and third hand information'.[182] The five mandate holders determined that they could better discharge their functions regarding human rights violations and Guantanamo Bay through submitting a single joint report rather than five separate ones.[183] However, it was the joint venture that, ultimately, resulted in none of the mandate holders visiting that facility.

The mandate holders had originally accepted the US invitation for only three of the five experts to visit Guantanamo Bay as well as other terms set out by the US.[184] Ultimately, a crucial reason why the Working Group

---

177 See, for example, Costa Rica, 2nd Session, 19 September 2006, in response to the President of the Working Group on Enforced Disappearances, Stephen Toope.

178 American delegate, 2nd Session, 19 September 2006, in response to the President of the Working Group on Enforced Disappearances.

179 See, for example, American delegate, 4th Session, 27 March 2007, in response to SR on Arbitrary Detention, Leila Zerrougui.

180 See, for example, American delegate, 4th Session, 27 March 2007, in response to SR on Extrajudicial Killings, Philip Alston.

181 Including, SR on Torture, Manfred Nowak; SR on the Independence of Judges and Lawyers, Leando Despouy; SR on the Right of Everyone to the Enjoyment of the Highest Attainable Standard of Physical and Mental Health, Paul Hunt.

182 American delegate, 2nd Session, 21 September 2006, in response to the Working Group on the Situation of Detainees.

183 ECOSOC, 'Situation of detainees at Guantánamo Bay', 27 February 2006, UN Doc E/CN.4/2006/120, para. 2.

184 *Ibid.*, para. 4.

decided to refuse the invitation was due to the US indicating that the Group would not be granted private interviews with detainees. The US had issued a letter on 28 October 2005 inviting three of the five mandate holders to visit Guantanamo Bay. However, the US stipulated that the mandate holders would not be able to conduct private interviews with detainees, citing national security reasons. In their response, dated 31 October 2005, the mandate holders accepted the invitation, stating that the visit would take place on 6 December 2005. However, the mandate holders asserted that excluding private interviews with detainees contravened the ability to undertake a fact-finding mission, and impeded an objective and fair assessment. The US failed to overturn that exclusion, and therefore, on 18 November 2005, the mandate holders cancelled the visit.[185]

In particular, the Special Rapporteur on Torture, Manfred Nowak, refused to accept the invitation to Guantanamo Bay without assurances that he would be allowed to talk to detainees in private. That position reflects the mandate holder's approach to country visits, and indeed was consistent with his later cancellation of a visit to Russia for the same reason,[186] and his agreement to visit China only after the authorities accepted this condition. The US expectation, framed in exceptionalist terms, that it be afforded different treatment than other states by the mandate holder demonstrated its continued exceptionalism regarding domestic human rights matters. That expectation is unworkable at the Council owing both to the body's mandate and to its founding principles of non-selectivity and universality.

The Working Group's report detailed and explained the problems set out above. However, the Working Group's oral statement to the Council asserted that a main reason why they had declined the invitation to visit Guantanamo Bay was the extension of it to only part of the group, as well as refusal to grant unhindered access to detainees, and a lack of standard terms for the visit.[187] These oral assertions were inconsistent with the written report which acknowledged the Working Group's initial acceptance of that invitation despite the restrictions set out by the US.[188] Indeed, the oral statement was more critical of the US than the written report had been, in particular by discussing issues that had not previously been raised. The Working Group's inconsistency indicates that some or all of the mandate holders were influenced, to some extent, by the political atmosphere within the body where many states adopted, or were allied with those who had, an anti-US position.

185 *Ibid.*
186 'Report of the Special Rapporteur on Torture and other Cruel, Inhuman or Degrading Treatment or Punishment, Manfred Nowak', 15 January 2007, UN Doc A/HRC/4/33, para. 13.
187 Oral intervention of Working Group on the Situation of Detainees Representative, Leila Zerrougui, 2nd Session, 9 September 2006.
188 ECOSOC, 'Situation of detainees at Guantánamo Bay', para. 3.

The Working Group orally stated that they regretted that there was 'no point' in visiting Guantanamo Bay[189] despite recognising, throughout the written report, the limitations that this placed on the information gathered and recommendations made. The US response, both orally and in a letter annexed to the report,[190] highlighted the flawed nature of the report owing to the failure to visit Guantanamo Bay and the 'flawed' premise that the US was not engaged in an international war. The US set out the 'need to work together to move forward' and its 'regret [regarding] the approach taken [by the Working Group] that they did not accept our invitation'[191] but failed to accept any of the recommendations given by the Working Group.

US intransigence towards mandate holders' recommendations was undoubtedly influenced by statements made by known human rights abusers during subsequent discussions on mandate holders' reports. During the discussion on the Working Group on the Situation of Detainees at Guantanamo Bay, the US argued that accusations, in the report, of US breaches of international law and violations of human rights were unfounded and incorrect.[192] These comments were followed by members such as China, Cuba, and Venezuela, as well as observers such as Iran and North Korea, supporting the assertions made in the report as well as criticising the US. The US was distressed by what it deemed as known abusers of human rights taking strident positions regarding the US treatment of detainees, despite the lack of first-hand evidence available in the report. The US ignored the fact that a wealth of information on abuses in, for example, Guantanamo Bay and Abu Graib, had been published by NGOs, the media, and other human rights actors. While Council members should, perhaps, have confined discussions to the report and its findings, the reality was that US abuses while countering terrorism was a highly contentious political issue on which many states had strong opinions. The US was held to higher standards than other states by other countries not only due to its global position, but also as a result of its ongoing human rights discourse on the one hand, and its simultaneous violations during its 'war on terror' on the other hand. However, the disproportionate reaction from other states, and the constant attack of the US in some countries' statements, reflected the general politicisation of the Council. Iran, for example, accused the US of lying to the Council,[193] while Venezuela asserted that the US was committing 'flagrant violations of human rights'.[194]

---

189 Oral intervention of Working Group on the Situation of Detainees Representative, Leila Zerrougui, 2nd Session.
190 ECOSOC, 'Situation of detainees at Guantánamo Bay', Annex II.
191 American delegate, 2nd Session, 9 September 2006, in response to Leila Zerrougui, Working Group on the Situation of Detainees.
192 *Ibid.*
193 Iranian delegate, 2nd Session, 9 September 2006, in response to Leila Zerrougui, Working Group on the Situation of Detainees.
194 Venezuelan delegate, 2nd Session, 9 September 2006, in response to Leila Zerrougui, Working Group on the Situation of Detainees.

These positions were not echoed by Western states, most of whom were more concerned with asking questions of the Special Rapporteurs rather than making sweeping criticisms of the US. However, even Western states known as allies of the US joined in the discussions on these issues, as there were clearly human rights violations that fell under the Council's protection mandate. Finland (on behalf of the EU) took the neutral approach that, whilst they were 'committed to the fight against terrorism, human rights law has to be respected'.[195] Switzerland criticised renditions of detainees to countries where torture was not prohibited. It questioned the US employment of such tactics.[196] Many Western states, particularly Western European ones, were highly critical, outside of the Council, of US abuses in the 'war on terror'. The US approach that those violations were legitimate as part of an ongoing 'war' demonstrated its exceptionalism and unilateralism. US attempts to justify those violations struck at the heart of the universal rights enshrined at the UN. The US did not respond directly to Western interventions or questions on these issues, instead preferring to deal solely with comments by countries such as Iran and Venezuela which, by attacking rather than questioning the US, were easier to deal with.

The US belief that it should not be held to disproportionately higher scrutiny arguably ignored the fact that the Council encouraged each state to strive constantly to improve its own human rights record. Therefore, countries such as Sweden were necessarily held to higher standards than, for example, Somalia, because each state was judged with reference to its available resources and abilities and not against a common standard. This reflects a general UN approach, such as for example in Article 2 of the International Covenant on Economic, Social and Cultural Rights.[197] The US world position and long-term stance on human rights resulted in it being expected, by other states and the body itself, to attain the highest possible standards of human rights. Arguably, owing to the negative effect of US violations on the fundamental notions of human rights, abuses by that country were regarded by other states as at least as serious as many violations in countries with limited capacity for human rights protection, authoritarian rulers or bad governance.

Although this concept does not appear too controversial, the US was the sole Western state constantly to condemn the scrutiny necessitated by such a process. The apparent US hypocrisy on human rights did, perhaps, contribute to its complaints and reluctance to discuss its domestic human rights record. Moreover, those complaints gave strength to those who argued that

195 Finnish delegate, 2nd Session, 9 September 2006, in response to Leila Zerrougui, Working Group on the Situation of Detainees.
196 Swiss delegate, 2nd Session, 9 September 2006, in response to Leila Zerrougui, Working Group on the Situation of Detainees.
197 GA Res. 2200A (XXI), 'International Covenant on Economic, Social and Cultural Rights', 16 December 1966, UN Doc. A/6316, *entered into force* 3 January 1976.

the US feared examination of its own record. However, the Council and its members placed the US under far more scrutiny than any other Western state aside from Israel, thus legitimising its complaints about selectivity and bias at the body. While US violations did require the body's attention under its mandate, the disproportionate scrutiny not only contravened the founding principles, but also resulted in other, often graver, abuses not being dealt with.

The US international human rights record. The Council was frequently used by states wishing to attack the US regardless of whether a relevant discussion was occurring. Certain countries, such as Iran, had well-known political motivations. The fact that such comments were allowed, without other states objecting nor the Chairperson intervening, despite their nature or their irrelevance to proceedings, was a significant cause of the US withdrawal from the Council. Whilst these attacks may be partially explained by incidents occurring around the time they were made, the vehemence and regularity of interventions made by a range of states must have contributed to the US decision to withdraw.

Unsurprisingly, given the long-standing poor relationship between those states, Cuba most often used the Council to criticise the US. Cuba's comments rarely related to topics under discussion at the body, and these assertions were supported only by Cuba's allies or states maintaining equally strained relations with the US. During a discussion on torture, for example, Cuba alleged, without drawing any link to issues of torture, and without evidence, that the CIA was training and developing terrorist groups to attack Latin American countries, and that it was involved in plots to kill the Cuban head of state.[198] Venezuela, also out of context and without evidence, expressed similar allegations against the US, stressing that 'we denounce those that protect and foster terrorism, specifically our neighbour to the north – America'.[199] These countries both have a history of bad relations with the US, and this was by no means the first time either country had attacked the US within UN bodies. Both countries have socialist governments with directly opposing political and economic views to the US. Targeting the US at the Council gave Cuba and Venezuela the opportunity to indirectly attack that state's political system.

Again offering no evidence, Cuba accused the US of 'coordinating diplomatic campaigns [. . .] in the Human Rights Council', alleging that NGOs with accreditation to the body were under American control.[200] Cuba further attacked the US through allegations that it was undermining the Council. For example, saying 'to those who attack, namely the US, the Council, they must show humility. Those who make the Council fail will be criticised

---

198 Cuban delegate, 4th Session, 27 March 2007, in response to SR on Torture, Manfred Nowak.
199 Venezuelan delegate, 7th Session, 6 March 2008, during general discussions.
200 Cuban delegate, 4th Session, 29 March 2007, during the 'related debate'.

by history'.[201] Cuba's remarks during non US-related discussions included, for example, calling it the 'main sponsor of the brutal regime of [Israeli] occupation'.[202] It also used similar tactics to allege that the UK was an American puppet, saying that its remarks on Cuba were 'prepared by Washington'.[203] While such remarks were, presumably, afforded little weight by other countries at the Council, the constant repetition and vociferous nature of these comments made them difficult for anyone, the US included, to ignore.

Syria supported Cuba's attacks on a number of occasions, and alleged that the country-specific mandate on Cuba was politically motivated due to the US position towards Cuba.[204] Again, the alliance between these two countries in this regard is akin to the old adage that 'my enemy's enemy is my friend', itself a form of 'virtual' regionalism. Cuba accused the US of ongoing human rights violations against it, stating that 'the policy of hostility maintained by the USA has used coercive measures as a fundamental tool and has had a serious impact on Cuba. Humanitarian damage has occurred especially in areas of public health and education.'[205] DPRK (North Korea) also attacked the US during Council discussions. It alleged that the US sought to 'destroy' its 'socialist system' through 'hostile policies' and 'conspiracies with the EU and Japan'.[206] DPRK accused the US of human rights abuses, asserting that 'it is a well-known fact that the US is the worst human rights violator in the world',[207] asking that a Special Rapporteur be 'placed in the US'.[208] The Palestinian delegate made similar comments, asserting that the US itself was a grave abuser of human rights, dubiously echoing Churchill, in exclaiming, 'Americans will always only do the right thing after they have exhausted all other alternatives'.[209]

Just as interesting were the approaches taken by allies of, or countries with a more neutral position towards, the US. The positions taken towards the US by such countries, especially those bordering on attacks or those which failed to apply the founding principles to discussions on the US, must

201 Cuba's MFA Felipe Perez Roque, 7th Session, 3 March 2008, during the High Level Segment.
202 Cuban delegate, 4th Session, 22 March 2007, in response to SR on the Occupied Palestinian Territories, John Dugard.
203 Cuban delegate, 2nd Session, 21 September 2006, in response to SR on Freedom of Religion, Asma Jahangir, and Special Rapporteur on Freedom of Expression, Ambeyi Ligabo.
204 Syrian delegate, 5th Session, 12 June 2007, in response to SR on Cuba, Christine Chanet.
205 Cuban delegate, 6th Session, 17 September 2007, during discussion on Agenda Item 3 'Protection and Promotion of All Rights'.
206 DPRK delegate, 23 March 2007, 4th Session, in response to SR on DPRK, Vitit Muntarbhorn.
207 DPRK delegate, 7th Session, 6 March 2008, during general discussions.
208 *Ibid.*
209 Palestinian delegate, 4th Session, 22 March 2007, in response to SR on the OPT, John Dugard.

have played a part in its decision to quit the Council. The US may have become used to being one of the few dissenting voices during Council debates, often joined only by Canada and at times Australia and New Zealand, while other Western states equivocated. However, being left isolated or even attacked by its allies, especially regarding such issues that they failed to criticise other known abusers about, might have been the final straw for the US in terms of its engagement at that time with the Council.

The EU, one such ally of the US, abstained from many votes on controversial issues, and often maintained a neutral position during related Council discussions. The EU's collective stance arguably was motivated by fear of upsetting dominant regional groups that targeted the US. However, its stance could also be viewed as resulting from fear of upsetting the US, or indeed those EU members which supported US actions, despite the critical opinions of the human rights abuses. Although the EU did, at times, criticise the US on topics where it may have been expected to ally itself with, or at least refrain from attacking, the US, it used non-confrontational tactics to do so. The EU's prevailing attitude towards the mandate 'Protection of Human Rights Whilst Countering Terrorism' was critical of US tactics, such as extraordinary rendition and detention without trial. The EU did not attack the US *per se*, but rather used discussions with Special Rapporteurs, or other related debates, to highlight its concerns in this regard. The EU's collective stance during such debates at the Council was rather ironic considering the role of some of its members, including the UK, in the counter-terrorism tactics being discussed.

The EU's interventions were typically placid, which neutralised its obvious disagreement with certain US practices. For example, the EU emphasised that 'the US should refrain from bringing [detainees] to other countries', before suggesting that international tribunals be used in order to ensure such detainees' rights.[210] The collective position negotiated amongst EU members would have taken into account opinions of all member states. There were EU members who supported the US tactics, or indeed engaged with them. Other states were, however, highly critical of violations that eroded the core of Western notions and aims of human rights. Some EU states were, therefore, restrained in their criticisms of the US during Council sessions due to the need to maintain the bloc's collective position.

Switzerland was critical of the US, especially in terms of its 'war on terror', but followed the EU in the manner of its criticisms rather than attacking the US, as Cuba and others chose to do.[211] Switzerland's comments were less reserved than those of EU countries, and it often posed pointed questions to mandate holders and experts that made clear its position towards the US international human rights record.

---

210 Finnish delegate, 21 September 2006, 2nd Session, in response to Working Group on Situation of Detainees.
211 Swiss delegate, *ibid*.

Russia and China may both have a history of difficult relations with the US, but their interactions at the Council have remained friendlier than at other UN bodies. Whilst China was conspicuous in its failure to criticise the US, possibly due to its fear of having its own human rights record scrutinised, Russia did, at times, condemn the US during discussions of certain issues. On one such occasion, Russia accused a US delegate of 'arrogance [. . .] in the way he talked about human rights situations', alleging that 'the US ignores the United Nations human rights mechanisms, and even stops financing them'.[212] The Russian attack on this occasion, which included references to Guantanamo Bay and extraordinary rendition, despite that state's own poor record on torture, enforced disappearances and the like, suggested political motivations that might be attributable to Russia's desire to maintain favourable relations with OIC members.

In many ways, the Western states' criticisms, or failures to insist on even-handed treatment, of the US probably impacted more upon the US decision to remove itself from the Council than other countries' comments. The US must have become used to venomous and vociferous attacks at UN bodies from countries such as Cuba and Iran. However, despite the belief by many within the US of an international culture of anti-Americanism extending even to Europe,[213] criticism from its allies, or at least those states it has good relations with, must have stung the US considerably. Moreover, those states noticeably failed to call for proportionate treatment of the US during Council discussions. Whether these positions struck a raw nerve in terms of its own human rights record, or whether the US was merely reacting to selectivity and bias against it, such interventions presumably played a role in its decision to withdraw from the body.

In order to understand why these comments may have encouraged the US to disengage from the Council due to alienation rather than fear of scrutiny, the regularity and nature of these attacks must be examined. One example of a particularly venomous attack on the US occurred at the Fourth Session in response to the High Commissioner for Human Rights' report. Iran, during its right to reply, launched into the following diatribe:

> Iran wants to draw the Council's attention to the most phenomenal irony of our era. The United States has been condemned as the most notorious violator of human rights by peoples of the world. The occupation and unilateral invasion of Iraq in 2003 was an unlawful and illegitimate invasion and has not only led to the violation and killing of innocent people. The United States is not referring to the very bitter cases of the rape of innocent women [. . .] The American action had led to violations of the right to life, killings, it has caused misery and destruction [. . .]

212 Russian delegate, 6th Session, 24 September 2007, during general debate on Agenda Item 4.
213 McGoldrick, *Permanent International Criminal Court*, p. 444.

referring to raping Iraqi girls and killing of their family. The invasion is an arrogant adventure [. . .] the United Nations is now not as credible any more [. . .] The barbaric treatment of prisoners in Guantanamo, which is by human rights criteria perfectly beyond description [. . .] in prisons in Iraq the United States resorts to the same approach, although it has failed. The situation in Iraq shocks the world. It has not tried to remedy the victims [. . .] the operation transferring prisoners to force them to confess under pressure and torture has the most ridiculous justification as a war on terror.[214]

That excerpt, alongside the fact that it was not controversial at the Council for such comments to be made, emphasises the anti-US sentiment that had become commonplace during the Council's first two years. The strength of feeling against the US may have reflected the general mood at the UN, but only served to isolate and ostracise it at the HRC.

7.6. US election to the Council

US withdrawal underscored its frustration with the Council's repetition of its predecessor's selectivity, bias and politicisation. The election of President Obama inspired hope that the change in the US administration would bring a new attitude to the Council. Eric Sottas, Director of the International Organisation against Torture, argued that the withdrawal was actually a political gesture. He said that:

[the US] has always clearly shown its opposition to the Council. This is a slightly more public way of putting pressure on it in order to raise the stakes. [. . .] [I]t reminds me of the time when the Nixon administration, which backed Pinochet in Chile, chastised the UN for criticising the Chilean dictator. But when Carter was elected in 1977, the American government took the floor at the Human Rights Commission to ask forgiveness. After a presidency like that of Bush, you can expect some important changes in US policy on human rights.[215]

This opinion was reinforced by the US election to the Council in May 2009, which the State Department spoke of as being 'in keeping with the Obama Administration's "new era of engagement" with other nations'.[216]

After the Presidential elections, a bipartisan group of over 30 senior foreign policy figures called for President-elect Barack Obama to strengthen relations

---

214 Iranian delegate, 4th Session, 15 March 2007, during interactive dialogue with UNHCHR, Louise Arbour.

215 Doole, 'US quits Human Rights Council?'.

216 Iranian delegate, 4th Session, 15 March 2007, during interactive dialogue with UNHCHR, Louise Arbour.

with the United Nations,[217] specifically urging Washington to re-engage and indeed to become a member of the Human Rights Council. One article reported on this statement:

> The statement urges Washington to join the Geneva-based HRC, an agency that has been singled out for scorn by Bolton and other hawks in and outside the Bush administration, since it replaced the U.N. Human Rights Commission in 2006 due to the presence there of governments accused of serious human rights abuses. Like its Western allies, the statement said Washington should 'work to influence [the HRC] from within'.
>
> 'The HRC has drawn a tremendous amount of fire, and the fact that you've got all these people coming together and saying that the best way to effect change in the institution is to have a seat at the table is very powerful,' said PSA Director Matthew Rojansky, who helped draft the statement.[218]

Another article stated that although 'the Bush administration has distanced itself from the U.N. Human Rights Council [. . .] the experts suggested the United States should now actively seek a seat on the "faltering" council and work to influence the body from within'.[219] During the Presidential campaign, Obama's views were mixed:

> With new leadership in Washington committed to human rights standards in deed as well as in word, the United States will again have the moral authority to lead the world on human rights issues. The United States should seek to reform the UN Human Rights Council and help set it right. If the Council is to be made effective and credible, governments must make it such. We need our voice to be heard loud and clear to shine a light on the world's most repressive regimes, end the unfair obsession with Israel, and improve human rights policies around the globe.[220]

217 The statement's signatories included three former National Security Advisors, former secretaries of state Madeleine Albright and Warren Christopher, and former defence secretaries Harold Brown and William Perry, a range of Republicans, and three former UN ambassadors. It was published in a full-page advertisement carried by the *New York Times* on 20 November 2008.

218 J. Lobe, 'US: Obama Urged to Strengthen Ties with UN', *Inter Press Services*, 19 November 2008.

219 S. Pleming, 'US Foreign Policy Experts Give Obama UN Advice', *Reuters*, 19 November 2008.

220 United Nations Association of the USA, 'Better World Campaign, 2008 Presidential Candidate Questionnaire on US–UN Relations', (Online). Available HTTP: <http://www.globalproblems-globalsolutions-files.org/bwc_website/candidate_questionnaires/Obama-Response.pdf> (accessed 16 October 2012).

However, the President has also criticised the Council, not least for passing 'eight resolutions condemning Israel, a democracy with higher standards of human rights than its accusers'.[221] He further asserted that the body 'only with difficulty adopted resolutions pressing Sudan and Myanmar [. . .] [and] has dropped investigations into Belarus and Cuba for political reasons, and its method of reporting on human rights allows the Council's members to shield themselves from scrutiny'.[222] Appointment of Hillary Clinton as Secretary of State demonstrated the new administration's desire for re-engagement with the Council. Some commentators pointed to Clinton's support for the UN, usually reserving her criticisms for individual member states, saying that she made clear her disapproval of the 'Bush administration's policy of "standing aside and not fully engaging"' with the Council.[223] Clinton has expressed strong opinions regarding the US standing for election to the Council, saying:

> Human rights are an essential element of American global foreign policy [. . .] With others, we will engage in the work of improving the UN human rights system to advance the vision of the UN Declaration of Human Rights. The United States helped to found the United Nations and retains a vital stake in advancing that organization's genuine commitment to the human rights values that we share with other member nations. We believe every nation must live by and help shape global rules that ensure people enjoy the right to live freely and participate fully in their societies.[224]

US unilateralism under the George W. Bush administration was of such a level that observers find it difficult to imagine any way but up for the US relationship with the UN.[225] Indeed, such a shift is deemed necessary by some for the UN's success.[226] However, despite the change in administration, and thus the change in policy towards the Human Rights Council, the US decision to work towards such change from the inside did not negate its positions regarding the Council's flaws and weaknesses. The impact of its withdrawal on the Council's credibility was significant, and parallels can and will be drawn with the demise of the body's predecessor. US disengagement only served to strengthen the arguments of the body's critics that the Council failed to adequately fulfil its mandate and to overcome the politicisation and selectivity that had plagued the Commission.

---

221 J. Rovenger, 'ANALYSIS: Obama vs. McCain on U.S.–U.N. Relations', Citizens for Global Solutions, 15 June 2008.

222 *Ibid.*

223 A. Avery, 'Hillary Clinton and the UN: How She Might Approach the Role of Secretary of State', 26 November 2008.

224 U.S. Department of State, 'Announcement on U.S. seat on U.N. Human Rights Council'.

225 Weiss, *What's Wrong with the United Nations*, p. 129.

226 *Ibid.*, p. 131.

7.7. Summary

The US never fully supported the creation of the Human Rights Council. It argued that neither the body's form nor Resolution 60/251 were sufficiently radical to effectively protect and promote human rights. Despite not standing for membership, the US participated in the first seven sessions as a permanent observer, expressing views on almost all issues raised during discussions and debates. The US arguably played as important a role as member states in the shaping of the new body. Its opinions and interventions were often more extensive than many Council members, although the US did not have the power to vote at the body.

The US relationship with the Council demonstrates that, from the outset, problems arose in relation to the body's fulfilment of its mandate and adherence to its founding principles. Those problems did not only occur in relation to the Council's treatment of the US, but were also highlighted and emphasised by that state in relation to the body's general work and proceedings. Exploring US involvement with, and disengagement from, the Council has enabled a more general assessment of the Council's formative years, particularly whether, and to what extent, the Council fulfilled its mandate, adhered to its founding principles, and overcame the politicisation that beset its predecessor. I shall explore the conclusions that have been drawn under three broad assessment criteria.

7.7.1 *Mandate*

GA Resolution 60/251 mandates the Council, under Paragraph 3, to 'address situations of human rights violations'. The US itself, and its own human rights record, became the focus of various Council discussions and of individual states' comments during debates. The US cannot boast a flawless human rights record. During the two years of the Council's existence before its withdrawal, the US committed serious abuses both domestically and internationally. For example, the Human Rights Committee[227] highlighted the following categories of serious human rights abuses by the US during 2006: renditions and secret detentions,[228] torture and other abuses[229] particularly at Guantanamo Bay,[230] widespread and systematic racial discrimination,[231] torture and ill-treatment in jails and police custody,[232] ill-treatment of female

---

227 UN Human Rights Committee, 'Concluding Observations of the Human Rights Committee, United States of America', UN Doc. CCPR/C/USA/CO/3 (2006).
228 *Ibid.*, paras 12 and 16.
229 *Ibid.*, para. 13.
230 *Ibid.*, paras 14–15.
231 *Ibid.*, paras 22–26.
232 *Ibid.*, paras 30 and 32.

prisoners,[233] and the disproportionate use of the death penalty on ethnic minorities and low-income groups.[234] These, and other, issues of serious concern were justifiably looked into by national and international human rights institutions, as well as NGOs.[235] The US accepted such attention, despite the scrutiny and criticisms that it entailed. The Council sought to discharge its mandate through attempts to protect victims of various US human rights violations. In terms of violations committed during the 'war on terror', the Council justifiably sought to protect victims from US abuses.

The body fulfilled its roles and functions while seeking to discharge its protection mandate; for example enabling information sharing, providing a forum for dialogue, and working with non-state actors. Paragraph 3 requires the Council to provide recommendations on situations requiring protection. However, despite discussing some recommendations within these debates, the Council did not provide formal recommendations on US violations. Kälin *et al.* noted that recommendations should include advice, assistance, or encouragement, rather than simply condemning violations.[236] However, discussions on the US reflected the Commission's culture of naming, shaming and blaming, rather than seeking to provide constructive advice, support or dialogue.

Discussions on protecting victims from US violations heard various allegations and comments from a range of states, groups and blocs. Comments made by countries with poor relations with the US had less impact, both on the US and on the Council, than criticisms from Western states and other US allies. Statements made by US allies were more constructive and less vociferous than those made by states seeking to attack the US. Yet, more weight was afforded to Western states' comments because those countries were clearly motivated by human rights concerns rather than by overt and unrelated political objectives. The Western states' interventions condemning the US mainly focused on human rights violations occurring during the 'war on terror'. The US failed to respond adequately to allegations and questions regarding extraordinary renditions, torture, arbitrary detention, and other tactics used in countering terrorism. The US, like many states at the Council, frequently reacted defensively to any founded criticism of its human rights record, rarely addressing the concerns raised. However, the US position arguably resulted from it being regularly condemned by the body with little constructive guidance.

233 *Ibid.*, para. 33.

234 *Ibid.*, para. 29.

235 See also, Amnesty International, *Annual Report 2007*, London: Amnesty International, 2008.

236 W. Kälin, C. Jimenez, J. Künzli and M. Baldegger, 'The Human Rights Council and Country Situations: Framework, Challenges and Models', Study commissioned by the Swiss Ministry of Foreign Affairs, Geneva: Institute of Public Law, University of Bern, 2006, p. 16.

The protection mandate was misused in two crucial ways. Firstly, a number of states used the guise of protecting human rights to attack the US, making unfounded allegations of the commission of domestic and international human rights violations. I shall explore this further in relation to the body's adherence to its founding principles and the impact of politicisation on the Council. Secondly, disproportionate focus on protecting victims of US violations resulted in the body failing to fulfil its mandate to address other, graver situations. The Council's mandate to protect human rights requires, necessarily, a degree of proportionality and even-handedness in order to ensure that sufficient time and resources are devoted to the range of human rights abuses occurring across the world at any one time. Criticism of the US was justified by that state's human rights violations and the body's express mandate to protect human rights through discussions and actions aimed at ceasing ongoing abuses. However, the Council did go beyond its protection mandate by disproportionately scrutinising the US human rights record to the exclusion of other, graver, situations.

Arguably, the US would have tolerated mildly disproportionate emphasis on its human rights record had the Council proceeded more strongly on other grave situations such as Darfur, Burma or Zimbabwe. Instead, the Council spent little time discussing situations such as these. The Council's failure to talk about, let alone take action against, repressive regimes that systematically violated human rights, such as Libya or Saudi Arabia, only emphasised the disproportionate focus on the US. Arguably, US withdrawal was cemented when it seemed that the disproportionate focus on its human rights record, under the guise of human rights protection, would continue indefinitely.

7.7.2 *Founding principles*

The US repeatedly called for adherence to the Council's founding principles, particularly of non-selectivity, impartiality and lack of bias. Those principles were emphasised through Resolution 60/251, underscoring the central importance of such aims for the body to successfully fulfil its mandate and overcome its predecessor's failings. The US stressed the importance of these principles during all discussions, including debates about Council working methods, country-specific human rights situations, and individual rights and responsibilities. Its fears that the body would repeat the Commission's mistakes were reflected in its efforts to steer the Council away from such pitfalls.

US displeasure with the Council for scrutinising its human rights record was particularly apparent within discussions on thematic issues where the US had few problems. As an intergovernmental body consisting of member states representing all regions and most political systems, none other than the most orthodox functionalists could expect the Council to be wholly apolitical. However, that the founding principles had been all but ignored from the outset underscored the US position that the new body and its constituent document did not go far enough to ensure a more effective body than the Commission that it replaced.

The US was highly critical of the Council's selective and partial treatment of its human rights record. In particular, the US repeatedly raised the issue of the body's non-adherence to its founding principles in its treatment of Israel. Indeed, the Council's selectivity and bias were stronger in relation to Israel than any other state including the US. As already discussed, a main criticism of the Commission had been the amount of time and resources that were spent on Israel and the Occupied Palestinian Territories to the detriment of other grave human rights situations. The US swiftly noted that throughout the Council's formative years, the body's discussions, mechanisms and work were being used for those same biased ends. Despite regular statements and assertions to that effect, the Council ignored US calls for adherence to the body's founding principles in relation to its treatment of Israel. The OIC, and some of its allies, frequently violated the founding principles in order to ensure that the Council repeated the Commission's treatment of Israel.

Had the Council fulfilled early expectations and followed its own idealistic principles, rather than becoming a forum for states, groups and blocs to pursue political objectives, the US would not have faced the predicament that led to its withdrawal. The US might have tolerated closer scrutiny of its human rights record had the Council been even-handed in its approach towards other states and their national records, as this would have gone some way to fulfilling the body's stated aims.

7.7.3 *Politicisation*

The US relationship with the Council highlights the problems of politicisation that beset the body from its creation. Pursuit of national agendas by states began during discussions creating the Council. Indeed the US pursued its own objectives in trying to ensure that the Council was composed of liberal democracies, reflecting its own position on human rights issues. US attempts to wield power over the Council's creation was a typically realist attempt of that powerful state to promote its own national policies by seeking to exert influence over weaker countries during negotiations. Mirroring similar behaviour at other UN bodies in the 1970s, when the US realised its policies were not fully being advanced, it chose not to stand for election to the Council.

Many Council members had anti-West, and in particular anti-US, national policies. As domestic politics play a large role in setting the agenda, proceedings would naturally feature disproportionate attention focused on the US and its allies. Indeed, it could be argued that the common interest between many Council members was the desire to challenge US supremacy. That can be shown through the combined will of many different states with whom the US had poor relations, for example Cuba and Venezuela joining forces with Syria, Iran and DPRK, resulting in targeting of the US. Those common agendas served to create a politicised atmosphere within the Council which, perhaps, affected the work of the independent mandate holders.

The Council's targeting of the US, whilst couched in human rights language, can be viewed as an indicator of international relations at that time. Archer comments that even functionalist bodies are riddled with political disputes that often have little, if anything, to do with their work.[237] Council membership included a large number of countries particularly concerned with US foreign policy, especially in regard to the 'war on terror', and ongoing situations in Iraq and Afghanistan. Many Council members belonged to the OIC, a group of Islamic countries which held a particular interest in the ongoing tensions between America and many parts of the Middle East. The significant politicisation of the Council in these, and other, regards played a considerable role in the US decision to withdraw.

Power politics dominated Council discussions on the US, with weaker states seeking to exert influence over the US through alliances with other members and regional groups. Long-standing US enemies, such as Cuba, allied themselves with newly powerful blocs, such as the OIC, which held their own cross to bear against America. Regionalism played a large role with groups of states exerting collective strength that exceeded the sum of its parts in the ongoing power struggles at the Council. Typical US allies, especially EU states, often abstained from contentious proceedings and votes, either because of displeasure about US violations or due to fear of reprisals from the powerful groups. Those abstentions enabled the Council to continue its lack of even-handedness regarding the US. The Council's proceedings and work over its early years demonstrates the primary importance of interstate power struggles.

Alliances between states pursuing national agendas were a cause of the politicisation that plagued the Commission during its final years. Most of these states were non-democratic countries with poor national human rights records. US displeasure with the Council's membership rules displayed fears that, with membership open to such countries, the body would become as politicised as its predecessor. Indeed, many such states were elected to the new body. During its formative years, the Council proved to be biased and selective, with members blocking meaningful debate about grave situations due to regional alliances, as well as failing to adequately deal with many of the issues brought to its attention. Furthermore, there were human rights situations that not only dominated the Council's discussions but were focused on to the detriment of worse abuses elsewhere.

Schoenbaum argues that US human rights violations are held to higher scrutiny than worse abuses in other states because of US power, wealth and

---

237 C. Archer, *International Organizations*, London: George Allen & Unwin, 1983, pp. 85–6.

influence, and because the US sets standards for other nations.[238] Whilst it is, at times, necessary to scrutinise some countries more than others, especially where a crisis or ongoing human rights situation occurs, the disproportionate focus given by the Council to certain states, such as the US, was due to political rather than humanitarian motivations. Moreover, whilst it may be acceptable to hold different nations to different standards in view of their respective levels of available resources, the Council again used political motivations as the basis for deciding those standards. Double standards, apparent at the Council from the outset, served to reiterate the position that the UN 'singles out Western and pro-Western states for obloquy, while winking at far worse excesses committed by socialist and Third World nations'.[239] Unlike bodies such as the Human Rights Committee or organisations such as Amnesty International, the Council's credibility as an impartial body was severely lacking.

238 Schoenbaum, *International Relations*, p. 283.
239 T.M. Franck, 'Of Gnats and Camels: Is There a Double Standard at the United Nations?', *The American Journal of International Law*, Vol. 78 (4), 1984, 811.

8 The Council's inaction on Darfur

8.0. Introduction to chapter

This chapter explores the impact of politicisation in the Council within an ongoing, country-specific situation. In particular, it examines problems arising as a result of regionalism. Regionalism occurs at the UN where a group of interdependent states form a subgroup within that universal organisation.[1] Allied countries use group tactics in the pursuit of common agendas, to protect individual members, or to further national policies of individual states. The Commission was criticised for regional groups blocking action on gross and systemic human rights violations. Regionalism at the Commission resulted in various problems that significantly contributed to its demise. The Commission's failure to take action against states such as Zimbabwe and Libya, or its weakened stance against known abusers such as China, were at the heart of criticisms levelled at that body.[2]

Specific reforms were proposed directly aiming to combat regionalism at the Council. One example was Kofi Annan's recommendation that there be 18 Council members as opposed to the Commission's 53.[3] That proposal would have resulted in no regional groups having sufficient members at the Council to be able to affect proceedings through group tactics. Kälin and Jimenez assert that such a proposal, had it been implemented, would have enabled the Council to work more efficiently.[4] Despite various reform

---

1 K. Kaiser, 'The Interaction of Regional Subsystems. Some Preliminary Notes on Recurrent Patterns and the Role of Superpowers', *World Politics*, Vol. 21 (1), 1968, 86.

2 See, for example, L. Rahmani-Ocora, 'Giving the Emperor Real Clothes: The UN Human Rights Council', *Global Governance*, Vol. 12 (1), 2006, 15–20; R. Wheeler, 'The United Nations Commission on Human Rights, 1982–1997: A Study of "Targeted" Resolutions', *Canadian Journal of Political Science*, Vol. 32 (1), 1999, 75–6; H. Harris, 'The Politics of Depoliticization: International Perspectives on the Human Rights Council', *Human Rights Brief*, Vol. 13 (3), 2006.

3 GA, Report of the Secretary-General 'In Larger Freedom: Towards Development, Security and Human Rights for All', 21 March 2005, UN Doc. A/59/2005, para. 183.

4 W. Kälin and C. Jimenez, 'Reform of the UN Commission on Human Rights', Study Commissioned by the Swiss Ministry of Foreign Affairs (Political Division IV), Geneva: University of Bern, 30 August 2003, pp. 6–7.

proposals aimed at combating regionalism, few were taken up at the Council's creation, leaving the body open to regional tactics similar to those that had dominated the Commission.

The human rights situation in Darfur has been brought to the attention of the Council at each of its regular sessions. This chapter does not examine in detail the conflict in Darfur. There are many, broader studies on Darfur, including Totten,[5] who examines the human rights violations in that region and Hassan and Ray,[6] who give a more detailed history and analysis of the conflict. By 2009, the conflict in Darfur, which began in 2003, had displaced up to 3 million people and caused up to 300,000 people to die from the combined effects of war, famine and disease. Sudan is only party to five[7] of the ten core human rights treaties whose implementation is monitored by UN treaty bodies.[8] Three of those five treaty-based committees, which had jurisdiction to do so, reported on Sudan during the conflict: the Committee for the Elimination of Racial Discrimination,[9] the Human Rights Committee[10] and the Committee on the Rights of the Child.[11] Reference to the Committee reports will be compared with the Council's discussions. This will provide a benchmark for assessing the HRC as well as, more broadly, for exploring the relationship between the Council and other UN human rights bodies.

The three Committees that reported on Sudan are each concerned with a limited set of rights, although the Committees tend to construe their mandates broadly. As such, I shall also refer to Amnesty International's reports, which provide coverage of a broader range of human rights than the Committees. Amnesty International reports on a wide range of human rights concerns across the world, aiming at an even-handed and proportionate approach.[12] As with the Committees at the UN, Amnesty International provides perhaps the most accurate, unified human rights sources from within the NGO community. Amnesty International's report from the year of the Council's creation will be used to give an overview of the human rights situation in Darfur in 2006:

> A Darfur Peace Agreement negotiated in Abuja, Nigeria, was signed
> in May by the government and one faction of the opposition armed

5 S. Totten, *Genocide in Darfur: Investigating the Atrocities in the Sudan*, London: Routledge, 2006.

6 S.M. Hassan and C.E. Ray, *Darfur and the Crisis on Governance in Sudan*, Ithaca, NY: Cornell University Press, 2009.

7 CCPR; CESCR; CERD; CRC; and CED.

8 CCPR; CESCR; CERD; CEDAW; CAT; SPT; CRC; CMW; CRPD; and CED.

9 CERD, 'Situation in Darfur: Sudan', 18 August 2004, UN Doc. CERD/C/65/Dec.1.

10 UN Human Rights Committee, 'Concluding Observations of the Human Rights Committee: The Sudan', 29 August 2007, UN Doc. CCPR/C/SDN/CO/3.

11 UN Committee on the Rights of the Child, 'Concluding Observations, Sudan', 21 June 2007, UN Doc. CRC/C/OPSC/SDN/CO/1.

12 E. Heinze and R. Freedman, 'Public Awareness of Human Rights: Distortions in the Mass Media', *International Journal of Human Rights*, Vol. 14 (4), 2010, 497–8.

groups in Darfur, but conflict, displacement and killings increased. The government failed to disarm the armed militias known as the Janjawid, who continued to attack civilians in Darfur and launched cross-border raids into Chad. Hundreds of civilians were killed in Darfur and Chad, and some 300,000 more were displaced during the year, many of them repeatedly. Displaced people in Darfur and Darfuri refugees in Chad were unable to return to their villages because of the lack of security. In August government forces launched a major offensive in North Darfur and Jebel Marra, which was accompanied by Janjawid raids on villages and continued at the end of 2006. The air force frequently bombed civilians. The African Union Mission in Sudan (AMIS) was unable to stop killings, rapes and displacement of civilians or looting. Government security services arbitrarily detained suspected opponents incommunicado and for prolonged periods. Torture was widespread and in some areas, including Darfur, systematic. Human rights defenders and foreign humanitarian organizations were harassed. Freedom of expression was curtailed. The authorities forcibly evicted displaced people in poor areas of Khartoum and people in the Hamdab area where a dam was being built. Armed opposition groups also carried out human rights abuses.[13]

Those and other grave violations continued throughout the Council's formative years. Sudan's government claimed to cooperate with international organisations and peacekeeping efforts. However UN bodies, independent experts, and NGOs constantly documented the government's collusion, and indeed active participation, in gross and systemic human rights violations within Darfur.

In 2005 the UN Commission on Human Rights appointed Sima Samar[14] as Special Rapporteur on Sudan.[15] Samar has reported on the situation to the Council since its creation. Despite her efforts, and those of individual states during various debates, no progress has been made. NGOs with a broad range of mandates, including such politically diverse groups as Human Rights Watch (2008), Nord-Sud XXI,[16] and UN Watch,[17] documented the gross and systemic violations perpetrated by all parties to the conflict. The Council regularly discussed Darfur and did pass resolutions which called, albeit weakly,

13 Amnesty International, *Annual Report 2006*, London: Amnesty International, 2007, pp. 242–3.

14 Dr Sima Samar (Afghanistan) is a medical doctor, former Deputy President and Minister for Women's Affairs under Hamid Karzai in Afghanistan's interim government, and currently serves as Chairperson of the Afghanistan Independent Human Rights Commission.

15 Human Rights Commission, 2005, UN Doc. E/CN.4/RES/2005/82. This mandate was subsequently extended by the Human Rights Council, 2007, UN Doc. A/HRC/RES/6/34.

16 Nord-Sud XXI, 'Darfur', (Online). Available HTTP: <http://nordsud21.ch/Darfour.htm> (accessed 16 October 2012).

17 UN Watch, 'UN Watch Action on Darfur', (Online). Available HTTP: <http://www.unwatch.org/site/c.bdKKISNqEmG/b.2607541/k.5D6E/UN_Watch_Action_on_Darfur/apps/nl/newsletter3.asp> (accessed 16 October 2012).

for action from the Sudanese government, other parties to the conflict, the African Union, and UN organs. Qualified experts insisted that the Council's resolutions and recommendations be implemented, and yet action rarely materialised. Despite calling on other actors to protect and promote human rights, the Council itself failed to take steps to fulfil its own mandate. The Council only provided broad, general recommendations, owing in no small part to the African Group and OIC insistence that Sudan's government not be singled out for scrutiny or criticism. Moreover, the body frequently did not follow up on the implementation of its recommendations, and the facts on the ground showed little improvement.

The Council's inaction on Darfur exemplifies the impact of regionalism. Sudan had many allies at the Council owing to its membership of both the African Group and the OIC. As such, Sudan largely was shielded from scrutiny or was protected by its allies from criticism about the situation in Darfur. The Council's inaction similarly resulted from regional alliances dominating proceedings whenever that situation was raised.[18]

8.1. Background positions within the political and regional alliances

Regionalism occurs where states form alliances based on common characteristics. Russett identifies geographic proximity, social homogeneity, and political or economic interdependence, as being some of the main characteristics of regional alliances.[19] The UN, as a universal organisation, is divided into various subgroups based on regional alliances. Some states belong to more than one alliance, where they share characteristics with more than one group. Harris comments that the Commission's main regional groups reflected Cold War divisions between Western states pushing for liberal democratic rights, and Communist countries alongside developing nations, which promoted collective and social rights.[20] Many developing states allied themselves with Communist positions, adopting a post-Marxist discourse on the use of human rights as a neo-colonial tool of oppression. They claimed that former colonial countries sought to undermine developing states through demands for human rights implementation despite those countries lacking national capabilities for such compliance. That discourse insists that ex-colonial states have a duty to assist decolonised countries with capacity-building. Weiss argues that the main division is now between the North and South, terms he uses to differentiate between developing and developed nations.[21]

18 See, for example, P. Scannella and P. Splinter, 'The United Nations Human Rights Council: A Promise to be Fulfilled', *Human Rights Law Review*, Vol. 7 (1), 2007, 61–2.

19 M. Russett, *International Regions and the International System: A Study in Political Ecology*, Chicago, IL: Rand-McNally, 1967, p. 2.

20 Harris, 'The Politics of Depoliticization'.

21 T.G. Weiss, *What's Wrong with the United Nations and How to Fix It*, Cambridge: Polity Press, 2008, p. 49.

At the Human Rights Council, regional groups have dominated discussions on specific situations such as the situation in Darfur. The alliances are used, either expressly or tacitly, to coerce states from other regional groups into action or silence, undermining the Council's ability to intervene. Power politics enters the arena through use of collective strength to determine whether the Council takes action regarding a human rights situation.

The alliances' members followed different patterns during discussions on Sudan. Individual states from the OIC, Arab Group and African Group tended to make statements, even where they all but echoed that made by the Group's chair. Use of large numbers of similar statements emphasised both the strength as well as the political aims of those groups. The other main regional groups – the Asian Group, the Western European and Others Group, the Eastern European Group, and GRULAC – tended to allow their elected chair to speak on their behalf in discussions on Darfur, unless there was something specific which the individual member wished to add. Therefore, many discussions lacked balance owing to the large number of repetitive statements by members of the African Group and the OIC compared with other states and their alliances. There is no substantive gain to be made from such tactics beyond using the allocated Council time for that agenda item, thus preventing potential negative statements from countries not allied to those groups. This tactic could be blocked by creating a procedural rule preventing states from making pronouncements that substantially repeat points made by the regional group representative. Such reform would allow the Council to spend more time on different discussions, whilst also preventing collective weight being exerted through repetition.

8.1.1 *The African Group as a regional group*

Sudan is a member of the African Group, satisfying all five of Russett's criteria for group membership. Although not a member of the Human Rights Council, Sudan was protected by its African Group allies. Representatives of the Group, followed by representatives of individual African states, generally supported the Sudanese government. They insisted that Sudan was doing everything possible to curb violations and to bring perpetrators to justice.

The Group's repeated declarations of solidarity with Sudan were accompanied by calls for international assistance. The Group's tacit and explicit refusals to ascribe any state responsibility to Sudan hindered the Council's ability to take action. Those positions mirrored China's position in 1997 that ex-colonial Western states were duty-bound to assist promotion of human rights in developing nations rather than criticise violations.

Not only did the African Group as a whole stand up for Sudan, but the vast majority of its individual members took similar positions during discussions and votes, even to the point of promoting obviously untenable, and clearly politicised, positions. In March 2007, for example, during a discussion about the Council-mandated Mission to Sudan, which the government had blocked from entering the country, the Tunisian delegate stated, 'Sudan continues to express its readiness to cooperate with Council.'[22]

The African Group's reluctance about allowing action against one of its members could have been simply shielding an allied state from Council action. However, there are realist arguments as to why Sudan was protected by the Group and its members. Many African Group members had poor human rights records. Blocking action against Sudan arguably would represent a common interest of group members in ensuring that similar action was not taken regarding their own human rights situations. That theory is supported by the behaviour of African states with stronger democratic regimes, such as Botswana[23] and Zambia,[24] which often contradicted the group position and supported proposed action on Darfur. Other than those states directly harmed by the conflict,[25] the only instances of African states breaking regional alliances were countries with more democratic regimes, although such instances were rare and unpredictable.

8.1.2 The OIC as an alliance

Sudan, in addition to being an African Group member, also holds membership of the Organisation of the Islamic Conference. Sharing geographic proximity, religious ties, as well as others of Russett's criteria, Sudan was afforded protection by the most powerful group at the Council. The OIC is the largest alliance of states within the UN. It calls itself the 'collective voice

22 Oral intervention of Tunisian delegate, 4th Session, 16 March 2007.
23 According to the Human Rights Committee, for example, 'The Committee notes with satisfaction the strong democratic culture of the State party as well as the establishing of universal basic education, and its considerable achievements in addressing the challenges posed by the HIV/AIDS pandemic.' 'Concluding observations of the Human Rights Committee: Botswana', 24 April 2008, UN Doc. CCPR/C/BWA/CO/1; According to the Foreign and Commonwealth Office, 'Botswana has a generally good human rights record, consistent with its reputation for democratic and constitutional governance', Foreign and Commonwealth Office, 'Country Profile: Botswana', (Online). Available HTTP: <http://www.fco.gov.uk/en/about-the-fco/country-profiles/sub-saharan-africa/botswana/> (accessed 16 October 2012).
24 According to the Human Rights Committee, for example, 'The Committee welcomes the establishment [. . .] of the Zambian Human Rights Commission, with the mandate to promote and protect human rights', 'Concluding observations of the Human Rights Committee: Zambia', 23 July 2007, UN Doc. CCPR/C/ZMB/CO/3/CRP.1; According to the Foreign and Commonwealth Office, 'Human rights are improving in Zambia. Although never particularly bad by regional standards, there were repressive policies associated with UNIP's one-party rule, and in response to alleged attempts to overthrow both UNIP and MMD governments. President Mwanawasa has notably commuted the death sentences given to the 1997 coup plotters and indicated his opposition to judicial execution', Foreign and Commonwealth Office, 'Country Profile: Zambia', (Online). Available HTTP: <http://www.fco.gov.uk/en/about-the-fco/country-profiles/sub-saharan-africa/zambia> (accessed 16 October 2012).
25 Chadian delegate, 4th Special Session, 13 December 2006.

of the Muslim world'. All of its members are developing states or those from the Global South. In 2006, 17 Council states were OIC members. Three of them, Algeria, Saudi Arabia and Azerbaijan, respectively, chaired the regional groups for Africa, Asia, and Eastern Europe. Schrijver had identified it as one of the newer groups holding considerable power at the Commission. From the outset, the OIC was the dominant group at the Council.[26]

OIC members almost invariably aligned themselves with the African Group's opinion on Sudan. Abebe, a delegate from Ethiopia, commented that the African Group and the OIC formed a 'natural alliance' based on agreement on several major Council issues.[27] Both groups were comprised of developing states, many from the South, and institutionalists might point to their various common interests as a leading factor for that alliance.

Peggy Hicks, Global Advocacy Director of Human Rights Watch commented, 'The OIC's mantra has been that the council should work cooperatively with abusive governments rather than condemn them. Since states tend to fear the airing of their own dirty laundry, many have bought into this argument.'[28] The OIC's shielding of an allied state, alongside group members' apparent desire to protect their own actions from scrutiny, bears a marked resemblance to the likely reasons for the African Group's position. The OIC's dominance allowed it to employ stronger tactics than the African Group in protecting Sudan. When Sudan was brought to the Council's attention, the OIC, like the African Group, emphasised its collective position by using large numbers of similar statements by individual states.

The impact of this alliance was especially apparent in the juxtaposition between Asian states belonging to the OIC, which therefore gave regular statements supporting Sudan, and other members of the Asian Group which did not often support nor criticise the regime. Apparent lack of interest from other Asian states could have been due to fear of reprisals at the Council from OIC or African Group members as opposed to mere disregard for the ongoing situation in Darfur.

Members of the OIC often blocked the Council from taking action on Sudan, or significantly weakened the body's attempts to protect human rights in Darfur. The OIC frequently used discussions on Darfur to raise unrelated issues, thus diverting time and focus away from the region. Raising unrelated issues also allowed the OIC to further its own objectives, especially where it diverted attention away from the human rights situation in Darfur by shining a spotlight on abuses in, for example, Israel or the US.

26 N. Schrijver, 'The UN Human Rights Council: A New "Society of the Committed" or Just Old Wine in New Bottles', *Leiden Journal of International Law*, Vol. 20 (4), 2007, 809–23.

27 A.M. Abebe, 'Of Shaming and Bargaining: African States and the Universal Periodic Review of the United Nations Human Rights Council', *Human Rights Law Review*, Vol. 9 (1), 2009, 32–3.

28 P. Hicks, 'How to Put U.N. Rights Council Back on Track', *The Forward*, 3 November 2006.

8.1.3 The EU as a regional group

The EU contains states which were once, individually, major world powers, reflected in Britain and France holding permanent Security Council seats. As a group, the EU is recognised as a serious force across all interest areas. However, Weiss observes that the EU has failed adequately to address various military, political and economic issues.[29] Perhaps such a reticence is motivated by the EU and its members' relationships with the US, whose power in some areas the EU would be challenging. Others have argued that the reconfiguration of global power, particularly in relation to the rise of China, India and Brazil, primarily at the expense of Western states, is the reason for EU passivity at the Council.[30]

As Sudan has no regional ties with the EU, that group's positions on the situation in Darfur ought to have been objective. However, political factors at times inhibited the EU in making statements regarding Darfur. The EU generally avoided strong criticism of Sudan, reflecting its overall approach to Council proceedings. The EU did attempt to ensure cooperation of Sudan and of the African Group by seeking to negotiate agreements with that group on how to best protect and promote human rights in Darfur. Those negotiations resulted in the creation of a Group of Experts with an innovative mandate which was somewhat short-lived despite some successes on the ground. Whether the EU's moderate stance on Sudan was attributable to a desire for cooperation, or internal politics within that bloc, or even due to fears of reprisals from Sudan's allies, the EU was notable for its effective abstention from much of the discussion on Darfur. The EU, perhaps noting post-colonialist discourses on human rights, undoubtedly took a more benign and neutral approach to human rights abuses in decolonised states than it did towards violations elsewhere.

Positions taken by the EU as a regional group are, supposedly, guided by ethical policies.[31] However, Khaliq notes inconsistencies in EU member states' relationships with non-democracies,[32] giving examples of friendly relations with Saudi Arabia, China, Pakistan, and others, but not with Zimbabwe or Myanmar. The EU therefore uses a lack of democracy as a selective, ideological weapon rather than as a decisive factor for determining foreign policies.[33] This is of particular importance because grave human rights situations often occur within non-democratic states.

The EU seeks to find common ground between member states, requiring negotiation and compromise. This requirement is especially difficult regarding

---

29 Weiss, *What's Wrong with the United Nations*, p. 128.
30 See, for example, Abebe, 'Of Shaming and Bargaining', 21.
31 U. Khaliq, *Ethical Dimensions of the Foreign Policy of the European Union: A Legal Appraisal*, Cambridge: Cambridge University Press, 2008, pp. 54–7.
32 On EU practice see, more generally, R. Youngs, *The European Union and the Promotion of Democracy*, Oxford: Oxford University Press, 2001.
33 Khaliq, *Ethical Dimensions of the Foreign Policy of the European Union*, p. 71.

foreign policy as member states have different interests, allegiances, priorities, and preferences. Khaliq comments that the process by which members adopt a common position is rarely straightforward.[34] At the Council, often the EU's group statement is shown to be a compromise between members, as states subsequently make individual statements taking positions to one side or the other of the common position. The EU position, being the lowest common denominator, does not always reflect the nuanced positions taken by individual members.

An agreed position does carry significant weight, not only because it is made on behalf of all members, but also because the group contains 'heavyweight foreign policy players',[35] such as France, Germany and the United Kingdom. Khaliq argues that the collective weight of the EU is more than a sum of its members.[36] However, the EU has taken a passive role at the Council despite its collective influence, partly due to the internal difficulties in adopting a common position and the inability of members to deviate from that position within the Council or to negotiate and compromise with other groups or blocs. EU passivity on contentious issues, such as Sudan, seemingly reflects a trend whereby states and regional groups seek to avoid damaging relations with OIC members owing to that group's collective weight.

8.1.4 Other groups and alliances

Latin American and Caribbean (GRULAC) states did voice the need to deal with the crisis in Sudan, but in ways that were neither internally nor mutually consistent. During different debates, an individual state which had previously expressed support for Sudan may subsequently be found to be silent, or even to have criticised the regime. The GRULAC states also lacked uniformity in the positions taken within any given debate. There were some regional exceptions, notably Cuba, which always supported Sudan. The alliance between Cuba and the OIC is demonstrated by Cuba frequently supporting OIC positions. The OIC's approach towards the West, and in particular the US, made it a natural group for Cuba to ally itself with.

The Asian Group did not take a collective stance, reflecting that Group's general trend on issues not directly affecting regional agendas. Many Asian states have conflicting alliances to each other, with some allied to the West and other members of the OIC, NAM or the Like-Minded Group.

The only countries consistently condemning Sudan and the atrocities taking place in Darfur were those belonging to the Western Group, albeit with the EU taking a more moderate approach than states such as Canada and Australia. There were a few states that were undeterred by the OIC's

---

34 *Ibid.*, p. 88.
35 *Ibid.*, p. 89.
36 *Ibid.*, p. 270.

tactics. Canada, the Netherlands, the United Kingdom, and Switzerland,[37] among others, were notable for both their condemnation of the situation in Darfur and their calls for action. Members of the Asian Group and GRULAC, and at times the EU, often remained silent or even deferred to the OIC's position in discussions, wishing to appear neutral rather than offend the OIC. Hicks, perhaps unduly idealistic about the repercussions of states' positions in the Council, strongly criticised the docility of such states towards the OIC, saying that these countries:

> [. . .] need to know that if they side with the Pakistans [*sic*] and Algerias [*sic*] [respectively chairs of the OIC and African Group at this time] of the Council to block efforts to address situations like Darfur, their conduct in Geneva will be made known, and they will pay a price both back home and in their international reputation.[38]

States appeared somewhat more concerned with the power and influence of OIC states within the Council, and their ability to use proceedings to raise political agendas attacking other states, than with any national or international repercussions for their positions on the situation in Darfur.

8.2. Council sessions' dealings on Darfur

The regional groups and political blocs have been explored in the abstract; it remains to be seen what occurs, in practice, when the groups interact at the Council. Positions taken by states, groups and blocs will be used to illustrate the impact of regionalism on the body's discussions and action on Darfur. The early sessions on Darfur demonstrate a trend for inaction that continued throughout the Council's work. The discussions focused less on Darfur from the Eighth Session onwards, with only the Ninth,[39] Eleventh[40] and Fifteenth[41] Sessions passing resolutions or decisions on the situation. Politicisation of early proceedings on Darfur arguably contributed to the situation later receiving less attention, alongside increasing pressures on the Council to deal with other situations.

A number of resolutions and decisions were passed on Darfur, many including recommendations to improve the situation. The African Group and the OIC ensured, through negotiations on the texts, that these contained

---

37 Switzerland joined the United Nations in 2002, thus allowing it to become a member of UN bodies.

38 Hicks, 'How to Put U.N. Rights Council Back on Track'.

39 HRC Res. 9/17, 'Situation of Human Rights in the Sudan', 18 September 2008, UN Doc. A/HRC/RES/9/17.

40 HRC Res. 11/10, 'Situation of Human Rights in the Sudan', 18 June 2009, UN Doc. A/HRC/RES/11/10.

41 HRC Res. 15/27, 'Situation of Human Rights in the Sudan', 7 October 2010, A/HRC/RES/15/27.

weaker language than the Western states would have preferred. The weakened language prevailed as states threatened to vote against strongly worded drafts. Such tactics affected, and at times altogether negated, the impact of these resolutions and decisions on the ground. This point was repeatedly made by individual states, as well as the Special Rapporteur on Sudan, when calling for recommendations to be implemented. A number of factors contributed to the lack of change in Darfur, not least the Sudanese government's unwillingness to allow UN forces to operate within Darfur, a matter in which the African Group and OIC colluded by blocking Council efforts to encourage or coerce the government to do so. A main motive for blocking these efforts lay, at least to some degree, in African countries' fears that such methods could be deployed in dealing with human rights abuses in other states.

An important aspect of proceedings on Darfur is the process of fact-finding employed by the Human Rights Council. Special Procedures mandate holders are tasked with carrying out fact-finding on the Council's behalf. For Darfur, the Council appointed, individual expert, Sima Samar to establish the facts regarding violations. The Special Rapporteur, in conjunction with the Office of the High Commissioner for Human Rights, was tasked with compiling reports, and delivering them to the Council during its sessions. Various missions were also sent by the Council to Sudan to ascertain the human rights situation in Darfur and to report their findings.

A main problem in fact-finding is where a country refuses entry to Council-appointed experts, as has occurred in, amongst others, Israel, Myanmar, and Sudan. Another common problem, which frequently arose during discussions on Darfur, is how to determine the facts when a state disputes the reports delivered to the Council. This method was employed not only by Sudan, but also by that state's allies in the African Group and the OIC. One solution would be to create an assumption that where a state refuses entry to a fact-finding mission without valid reason, that mission's report will be given greater weight than the concerned state's assertions. This would encourage cooperation with mandate holders and stop states from circumventing Council investigations.

8.2.1 The Second Session

The Second Session[42] opened with the UN Secretary-General Kofi Annan[43] and the High Commissioner for Human Rights Louise Arbour both drawing attention to Darfur. Both speakers emphasised the grave violations occurring within that region. Arbour spoke about the further deterioration of the

---

42 2nd Session, 18 September–6 October 2006 (first part), 27–29 November 2006 (resumed).

43 'You [the Council] were rightly concerned with the situation in the Middle East, I feel confident that you will draw the same attention to other situations. At this time, I feel I must draw your attention on issue on Darfur', Kofi Annan UN Secretary-General, 2nd Session, 18 September 2006.

humanitarian situation despite the Darfur Peace Agreement.[44] She noted Sudan's refusal to allow UN peacekeeping troops into the region, and the insufficient mechanisms for dealing with violations.[45] The inclusion of Darfur in these speeches set the tone for the session, with a number of mandate holders' reports raising concerns about the region. Walter Kälin, the Special Representative of the Secretary-General on Human Rights of Internally Displaced Persons, expressed 'grave concerns', especially with regard to the internally displaced persons hoping to return to Darfur.[46] Yakin Ertuk, the Special Rapporteur on Violence Against Women discussed the lack of improvement[47] since the Comprehensive Peace Agreement (CPA) of 2005.[48] Jean Ziegler, the Special Rapporteur on the Right to Food, spoke about the 'millions of displaced people [in Western Sudan and Darfur who were] seriously and constantly undernourished'.[49] Radhika Coomaraswamy, the Special Rapporteur on Children in Armed Conflict expressed concern about violations of children's rights, especially with regard to non-state actors, closely associated with the state, who recruit children.[50] These mandate holders' focus on Sudan highlights the ongoing gross and systemic violations and also demonstrates the strength and importance of the Council's information sharing function.

44 Negotiated in Abuja, Nigeria in May 2006 and signed by the government and one faction of the opposition armed groups. Amnesty International reported, 'A Darfur Peace Agreement (DPA) was signed in May by the government and one faction of the Sudan Liberation Army (SLA) led by Minni Minawi. Other armed opposition groups, including the SLA and the Justice and Equality Movement, refused to sign. Most displaced people opposed the agreement, which was felt to lack guarantees for safe return and compensation. In demonstrations which turned into riots in many camps for the displaced, there were deaths, including of police officers, and numerous arrests. Some individuals and groups later signed the peace agreement. Under the DPA's terms, Minni Minawi was appointed Senior Assistant to the President.' *Annual Report 2006*, pp. 273–4.

45 'In light of the continued failure or willingness [of the Sudanese government] to hold perpetrators to account, states must give support to the International Criminal Court and remind Sudan that its cooperation is not optional, it is a Chapter 7 decision of the Security Council.' UNHCHR, Louise Arbour, 2nd Session, 18 September 2006.

46 Oral intervention of SR on Internally Displaced Persons, Walter Kälin, 2nd Session, 19 September 2006. These concerns are reflected by Amnesty International, which reported, 'On 16 August, without prior warning, bulldozers began to demolish homes in Dar al-Salam, an IDP settlement 43km south of Khartoum housing some 12,000 internally displaced persons. Many had fled droughts and famine in Darfur in the 1980s. Armed police and Special Forces used violence and tear gas against residents, and carried out arrests. Four people died, including a child, and many were injured.' *Annual Report 2006*, p. 245.

47 Oral intervention of Yakin Ertuk, 2nd Session, 20 September 2006. This can be evidenced in Amnesty International reporting, for example, 'Janjawid accompanying the armed forces offensive in North Darfur in September captured five girls and women aged between 13 and 23 in the village of Tarmakera, south of Kulkul. They were reportedly raped and severely beaten before being released the following day.' *Annual Report 2006*, p. 244.

48 The Comprehensive Peace Agreement 2005 between the government and the Sudan People's Liberation Army.

49 Oral intervention of Jean Ziegler, 2nd Session, 22 September 2006.

50 Oral intervention of Radhika Coomaraswamy, 2nd Session, 29 September 2006.

Owing to the gravity of the situation, the Council heard a report from Sima Samar. Her report covered three missions to Sudan that had been conducted during 2005 and 2006. Despite the Interim National Constitution[51] and the CPA creating a framework for human rights, Samar observed, 'the government has failed in its responsibility to protect its civilians'.[52] According to Samar, rape and sexual violence were continuing in Darfur, and 'the authorities have often failed to bring the perpetrators to justice'.[53] Her recommendations included investigation of violations, government cooperation with the International Criminal Court, protection of civilians by the African Union mission, and for the international community to support human rights facilities and inclusive dialogue.

8.2.1.1 Sudan

Sudan always exercised its right of reply at the Council. The state representative put forward the government's position, mostly a propaganda exercise. He argued, for example: 'The policy of the Sudanese government is to offer unlimited cooperation with institutions of the international community and with human rights institutions.'[54] The comments also included Sudan asking for assistance, for example, 'We need support, especially financial support, from the international community. We would require 200 billion dollars to settle the problem in Darfur.'[55] Sudan's statement seemingly perverted the otherwise legitimate link between resources and human rights by insisting that financial assistance was required for the violations to cease.

The Sudanese delegate questioned the legitimacy of mandate holders' reports, stating, 'the Special Rapporteur said that regarding Sudan you relied on reliable information. What kind of information is that? Why does the [Sudanese] government not have this information?'[56] Sudan further questioned the motives of the international focus on Darfur:

> In Sudan there are many investigators from human rights institutions, especially in Darfur [. . .] There are many reports on this within the UN framework [. . .] I leave it to you to understand the real motivation

---

51 A transitional legal framework entered into in July 2005, after the CPA ended decades of conflict between Khartoum and Southern Sudan. The Interim National Constitution changed the legal and governance system in Sudan, as well as providing a comprehensive Bill of Rights.

52 Oral intervention of Sima Samar, 2nd Session, 27 September 2006.

53 *Ibid.*

54 Sudanese delegate, 2nd Session, 27 September 2006, in response to Samar, Special Rapporteur on Sudan.

55 Sudanese delegate, 2nd Session, 18 September 2006, in response to UNHCHR, Louise Arbour.

56 Sudanese delegate, 2nd Session, 20 September 2006, in response to Ertuk, Special Rapporteur on Violence Against Women.

of some states to continuously put pressure on Sudan [. . .] This is just making the situation more difficult for the victims.[57]

It also reminded the Council of the body's founding principles and the need for impartiality, saying 'the Human Rights Council should have no politicisation [. . .] selectivity [. . .] or double standards'.[58] Taken at face value, Sudan's comments appear in line with the idealist language under-pinning the Council's creation. Similar comments were repeated throughout the sessions, with calls for non-politicisation being used as a defence against the Council's attempts to protect and promote human rights in Darfur. How-ever, Sudan's objections were unsubstantiated, and it failed to identify unrelated political agendas regarding the international focus on Darfur. Rather, the focus on that region resulted from the widespread and systematic human rights violations including rapes, killings, violence and displacement of civilians.

The situation in Darfur arguably constituted one of the gravest human rights situations[59] during the Council's formative years, thus necessitating more attention and resources than other situations in, for example, Myanmar, Israel, or Sri Lanka.[60] Indeed, the situation has been identified by many as a genocide.[61] In July 2010, the International Criminal Court issued a second arrest warrant for Sudan's President, Omar Al-Bashir, adding genocide to its original list of charges for crimes allegedly committed in Darfur.[62] Sudan's claims of selectivity and politicisation were arguably nothing more than that state's attempt to deflect attention from its gross and systemic violations.

8.2.1.2 The African Group

Algeria (speaking on behalf of the African Group) pointed out that Samar's report had been written six months before the Peace Agreement of June 2006, since which time improvements had occurred, a point which it felt Samar had unfairly overlooked. However, Algeria's assertion that the Sudanese

---

57 Sudanese delegate, 2nd Session, 27 September 2006.
58 *Ibid.*
59 In 2005, the Security Council-appointed Commission of Inquiry on Darfur emphasised that its conclusion that genocide was not occurring in the region 'should not be taken in any way as detracting from the gravity of the crimes perpetrated in that region. Inter-national offences such as the crimes against humanity and war crimes that have been committed in Darfur may be no less serious and heinous than genocide', 'Report of the International Commission of Inquiry on Darfur to the United Nations Secretary-General', 25 January 2005, Part II, p. 4 (Online). Available HTTP: <http://www.un.org/News/dh/sudan/com_inq_darfur.pdf> (accessed 25 June 2012).
60 All of which also received Council attention through various mechanisms, including agenda items, resolutions, fact-finding missions and special sessions.
61 E. Sanders, 'Is the Darfur Bloodshed Genocide? Opinions Differ', *LA Times*, 4 May 2009.
62 International Criminal Court Second Warrant of Arrest for Omar Hassan Ahmad Al Bashir, in the case of *The Prosecutor v. Omar Hassan Ahmad Al Bashir* (*'Omar Al Bashir'*), 12 July 2010, ICC-02/05-01/09.

government was dealing with, rather than contributing to, the human rights situation contradicted the Amnesty International *Annual Reports 2006* at that time, that merely a month prior to this Council session, government-backed attacks had occurred in the region.[63] Algeria nevertheless insisted that Council action should be limited to material and institutional support: 'The international community at large, and donor countries in particular, [must] provide financial and technical assistance to Sudan.'[64]

Those positions were typical of the African Group's support for Sudan; that group frequently sought to undermine the Council's information sharing function and often called for Sudan to receive solely material and technical assistance. The African Group adopted a post-Marxist approach, reflecting post-colonialist theories which argue that developing states should not be criticised for human right abuses by ex-colonial countries, but rather assisted in creating mechanisms to protect and promote human rights. This assertion, combined with developing states' dominance at the Council, enables countries to use post-Marxist discourses to avoid scrutiny and criticism even where there are gross and systemic violations.

8.2.1.3 The OIC

Pakistan (OIC) expressly associated itself with the African Group's statement on 27 September 2006. It reiterated that the groundwork had been built for the implementation of human rights in Darfur as well as 'commend[ing] the Sudanese government for its efforts [. . .] and for its international cooperation'.[65] The OIC called on the international community to assist the Sudanese government, stating that, 'justice and human rights should be absolute priorities [. . .] We have to support this [. . .] to strengthen the Sudanese government [. . .] and provide moral support and technical assistance.'[66] The OIC's support for the Sudanese government's efforts[67] can be contrasted with Amnesty International's reports of government offensives at this time.[68] That

---

63 'In August government forces launched a major offensive in North Darfur and Jebel Marra, which was accompanied by Janjawid raids on villages.' Amnesty International, *Annual Report 2006*, p. 242.

64 Algerian delegate, 2nd Session, 27 September 2006, in response to Samar, Special Rapporteur on Sudan.

65 Pakistani delegate, 2nd Session, 27 September 2006, in response to Samar, Special Rapporteur on Sudan.

66 *Ibid.*

67 'The Government does its part to achieve reconciliation [. . .] It is a nightmare to disarm people in Darfur because there are so many small arms. [. . .] Sudan also cooperates with the Security Council [. . .] All parties must come to the negotiation table like the Special Rapporteur suggests', Pakistani delegate, 2nd Session, 27 September 2006, in response to Samar, Special Rapporteur on Sudan.

68 'After a massive troop build-up in Darfur in August, the government launched an offensive against areas controlled by those groups in North Darfur and Jebel Marra. Government aircraft indiscriminately or directly bombed civilians.' Amnesty International, *Annual Report 2006*, p. 244.

group, with its various cultural, regional and religious ties to Sudan, advanced national agendas, including self-protection of members with similar dubious records, through its support of Sudan.

8.2.1.4 The EU

The EU's position was markedly different to the African Group and OIC, especially in how it viewed the Sudanese government's role in the conflict. For example, in response to the High Commissioner, the EU said that it was 'alarmed by the new fighting in Darfur, especially the systematic bombings of villages. It is the responsibility of the government to protect its own citizens and to hold perpetrators accountable [. . .] Do not forget the lessons learned in Rwanda.'[69]

A similar position was repeated when Finland (EU) expressed 'strong support for Ms Sima Samar's mandate' and asked for her opinion on the best way to protect civilians. Finland noted Samar's warning that further deterioration would be likely if steps were not taken. Finland claimed that Samar's 'fears have become reality'. The EU, seemingly ignoring the political realities and adopting a social constructivist approach, emphasised that 'the Human Rights Council cannot remain silent about the killings and violations in Darfur'.[70]

8.2.1.5 Canada

Whilst Canada acknowledged the government's efforts, it spoke at greater length of the increase in violence and the need for international intervention. Canada expressed its concerns in a Joint Statement:

> we are deeply concerned about the situation in Sudan [. . .] some two million people have been displaced [. . .] We welcome the efforts of the UN, the EU and the government of Sudan [. . .] Despite the Peace Agreement, there is more and more violence, also towards aid workers. We call on all parties to immediately cease violence towards civilians and aid workers and to enable the UN mission in Darfur.[71]

Canada questioned the most effective ways for assistance to be provided to the civilians in Darfur, for example asking whether the High Commissioner thought that 'monitoring the situation [in Darfur] makes a difference?' as

---

69 Finnish delegate, 2nd Session, 18 September 2006, in response to UNHCHR, Louise Arbour.
70 Finnish delegate, 2nd Session, 27 September 2006, in response to Samar, Special Rapporteur on Sudan.
71 Joint statement on behalf of Canada, Australia and New Zealand, 2nd Session, 27 September 2006, in response to Samar, Special Rapporteur on Sudan.

well as questioning whether 'there is anything the Council can do to assist you in this regard?'[72]

Canada voiced concerns about protection of women in the region, saying, 'Canada sees that there is an increase in violence, despite of the peace agreement [. . .] Internally displaced women are particularly vulnerable [. . .] Sudanese police failed to act with due diligence.'[73] Canada asked Samar 'how can the OHCHR and international community assist Sudan to protect women?'[74]

8.2.1.6 *Other states*

Whilst many states spoke about Sudan, one country's comments on the situation were unique. China spoke of the challenges presented by poverty which, in its opinion, significantly contributed to the human rights situation within Sudan[75] before praising the government's 'efforts to protect and promote human rights'.

Towards the end of the session, the President postponed all proposed resolutions and decisions owing to delay caused by informal consultations. It is interesting to note that whilst members of GRULAC had remained somewhat passive during the discussions on Sudan, several of these same states criticised the Council for not taking any substantive decisions, especially in relation to Darfur. Those countries expressed disappointment about the Council's failure to fulfil its protection and promotion mandates in relation to Darfur. For example, Uruguay pointed out that 'any gap on substantive issues is a lack of protection for victims'.[76]

8.2.1.7 *Decision on Darfur*

The Second Session produced a Decision on Darfur[77] which called on all parties to sign and adhere to the Darfur Peace Agreement[78] and to cease violations of international humanitarian law.[79] It reminded the international community of its obligations, calling on states to honour their promises of assistance.

---

72 Canadian delegate, 2nd Session, 18 September 2006, in response to UNHCHR, Louise Arbour.
73 Canadian delegate, 2nd Session, 27 September 2006, in response to Samar, Special Rapporteur on Sudan.
74 *Ibid.*
75 'Sudan is [. . .] struggling with poverty and diseases. The Council should take into account the special difficulties which the government of Sudan faces.' Chinese delegate, 2nd Session, 27 September 2006, in response to Samar, Special Rapporteur on Sudan.
76 Uruguay delegate, 2nd Session, 6 October 2006, general discussion on other issues, initiatives, and decisions.
77 Human Rights Council Decision 2/115, 'Darfur', 28 November 2006, UN Doc. A/HRC/DEC/2/115.
78 Darfur Peace Agreement signed in Abuja.
79 Human Rights Council, Decision 2/115, 'Darfur', UN Doc.A/HRC/DEC/2/115, para. 2.

The decision repeatedly stressed the need for 'all parties' to uphold general human rights obligations, mentioning women, children and internally displaced persons[80] but without reference to specific violations or obligations. This text can be compared with the Human Rights Committee's report on Sudan,[81] which highlighted specific rights that were violated and indicated how the government should ensure compliance with its obligations regarding those rights.

After weeks of delay owing to informal consultations,[82] the draft Decision[83] was presented by Algeria (African Group).[84] The EU proposed revisions in a separate Draft,[85] with the apparent intention to strengthen the text. One difference was whether 'the' or 'a' should precede 'report' in the text of the Decision, which would determine whether to require a specific follow-up report. The African Group deemed this 'extremely sensitive', saying 'one of the reasons why the Commission was not successful was because of the naming and shaming [of states]',[86] reflecting the language of criticisms levelled at country-specific discussions at the Council's predecessor. The African Group insisted that this issue directly related to the founding principle of non-selectivity. The African Group strenuously disagreed with the EU's position that the 'situation of Darfur really requires special reporting'.[87]

That difference of opinion on a seemingly technical matter actually struck at the heart of the issue of how the Council would attempt to avoid the pitfalls of its predecessor; that is, the issue of whether country-specific focus could – or even should – occur in certain circumstances. Whilst it was agreed that the Council should generally avoid politicisation and selectivity, the question was whether this should apply during a humanitarian crisis such as the one in Darfur. African Group members demonstrated a disregard for the founding principles by seeking to use them to divert attention away from human rights violations.

The EU also raised substantive issues, especially in relation to impunity. It argued that nothing would change through monitoring, and that the text needed to include places of detention for perpetrators. Canada voiced support for the proposed amendments, stating that, whilst Algeria's efforts were appreciated, they 'fail[ed] to address essential issues'. Some states supported Canada's

80 *Ibid.*, para. 2.
81 UN Human Rights Committee, 'Concluding Observations of the Human Rights Committee: The Sudan', UN Doc. CCPR/C/SDN/CO/3.
82 Despite ongoing escalation of violence in Darfur at this time, as reported by Amnesty International, for example, 'In November at least 50 civilians were killed, including 21 children under 10, when Janjawid attacked eight villages and an IDP camp in Jebel Moon in West Darfur. AMIS forces arrived the day after the attack.' *Annual Report 2006*, p. 244.
83 Human Rights Council, Draft Decision 2/L.44, 'Darfur', 28 November 2006, UN Doc. A/HRC/2/L.44.
84 Algerian delegate, 2nd Session, 28 November 2006.
85 HRC, 'Amendment to decision L.44 entitled "Darfur"', 28 November 2006, UN Doc. A/HRC/2/L.48.
86 Algerian delegate, 2nd Session, 28 November 2006.
87 Finnish delegate, 2nd Session, 28 November 2006.

position that 'people in Darfur should not wait for another six months until the Council meets again'.[88] However, the African Group did not share the concern that the situation in Darfur was deteriorating, instead the Group spoke about recent 'positive developments' in the region.

The EU expressed 'deep disappointment'[89] at the defeat of its proposed amendments, asserting that the draft resolution did not adequately address the deteriorating situation. The UK expanded on this statement, saying 'it is hard to imagine a situation where it would be more appropriate for the Council to act'. Despite hopes that the Council would take action where the Commission had failed to do so, inaction had prevailed through regionalism.

8.2.2 *The Third Session*

The Third Session[90] opened with the High Commissioner's overview of missions. She spoke of the crisis in Darfur, noting that it had 'spilled over'[91] into Chad and Central African Republic,[92] and that attacks on villages, killings, displacement and rape had continued,[93] with up to two million people now displaced, alongside other 'horrific levels of violations'.[94] The High Commissioner, relying on information provided by the OHCHR about attacks by government-sponsored militia, reported that up to four million people were in need of aid, urging the international community to ensure cessation of human rights violations.

The session heard calls for a Special Session to be convened on Darfur, primarily from Western and GRULAC States.[95] It was later announced[96] that the Special Session on Darfur would occur immediately after the Third Session. Discussions focused on the need for the Special Session and the way it would be conducted.

88 Canadian delegate, 2nd Session, 28 November 2006.

89 Finnish delegate, 2nd Session, 28 November 2006.

90 29 November–8 December 2006.

91 Oral intervention of UNHCHR, Louise Arbour, 3rd Session, 29 November 2006.

92 An escalation reported by Amnesty International, 'Attacks across the border resumed in October, in which some 500 civilians were unlawfully killed, many more were raped, thousands were driven from their homes, and villages were destroyed', *Annual Report 2006*, p. 244.

93 For example, Amnesty International reported, 'In November at least 50 civilians were killed, including 21 children under 10, when Janjawid attacked eight villages and an IDP camp in Jebel Moon in West Darfur. AMIS forces arrived the day after the attack. The Governor of West Darfur promised an inquiry but no findings had been made public by the end of 2006', *Annual Report 2006*, p. 244.

94 'The Chief Prosecutor said [at this time] that the office had documented killings and massacres and there is a lot of information indicating deaths, destruction of food stocks and livestock which has deprived citizens of their means of survival', Louise Arbour, High Commissioner for Human Rights, 3rd Session, 29 November 2006.

95 Including; the Netherlands, Ecuador, Poland, Australia, Chile, Sweden, and Norway, 29 November 2006.

96 Oral statement of HRC President, Luis Alfonso de Alba (Mexico), 3rd Session, 30 November 2006.

8.2.2.1 *Sudan*

Sudan's response to the High Commissioner's report followed similar patterns to its comments in the previous session. Sudan dismissed the Council's information sharing function, alleging that there was an 'intentional campaign to offer false information on the situation',[97] and that the 'Resolution of the Council was based on false information'.[98] Sudan further emphasised this by saying 'there are repeated attempts to spread false information in regard to rape [. . .] it was said that dozens of cases took place [. . .] we proved that rumours spread by some NGOs are not true'.[99] Having made such accusations, Sudan invited 'the High Commissioner and the OHCHR to come to Darfur to see what the situation looks like'.[100]

Sudan again insisted that focus on Darfur was caused by politicisation and selectivity. During discussions regarding a Special Session on Darfur, Sudan alleged that it was being singled out and treated unfairly, for example saying 'there are violations in many parts of the world . . . the question of Darfur is different to other situations, because it is highly and heavily politicised [. . .] we were not able to change this'.[101]

Sudan's attempts to present a positive image included assuring the Council that the '[peace] agreement has led to very positive developments',[102] and asserting that 'those responsible [for attacks] are those who have not signed the peace agreement'.[103] Sudan again showed its ties with the African Union, saying:

> The African Union has stated, and it is the most credible, that the security situation has improved [. . .] [there have been] improved levels of nutrition [. . .] internally displaced persons have better access to water than others in Darfur [. . .] [there has been] improvement in the rates of child deaths [. . .]. [and has been] tribal reconciliation.[104]

This information, again, contradicted independent NGO reports from this time.[105]

---

97 Sudanese delegate, 3rd Session, 29 November 2006, in response to UNHCHR, Louise Arbour.
98 *Ibid.*
99 *Ibid.*
100 *Ibid.*
101 Sudanese delegate, 3rd Session, 1 December 2006, general discussion on 'other issues'.
102 *Ibid.*
103 Sudanese delegate, 3rd Session, 29 November 2006.
104 *Ibid.*
105 For example, Amnesty International reported that 'The Gereida region was insecure throughout 2006, with scores of villages destroyed in attacks by Janjawid or other armed groups. Some 80,000 people fled the camp for Internally Displaced Persons (IDP) in Gereida after fighting between forces of the SLA Minawi faction and the Justice and Equality Movement in October', *Annual Report 2006*, p. 244.

8.2.2.2 *The African Group*

Following the High Commissioner's speech, the sole focus of the African Group's statement was to complain that five paragraphs of her report had been dedicated to Darfur as compared with one paragraph on the crisis caused by the invasion in Iraq. Echoing the Sudanese position, the African Group accused the High Commissioner of bias and selectivity.[106] Moreover, the group blamed the worsening of the Sudanese crisis on the 'politicisation' of the situation. Algeria (African Group) claimed that the Sudanese government was cooperating with the ICC, and that security was improving in the region; developments which Algeria said were yet to be recognised by the Council or the OHCHR – which the African Group alleged was unfair[107] and biased against the government.[108]

The African Group and its members mostly remained silent during the calls for a Special Session on Darfur. However, Algeria did strongly oppose Canada's proposals regarding the Special Session, alleging that strict procedural rules would hinder the Council in terms of addressing substantive issues in a flexible manner. It went on to state, 'The Council must make sure that we do replicate the model of the three previous sessions [. . .] [to] avoid the impression that there is selectivity, politicization and a particular desire to attack a particular State that is a member of the African Group.'[109]

8.2.2.3 *The OIC*

The OIC and its individual members also remained silent during both the discussion of the High Commissioner's report and the calls for a Special Session. This silence can at least partially be explained by the High Commissioner's speech mentioning the situation in the Occupied Palestinian Territories, which subsequently became the focus of almost all OIC members' statements.[110] The OIC's focus on the OPT might have been a specific

---

106 In fact, the High Commissioner said in her response that the reason for doing so was due to the situation in Iraq having been the subject of 8 reports between 2004–2006. This was a direct result of the Human Rights Office within the UN Assistance Mission in Iraq being established in 2004. For reports see, United Nations Human Rights: Office of the High Commissioner for Human Rights, 'UNAMI Human Rights Reports', in *Countries: Iraq* (Online). Available HTTP: <http://www.ohchr.org/EN/Countries/MENARegion/Pages/UNAMIHRReports.aspx> (accessed 16 October 2012).

107 'The meeting on the 12th of November welcomed information that the security situation in Sudan is improving [. . .] encouraged by outcome of high level consultation on the 16th of November [. . .]', Algerian delegate 3rd Session, 29 November 2006, in response to UNHCHR, Louise Arbour.

108 'The alleged links between the government and the militias referred to by the High Commissioner have yet to be documented in an objective way', Algerian delegate, *Ibid.*

109 Algerian delegate, Organisational Meeting, 7 December 2006.

110 See, for example, delegates of Pakistan, Morocco, Bahrain, Bangladesh, and Tunisia, 3rd Session, 29 November 2006, in response to UNHCHR, Louise Arbour.

diversionary tactic. Alternatively, that bloc was pursuing its own political interests, unrelated to Darfur, to the extent that they altogether failed to address the ongoing human rights violations within that region.

8.2.2.4 The EU

Finland (EU) condemned the situation in Darfur, calling on the Council to convene a Special Session and to take action. It declared:

> Acts of violence against vulnerable groups in Darfur, especially against children, must stop. Ethnically targeted violence against women and children, especially against internally displaced persons, must stop [. . .] put an end to impunity [. . .] [the Council must] exercise responsibility to adequately address the situation in Darfur.[111]

The EU did not explicitly criticise the Sudanese government, although some of its members did do so in their individual statements.[112]

8.2.2.5 Canada

Canada argued that setting procedural rules would enable the Special Session to be as effective as possible. It suggested that four working days should pass between the end of the Third Session and the beginning of the Special Session, thus ensuring adequate preparation time for all delegations. Canada asked the OHCHR to provide background information on Darfur from a variety of different UN sources. After a number of states opposed these proposals,[113] Canada explained that the aim was not to restrict nor set limits and that its suggestions would merely be guidelines in terms of ground rules. Canada again expressed the idealist hope that the Council's work be directed towards making changes on the ground, and that it should not become a political chamber.

8.2.2.6 Other states

During the discussions on 29 November 2006 some states urged the Council not to selectively focus all of its attention on one region alone. Australia

---

111 Finnish delegate, 3rd Session, 1 December 2006, general discussion on 'other issues'.
112 For example, '[e]ven if all parties are guilty of serious breaches of international law, responsibility lies with the government', Swedish delegate, 3rd Session, 29 November 2006, in response to UNHCHR, Louise Arbour.
113 See discussion regarding convening a Special Session on Darfur, including: Algeria's objections, 3rd Session, 30 November 2006; Cuba opposed Canada's proposal, arguing that the session was of such urgency that it could not wait for another four working days to pass, 3rd Session, 30 November 2006; The Philippines said that the nine proposed procedural points were excessive, 3rd Session, 30 November 2006; Brazil concurred, saying that such a 'heavy instrument' was unnecessary, 3rd Session, 30 November 2006.

reiterated that 'there are more situations than just the Middle East that have to be addressed [by the Council]'.[114] Chile also called on the Council to 'not forget that human rights are universal'.[115] The UK took a slightly different position and called for equal attention to be paid to the crisis in Darfur as the Council had already given to the Middle East. That statement moved beyond emphasising the principle of non-selectivity; the UK proposed that the Council be more even-handed in its approach to grave human rights situations. These comments reflect the growing disappointment that the Council was already mirroring its predecessor in devoting disproportionate time and resources to Israel and the OPT at the expense of other grave situations such as Darfur.

8.2.2.7 *No decisions or resolutions on Darfur*

The Third Session's lack of decisions or resolutions on Darfur can be explained by the announcement that a Special Session on Darfur would take place immediately after the session. Member states, aware that an arena would be immediately provided for discussions, decisions and resolutions on Darfur, arguably had no reason to raise the situation or table draft texts during the regular session.

8.2.3 **Special Session on Darfur**

The Special Session on Darfur[116] took place over two days. It opened with a video address by the Secretary-General[117] and a speech by the High Commissioner,[118] both of whom expressed grave concerns about the conditions in Darfur and called on the Council to send a clear message to the victims that change would occur. Representatives of a number of agencies[119] delivered statements, including Jan Egeland – the Under-Secretary-General for Humanitarian Affairs and Emergency Relief Coordinator – who accused the government of Sudan of 'allowing more freedom to those committing atrocities than those there to protect'.[120] Several elements of UNICEF's intervention directly

---

114 Australian delegate, 3rd Session, 29 November 2006, in response to UNHCHR, Louise Arbour.
115 Chilean delegate, 3rd Session, 29 November 2006, in response to UNHCHR, Louise Arbour.
116 4th Special Session on the Human Rights Situation in Darfur, 12–13 December 2006.
117 Secretary-General Kofi Annan, Address to the Human Rights Council, 4th Special Session, 12 December 2006.
118 UNHCHR Louise Arbour, Address to the Human Rights Council, 4th Special Session, 12 December 2006.
119 See, for example, UNHCR statement, 4th Special Session, 12 December 2006.
120 Written statement of Jan Egeland, read by Office for the Coordination of Humanitarian Affairs representative, 4th Special Session, 12 December 2006.

contradicted claims made by Sudan at the Session, especially with regard to malnutrition, food insecurity, and violence against women and children.[121]

NGO contributions[122] followed similar patterns to the regional alliances; some organisations sought to address human rights issues, while others used the Council to further their own political objectives. Human Rights Watch spoke about the failures of the government of Sudan, accusing it of arming the militias and denying the factual records. Amnesty International read representative testimony sent from an individual in Darfur.[123] Nord-Sud XXI[124] brought a Darfuri as their speaker, and criticised the OIC for denying the facts of Sudan's participation in the ongoing violations. The Lutheran World Federation[125] made neutral comments and did not criticise Sudan, whilst the Union des Juristes Arabes[126] and Tupaj Amaru[127] sought to shift the focus away from Darfur and onto Israel,[128] which bore obvious similarities to tactics used by the OIC.[129]

121 UNICEF statement, 4th Special Session, 12 December 2006.

122 NGO statements occurred on 13 December 2006.

123 Amnesty International, 'Meeting the Challenge: Transforming the Commission on Human Rights into a Human Rights Council', 12 April 2005, AI Index IOR 40/008/2005.

124 Nord-Sud XXI is an NGO which 'strives to support the work of the United Nations in the fields of human rights and development by providing a voice for concerns of individuals in the southern hemisphere' and is strongly anti-war. Its founders include Mr Ahmed Ben Bella, the first President of Algeria, Mr Nelson Mandela, the first President of South Africa after apartheid, and Mr Ramsey Clark, a former US Attorney General and leading human rights lawyer. See, generally, Nord-Sud XXI, 'Darfur'.

125 The Lutheran World Federation provides relief and education in developing countries. See, The Lutheran World Federation (Online). Available HTTP: <http://www.lutheranworld.org/> (accessed 16 October 2012).

126 'The Union of Arab Jurists, founded in 1975, is an international organisation that aims to bring together associations of practicing lawyers and other members of the legal community in the Arab world to promote the rule of law.' See, Arab Inter-Parliamentary Union (Online). Available HTTP: <http://www.arab-ipu.org/english/> (accessed 16 October 2012).

127 Tupaj Amaru is an NGO which advocates for the rights of indigenous populations of the Americas known for its anti-West stance. It had its consultative status suspended for a year in 2004 when at the '59th session of the Commission on Human Rights in 2003, two representatives of the organisation had rushed towards [USA's] delegation carrying a large cylindrical object, had unfurled a banner and had chanted anti-American slogans.' See, Tupaj Amaru (Online). Available HTTP: <http://www.pusinsuyu.com/english/html/tupaj_amaru_english.html> (accessed 16 October 2012). Tupaj Amaru said that the solution to the crisis in Darfur required the political will of the government of Iran – which gives some indication of their desire to echo Iran's focus on Israel at this session – and that Western powers were solely responsible for the conflict in Darfur.

128 Union des Juristes Arabes suggested that international interests in Darfur were due to oil, minerals and colonial intentions, and said that the West did not really want democracy because 'it responded to democracy in Palestine with a siege against the Palestinian people'.

129 See Section 8.4.2.

8.2.3.1 *Sudan*

Sudan's comments[130] can be divided into three categories: its efforts to curb human rights violations and calls for assistance to continue to do so; the inaccuracy of reporting on Darfur; and the alleged bias and politicisation against the government. Sudan cited numerous statistics, many of which it claimed had been documented by the African Union, as proof that the conflict in Darfur was 'tribal struggles' that the 'government is aware of and settling through agreements'. It asserted that it was actively working to protect its citizens, and that rebel groups which had not signed the Darfur Peace Agreement were committing atrocities such as recruiting children, raping women and committing mass killings.

Sudan repeatedly alleged that information presented to the Council, and also apparent in the Western media, was inaccurate. Sudan accused Western states of attempting 'to undermine the dignity and sovereignty of weak states'. It questioned the motives of some states who had called for the Special Session, alleging that this was a tactic to divert attention away from atrocities being committed by the West in Iraq and elsewhere.[131] Sudan highlighted its regional alliances, emphasising that 'we have chosen to belong to the African community, the Arab community, and the Islamic community', perhaps in an attempt to underscore its power and strength at the Council through regionalism. Sudan set out the differences that it saw between Western and other states, saying 'we distinguish between genuine concerns for human rights, and ideological and political drives pushed by countries and organisations that control power, wealth and media'.

Alongside alleging that the West and the media were partial and unfair, Sudan accused the High Commissioner of being 'clearly biased', citing her focus on Sudan at the Third Session as evidence, before saying 'the High Commissioner has adopted an unprofessional position [. . .] [she] is partial to opinions of certain countries'. Sudan's position towards the High Commissioner reflected some states' treatment of the secretariat and Council-appointed experts where the information provided is unpalatable to, or disputed by, the country concerned.[132] Sudan did not provide evidence to support its accusations of bias and selectivity, leaving its statements open to the interpretation that they were an attempt to undermine the High Commissioner's credibility and thus the report delivered to the Council.

130 All comments made by the Sudanese delegate, 4th Special Session, 12 December 2006.
131 '[the West] seeks to divert attention from cities air-bombarded where every morning more than 400 people die. Also attempts to divert attention from agony of people under occupation, detainees under secret detention, here in Europe, without anyone doing anything about it.' Sudanese delegate, 4th Special Session, 12 December 2006.
132 See Chapter 5, Section 5.2.

8.2.3.2 *The African Group*

Algeria (African Group) delivered a statement that supported many of Sudan's assertions. Algeria criticised the Western media for trying to 'undermine the sovereignty of an African government',[133] later emphasising this position by stating:

> We are gathered to make an objective diagnosis for an appropriate road map. We must be driven by facts obtained on the ground, not simply by media-driven interpretations as a heavy-handed response aimed at naming and shaming an African government.

Algeria also insisted that the Special Session was being used for political purposes, including diverting attention away from Iraq, for example saying, 'human rights protection was more needed in Africa than any other continent during the slave trade. [. . .] Today, [the human rights situation in Africa] pales in comparison with Iraq [where there are] hundreds of thousands of deaths.' Mentioning Iraq not only diverted attention away from Sudan, its regional ally, but also advanced the national agendas of those African states, including Algeria, with ties to Iraq through OIC membership.

The African Union alleged that facts had been misrepresented to the Council, saying:

> [there have been] far-reaching propaganda campaigns where human rights situations are politicised [. . .] Thus, one major first-world NGO calls this an 'apocalyptic conflict where an Arab government with its militia attacks non-Arab tribes' [. . .] [However] the Chairman of Commission of the African Union says that the situation is 'improving slightly in some parts while deteriorating in others'.

Algeria queried the fact-finding process, questioning whether reports were valid. Such tactics mirrored Sudan's position towards the High Commissioner, appearing to be attempts to undermine the credibility of the fact-finding process. Algeria spoke of the need to 'find out first-hand what the facts really are' in order for innovative solutions rather than 'just maintaining the status quo', something which the African Group stressed was 'not an option'.

8.2.3.3 *The OIC*

Pakistan (OIC) again commended the Sudanese government for its cooperation, its efforts and the information provided, asserting that 'no government has been more forthcoming than Sudan'.[134] It said that other parties to the

---

133 All comments made by the Algerian delegate, 4th Special Session, 12 December 2006.
134 All comments made by the Pakistani delegate, 4th Special Session, 12 December 2006.

conflict bore responsibility for the violence and atrocities, and requested further funds and assistance in the region. The OIC called for the outcomes of the session to 'not be one-sided' against the Sudanese government.

The OIC again used its statement to shift the focus from Darfur and onto the Middle East. Pakistan criticised Kofi Annan, alleging that his call for the Council to address problems outside of the Middle East was a 'tit for tat' approach. Pakistan enquired why the Secretary-General had not spoken at the previous Special Sessions, at one point asking 'were the situations in Gaza or Lebanon not worthy of a message from the Secretary-General?'

8.2.3.4 *The EU*

The EU repeated some points which had already been presented to the Council, emphasising the importance of the factual information that had been delivered. It spoke of a 'grave crisis', of which the 'magnitude is profoundly shocking', before citing numbers including 'more than 200,000 dead' and 'two million who have left their homes'.[135] Finland (EU) called on the Council to act by saying 'an assessment mission should be sent to Darfur [. . .] including the Special Rapporteur [. . .] the mission should build on OHCHR experience, and recommendations should be given to Sudan on how to implement proposals'.

The EU did not explicitly criticise Sudan, but did express the need for the Sudanese government to take action to change the situation in Darfur. It emphasised that 'the cooperation of the government of Sudan is essential [. . .] We call on Sudan to cooperate with follow-up mechanisms [. . .] We appeal to all of you to cooperate [on behalf of] the people of Darfur.'

8.2.3.5 *Canada*

Canada reminded the HRC why the Special Session had been convened, noting that 'it is high time that the Council act in accordance with its mandate' of promoting and protecting human rights.[136] It said of the international community's duties:

> we are here to signal that we haven't forgotten the people of Darfur [. . .] to show that the international community is ready to act [. . .] the international community must do all that it can to provide protection [. . .] the international community must do the monitoring, provide technical assistance for human rights education.

When speaking about solutions, Canada expressed 'support [for] the decision for an independent human rights assessment mission with suitable expertise

135 All comments made by the Finnish delegate, 4th Special Session, 12 December 2006.
136 Canadian delegate, 4th Special Session, 12 December 2006.

to provide recommendations on practical short-term actions to improve the situation'. Canada further said that '[we are here] to remind the government of Sudan that it has primary responsibility to protect this region', before calling on 'all parties to implement recommendations [. . .] and resolutions'.

8.2.3.6 Other states

Zambia, once again, took a different position to the African Group, speaking out forcefully against 'burying our heads in the ground'.[137] It accused other African governments of previously taking an ostrich approach to the atrocities in Rwanda and of again doing so regarding Darfur. Zambia criticised other African states for being quick to call for UN action outside of Africa, but being much slower to respond to problems occurring within their continent. On the other hand, despite its democratic tendencies, South Africa's statement neither criticised Sudan nor departed from the African Group's sentiments, reflecting a similar stance taken by that state towards fellow African Group members such as, for example, Zimbabwe.

The Netherlands notably spoke strongly, repeatedly blaming the Sudanese government for the violations as well as accusing it of lying to the Council.[138] Some GRULAC[139] states spoke strongly in support of the High Commissioner, especially after many of the OIC countries had strongly criticised her, and Armenia commented that doubting UN sources' credibility was akin to 'questioning the integrity of the UN'.[140]

Special Sessions, as will be explored in Chapter 9, are an innovative mechanism designed to combat the Commission's failure to take action on crisis situations. The Council's Special Session on Darfur was its fourth such session and the first to be convened on a country other than Israel. Examining that session in detail has shown that the problems at the Council impacted upon Special Sessions' effectiveness for protecting human rights. It also underscores the politicisation, through regionalism and other tactics, which continued to plague the Council and to hamper the body's ability to fulfil its mandate.

8.2.3.7 Decision on the situation of human rights in Darfur

The Council adopted, by consensus, a Decision which created a High Level Mission to Sudan.[141] The Decision neither condemned Sudan nor used the

---

137 Zambian delegate, Canadian delegate, 4th Special Session, 12 December 2006.
138 Dutch delegate, Canadian delegate, 4th Special Session, 12 December 2006.
139 See, for example, Uruguayan and Argentine delegates, Canadian delegate, 4th Special Session, 12 December 2006.
140 Armenian delegate, Canadian delegate, 4th Special Session, 12 December 2006.
141 HRC Dec. S-4/101, 'Situation of Human Rights in Darfur', 13 December 2006, UN Doc. A/HRC/S-4/101.

word 'violation', making it weaker than the Western states had proposed. This highlights the inherent problem with seeking a compromise between states on human rights matters. The emphasis in the text was on promoting rather than protecting human rights, with references to advisory services and technical assistance.[142] Even in terms of the promotion mandate, the Council failed adequately to discharge its duties, with the Decision's text and language remaining general and neutral. Again, in contrast with the Human Rights Committee's approach,[143] the Council failed to set out which specific human rights need protecting, and failed to provide recommendations for how the Sudanese government should comply with its obligations. The Decision set out that the President should select the five members of the Mission to Sudan, although it specified that the SR on Sudan would also participate in the mission.

Algeria spoke before the vote, and 19 other Council members[144] spoke afterwards, all lauding the Council for its cooperation, compromise, and congenial approach, with some making it clear that they saw the consensus as proving the legitimacy of the Council.[145] Cuba said that one of the best things about the Decision was that it left aside 'inflammatory language' and the desire to impose 'unnecessary condemnation', despite the fact that Cuba does not possess an unblemished record in this regard. The UK repeated its hope that the Council use this constructive spirit to move its focus away from being solely on the Middle East, and the President invited Council members to 'maintain this spirit when we deal with other situations'.

8.2.4 The Fourth Session

Despite institution building being the primary focus of the Fourth Session,[146] Darfur was extensively discussed during the High Level Segment,[147] and some states used the situation as an example when criticising the non-implementation of Council decisions.[148] Darfur was also spoken about in

---

142 *Ibid.*, para. 5.

143 UN Human Rights Committee, 'Concluding Observations of the Human Rights Committee: The Sudan', UN Doc. CCPR/C/SDN/CO/3.

144 7 OIC countries, 5 EU countries, 4 GRULAC (including Cuba), and India, Russia, China, and Zambia.

145 Including India, China, Saudi Arabia and Tunisia.

146 12–30 March 2007.

147 The IBP mandates a High Level Segment to take place annually during the main session of the Council. HRC Res. 5/1, 'Institution Building of the United Nations Human Rights Council', 18 June 2007, UN Doc. A/HRC/RES/5/1, para. 116. A High Level Segment is a discussion where state dignitaries or government representatives of ministerial or higher rank address the Council. For an example of High Level Segment modalities see (Online). Available HTTP: <http://www2.ohchr.org/english/bodies/hrcouncil/docs/modalitieshls2june.doc> (accessed 25 June 2012).

148 See, Lithuanian delegate, 4th Session, 14 March 2008, High Level Segment.

response to reports by the Special Representative of the Secretary-General on Internally Displaced Persons (Walter Kälin)[149] and the Council-appointed Special Rapporteur on Violence against Women[150] (Yakin Ertuk), as well as in the High Commissioner's report[151] which noted increased levels of violence. States, NGOs, and agencies called for increased international presence, stressing the necessity of such action in order for civilians to be best protected.

Similar themes were apparent in the Mission to Sudan's report which spoke of the 'pattern of counter insurgency by the government and the Janjawid militia',[152] and described grave and systematic human rights abuses. The report noted that 'the region is a stranger to the rule of law' and that as the 'conflict continues, abuse feeds on abuse'.[153] It strongly condemned violations, calling on the international community to 'take urgent action to ensure effective protection [of civilians]'.[154] Its recommendations included; the deployment of a UN peacekeeping force, independent monitoring of the situation, and international prosecution of Sudanese war criminals – none of which had previously been implemented effectively.

8.2.4.1 Sudan

Sudan repeated its pattern of comments in responding to the issues raised at this session. It again spoke of its willingness to protect human rights and its efforts to do so, for example saying 'we showed unprecedented cooperation and flexibility, and believed that would be sufficient to help the international community help us to achieve peace'.[155] These comments were made despite the fact that it had denied entry to Bertrand Ramcharan.[156] As a result, the entire Mission could not enter Darfur.[157] Sudan protested innocence over that incident, alleging that it merely denied a visa to one member of the mission. Sudan failed to acknowledge that its objection to Ramcharan's inclusion caused the denial of entry to the Mission and the resulting fallout at the Council.

Sudan again condemned the Council's 'politicisation' of the situation, and urged the body not to repeat the 'politically-motivated naming and shaming'

---

149 See, Canadian delegate, 4th Session, 21 March 2007, in response to SR on Internally Displaced Persons, Walter Kälin.
150 See, Maltese delegate, 4th Session, 22 March 2007, in response to SR on Violence Against Women, Yakin Ertuk.
151 UNHCHR Louise Arbour, 4th Session, 14 March 2008, High Level Segment.
152 Oral intervention of Mission to Sudan's representative, Jody Williams, 4th Session, 16 March 2007.
153 *Ibid.*
154 *Ibid.*
155 Sudanese delegate, 4th Session, 16 March 2007.
156 See, Jody Williams, 4th Session, 16 March 2007.
157 HRC Res. 4/8, Follow-up to decision S-4/101 of 13 December 2006 adopted by the Human Rights Council at its fourth special session entitled 'Situation of Human Rights in Darfur', 30 March 2007, UN Doc. A/HRC/RES/4/8, para. 1.

of its predecessor.[158] Sudan reminded the Council that the body had been created 'to move away from selectivity and double standards', and claimed that these aims were being violated – 'today we witness a conspiracy against Sudan for political objectives'.[159] Sudan again challenged the impartiality of UN employees, and questioned the mission's neutrality.[160] It queried the impartiality of the OHCHR, doubting the validity of the recommendation for an international presence in the region.[161] Sudan condemned the Mission's 'faulty report',[162] alleging that various findings were exaggerated or false.[163]

8.2.4.2 The African Group

The African Group stated that it refused to accept the legitimacy of the mission owing to it not having entered Sudan, and owing to its report being written whilst the mission was in neighbouring countries. The African Group failed to criticise Sudan for denying entry to the mission, or to acknowledge the reason why the report had been compiled outside of that state. Instead it asserted 'the assessment is incomplete and the needs of Sudan were never fulfilled'.[164]

Despite expressing concerns about 'the gravity of the situation', Algeria said that there had been 'progress in the situation of human rights in Darfur'. The African Group repeated its support for the government, saying 'we welcome the commitment of Sudan's government to cooperate with international support [. . .] [and] continuing to permit humanitarian support for people in Darfur'.[165]

8.2.4.3 The OIC

Pakistan agreed with the African Group's positions, saying that the OIC was 'unable to comment on the substance of the report' of the mission owing to it not having entered Sudan in order to fulfil its mandate.[166] It further

---

158 Sudanese delegate, 4th Session, 13 March 2007, High Level Segment.
159 Sudanese delegate, 4th Session, 16 March 2007, in response to Williams, representative of Mission to Sudan.
160 '[Sudan has] reservations towards the head of the [fact-finding] mission. That person was from a country known for having a hostile position regarding Sudan. The subsequent behaviour of the mission's head confirmed that our fears were correct [. . .]', Sudanese delegate, 4th Session, 13 March 2007.
161 'Report of the High Commissioner for Human Rights and follow-up to the World Conference for Human Rights', 2 March 2007, A/HRC/4/49, page 11, para. 42.
162 Sudanese delegate, 4th Session, 16 March 2007.
163 *Ibid.*
164 Algerian delegate, 4th Session, 16 March 2007, in response to Williams, representative of Mission to Sudan.
165 *Ibid.*
166 Pakistani delegate, 4th Session, 16 March 2007, in response to Williams, representative of Mission to Sudan.

commented that 'the concept of the responsibility to protect was not reflected' by the mission, and that its report 'has multiple political and security dimensions that go beyond its mandate'. The OIC supported Sudan, saying:

> The government was asked to continue and intensify its cooperation [. . .] the Council must build on that [. . .] there should be no selectivity and targeting [. . .] the interests of the Sudanese people are not served by a list of recommendations. The situation can only be improved by the government of Sudan and the assistance of the international community.[167]

8.2.4.4 The EU

The EU criticised Sudan for denying entry to the mission. It reminded the Council that the Special Session had been held 'because of the extreme seriousness of the human rights situation in Darfur'[168] and that 'the government of Sudan welcomed the decisions' made at that session. The EU said that this made it even more regrettable that 'the government did not extend that cooperation to the mission'.

Germany (EU) commented that 'the legitimacy of the mission is not in question, because it fulfilled its mandate and provided a good report'. Germany emphasised the report's findings, particularly that government troops were committing violations in Darfur. Using the report as its basis, Germany called for Sudan's government, the Council and the international community to take further action to cease the ongoing human rights violations.

8.2.4.5 Canada

Canada voiced support for the mission and its report and expressed concerns about the Sudanese government, for example saying 'Canada had welcomed the commitment by the government to cooperate [. . .] but regrets that the mission was not allowed into Sudan.'[169] Having expressed these concerns, Canada insisted that 'the international community must act when a country is unwilling or unable to do so'.[170]

8.2.4.6 Other states

Like Zambia, Botswana was a notable exception to the general African silence regarding Sudan at the High Level Segment, telling the Council of their

---

167 *Ibid.*
168 German delegate, 4th Session, 16 March 2007, in response to Williams, representative of Mission to Sudan.
169 Canadian delegate, 4th Session, 16 March 2007, in response to Williams, representative of Mission to Sudan.
170 *Ibid.*

peacekeeping contribution, and expressing concern about the 'suffering of internally displaced persons and refugees' in the region.[171] Ghana also broke regional alliances, this time during the discussion on the Mission to Sudan, saying 'the situation in Sudan needs urgent attention [. . .] concerning the promotion and protection of human rights. The report by Jody Williams underlies the need for urgent action.'[172]

Ireland,[173] speaking as an observer at the Council, expressed grave concerns regarding the situation, saying that the mission's findings were a 'badge of shame for the international community' and 'urge[d] the Council to act consensually to adopt the conclusions of the mission'. Ireland was careful to point out that it had 'no strategic interest in Sudan' nor 'motive to stand up for Darfur' other than the desire to 'promote human rights'. This was a direct reference to an earlier accusation that the Western interest in this region was motivated by oil.[174]

8.2.4.7 *Resolution on the Follow-Up to Decision S-4/101*

At the Fourth Session a resolution[175] was adopted, by consensus, following-up the Special Session's Decision. The Resolution was the first Council text on Darfur which documented violations of specific human rights[176] and provided recommendations and a mechanism aimed at protecting human rights.[177] Alongside calling on all parties to uphold human rights,[178] the Resolution further, for the first time, identified the Sudanese government's obligations to protect human rights.[179] It was written and co-sponsored by the EU and the African Group. This joint initiative between the African Group and EU resulted from the two groups working together closely in order to ensure the cooperation of African states with the Council's action on Darfur. Germany (EU) said that its adoption showed that 'the Human Rights Council does not close its eyes to the suffering of the people of Darfur'. It further said that 'this [resolution] is not about political games, diplomatic manoeuvres [but is] solely about the realisation of human rights'.[180]

---

171 Botswana delegate, 4th Session, 13 March 2007, High Level Segment.
172 Ghanaian delegate, 4th Session, 16 March 2007, in response to Williams, representative of Mission to Sudan.
173 Irish Minister for Human Rights, 4th Session, 13 March 2007, High Level Segment.
174 Palestinian delegate, 4th Session, 16 March 2007, in response to Williams, representative of Mission to Sudan.
175 HRC Res. 4/8, 'Resolution on the Follow-Up to Decision S-4/101 of 13 December 2006 Adopted by the Human Rights Council at its Fourth Special Session Entitled the Human Rights Situation in Darfur', UN Doc. A/HRC/RES/4/8.
176 *Ibid.*, para. 3.
177 *Ibid.*, paras 4, 6, 7.
178 *Ibid.*, paras 4, 5.
179 *Ibid.*, paras 7, 8.
180 German delegate, 4th Session, 30 March 2007.

As a result of the mission not visiting Darfur, the Council established a Group of Experts on Darfur. The Group of Experts was the first group created by either the Council or its predecessor with the purpose of following up recommendations made by human rights bodies. It was innovative for a UN human rights body to implement a follow-up process. Previously, each new resolution sent out, for example, commissions of enquiries which required the fact-finders or experts to begin new enquiries even when a territory had been visited the previous year. By creating a mission to follow up recommendations, the Council demonstrated its intent that the Group focus on implementation rather than on making new recommendations.

The joint initiative to establish the Group of Experts focused on cooperation, not only of Sudan but also of that state's regional allies in the African Group. Cooperation is a founding principle at the Council, underscoring its importance for effective promotion and protection of human rights within a state's domestic jurisdiction. Negotiations and compromise between the EU and the African Group sought to ensure that Council action on Sudan would be more palatable to that state and therefore facilitate the body better fulfilling its mandate with regard to Darfur. However, that compromise required the body to weaken action it might otherwise have taken in order to retain the cooperation of Sudan and its allies. This initiative failed to achieve many positive results in terms of Sudan's implementation of the Group's recommendations although, arguably, some work was done which may not have been achieved without the atmosphere of cooperation and dialogue engendered within this joint initiative.

Despite their close cooperation, the EU and the African Group took somewhat different positions during Council discussions on the Resolution. The EU sought to avoid the appearance of politicisation, and to encourage the Council to take action on violations. The African Group took a different approach to the EU, stressing the importance of unanimity in decision-making. Despite these comments, the African Group had devoted considerable effort to blocking meaningful discussions, let alone action, on Darfur.

8.2.5 The Fifth Session

Darfur was raised at the Fifth Session[181] by Jean Ziegler, the Special Rapporteur on the Right to Food[182] and Arjun Sengupta, the Independent Expert on Extreme Poverty.[183] Sima Samar, the Special Rapporteur on Sudan[184] presented a report and made a number of recommendations. Darfur was also mentioned during the report on the situation in Israel and the OPT in

---

181 11–18 June 2007.
182 Oral intervention of SR on the Right to Food, Jean Ziegler, 5th Session, 11 June 2007.
183 Oral intervention of SR on Extreme Poverty, Arjun Sengupta, 5th Session, 11 June 2007.
184 Oral intervention of Sima Samar, SR on Sudan, 5th Session, 13 June 2007.

terms of the universality of human rights, with the head of the mission[185] saying 'it is important that this Council has sought to investigate the situation in Darfur'.

8.2.5.1 *Sudan*

Sudan denounced Ziegler's report, asserting that there were factual inaccuracies, and alleging that humanitarian food aid was being blocked by those parties to the conflict who had not signed the Peace Agreement.[186] Sudan also blamed militia groups, especially the Janjawid, for causing the problems set out in the session. It denied government responsibility for the social exclusion and the impeding of Darfuris' ability 'to enjoy the essential freedoms in life'.[187] Sudan again asked for international support, for example saying 'the government of Sudan asks this Council to call on the United Nations [. . .] to provide us with aid'.[188]

Sudan reiterated their 'commitment to cooperate with the Council and the Group of Experts', emphasising their alleged efforts to improve the situation in the region before again requesting assistance in doing so, expressing that 'the United Nations and the international community must render support to Sudan for an action plan to deal with Darfur'.[189]

8.2.5.2 *The African Group*

Algeria repeated its support for the Sudanese government, for example by saying 'the dialogue between Sudan and the Group of Experts was open and frank'.[190] The African Group stated that it supported the recommendations made by the Group of Experts, insisting that, thus far, it had been successful:

> We particularly [welcome] the consultation that went on between the Group of Experts and the regional groups. [. . .] This Group made a selection of various recommendations that fall within responsibility of this council [. . .] They also established a timeframe in terms of short and long term action [. . .] The African Group has been involved in addressing Darfur at the level of the Council [. . .] I am confident that we will achieve yet another consensus in terms of this very delicate issue [. . .] What is important is the consensus on the ground.[191]

185 Oral intervention of Mission to OPT representative, Desmond Tutu, 5th Session, 13 June 2007.
186 Sudanese delegate, 5th Session, 11 June 2007, in response to SR on the Right to Food, Jean Ziegler.
187 Arjun Sengupta, 5th Session, 11 June 2007.
188 Sudanese delegate, 5th Session, 11 June 2007.
189 Sudanese delegate, 5th Session, 13 June 2007, in response to Samar, SR on Sudan.
190 Algerian delegate, 5th Session, 13 June 2007, in response to Samar, SR on Sudan.
191 *Ibid.*

Furthermore, in picking up on comments by Desmond Tutu, the African Group said, 'today I have the pleasure of knowing that we have moved forward in Darfur [. . .] I just pray and hope that the progress we are making continues'.[192]

8.2.5.3 The OIC

Pakistan also spoke positively about the Group of Experts and Sudan's cooperation with those mandate holders, saying:

> The work in this area shows how cooperation leads to results [. . .] The government of Sudan has worked well with the UN to implement the existing resolutions [. . .] We support the recommendation that the experts continue their work for another fixed period of time [. . .] We appreciate having a focal point to coordinate assistance to Sudan.[193]

8.2.5.4 The EU

Germany (EU) questioned the usefulness of the report, saying that the members of the Council 'all know of the problems in Darfur', and that rather than giving new recommendations the Council should be trying to ensure that existing ones are implemented. The EU's position was that 'it is essential that we actually change the situation on the ground [. . .] because as we consider the report, the violence goes on'.[194] During the discussion on the right to food,[195] Germany expressly condemned the Sudanese government for its role in violating that right, and criticised the lack of access to food in Darfur as well as the use of food and water as a political tool in the region.[196]

8.2.5.5 Canada

Canada was more positive than the EU about Samar's report, saying:

> We welcome the report [. . .] We believe after this report that the government of Sudan can now show its commitment to human rights [. . .] We welcome the dialogue that has taken place between Sudan and the international community, and we note that all parties, including rebel groups and regional neighbours, should be involved.[197]

192 *Ibid*.
193 Pakistani delegate, 5th Session, 13 June 2007, in response to Samar, SR on Sudan.
194 German delegate, 5th Session, 13 June 2007, in response to Samar, SR on Sudan.
195 Jean Ziegler, 5th Session, 11 June 2007.
196 German delegate, 5th Session, 11 June 2007, in response to SR on the Right to Food, Jean Ziegler.
197 Canadian delegate, 5th Session, 13 June 2007, in response to Samar, SR on Sudan.

However, Canada did speak of the ongoing violations in Darfur and the need to deal with this situation, saying that 'since March 2007, there has been tremendous sexual violence in Darfur [. . .] Humanitarian assistance is compromised by all parties to the conflict [. . .] We call on all parties to bring the violence to an immediate halt.'[198] Whilst noting some improvements, Canada reiterated its usual position that the international community 'needs to do better to help the people of Darfur [. . .] We can start by implementing these recommendations.'[199]

8.2.5.6 *Other states*

Most countries used the discussions to reiterate their previous positions on the situation, but there were a few statements of particular interest. Central African Republic, a neighbour of Sudan affected by the conflict, broke regional trends in condemning the situation:

> Darfur, after the two world wars, is the worst humanitarian disaster the world has witnessed. It is a shame for all mankind. Failing to have dealt with Darfur has encouraged the abuse of human rights around the world. We must stop this catastrophe and protect the fundamental rights that the people of Sudan are entitled to.[200]

The United States called for sanctions to be imposed against Sudan[201] in order to encourage the government to fulfil its international obligations and cooperate fully.

China again adopted a post-colonial discourse, asserting that poverty was the fundamental problem in Darfur. China insisted that the economic and social issues which contributed to the situation had to be addressed.[202] Syria brought up the politicisation of the conflict, declaring that:

---

198 *Ibid.*

199 *Ibid.*

200 Central African Republic delegate, 5th Session, 13 June 2007, in response to Samar, SR on Sudan.

201 'This Council has yet to adequately address the human rights violations in Sudan. The targeting of women and children remain a grave concern [. . .] The US has imposed sanctions on Sudan to bring about a peaceful resolution to this conflict. We wish to end the suffering of millions of Sudanese [. . .] At the Security Council the US is working on a resolution to widen sanctions against Sudan. We call on Sudan to disarm the Janjaweed, demonstrate commitment to peace, cease aerial bombardments, stop obstructions and allow peacekeepers and humanitarian workers access to internally displaced persons' camps', American delegate, 5th Session, 13 June 2007, in response to Samar, SR on Sudan.

202 'The fundamental problem is poverty [. . .] we must address the economic and social issues that contribute [to the conflict]', Chinese delegate, 5th Session, 13 June 2007, in response to Samar, SR on Sudan.

[alongside] other countries, we are concerned with the politicisation of the situation in Darfur with external parties exploiting the situation to achieve their own objectives, particularly in oil. There will be no improvement until there is an end to external interference.[203]

8.2.5.7 *Resolution on the Group of Experts*

Having seen relatively little improvement in Darfur as a result of the work of the Group of Experts,[204] at the Fifth Session the EU and the African Group jointly tabled[205] a draft resolution following up Resolution 4/8 on Darfur.[206] They proposed a six-month extension of the mandates of the Special Rapporteur on Sudan and the Group of Experts. Despite the extension being passed, the Group of Experts' work was not finished, nor their recommendations implemented, by the end of the year,[207] and, as will be explored, the Council chose not to extend their mandate at the following session.[208]

8.2.6 *The Sixth Session*

Having postponed its follow-up at the Fifth Session, the Council heard an update from the Group of Experts[209] during the Sixth Session.[210] The government of Sudan was urged to cooperate with the group and to implement its recommendations, and the situation in Darfur was, again, raised a number of times during general debates. The first day of the resumed Sixth Session[211] coincided with the 60th anniversary of the Universal Declaration on Human

---

203 Syrian delegate, 5th Session, 13 June 2007, in response to Samar, SR on Sudan.

204 For example, 'In March the Council convened a group of experts to pursue previous recommendations made by UN human rights bodies on Darfur. The Sudanese government-appointed Human Rights Advisory Council responded to these recommendations but according to the report presented to the Council in November, few of the recommendations were implemented.' Amnesty International, *Annual Report 2007*, London: Amnesty International, 2008, p. 280.

205 Consideration of all resolutions and decisions were postponed at this Session, see HRC, 'Postponement of consideration of all pending draft resolutions and decisions, and of the draft report', 18 June 2007, UN Doc. A/HRC/DEC/5/102.

206 HRC, 'Follow-up to Resolution 4/8 of 30 March 2007 adopted by the Human Rights Council at its fourth session entitled "Follow-up to decisions S-4/101 of 13 December 2006" adopted by the Human Rights Council at its fourth special session entitled "Situation of Human Rights in Darfur"', 15 June 2007, UN Doc. A/HRC/5/L.6.

207 'In December the Council urged Sudan to implement all outstanding recommendations identified by the group of experts on Darfur'. Amnesty International, *Annual Report 2007*, p. 281.

208 HRC Res. 6/35, 'Resolution on the Human Rights Council Group of Experts on the Situation of Human Rights in Darfur', 14 December 2007, UN Doc. A/HRC/RES/6/35.

209 Oral intervention of the Group of Experts representative, Walter Kälin, 6th Session, 24 September 2007.

210 10–28 September 2007.

211 10–14 December 2007.

Rights. The report of the High Commissioner[212] spoke of 'grave violations' in Sudan since September, saying that 'more needs to be done by the government in Khartoum and the international community to ensure protection for civilians', and that the 'rule of law needs to be strengthened, especially in Darfur where lawlessness abounds'.[213]

At the resumed Sixth Session, the Chair of the Group of Experts[214] presented its final report.[215] The Group stressed Sudan's 'primary duty to respect human rights and to comply with international obligations', and expressed continuing concerns about lack of governmental action. The Sudanese government's 'cooperative behaviour' in certain regards was noted, but Samar then stated:

> In terms of substance, not much impact has occurred [since the Group of Experts was set up] [. . .] A lot of the recommendations made could have been implemented in a few months with minimal cost [but this has not occurred] [. . .] The Group remains concerned that efforts have not led to improvement of the human rights situation in Darfur.[216]

8.2.6.1 Sudan

In a statement on Human Rights Day, Sudan described the situation in Darfur as 'a difficult period in Sudan's history'.[217] It reiterated its commitment to improving the situation, assuring the Council that 'no efforts have been spared by Sudan to ensure human rights in the country'.[218]

Sudan continued to take this position during the session, stating its firm commitment to the implementation of resolutions and trying to convince the Council that it had recently undertaken activities complying with the recommendations. Sudan's response to the High Commissioner asserted that

212 Oral intervention of UNHCHR, Louise Arbour, 6th Session, 11 December 2007.

213 *Ibid.*

214 Oral intervention of Chair of Group of Experts, Sima Samar, 6th Session, 11 December 2007.

215 HRC Rep. 6/19, 'Final report on the situation of human rights in Darfur prepared by the United Nations Experts Group on Darfur, presided by the Special Rapporteur on the situation of human rights in Sudan and composed by the Special Representative of the Secretary-General for children and armed conflict, the Special Rapporteur on extrajudicial, summary or arbitrary executions, the Special Representative of the Secretary-General on the human rights defenders, the Representative of the Secretary-General on human rights internally displaced persons, the Special Rapporteur on the question of torture and the Special Rapporteur on violence against women, its causes and consequences', 28 November 2007, UN Doc. A/HRC/6/19.

216 Oral intervention of Sima Samar, 6th Session, 11 December 2007.

217 Sudanese delegate, 6th Session, 10 December 2007, general discussion on 'Human Rights Day'.

218 Sudanese delegate, 6th Session, 11 December 2007, in response to Chair of Group of Experts, Sima Samar.

the regime 'respects all conventions of human rights' and that the government 'promotes human rights protection [in Darfur]'.[219] Sudan responded to Samar's report in a similar manner, again trying to assure the Council of its 'cooperation with the Human Rights Council, Special Rapporteur and Group of Experts [which] has given the fledgling Council the chance of credibility'.[220] These comments were made despite reports of worsening conditions and ongoing violations at this time.[221]

Sudan repeated its earlier positions, again calling on the Council to ensure that it did not have 'double standards or selectivity when it comes to protecting vulnerable groups and promoting human rights'.[222] Sudan also repeated its request for assistance. Whilst arguing that 'the situation in Darfur is improving', Sudan claimed that 'many factors exert influence on the situation' and asked the international community 'to help us try to find solutions'.[223]

8.2.6.2 *The African Group*

The African Group discussed 'positive developments and improvements' in Darfur and attributed them to 'the strong will of the government of Sudan to improve the situation'.[224] Egypt spoke of 'the high level of cooperation shown by the government of Sudan'.[225] At the resumed Session, Egypt repeated this position, saying:

> We had hoped that the High Commissioner would acknowledge the efforts of the Sudanese government to improve the situation on the ground, as noted by the Expert Group on Darfur. The Sudanese authorities have taken tangible steps to improve the situation on the ground.[226]

Egypt asserted that the international community 'has failed to truly assist' Sudan and the Darfur region, a position that seemingly ignored the Sudanese government's resistance to various initiatives and recommendations. Egypt also asserted that the 'international community and agencies must assist

---

219 Sudanese delegate, 6th Session, 11 December 2007, in response to UNHCHR, Louise Arbour.
220 Sudanese delegate, 6th Session, 11 December 2007.
221 For example, 'As a result of attacks, particularly by government and paramilitary groups, some 280,000 people were displaced bringing the number of displaced in Darfur to more than 2,387,000.' Amnesty International, *Annual Report 2007*, p. 281.
222 Sudanese delegate, 6th Session, 11 December 2007.
223 *Ibid.*
224 Egyptian delegate, 6th Session, 24 September 2007, in response to Group of Experts representative, Walter Kälin.
225 *Ibid.*
226 Egyptian delegate, 6th Session, 11 December 2007, in response to UNHCHR, Louise Arbour.

Sudan'.[227] These requests were reiterated, with the African Group saying, '[w]e call on the OHCHR to continue to provide technical support [. . .] and we call on the international community to help provide the resources needed to improve the situation'.[228]

8.2.6.3 The OIC

The OIC expressly aligned itself with the African Group's statements on Sudan. It did not comment extensively on Sudan, setting out its desire to avoid mentioning specific countries during general discussions because of the need to then 'talk about all the issues'.[229] The sole position expressed by the OIC regarding Sudan was its statement of ongoing support for the government. Pakistan focused its comments on international assistance for the government to deal further with the situation in Darfur, for example saying that 'the Sudanese government's efforts need concrete support from the international community'.[230]

8.2.6.4 The EU

In response to the Group of Experts, the EU welcomed the 'great cooperation of the government of Sudan'. However, unlike the African Group, the EU expressed concerns about the continuing situation of human rights in Sudan, saying 'we urge Sudan to demonstrate its willingness to fight violations of human rights in Darfur and to combat impunity'.[231] Similarly, after the High Commissioner's report, Portugal (EU) voiced 'grave concern over human rights abuses in Darfur' before calling for an 'end to impunity' and for perpetrators to be brought to justice.[232] This acknowledgement of the government's efforts, alongside condemnation of the situation and calls for further changes, was repeated after the Group of Experts' report in December. In this statement, Portugal again urged the Sudanese government to end the human rights violations in Darfur and to fulfil its international obligations.[233]

---

227 Egyptian delegate, 6th Session, 24 September 2007.

228 Egyptian delegate, 6th Session, 11 December 2007.

229 Pakistani delegate, 6th Session, 11 December 2007, in response to UNHCHR, Louise Arbour.

230 Pakistani delegate, 6th Session, 11 December 2007, in response to Chair of Group of Experts, Sima Samar.

231 Portuguese delegate, 6th Session, 24 September 2007, in response to Group of Experts representative, Walter Kälin.

232 Portuguese delegate, 6th Session, 11 December 2007, in response to UNHCHR, Louise Arbour.

233 Portuguese delegate, 6th Session, 13 December 2007, in response to Samar, Special Rapporteur on Sudan.

8.2.6.5 *Canada*

Canada again took a stronger position than the EU, voicing its 'ongoing concern' about the violence and documenting various violations.[234] Canada said that it was 'appalled' at the appointment of Ahmad Mohammed Harun as co-chairman of a national committee charged with addressing human rights violations in Darfur.[235] The Council was informed that Harun had been formally charged with crimes by the International Criminal Court[236] and Canada asserted that his appointment 'casts doubt' on the government of Sudan's commitment to improve the human rights situation in Darfur.

In December, Canada stressed that improvements on the ground would only occur if the Group of Experts' recommendations were implemented. It criticised the government for saying much and doing little, saying 'we are concerned that the failure to implement many of the recommendations shows that there is rhetoric, but little concrete action'.[237]

8.2.6.6 *Other states*

The US, an observer state, denounced the poor human rights records in a number of countries including Sudan, and questioned the relevancy of a body which ignores ongoing human rights abuses.[238] Zambia again broke regional alliances, urging the Sudanese government to cooperate with the Council and the international community in order to 'improve the human rights situation on the ground'. In expressing its concerns, Zambia said that 'attacks still continue, which is of great concern because the people of Darfur should be able to have their lives return to normal, and to close the chapter on this issue'.[239]

Algeria retained its regional alliances despite no longer chairing the African Group. Having congratulated Sudan for its 'excellent cooperation', it expressed deep alarm at the 'exaggerated disinformation' on Darfur, saying that the situation received disproportionate coverage in the media.[240] Algeria then

234 Canadian delegate, 6th Session, 24 September 2007, in response to Group of Experts representative, Walter Kälin.

235 See, for example, Trial (Website), 'Ahmad Mohammed Harun', in *Trial Watch*, (Online). Available HTTP: <http://www.trial-ch.org/en/trial-watch/profile/db/legal-procedures/ahmad-mohammed_harun_621.html> (accessed 16 October 2012).

236 Warrant for the Arrest of Ahmad Harun, in the case of *The Prosecutor v. Ahmad Muhammad Harun*, 27 April 2007, ICC-02/05-01/07.

237 Canadian delegate, 6th Session, 11 December 2007, in response to Chair of Group of Experts, Sima Samar.

238 'This council is becoming less and less relevant [. . .] because it continues to ignore the oppressing situations in many countries', American delegate, 6th Session, 24 September 2007, in response to Group of Experts representative, Walter Kälin.

239 Zambian delegate, 6th Session, 24 September 2007, in response to Group of Experts representative, Walter Kälin.

240 Algerian delegate, 6th Session, 24 September 2007, in response to Group of Experts representative, Walter Kälin.

used an African Group and OIC tactic, shifting the focus away from Sudan by asserting that the Council should instead be discussing the situations in Iraq and Palestine.[241] That rhetoric on Darfur is an exact mirror image of that given by OIC states regarding Israel.

8.2.6.7 *Resolutions on the Mandate of the Special Rapporteur*

The review of the mandate of the Special Rapporteur on Sudan occurred at the resumed Sixth Session.[242] The African Group argued that, bearing in mind that Sudan would be subject to Universal Periodic Review,[243] the mandate should be eliminated.[244] Sudan said that 'there is a politicisation that led to the dismantling of the Commission which has started once again to infiltrate the work of this Council'. It called on the SR 'to reflect very carefully on the information provided by the Sudanese authorities'.[245]

The EU expressed its 'strong support of the mandate and the excellent work of the Special Rapporteur', and asserted that 'the Special Rapporteur can play a very important role on combating impunity, but it is the responsibility of Sudan to respect and ensure human rights'.[246] The EU hoped that 'the renewal of the mandate will be adopted by consensus',[247] a position that was supported by other Western States.[248] Emphasis on consensus reflects the EU's social constructivist approach regarding commonality of interest at the Council. The Resolution on the Mandate of the Special Rapporteur on the Situation of Human Rights in the Sudan[249] was passed by consensus. The Resolution focused on capacity-building and technical assistance,[250] emphasising the founding principles of cooperation and dialogue,[251] but again failed to mention any specific rights or violations.

---

241 The Council passed nine resolutions on Israel as compared with three non-condemnatory resolutions on Sudan during its first year.

242 13 December 2007.

243 Universal Periodic Review applies to all UN member states.

244 This position was supported by states such as Cuba and Russia, which said that the SR on Sudan would only be effective if it was adopted with the consent of the Sudanese authorities, oral statements at the 6th Session, 14 December 2007.

245 Sudanese delegate, 6th Session, 13 December 2007, in response to Samar, Special Rapporteur on Sudan.

246 Portuguese delegate, 6th Session, 13 December 2007, in response to Samar, Special Rapporteur on Sudan.

247 *Ibid.*

248 For example, the US said that 'the Council cannot ignore the ongoing crisis in Sudan [. . .] [We] fully support the renewal of the mandate and resist all efforts to weaken it', American delegate, 6th Session, 14 December 2007.

249 HRC Res. 6/34, 'Mandate of the Special Rapporteur on the Situation of Human Rights in the Sudan', 14 December 2007, UN Doc. A/HRC/RES/6/34.

250 *Ibid.*, para. 3.

251 *Ibid.*, para. 5.

The Council also passed a resolution which acknowledged the Group of Experts' work, which had reported on human rights abuses in Darfur, but effectively abolished its mandate by omitting any reference to its future work.[252] The Resolution welcomed the Group's report and called on the government of Sudan to take action against 'serious violations of human rights'.[253] The strong language in this Resolution and the documenting of specific grave violations was markedly different from the Council's previous texts, and appeared closer to that of the Human Rights Committee. Perhaps because of the expertise of its members, or owing to the cooperation of the EU and the African Group, the Group was viewed as both stronger and more influential than the Special Rapporteur. Arguably, that was a main reason for the mandate's abolition by states seeking to shield the Sudanese government, thereby prioritising political objectives over protecting human rights. The Resolution that effectively abolished the Group of Experts was adopted by consensus, having been co-sponsored by Egypt on behalf of the African Group, and Portugal on behalf of the European Union. It appears, then, that negotiations outside of the Council chamber, and thus not available on public record, resulted in the EU and the African Group accepting the termination of the mandate despite having established the Group of Experts and supported its work.

8.2.7 *The Seventh Session*

At the beginning of the Seventh Session,[254] during the High Level Segment, a number of Western states[255] raised the situation in Darfur. The High Commissioner noted the escalating violence in West Darfur during her presentation of the OHCHR Annual Report.[256] Western States again spoke about Darfur during the general debate on Agenda Item 4.[257] The report of the Special Rapporteur on Sudan condemned the 'culture of impunity' in Sudan, and voiced concerns about the 'persistent violence, military force, and the government's failure to protect citizens' in Darfur.[258]

8.2.7.1 *Sudan*

Sudan again followed its pattern of assuring the Council that the government would 'continue to cooperate with the Group of Experts and the Special

---

252 HRC Res. 6/35, 'Human Rights Council Group of Experts on the Situation of Human Rights in Darfur', UN Doc. A/HRC/RES/6/35.
253 *Ibid.*, para. 5.
254 3–28 March 2008.
255 Including oral interventions of: Switzerland's Micheline Calmy-Ray, Luxembourg's Vice Prime Minister Jen Asselborn, and France's State Secretary for Foreign Affairs and Human Rights Rama Yade, all 6th Session, 3 March 2008, High Level Segment.
256 Oral intervention of UNHCHR, Louise Arbour, 7th Session, 7 March 2008.
257 Including delegates of: the Netherlands, Switzerland, Ireland, and Australia, all 7th Session, 14 March 2008, general debate on Agenda Item 4.
258 Oral intervention of SR on Sudan, Sima Samar, 7th Session, 17 March 2008.

Rapporteur on Sudan'.[259] It spoke of improvements to the situation in Darfur and initiatives taken by the government. Sudan's response to the High Commissioner's report was to assert that the situation in West Darfur was under control, saying that the government had 'already put forward the peaceful solution in its right, appropriate way'.[260] Sudan repeated another of its usual positions in alleging that there were factual inaccuracies in the Special Rapporteur on Sudan's report, saying 'we believe that the facts of the report are not represented by the facts [on the ground]'.[261]

During the High Level Segment, Sudan attempted to shift the focus from its own crisis onto the situation in Israel and the OPT, declaring that:

> The entire world is watching with sadness the massacres in the OPT [. . .] we strongly condemn Israeli aggressions. We call on the Human Rights Council to protect the innocent civilians and children and women who are being killed on a daily basis and in cold blood.[262]

Sudan's comments arguably both demonstrated their allegiance with the OIC and the Arab Group, as well as sought to divert attention from the crisis on its own soil.

8.2.7.2 *The African Group*

The African Group reiterated its 'appreciation' for the Sudanese government's efforts and cooperation, citing the Special Rapporteur's activities across the country as evidence of 'Sudan's willingness to comply with the United Nations'. Its speech focused on the 'cooperative spirit that has gone on in regards to Sudan', and expressed the hope that this would continue.[263]

8.2.7.3 *The OIC*

Pakistan expressed similar sentiments to the African Group, saying, 'the Special Rapporteur acknowledged the progress of the Sudanese government [. . .] they are noteworthy and must be encouraged [. . .] We appreciate the consistent efforts of the Sudanese government.'[264] The OIC also called for further assistance to the region, saying 'the government requires international support without political qualifications', a position reiterated in its later calls for 'support without political criteria'.

259 Sudanese Minister of Justice, 7th Session, 3 March 2008, High Level Segment.
260 Sudanese delegate, 7th Session, 7 March 2008, response to the UNHCHR, Louise Arbour.
261 Sudanese delegate, 7th Session, 17 March 2008, response to SR on Sudan, Sima Samar.
262 Sudanese Minister of Justice, 7th Session, 3 March 2008.
263 Egyptian delegate, 7th Session, 17 March 2008, response to SR on Sudan, Sima Samar.
264 Pakistani delegate, 7th Session, 17 March 2008, response to SR on Sudan, Sima Samar.

8.2.7.4 *The EU*

During the general debate on Agenda Item 3, the EU deplored the 'many instances of discrimination against lesbian, gay, bisexual and transgender people in Sudan'[265] as well as condemning the renewal of violence in West Darfur. Concerns were also raised after the Special Rapporteur on Sudan's report, with Slovenia asking what could be done to ensure access to humanitarian aid, to bring perpetrators to justice, to halt the violence against women, and to protect journalists.[266] The EU criticised the Sudanese government for failing adequately to address these issues.[267]

8.2.7.5 *Canada*

Canada, perhaps realising the futility of continuing to repeat its idealist statements on the situation, said relatively little in relation to Sudan at this session. Its primary focus was to question the Special Rapporteur on Sudan about the best ways to change the situation on the ground in Darfur. In particular, Canada asked 'how can we [the Council] assist the Special Rapporteur to carry out the recommendations in your report?'

8.2.7.6 *Other states*

Cuba repeated its previous opinion that 'all of these scourges were caused by colonialism',[268] although it neither expanded upon nor explained this position. Other individual states and observer missions commending the Sudanese government at this Session included; Palestine, Algeria, Pakistan (OIC), Saudi Arabia, Cuba, China, Russia, and Zimbabwe. The UK voiced what appeared to be the strongest condemnation of Sudan, saying 'the situation has not fundamentally changed, including the indiscriminate killing on both sides. The Special Rapporteur's reports remain the same from one year to the next and we call on the Sudanese government to address this issue.'[269]

8.2.7.7 *Resolution on Human Rights in Sudan*

At the Seventh Session a Resolution on Sudan[270] was submitted by the African Group and co-sponsored by the UK. The EU joined the consensus, and expressed its belief that the Resolution highlighted the deep concern of the

---

265 Slovenian delegate, 7th Session, 13 March 2007, general debate on Agenda Item 3.
266 Slovenian delegate, 7th Session, 17 March 2008, response to SR on Sudan, Sima Samar.
267 *Ibid.*
268 Cuban delegate, 7th Session, 17 March 2008, response to SR on Sudan, Sima Samar.
269 UK delegate, 7th Session, 17 March 2008, response to SR on Sudan, Sima Samar.
270 HRC Res. 7/16, 'Situation of Human Rights in the Sudan', 27 March 2008, UN Doc. A/HRC/RES/7/16.

Council. Canada voiced its disappointment that, again, the resolution fell short and 'fails to reflect the recent deterioration of the situation'.[271] Canada's position arguably reflects the Council's failure, once more, to discharge its mandate adequately. Although the Resolution did identify some categories of violations, and did call for the Sudanese government to comply with its human rights obligations, the text again sought to shield the government and to identify other actors as abusers.

Canada recalled recent reports showing grave violations, and spoke of its regret that this Resolution was not more 'robust'. Although Canada joined the consensus, it asserted that the people of Sudan deserved better. Again, the weakening of the text can be explained by the need for compromise in order to ensure that the resolution was passed, let alone to gain consensus. The result was, once again, a resolution lacking weight in language and substance.

8.3. Patterns and impact of regional alliances

As has been demonstrated, regional alliances played a large role in shaping Council discussions and actions on the situation in Darfur. Regular discussions on the situation in Darfur displayed differing positions taken by regional groups, often depending on their own objectives. The pattern that emerged was that the Council was split between two sets of groups and states; those who expressed the opinion that the Sudanese government was cooperating fully and required further international assistance, and those who believed that the government was not doing all that it could and who called on it to comply with its international obligations and improve the situation. The former often resorted to accusing the Council, its mandate holders, or even member states, of politicisation in order to block intervening action. The term 'politicisation', often supported with references to post-colonial discourses on human rights, had become a rallying cry against action proposed by Western states. It was used to accuse Western states and mandate holders of falsifying information. However, the reports from UN bodies and NGOs often independently verified the information being called into question.[272]

States' accusations of falsification were, at least partially, aimed at undermining the Council's information activities regarding the situation in Darfur. Information activities are a main function of the body, and attempts to delegitimise that function resulted from political objectives of certain states, particularly Sudan's regional allies. Politicisation can be seen on the part of those who were bandying around that same accusation against others. Parallels can be drawn with America's accusations of politicisation at UNESCO in the 1970s.

271 Canadian delegate, 7th Session, 27 March 2008.
272 cf. Amnesty International, *Annual Report 2006*; Amnesty International, *Annual Report 2007*.

Advancement of states' national political aims, including protecting Sudan from Council scrutiny in order to protect themselves from similar scrutiny in the future, demonstrated realist tendencies already prevalent at the new body. National policies combined with regional alliances allowed these agendas to dominate proceedings and to impact greatly upon the Council's ability to fulfil its mandate.

8.3.1 *The African Group*

African Group members almost always shielded Sudan. Many African states also had dubious human rights records, and were advancing national objectives by seeking to ensure that the Council was unable to take strong action against Sudan that might be replicated in the future against other African regimes. In order to shield Sudan from Council action, the African Group employed various tactics during Council discussions and votes on resolutions. The Group used its collective weight to ensure that discussions were steered away from the specific violations, and ensured that resolutions were as weakly worded as possible.

The African Group constantly sought to undermine information sharing activities regarding Sudan. It frequently expressed the opinion that the Sudanese government was doing all that it could to ensure resolution of the crisis, and that other parties to the conflict were to blame for the situation. For example, at the Third Session, Algeria said 'the alleged links between the government and militias referred to by the High Commissioner have yet to be documented in an objective way'.[273] However, not only had documentation compiled by OHCHR been presented to the Council by the High Commissioner at the beginning of the Session,[274] but it was also verified by independent information from NGOs.[275]

Individual members of the African Group reiterated that collective position during discussions, even where their opinions contradicted independent evidence. For example, Egypt, a member of both the African Group and the OIC, said 'we commend Sudan for her cooperation and efforts to disarm militias, despite practical challenges'.[276] However, Amnesty International contradicted these statements, reporting that 'a government promise to disarm the Janjawid was broken, as it had been after numerous previous agreements, and none of the agreed commissions was operating by the end of 2006, including the Compensation Commission'.[277]

---

273 Algerian delegate, 3rd Session, 29 November 2006.
274 *Ibid.*
275 See, for example, 'In August government forces launched a major offensive in North Darfur and Jebel Marra, which was accompanied by Janjawid [sic] raids on villages and continued at the end of 2006.'Amnesty International, *Annual Report 2006*, p. 242.
276 Egyptian delegate, 4th Special Session, 12 December 2006.
277 Amnesty International, *Annual Report 2006*, p. 244.

The African states which did, at times, break regional alliances in discussing Darfur, were those known to be more benign or democratic than their neighbours.[278] The more democratic African regimes were more likely to deviate from the African Group's position perhaps owing to less fear of Council scrutiny of their own human rights records. For example, at the Special Session on Darfur, Zambia said 'despite the peace agreement, there is a lack of political will of the government of Sudan to protect civilians [. . .] The government must care for the welfare of all people regardless of racial or religious background.'[279] This sentiment was not often expressed by African states, and was buried in the vast amount of statements of support for the Sudanese government from this region.

8.3.2 The OIC

The OIC frequently aligned itself with the African Group's statements on Sudan. It also employed the tactic of using large numbers of states giving similar comments during discussions in order to emphasise the collective position. At the Second Session, individual states from the OIC expressing confidence in the Sudanese government's ability and willingness to improve the situation in Darfur included Bahrain (Chair of the Arab Group), Tunisia, Morocco, Jordan, Malaysia, Senegal, Azerbaijan and Bangladesh. The use of large numbers of states making broadly similar comments in order to emphasise a collective opinion was a tactic which continued to be employed at subsequent sessions. The OIC sought to protect Sudan, a member of the group, from scrutiny, often by advancing members' common national agendas of keeping the spotlight on human rights abuses committed by non-allied countries. The OIC sought to protect Sudan through constantly shifting attention onto other human rights situations, particularly in Israel and the OPT.

OIC members include many countries with foreign policy aims to delegitimise Israel. Its members pursued those political objectives at the Council by raising issues regarding Israel during discussions on Sudan. At the Special Session on Darfur,[280] for example, the discussion became sidelined by members of the OIC, including the representative of Palestine, who accused Kofi Annan of being partial to the developed world, and the High Commissioner of ignoring the occupation of Palestine. Iran later spoke at length about the '60-year Holocaust in Palestine' and accused the Council of ignoring the conflict in this region. The attempt to divert attention away from Sudan,

---

278 On Botswana see 'Concluding observations of the Human Rights Committee: Botswana', 24 April 2008, UN Doc. CCPR/C/BWA/CO/1. On Zambia see 'Concluding observations of the Human Rights Committee: Zambia', 23 July 2007, UN Doc. CCPR/C/ZMB/CO/3/CRP.1

279 Zambian delegate, 4th Special Session, 12 December 2006.

280 4th Special Session, 12–13 December 2006.

where Arab militia[281] were being accused of atrocities, and to shift the focus onto Israel, must be viewed in context of the fact that not only had a Special Session already taken place about Israel a month earlier[282] but that there had also been a Special Session on Israel four months prior to that.[283] Therefore, the shifting of focus by OIC members onto Israel during a Special Session convened on Darfur showed that the undercurrent of selectivity was still apparent within the main UN human rights body.[284] This was something picked up by other states, for example the UK said that 'when [the Council] focuses on the Israel and Palestine situation without focusing on other issues, some will wonder what this Council is doing'.[285]

8.3.3 Other regional groups

The EU consistently took a fairly neutral approach, unusually for that Group owing to its 'ethical foreign policy' normally guiding its approach to such situations.[286] The EU commended Sudan's efforts and cooperation, and it called for further assistance to support the government's efforts, whilst also condemning the human rights situation in Darfur and calling for action in this region. For example, after the Group of Experts' report at the resumed Sixth Session, it said:

> The report gives us some encouragement regarding potential positive results of this exercise. It also demonstrates clearly that much still has to be done. We welcome the open and constructive dialogue which has been taking place. However, little, or no, tangible impact has been reported of the few recommendations that have been implemented [. . .] Lots of recommendations have not been implemented [. . .] Some displaced persons have returned, but more have been displaced during this time [. . .] violence has increased [. . .] the Sudanese government is responsible for protecting its people, and they have not done so. [. . .] We must all help to stop these human rights violations.[287]

Moss has commented that even 'democratic countries are often reluctant to join in condemnation of other countries when doing so could harm the many other interests and ties – economic, political, security, regional, cultural,

---

281 Most notably the Janjaweed militia.
282 3rd Special Session (regarding Israel and the Occupied Palestinian Territories), 15 November 2006.
283 2nd Special Session (regarding the war between Israel and Lebanon), 11 August 2006.
284 Despite the founding principles of universality, impartiality, objectivity and non-selectivity, amongst others.
285 UK delegate, 2nd Session, 28 November 2006.
286 See, for example, Khaliq, *Ethical Dimensions of the Foreign Policy of the European Union*.
287 Portuguese delegate, 6th Session, 11 December 2007.

or religious – they have with those countries.[288] EU states' neutrality on the situation in Darfur reflected its reticence about endangering its overall relationship with Sudan's allies.

GRULAC members took neither consistent nor uniform positions regarding Sudan and the situation in Darfur, which emphasises that regional group's lack of political interest in Darfur. Whilst individual states did, at times, call for action or condemn the government, none did so regularly over the two-year period. Many states remained silent during discussions. Cuba, unsurprisingly given its political alliances, consistently aligned itself with the OIC and African Group's position, commending the Sudanese government for its efforts and cooperation. This position contradicted comments of other GRULAC members during the same discussions.

Canada, whose statements were often joined by Australia and New Zealand, took a stronger approach than the EU or GRULAC members, consistently condemning the Sudanese government for its role in the situation, and calling for action to be taken and recommendations to be implemented. Canada often questioned mandate holders as to how assistance could best be provided to help the civilians in Darfur. It spoke out against the weakening of resolutions and decisions, and was consistent in its calls for the Council to take a proactive approach. Canada's positions did not escape the OIC's attention, as will be explored directly below.

8.3.4 An example of the impact of regional alliances

The repercussions for a state taking a stand against the OIC can be seen in its subsequent treatment by the OIC and the African Group. This deterrent undoubtedly played a role in the weakening of the Council's resolutions and decisions. The Resolution passed at the Second Session was weaker in its wording than Western states and others had urged. The EU's proposals to strengthen the language, including the use of the words 'grave concern', were overwhelmingly defeated by the OIC and African Group. To understand why the weakened text was adopted, it must be examined within the context of an incident occurring during the resumed session. Canada had been the sole opposing vote against the OIC's resolutions on Israel,[289] with many Western states choosing to abstain. Ignoring the reasons given for Canada's 'no' votes,[290] the OIC showed its displeasure by using its collective weight

---

288 L.C. Moss, 'Will the Human Rights Council have Better Membership than the Commission on Human Rights?', *Human Rights Brief*, Vol. 13 (3), 2006, 10–11.

289 HRC Res. 2/3, 'Human Rights in the Occupied Syrian Golan', 9 January 2007, UN Doc. A/HRC/RES/2/3; HRC Res. 2/4, 'Israeli Settlements in the Occupied Palestinian Territory, Including East Jerusalem, and in the Occupied Syrian Golan', 9 January 2007, UN Doc. A/HRC/RES/2/4.

290 Which included the fact that the resolutions were biased and only addressed the human rights violations of Israel, which contradicted the Council's principles of non-selectivity, universality and equality.

to pass a last minute motion postponing three non-controversial Canadian Draft Resolutions.[291]

The OIC's flexing of its collective muscle, alongside that of their usual supporters,[292] sent a clear message to the Council. Power politics undoubtedly made an impact upon other members of the Council that witnessed this tactic. Morgenthau argued that all politics, including international affairs, can be categorised as one of three types: 'A political policy seeks either to keep power, to increase power, or to demonstrate power'. OIC members' behaviour at the Council clearly sought to achieve all three objectives.[293] The OIC aimed to retain power by discouraging other states from challenging its power. It aimed to increase power through deterring other states from taking contradictory stances, as Canada had done. It further demonstrated power through displaying its collective strength. Therefore, when it came to the language of the Resolution on Darfur, the Western states stood little chance of being able to convince other countries to stand against the OIC and African Group.

8.4. Summary

The human rights situation in Darfur was ongoing and grave, requiring the Council's attention from the body's outset. Unlike other situations, for example in Zimbabwe, the Council did focus attention on the gross and systemic abuses in Darfur. The body sought to discharge its protection, and indeed promotion, mandate through pre-existing and innovative mechanisms. The Council focused on the founding principles of cooperation, inclusiveness and dialogue with Sudan and its regional allies in the African Group. Despite the time and resources devoted to Darfur, there was little improvement on the ground. This chapter has presented a case study which demonstrates, through detailed analysis of Council sessions, that politicisation through regionalism prevented the body from adequately fulfilling its mandate. Political agendas, particularly protecting an ally and deflecting attention away from abuses within other allied states, resulted in weakened action on Darfur and less pressure on Sudan to fulfil its human rights obligations and implement recommendations. I shall explore conclusions on the Council's inaction on Darfur under the three headings used in Chapter 7 – the body's mandate, its founding principles, and politicisation.

---

291   One of which – HRC Res. 2/5, 'Effective Implementation of International Instruments on Human Rights', 28 November 2006, UN Doc. A/HRC/RES/2/5 – was later negotiated to be presented the following day, and passed by consensus. The other two – HRC Draft Decision 2/L.44, 'Darfur', 28 November 2006, UN Doc. A/HRC/2/L.44 and HRC Draft Decision 2/L.44, 'Impunity', 28 November 2006, UN Doc. A/HRC/2/L.38 – were presented at a different Council Session.
292   Including Cuba, China and Russia.
293   H.J. Morgenthau, *Politics Among Nations*, New York: Alfred A. Knopf, 1960, p. 39.

8.4.1 *Mandate*

The Council utilised a number of tools and undertook various functions in attempting to fulfil its mandate. The body enabled fact-finding missions, information sharing, dialogue between state and non-state actors, and support, advice, and capacity-building for Sudan's government. All of these sought to protect victims of abuses within Darfur. The body further utilised its mechanisms, including convening a Special Session on Darfur, and sought to use its powers, including decisions and resolutions, to place pressure on the Sudanese government to comply with its human rights obligations. Alongside the UN-appointed Special Rapporteur on Sudan, the Council upheld a joint initiative between the EU and the African Group creating a Group of Experts on that region. The Group of Experts was an innovative mechanism aimed at discharging the Council's protection mandate and adhering to the principles of cooperation, inclusiveness and constructive dialogue. The Group's short existence, however, proved insufficient for its work to have a serious impact on the ground.

The body's attempts to discharge its mandate were repeatedly thwarted. Resolutions and decisions were mainly expressed in general terms, and often failed to specify the violations, condemn the ongoing abuses, or ascribe responsibility to the government. Those weak texts, particularly when compared with reports from such bodies as the Human Rights Committee or indeed with Council resolutions on states such as Israel, resulted in little political or other pressure on the Sudanese government. Arguably emboldened by the Council's weak attempts to fulfil its mandate, the government often ignored the body's work. For example, Sudan was expected formally to accept at least some of the recommendations made by the Group of Experts, but this did not occur in practice. In its final report, the Group of Experts concluded that:

> while certain recommendations have been partially implemented, it is not in a position to report that a clear impact on the ground has been identified. Regarding other recommendations, first steps towards implementation have been taken in some cases, whereas in others, recommendations remain to be implemented. The Group of Experts regrets that certain short term recommendations were not addressed by the Government at all or, in other cases, information provided was unrelated to them.[294]

The Council did achieve some successes under its protection mandate, and indeed the Group of Experts did provide Sudan with important proposals

---

294 HRC, 'Interim report on the situation of human rights in Darfur prepared by the group of experts mandated by the Human Rights Council in its resolution 4/8', 22 September 2007, UN Doc. A/HRC/6/7, p. 3.

and recommendations. One example where the Council effectively protected human rights was by improving the reporting requirements and procedures for rape victims. Those successes were, however, offset by continuing, and sometimes worsening, human right abuses. Hafner-Burton argues that naming and shaming of states for human rights violations results in some improvements regarding the abuses in the spotlight, but a worsening of other human rights abuses within that country.[295] This analysis is supported when examining Sudan's human rights record in Darfur during the Council's early sessions.

The failure of the Group of Experts to encourage 'concrete improvements on the ground in Darfur'[296] is representative of a more general problem with the Council's attempts to secure the cooperation of Sudan despite that state's clear disregard for the body's work. Attempts to ensure cooperation impacted upon the Council's work, for example by weakening both the language of decisions on the situation in Darfur and the pressure on Sudan to cease human rights violations. The Council's desire for inclusiveness did not achieve results on the ground because the Sudanese government failed to implement recommendations to which it had agreed, and disregarded much of the body's work on Darfur. Sudan was supported in this stance by its allies, particularly within the OIC and the African Group.

The promotion aspect of the Council's mandate was manipulated by states as a method for shifting focus away from the Sudanese government. The Council was constantly asked to focus on capacity-building and technical assistance despite the crisis situation requiring focus on the need for immediate protection of victims. These invocations were repeatedly made by states seeking to protect Sudan. Calls for further assistance for Sudan was a theme apparent within all discussions of Darfur, and one which masked the attempts by regional groups to block intervention. Furthermore, these calls for assistance often came from members of those alliances which were weakening attempts to intervene in Darfur. These statements often used a post-colonialist discourse, seeking to shift attention away from the Sudanese government by blaming the international community for the escalating and continuing crisis.

8.4.2 Founding principles

The Council's attempts to discharge its mandate in relation to Darfur were constantly undermined by states seeking to protect Sudan for subjective and partial motives. The Council, therefore, saw its efforts to adhere to its founding principles of objectivity and impartiality thwarted by states, groups and blocs which sought to achieve their own objectives. It is clear from the

295 E.M. Hafner-Burton, 'Sticks and Stones: Naming and Shaming – The Human Rights Enforcement Problem', *International Organization*, Vol. 62, 2008, 689–716.
296 *Ibid.*

Council's work on Darfur that the idealist principles were unable to withstand some states' realist aims and power politics.

The Council did attempt to secure cooperation, inclusiveness and dialogue, all of which are founding principles. Cooperation was stressed in decisions and resolutions, particularly through highlighting the need for Sudan's consent. However, emphasis on cooperation was often used as an excuse to weaken the texts. Despite some states and groups, particularly the EU, seeking to ensure cooperation, a main obstacle was the Sudanese government's refusal to cooperate with the body.[297] Sudan's constant downplaying – or, at times, outright denial – of its role in the atrocities being committed in Darfur was consistently strengthened by the comments and actions of the African Group, the OIC and other allied states such as Cuba and China.

8.4.3 Politicisation

A main tactic deployed by regional groups was collective voting to block action being taken against Sudan. Mirroring the same issue at the Commission, most of the states using these tactics at the Council themselves had somewhat dubious human rights records. Blocking action against Sudan furthered these states' national objectives by creating obstacles to similar Council scrutiny of their own records.

Another tactic was the OIC's use of its dominance at the Council to promote its policies on Sudan. The tactic of ostracising countries which vocalised their disagreement with the OIC's collective stance was employed to intimidate other non-OIC states and to ensure that they did not speak out against the alliance's stance. The OIC's collective action against Canada, at the Second Session, provided an early indication of the tactics which that bloc was willing to deploy. States were given a clear message that disagreement with the OIC would result in repercussions beyond those particular discussions or issues. Reluctance about disrupting relations with that influential group arguably went beyond repercussions at the Council. Fears of damaging economic, security, political, and other ties, resulted in a number of states, especially EU members, taking neutral positions on Darfur to avoid conflict with that group.

---

297 See, for example, Schrijver, 'A New "Society of the Committed"'.

9 Innovative mechanisms

Assessment of the Council requires an examination of the two new mechanisms. Universal Periodic Review (UPR) was aimed at supporting Council efforts to universally promote human rights. Special Sessions were designed to enable protection of human rights within grave and crisis situations.

9.1. Universal Periodic Review

Universal Periodic Review, through its universality, directly deals with criticisms of selectivity and politicisation at the Council's predecessor.[1] Sweeney and Saito comment that the UPR is the one completely innovative mechanism that distinguishes the new body from the Commission.[2] However, while the UPR has been mooted, and widely accepted, as an innovative mechanism,[3] Alston draws a historical parallel between the UPR and a 1950 proposal for a periodic review.[4] Although this comparison has been criticised,[5] I shall use it as a starting point for exploring the UPR's background.

In 1950, France proposed a system to examine states' adherence to their human rights commitments. Yugoslavia raised the issue of capacity-building during these discussions, insisting that assistance be given to states lacking the national resources to implement human rights standards.[6] That issue is

1 C. Callejon, 'Developments at the Human Rights Council in 2007: A Reflection of its Ambivalence', *Human Rights Law Review*, Vol. 8 (2), 2008, 334.

2 G. Sweeney and Y. Saito, 'An NGO Assessment of the New Mechanisms of the UN Human Rights Council', *Human Rights Law Review*, Vol. 9 (2), 2009, 203.

3 Callejon, 'Developments at the Human Rights Council in 2007', p. 334; J. Carey, 'The U.N. Human Rights Council: What Would Eleanor Roosevelt Say?', *ISLA Journal of International and Comparative Law*, Vol. 15 (2), 2008–2009, 460.

4 P. Alston, 'Reconceiving the UN Human Rights Regime: Challenges Confronting the New UN Human Rights Council', *Melbourne Journal of International Law*, Vol. 7, 2006, 207.

5 cf. A.M. Abebe, 'Of Shaming and Bargaining: African States and the Universal Periodic Review of the United Nations Human Rights Council', *Human Rights Law Review*, Vol. 9 (1), 2009, 5. Arguing that there are few similarities between the two mechanisms.

6 'Yugoslavia: Amendments to the Draft Resolution on Annual Reports (E/CN.4/L.266) Submitted by the United States of America', UN Doc. E/CN.4/L.305/Rev.1 (1953) in CHR, 'Report of the Ninth Session of the Commission on Human Rights', 30 May 1953, UN Doc. E/2447, p. 266.

still raised in relation to human rights and the expectations placed on weaker, particularly developing, states. Cold War tensions initially blocked the proposal, with Western and Latin American states[7] fearing that 'democratic states' would be the sole countries to submit reports.[8] In 1953, however, the US, seeking to deflect criticism from its pronouncement that it would not ratify human rights treaties,[9] built on France's proposal, suggesting annual voluntary state reports on particular human rights issues.[10] The US proposal particularly focused on fact-finding, information sharing, and the role of administrative staff and states in providing peer-led practical advice and guidance on implementing human rights standards.[11]

Neither proposal bore fruit until 1956. Even then, Alston comments, they were watered down in an effort to achieve compromise, resulting in a number of failings of the reporting system.[12] These failings are key to understanding the UPR and the potential problems that it faces. State reports to the Commission regularly downplayed or ignored issues of compliance. The potential for such abuse stems from allowing states, rather than independent experts, to submit reports on their human rights situations. Another main flaw was that rather than allowing the Secretary-General to analyse state reports, he was only mandated to summarise them. Alston comments that this undermined the reporting system's effectiveness.[13] A third issue relevant for the UPR was that recommendations were qualified by the requirement that they be 'general and objective', thus limiting the ability of the mechanism to deal with specific human rights issues or situations.[14]

The Commission's reporting procedure lasted for 25 years, but made little impact on the protection and promotion of human rights. Alston comments that the procedure's 'achievements could readily be measured in terms of trees destroyed'.[15] Its main success was to give the impression that governments were cooperating with the Commission. One of the UPR's main tasks will be to ensure that it does more than merely giving the appearance of human rights protection.

Alston summarises four main lessons that the Council can learn from the Commission's review system: transparency and fairness; strong and reliable information; concise, focused recommendations tailored to individual situations; and tangible outcomes.[16] This section examines the UPR, state positions

---

7 CHR, 'Report of the Sixth Session of the Commission on Human Rights', 19 May 1950, UN Doc. E/1681, p. 8.
8 Alston, 'Reconceiving the UN Human Rights Regime', 208.
9 See Chapter 7, Section 7.1.
10 Alston, 'Reconceiving the UN Human Rights Regime', 208–209.
11 *Ibid.*, 209.
12 *Ibid.*, 211.
13 *Ibid.*, 212.
14 *Ibid.*, 212.
15 *Ibid.*, 213.
16 *Ibid.*, 214.

taken during its creation, and sessions from the first cycle, in order to assess whether it has learned lessons from the previous review system and, indeed, has achieved its objectives.

9.1.1 *Background*

Adoption of a 'peer review' was first proposed by the then Secretary-General Kofi Annan in April 2005[17] during the Commission's final session. The concept was introduced as part of Annan's proposal to replace the Commission.[18] The mechanism was intended to implement universal and indivisible human rights.[19] The review was expected to assist the UN human rights machinery to overcome the Commission's politicisation and selectivity,[20] and was seen as 'the main drive to depoliticization' of the human rights body.[21]

Alston notes the proposal's main attractions: universality; avoidance of the politicisation that had undermined the Commission; and provision of practical human rights support and advice.[22] Peer review was expected to overcome selectivity by assessing every state's fulfilment of human rights obligations.[23] Annan proposed that each country be reviewed periodically[24] to ensure regular and universal application. Annan insisted[25] that subjecting all states to a review would remove the 'selectivity bias that had kept some states perennially on or off the commission's agenda',[26] and 'eventually combat the Council's selectivity in addressing human rights violations in the world'.[27] The mechanism would avoid selectivity and politicisation as it would not single out known human rights abusers for scrutiny.[28] Rather than eliminating

---

17 Speech of Secretary-General Kofi Annan to the Commission on Human Rights, 'Reforming UN Human Rights Machinery', 7 April 2005, UN Press Release SG/SM/9808 HR/CN/1108.

18 N. Schrijver, 'The UN Human Rights Council: A New "Society of the Committed" or Just Old Wine in New Bottles', *Leiden Journal of International Law*, Vol. 20 (4), 2007, 814.

19 GA, 'Secretary-General Report, Addendum, Human Rights Council, Explanatory Note by the Secretary-General', 23 May 2005, UN Doc. A/59/2005/Add.1, para. 6.

20 *Ibid.*

21 M. Davies, 'Rhetorical Inaction? Compliance and the Human Rights Council of the United Nations', *Alternatives: Global, Local, Political*, Vol. 35, 2010, 457.

22 Alston, 'Reconceiving the UN Human Rights Regime', p. 207.

23 GA, 'Secretary-General Report, Addendum, Human Rights Council, Explanatory Note by the Secretary-General', 23 May 2005, UN Doc. A/59/2005/Add.1, para. 6.

24 *Ibid.*, paras 6 and 7.

25 *Ibid.*, para. 3.

26 Davies, 'Rhetorical Inaction? Compliance and the Human Rights Council of the United Nations', 456.

27 M. Nowak, M. Birk, T. Crittin and J. Kozma, 'UN Human Rights Council in Crisis – Proposals to Enhance the Effectiveness of the Council', in W. Benedek, F. Benoit-Rohmer, W. Karl and M. Nowak (eds.), *European Yearbook on Human Rights*, Vienna: European Academic Press, 2011, p. 45.

28 F.D. Gaer, 'A Voice Not an Echo: Universal Periodic Review and the UN Treaty Body System', *Human Rights Law Review*, Vol. 7 (1), 2007, 111.

country scrutiny altogether, the review would place the burden of scrutiny on 'peers' – other member states.[29] Moreover, as it aimed to prevent any country from avoiding human rights scrutiny, the proposal was seen as the embodiment of a genuinely reformed human rights body.[30]

Alston comments that 'peer review' has no meaning other than involvement of other states, despite the term's frequent use within international organisations.[31] Annan did not expand upon the 'peer' element of his proposal, and the term 'peer review' was absent from Resolution 60/251,[32] which instead required the Council to 'undertake a universal periodic review'.[33] Change from 'peer' to 'periodic' appears to have had little impact on the mechanism which, as shall be explored, undertakes a periodic and peer review of all states. It does, however, allow other stakeholders to participate alongside states in the review,[34] although that participation is limited. Change in language perhaps reflects concerns regarding the phrase's lack of definition, or counters any potential state arguments about who constitutes a 'peer'.

Idealism featured prominently in Annan's proposals. Gaer comments that Annan, supported by the former High Commissioner for Human Rights Louise Arbour, had 'a grand vision' in which various UN mechanisms would be utilised to implement UN human rights norms and standards.[35] However, little discussion occurred on the review's modalities, nor how it would achieve the stated aims.[36] Idealist language and hopes were expressed with little regard to the practicality, nor even the possibility, of implementation. Indeed, Annan failed to discuss whether or how the UPR, itself an intergovernmental mechanism, might avoid the same politicisation that it sought to help the UN human rights body to overcome.[37] Perhaps, in the throes of idealistic vision, Annan did not consider the very possibility that UPR was always going to be placed under pressure as an intergovernmental mechanism mandated to conduct itself without politicisation.

In keeping with Annan's idealist aims, the General Assembly's first pronouncement on the new mechanism[38] stated that the 'Council shall have the ability to periodically review the fulfilment of all human rights obligations

---

29 *Ibid.*, 110.
30 *Ibid.*, 110.
31 Alston, 'Reconceiving the UN Human Rights Regime', 207.
32 Gaer, 'A Voice Not an Echo: Universal Periodic Review and the UN Treaty Body System', 112.
33 GA Res. 60/251, 'Human Rights Council', 15 March 2006, UN Doc. A/RES/60/251, para. 5 (e).
34 Callejon, 'Developments at the Human Rights Council in 2007', 334.
35 Gaer, 'A Voice Not an Echo: Universal Periodic Review and the UN Treaty Body System', 113.
36 Sweeney and Saito, 'An NGO assessment of the new mechanisms of the UN Human Rights Council', 204.
37 *Ibid.*
38 Draft released by the General Assembly President, dated 3 June 2005.

of all Member States'.[39] The August draft similarly called for periodic review of all human rights obligations of all states.[40] However, the September draft downgraded the review from fulfilment of human rights obligations to compliance with such obligations.[41] Observers have noted the fundamental difference between 'fulfilment' and 'compliance',[42] arguing that the former requires states to take proactive steps to ensure individuals' rights.[43] These early changes mirror the Commission's review procedure, whereby key elements for protecting and promoting human rights were undermined or downplayed in order to maintain state support for the fledgling proposal.

All states saw UPR as a mechanism that would deal with the UN human rights machinery's credibility issues after the Commission's demise. As a universal procedure it was expected that no states, not even powerful or well-connected countries, would be able to avoid scrutiny.[44] However, the North–South divide demonstrated different motivations for wanting the UPR and different expectations for the mechanism's outcomes. Steiner *et al.* comment that the UPR was heralded by developing countries, particularly the Like-Minded Group, as they had opposed the Commission's selective focus on grave violations within a few states.[45] UPR offered a universal mechanism that would focus on a range of human rights abuses, not just gross and systemic situations. Western Governments and NGOs also welcomed UPR as an opportunity to hold regular, in-depth reviews on all states' human rights records.[46] Alston comments that, in practice, there will be divergence between North and South expectations.[47] Western states will seek probing reviews resulting in critical country-specific recommendations. Developing

39 GA Report, 'Draft Outcome Document of the High Level Plenary Meeting of the General Assembly of September 2005 submitted by the President of the General Assembly', 8 June 2005, UN Doc. A/59/HLPM/CRP.1, para. 88; see UN Press Release, 'Assembly President Previews Possible Outcome of Summit on UN Reform', 3 June 2005 (Online). Available HTTP: <www.un.org/news> (accessed 22 July 2012).
40 GA Report, 'Revised Draft Outcome Document of the High Level Plenary Meeting of the General Assembly of September 2005 submitted by the President of the General Assembly, 10 August 2005, UN Doc. A/59/HLPM/CRP.1/Rev.2, para. 139.
41 Gaer, 'A Voice Not an Echo: Universal Periodic Review and the UN Treaty Body System', 111.
42 See, for example, Gaer, 'A Voice Not an Echo: Universal Periodic Review and the UN Treaty Body System', 111.
43 For more on this see, Committee on Economic, Social and Cultural Rights General Comment No. 16, 'The equal right of men and women to the enjoyment of all economic, social and cultural rights (Article 3)', 11 August 2005, UN Doc. E/C.12/2005/4; Human Rights Committee General Comment No. 31, 'The Nature of the General Legal Obligations Imposed on States Parties to the Covenant', 26 May 2004, UN Doc. HRI/GEN/1/Rev.7, para. 192.
44 Gaer, 'A Voice Not an Echo: Universal Periodic Review and the UN Treaty Body System', 110.
45 H.J. Steiner, P. Alston and R. Goodman, *International Human Rights in Context*, 3rd edn., Oxford: Oxford University Press, 2008, p. 806.
46 *Ibid.*
47 Alston, 'Reconceiving the UN Human Rights Regime', 206.

states will seek a general, open-ended, non-condemnatory process. Alston, writing before the UPR's first cycle, argued that the mechanism will ultimately be shaped by states not aligned with the North or South, such as Latin American countries and those African states not members of the OIC.[48] That assertion was correct to a certain extent, as will be demonstrated through examining the debates on the UPR's creation and modalities, as well as its first cycle.

9.1.2 UPR creation

Canada circulated two non-papers[49] on Peer Review during 2005.[50] The first offered two approaches for the review – the Comprehensive Approach and the Interactive Dialogue.[51] Gaer explains that the Comprehensive Approach[52] comprised compiling a comprehensive state report, giving recommendations, a formal interactive dialogue, and publication of conclusions.[53] The Interactive Dialogue proposed a three-hour discussion of a state's pre-published statement on its national human rights situation, with extra information made available by the OHCHR,[54] with a published summary to which the concerned states could respond within six months.[55] The latter was a simpler but less rigorous approach.[56]

Canada's second non-paper combined the two approaches. OHCHR would compile all available information on the reviewed state to which that state would respond. A committee 'of experts appointed by the [12] "peer states"' would hold an interactive dialogue, with a state presentation, questions and comments, and state response. A summary would be published to which the state could respond. All documents would then be submitted to the Council.[57]

Canada's proposals clearly guided and shaped the UPR, as I shall demonstrate when examining the mechanism's modalities. Although not explicitly stated by Canada, that country hoped that UPR would enable the UN human rights body to move away from politicisation and towards cooperation.[58] Canada, a Western and developed state, aligned itself with a typically South

48 *Ibid.*
49 Non-papers are authoritative but unofficial documents used to present ideas about and test state reactions to policies.
50 Gaer, 'A Voice Not an Echo: Universal Periodic Review and the UN Treaty Body System', 113.
51 *Ibid.*, 114.
52 Based on OECD, ILO, and World Trade Organisation peer review mechanisms, as well as the African Peer Review Mechanism.
53 Gaer, 'A Voice Not an Echo: Universal Periodic Review and the UN Treaty Body System', 114.
54 Such as treaty body reports, information from other procedures, and statements from interested parties.
55 Gaer, 'A Voice Not an Echo: Universal Periodic Review and the UN Treaty Body System', 114.
56 *Ibid.*
57 *Ibid.*, 115.
58 *Ibid.*, 115.

position that naming, shaming and blaming states achieves less than encouraging a cooperative culture of practical assistance. Canada does have a strong reputation at the UN for its peacekeeping initiatives, and is seen as a benign Western nation by many developing countries and groups. Therefore, Canada's taking up the South's mantle in this regard is not wholly surprising. Canada has nevertheless found itself ostracised at the Council by some regional groups and political blocs owing to the positions that it has taken at the Council, particularly regarding Israel.[59] Canada's general position against naming, shaming and blaming, and its interest in avoiding politicisation, particularly regarding country-specific issues, was mirrored in its proposals for the UPR.

The UPR's general outline was established by GA Resolution 60/251. However, the modalities were left to the Council, with only guiding principles and concepts set out in Paragraph 5(e), which says that the Council shall:

> Undertake a universal periodic review, based on objective and reliable information, of the fulfilment by each State of its human rights obligations and commitments in a manner which ensures universality of coverage and equal treatment with respect to all States; the review shall be a cooperative mechanism, based on an interactive dialogue, with the full involvement of the country concerned and with consideration given to its capacity-building needs; such a mechanism shall complement and not duplicate the work of treaty bodies; the Council shall develop the modalities and necessary time allocation for the universal periodic review mechanism within one year after the holding of its first session.[60]

Alston comments that Resolution 60/251 'faithfully reflects' Annan's vision.[61] However, as with Annan's original proposal, the Resolution sets out nothing more than the mechanism's general skeleton. Annan's explanatory note on the Council's creation[62] added a similarly vague and broad statement that the UPR should give 'an evaluation of fulfilment of all human rights for all persons'.[63] The language used reflects idealist language found in other UN documents. Ghanea comments that such idealist language is 'worrisome', particularly as requiring cooperation will reduce the Council's ability to deal with the gravest situations where an abuser state is unlikely to cooperate with the Council.[64]

---

59 See Chapter 8, Section 8.3.4; see, also, Canada's UPR, Section 9.1.4.2.

60 GA Res. 60/251, 'Human Rights Council', para. 5 (e).

61 Alston, 'Reconceiving the UN Human Rights Regime', 207.

62 'Human Rights Council, Explanatory Note by the Secretary-General', UN Doc. A/59/2005/ Add.1, para. 6.

63 *Ibid.*

64 N. Ghanea, 'From UN Commission on Human Rights to UN Human Rights Council: One Step Forwards or Two Steps Sideways?', *International and Comparative Law Quarterly*, Vol. 55 (3), 2006, 703.

Rather than dealing with the UPR's specifics, Resolution 60/251 directed the Council on certain fundamental criteria that it should fulfil: it should be based on objective and reliable information; it must review state fulfilment of human rights obligations and commitments; the review must ensure universality of coverage and equal treatment of all states, with consideration given to a state's capacity-building needs; it shall be a cooperative mechanism; and it involves an interactive dialogue with the state's full involvement.[65]

Interpreting this idealist language, and ensuring practical implementation of these requirements, presented various issues, including: the information to be used; involvement of the state; how to ensure universal coverage and equal treatment; UPR's interactions with Council plenary sessions; and the formal reports to be submitted. North–South tensions existed from the outset, with developing nations and groups taking very different positions to Western and other developed countries. One example was the debate on whether non-ratified treaty obligations should form part of the review. Reviewing a state's universal coverage of human rights obligations was innovative, and can be contrasted with treaty body reviews which only deal with states' obligations under ratified treaties.[66] Treaty ratifications vary greatly.[67] Gaer comments, for example, that many Asian states are not parties to the Convention Against Torture.[68] Unsurprisingly, states arguing that the UPR should not examine obligations under non-ratified treaties were invariably themselves, or allied with states, not party to such treaties. Algeria (African Group) said that '[n]o State can be held accountable for obligations pertaining to a treaty that they have not ratified'.[69] Singapore argued that the Resolution:

> clearly precludes judging States against treaties and conventions that they have not ratified, since they are neither obligated to fulfil them nor have made a commitment to do so [. . .] Instead, the review should examine broader obligations under the Universal Declaration of Human Rights as well as commitments made by individual States, such as the voluntary pledges made while seeking membership in the [Council].[70]

---

65 Although the UPR's relationship with treaty body mechanisms shall not be explored in this book, it must be noted that Resolution 60/251 went beyond earlier stipulations that the mechanism not interfere with the system of reporting to treaty bodies, instead directing that the procedure 'shall complement and not duplicate the work of the treaty bodies'.

66 Gaer, 'A Voice Not an Echo: Universal Periodic Review and the UN Treaty Body System', 125.

67 For example, 192 states are party to the CRC, 141 to CAT and only 34 to the CMW.

68 Gaer, 'A Voice Not an Echo: Universal Periodic Review and the UN Treaty Body System', 125.

69 Algeria, Oral Statement (on behalf of the African Group), 21 July 2006.

70 Singapore, Oral Statement, 21 July 2006.

9.1.3 *Finalising the UPR*

One of the Council's initial tasks was to establish the UPR's modalities. An open-ended Working Group,[71] comprised of state delegates rather than independent experts, was established to create the mechanism's modalities. Morocco's Ambassador Mohammed Loulichki was appointed as facilitator. It held numerous meetings and consultations, including a one-day conference in Switzerland, during which Canada's proposals were examined at length and presentations given on similar review processes.[72] The modalities were drafted over three sessions in 2006–2007, and were observed to have been 'the least contentious component of the institution-building phase'.[73]

Abebe, an Ethiopian delegate to the Council, comments that institution-building was heavily dominated by political agendas, with only 'a minimal professional and expert input'.[74] Creating the UPR mechanism followed similar patterns to, but to a lesser extent than, other institution-building tasks, perhaps owing to the central importance of ensuring the mechanism's success. Key areas of divergence included concern about the roles of NGOs and independent experts, the sources of information to be used, and the composition of the working group facilitating the review.[75] It was determined that the UPR would be an evolving mechanism, with its modalities reviewed at the end of the first four-year cycle.[76]

The facilitator's final non-paper[77] was reproduced in the IBP to enshrine the UPR's modalities. Sweeney and Saito argue that consensus on this document was easily achieved as the mechanism's success was recognised as key for the Council's success.[78] The need for consensus was particularly important to give credibility to this new mechanism. Without such consensus the UPR would have been weakened both in practice and in the eyes of the UN and observers.

9.1.3.1 *How it works*

UPR is not based on a treaty or legal instrument; its legal foundations are Resolution 60/251 and the IBP. As Resolution 60/251 simply sets out the

---

71 Human Rights Council Decision 1/103, 'The Universal Periodic Review', 30 June 2006, UN Doc. A/HRC/DEC/1/103.

72 Scannella and Splinter, 'The United Nations Human Rights Council', 63–4.

73 Sweeney and Saito, 'An NGO assessment of the new mechanisms of the UN Human Rights Council', 205.

74 Abebe, 'Of Shaming and Bargaining', 3.

75 For critical summaries, see ISHR's 'Overview reports of the Working Group sessions' and 'Daily Highlights of the final session of the Working Group' (Online). Available HTTP: http://www.ishr.ch/index.php?option=com_content&task=view&id=248&Itemid=444 (accessed 22 July 2012).

76 Callejon, 'Developments at the Human Rights Council in 2007', 337.

77 HRC, 'Non-paper on the universal periodic review mechanism', 27 April 2007, UN Doc. A/HRC/5/14.

78 Sweeney and Saito, 'An NGO Assessment of the New Mechanisms of the UN Human Rights Council', 205.

UPR's general principles and objectives, the IBP must be examined to understand how the mechanism works. Part I of the IBP identifies the roles, functions, principles and objectives of the review. It then sets out the modalities, including: periodicity and order of the review; process of the review; documents to be used, and the review's outcome and follow-up. Each UPR Working Group session reviews 16 states. Three reviews take place per year, thus covering 48 states, with all states reviewed during the four-year cycle.

The first stage involves gathering and collating information on the reviewed state's human rights situation. State cooperation is an essential component of the process. Many states viewed UPR as a cooperative rather than con-frontational mechanism, as is reflected in the IBP's emphasis on cooperation.[79] It has generally been accepted that states are obligated to participate in the process, and as such there are no provisions for how to deal with a state that does not engage with the mechanism.[80] However, it has been argued that requiring a 'cooperative mechanism' may cause problems[81] as much of the UPR's success, or otherwise, depends on the nature and quality of the documents used to conduct the review.[82] State cooperation is key to the collation of such material. Gaer argues that the UPR's ambiguity on state cooperation, and the conflicting visions of the Council's general role in protecting and promoting human rights, casts doubt on whether such issues will be adequately resolved to allow the UPR to achieve its objectives.[83] During the first cycle, the majority of states cooperated to a large extent with collation of relevant materials. Exceptions predominantly fell into two categories: (1) states, such as the DPRK,[84] that might have been expected altogether to refuse to cooperate with the review process and, therefore, for whom failure fully to cooperate was still a 'success'; and (2) states, such as Comoros,[85] with limited resources for collating relevant materials. States falling under those categories arguably are more likely to have poor human rights records. As Nowak *et al.* point out, it is those states which 'most need external scrutiny' and, yet, are least likely to cooperate with, and therefore be impacted by, the UPR process.[86]

79 Callejon, 'Developments at the Human Rights Council in 2007', 335.
80 Abebe, 'Of Shaming and Bargaining', 7.
81 Gaer, 'A Voice Not an Echo: Universal Periodic Review and the UN Treaty Body System', 137.
82 Callejon, 'Developments at the Human Rights Council in 2007', 336.
83 Gaer, 'A Voice Not an Echo: Universal Periodic Review and the UN Treaty Body System', 137.
84 Sixth Session of the Working Group of the Universal Periodic Review, 7 December 2009; HRC Res. 13/13, 'Report of the Working Group on the Universal Periodic Review, Democratic People's Republic of Korea', 4 January 2010, UN Doc. A/HRC/13/13.
85 Fifth Session of the Working Group of the Universal Periodic Review, 13 May 2009; HRC Res. 12/16, 'Report of the Working Group on the Universal Periodic Review, Comoros', 3 June 2009, UN Doc. A/HRC/12/16.
86 Nowak *et al.*, 'UN Human Rights Council in Crisis – Proposals to Enhance the Effective-ness of the Council', 46.

States' national reports are limited to 20 pages. The General Guidelines[87] require a brief description of a state's human rights situations, the challenges it faces and the assistance it requires. Abebe comments that requiring states 'to present a colossal and factually dense report' would have been burdensome. This is particularly true for poorer countries.[88] Presenting a major report would also take longer, thus limiting the number of reviewed states per session. The General Guidelines also 'clearly differentiate the UPR from treaty body periodic reports',[89] thus ensuring that the UPR complies with para. 5 (e), GA Resolution 60/251 by complementing and not duplicating the work of other human rights bodies.[90] States are required to include within the national reports the 'broad consultation process followed for the preparation of information provided'.[91] Alongside the national report, the review considers the OHCHR's compilation ten-page report of UN information[92] and the OHCHR's ten-page summary of 'credible and reliable information provided by other relevant stakeholders'. As Callejon notes, the OHCHR has a difficult task in condensing the collated information into ten pages.[93]

The UPR Working Group, consisting of all Council members and observer states, conducts the three-hour review. Davies asserts that a 'mere' three hours 'renders the review more of a schematic overview of the situation in any given country, rather than a detailed appraisal'.[94] The review is led by the troika of rapporteur states[95] which consists of three Council members, drawn by lots, each from different regional groups. Conducting the review with all Council members sitting as a Working Group rather than at a plenary

---

87 'As their name indicates, the guidelines include general requirements, *inter alia* the normative and institutional framework, particularly the scope of international human rights obligations identified as the basis of the review and their implementation, identification of achievements, best practices, challenges and constraints. The guidelines also include a description of the methodology and the consultation process at the national level, which should ensure consultation of civil society by the concerned State.' Callejon, 'Developments at the Human Rights Council in 2007', 337.

88 Abebe, 'Of Shaming and Bargaining', 10.

89 J. Vengoechea-Barrios, 'The Universal Periodic Review: A New Hope for International Human Rights Law or a Reformulation of Errors of the Past?', *International Law: revista colombiana de derecho internacional*, Vol. 12, 2008, 109.

90 See Chapter 3, Section 3.2.3.

91 HRC Decision 6/102, 'General Guidelines for the Preparation of Information Under the Universal Periodic Review', 27 September 2007, UN Doc. A/HRC/DEC/6/102, para. A.

92 HRC Res. 5/1, 'Institution Building of the United Nations Human Rights Council', 18 June 2007, UN Doc. A/HRC/RES/5/1, para. 15(b) stating 'information contained in the reports of treaty bodies, special procedures, including observations and comments by the State concerned, and other relevant official United Nations documents'.

93 Callejon, 'Developments at the Human Rights Council in 2007', 337.

94 Davies, 'Rhetorical Inaction? Compliance and the Human Rights Council of the United Nations', 462.

95 HRC Res. 5/1, 'Institution Building of the United Nations Human Rights Council', UN Doc. A/HRC/RES/5/1, para. 18 (d).

session was a compromise to allow all members to participate without taking time away from other Council matters.[96] A reviewed state may request that one troika member be from its own region, enabling countries to have a regional ally that understands its cultural sensitivities and/or issues relating to capacities for human rights protection and promotion. All African countries selected for review, bar Ghana, did indeed request a regional rapporteur during the UPR's first two sessions.[97] Conversely, a state may decline a position on the troika, as occurred where Pakistan declined to be part of the troika reviewing India, owing to the long-standing political tensions between those two countries.

The reviewed state's presentation is followed by comments, questions and recommendations from other states which the concerned state may respond to at any stage. NGOs do not actively participate in the review.[98] The UPR's basis as a cooperative mechanism results in the state under review being able to determine to which, if any, comments and questions it will respond. Focus on cooperation and consent 'promote[s] the necessity of discussion, compromise, and agreement' and enables the 'open debate and discussion' required to achieve the UPR's objectives.[99] However, it is clear that this approach is open to abuse, particularly from states unwilling to enter into discussion on particular human rights violations.

The OHCHR compiles an outcome report within two days for the troika's and the reviewed state's approval. The report summarises which, if any, recommendations the state initially accepts or rejects. The state may reserve judgement on any or all recommendations. The report is then presented to the UPR Working Group for editing and adoption. At the next scheduled Council Session, the report is considered and adopted. The reviewed state has two minutes to present its acceptance, rejection or reservation on recommendations and reasons, which are recorded in an amendment to the original draft as are states' written submissions. Member and Observer States are allowed to make comments on the outcome of the review and NGOs make 'general comments'. These contributions are summarised in the report of the Council session and included in the final report, which is then formally adopted by the Council.

9.1.3.2 Basis of the review

UPR is based on a number of instruments: the UN Charter, the UDHR, UN human rights treaties to which a state is party, a range of human rights

---

96 Callejon, 'Developments at the Human Rights Council in 2007', 334.

97 Abebe, 'Of Shaming and Bargaining', 14.

98 NGOs are entitled to observe the review in the room, and may conduct parallel events at the time of the review in the Working Group, but they are only entitled to take the floor later during the consideration and adoption of reports in the Council plenary.

99 Davies, 'Rhetorical Inaction? Compliance and the Human Rights Council of the United Nations', 458–9.

regardless of treaty ratification, and states' voluntary pledges and commit-ments.[100] Redondo emphasises the review's comprehensiveness as it incor-porates legally binding and non-legally binding human rights standards.[101] For example, voluntary commitments and pledges take on a greater importance during the UPR than, for example, as membership criteria. Some countries[102] argued for international humanitarian law to be included, whereas other states[103] insisted that review's basis should be exclusively human rights norms.[104] The IBP provides that UPR should take international humanitarian law (IHL) into account.[105] However, IHL often relates to issues such as conflict situations, and its relationship with human rights is not agreed upon by all states, thus its inclusion could cause difficulties. Callejon comments that inclusion of IHL was outside of the Council's mandate as it does not have the competency to deal with this body of law.[106]

A broad consultation is undertaken with NGOs and other stakeholders, as set out in the General Guidelines. OHCHR summarises and publishes these submissions on its website. The summary is an official UN document, giving it more weight than NGO submissions to other treaty bodies. Sweeney and Saito note that most NGOs are satisfied with these summaries.[107] The African Group, alongside other developing nations, argued against NGO involvement, emphasising the need for a peer-led mechanism.[108] Such positions were perhaps motivated from fear that NGO submissions would dispropor-tionately affect developing nations. Poorer states, and countries with newer and weaker democracies, let alone those with autocratic rule, invariably have graver and more widespread human rights issues than richer, more democratic – i.e., Western – states. Developing nations might also argue that many of the main NGOs follow Western, liberal notions of human rights, and are funded by supporters and governments that push such rights. Although NGO involvement was enshrined in the IBP, the deadline for submissions has been far earlier than for state submissions.[109] There are a number of

100 HRC Res. 5/1, 'Institution Building of the United Nations Human Rights Council', UN Doc. A/HRC/RES/5/1, para. 1.

101 E.D. Redondo, 'The Universal Periodic Review of the UN Human Rights Council: An Assessment of the First Session', *Chinese Journal of International Law*, Vol. 7 (3), 2008, 721–34.

102 For example, Switzerland.

103 Including members of the African Group and some Western countries such as the US.

104 Abebe, 'Of Shaming and Bargaining', 5–6.

105 HRC Res. 5/1, 'Institution Building of the United Nations Human Rights Council', UN Doc. A/HRC/RES/5/1, para. 2.

106 Callejon, 'Developments at the Human Rights Council in 2007', 336.

107 Sweeney and Saito, 'An NGO Assessment of the New Mechanisms of the UN Human Rights Council', 207.

108 Abebe, 'Of Shaming and Bargaining', 10.

109 The deadline for the 3rd and 4th sessions was five months prior to the review. It is six months prior to the review for the 5th session and seven months for the 6th session, see: OHCR (Website), (Online). Available HTTP: <http://www.ohchr.org/EN/HRBodies/UPR/Pages/NewDeadlines.aspx> (accessed 22 July 2012).

practical considerations for this discrepancy, but it has caused some difficulties.[110] Clearly, despite involvement, NGOs are not equal players in the UPR process.

The OHCHR's role includes overall supervision of the process, advice to the troika, as well as collection and compilation of information. A number of states contested such strong involvement, asserting that the process should be peer-led rather than directed by an administrative body. African countries argued that the OHCHR 'is not adequately accountable to Member States of the United Nations and its function is highly influenced by members of the Western Group and civil society organisations'.[111] Despite this argument, the OHCHR's role remains integral. However, such discussions demonstrate the North–South divide, and developing nations' ongoing position that the UN was set up by imperialist, Western states for imperialist, Western states.

9.1.3.3 UPR and politicisation

Gaer notes that, from the outset, states and non-state actors hoped that the UPR would ensure fair scrutiny of human rights in all states, and as such enhance UN human rights' credibility.[112] In particular, the requirement for all member states to be reviewed was central to fulfilment of these expectations.[113] Universality and equal coverage distinguishes UPR from the treaty body review mechanisms already in place. However, the UN tends to view universality as devoting equal time, treatment and resources.[114] That view is problematic, as it can result in too much attention being devoted to states which do not proportionately require it, while gross and systemic violations are occurring elsewhere.[115] As has been discussed, the need for proportionate treatment is in many ways more important than equality.

As a state-driven mechanism, UPR is an intergovernmental mechanism. Abebe comments that it is therefore 'a profoundly political undertaking'.[116] Although the OHCHR plays a supervisory and information sharing role, and NGOs are consulted during the process, UPR remains a state-led process. Indeed, human rights experts are deliberately excluded from direct participation,[117] leaving states to analyse the information and prepare the outcome reports and recommendations. It is analysis that is key to the process,

---

110 Sweeney and Saito, 'An NGO assessment of the new mechanisms of the UN Human Rights Council', 207.
111 Abebe, 'Of Shaming and Bargaining', 8.
112 Gaer, 'A Voice Not an Echo: Universal Periodic Review and the UN Treaty Body System', 135.
113 *Ibid.*
114 *Ibid.*, 137.
115 *Ibid.*, 137.
116 Abebe, 'Of Shaming and Bargaining', 8.
117 *Ibid.*

as much of the information used in the UPR has already been shared within the UN human rights machinery.[118] Clearly, the modalities leave much room for potential politicisation, either through direct tactics used to protect allies, or indirectly through lack of expertise amongst the troika.

Indeed, the troika rapporteur states placed a large reliance on their Geneva-based diplomats, particularly developing states which could not afford to bring experts over to Switzerland for the review. Reliance on diplomats impacted upon the expertise and effectiveness of the troika, resulting in visible discrepancies depending on the troika's composition.[119] The outcome of each review depends on the troika's knowledge and expertise, and their protection from pressure or influence from the reviewed state or its allies. Gaer argues that the UN secretariat's role in this regard is essential, as is the information and expertise provided by NGOs and other relevant stakeholders.[120]

9.1.4 The first cycle

The first cycle began in April 2008 – delayed from 2007 – and was completed in October 2011. Thirty-two states[121] were selected[122] for the first two review sessions. The first review took place despite various procedural issues remaining.[123] A majority of states wished to begin the exercise whilst simultaneously conducting negotiations and consultations on the remaining

---

118 Gaer, 'A Voice Not an Echo: Universal Periodic Review and the UN Treaty Body System', 136.

119 Abebe, 'Of Shaming and Bargaining', 22–3.

120 Gaer, 'A Voice Not an Echo: Universal Periodic Review and the UN Treaty Body System', 136.

121 States under review at the first session were, in order: Bahrain, Ecuador, Tunisia, Morocco, Indonesia, Finland, the United Kingdom, India, Brazil, Philippines, Algeria, Poland, the Netherlands, South Africa, the Czech Republic and Argentina. States under review at the second session were, in order: Gabon, Ghana, Peru, Guatemala, Benin, Republic of Korea, Switzerland, Pakistan, Zambia, Japan, Ukraine, Sri Lanka, France, Tonga, Romania and Mali. See the OHCHR extranet (Online). Available HTTP: <http://portal.ohchr.org/portal/page/portal/HRC_Extranet/6thSession/OralStatements/210907/Tab16> (accessed 22 July 2012) and ISHR, Daily Update, 21 September 2007 (Online). Available HTTP: <http://www.ishr.ch/hrm/council/daily_updates/session006/21september2007.pdf> (accessed 22 July 2012).

122 The selection process, which accounts for geographical representation, the percentage of Council member and observer states and the status of development of states, was inordinately complex and required the creation of an algorithmic software programme that many delegations found very difficult to comprehend. For a summary explanation, as well as state and NGO responses, see 'Main steps to be taken regarding the establishment of the UPR work programme (for the first year): draft Note from the Secretariat – version 11, 12 September 2008' on the OHCHR extranet. For a summary of the simulation process, see ISHR, Daily Updates, 12 and 19 September 2008, (Online). Available HTTP: <http://www.ishr.ch/index.php?option=com.content&task=view&id=115&Itemid=176> (accessed 22 July 2012).

123 Abebe, 'Of Shaming and Bargaining', 8.

issues.[124] The Working Group made a number of procedural decisions, on issues where the IBP was silent, during the first session, in order to enable the reviews to take place.[125]

Although Switzerland and Colombia volunteered for review during the first session of the UPR Working Group, the order of review for other states was done by drawing lots. OHCHR designed a mathematical model for selection that takes into account considerations such as regional representation, reviewing Council's members during their term of membership and accommodating volunteers.

Reviewed states mainly had large delegations, often including ministerial level representatives,[126] demonstrating the seriousness afforded to the process.[127] Abebe notes that the Council, OHCHR and states stressed the importance of ministerial representation, although the general feeling was that states should determine, rather than be directed, who to send.[128] The types of ministers representing states signified how the countries viewed the UPR. For example, Ministers of Foreign Affairs sent by Bahrain, Indonesia and Algeria showed that they viewed the UPR as a foreign relations exercise.[129] Although other states sent Ministers of Justice, thus affording the process the national legal clout that it deserved, commentators have noted with concern that, throughout the first cycle, many countries deemed it appropriate to send delegates from foreign ministries rather than ministers with legal or human rights expertise.[130] Although each report was allocated one hour,[131] at the initial sessions some countries, including Argentina, Ghana, Peru, Romania and Sri Lanka,[132] used at least double the allocated 20 minutes when presenting their reports, thus reducing the time for interactive dialogue.[133]

---

124 For example, the troika members' responsibilities prior to the actual review, the length of states' speaking time, and the preparations of the report of the Working Group, all required last minute decisions.

125 Abebe, 'Of Shaming and Bargaining', 9.

126 For example, India–Solicitor General, the Netherlands–Secretary of State for Justice, Ecuador–Minister of Justice, Tunisia–Minister of Justice, Morocco–Minister of Justice, Finland–Secretary of State, and the United Kingdom–Minister of State.

127 Sweeney and Saito, 'An NGO Assessment of the New Mechanisms of the UN Human Rights Council', 209.

128 Abebe, 'Of Shaming and Bargaining', 12.

129 Sweeney and Saito, 'An NGO Assessment of the New Mechanisms of the UN Human Rights Council', 209.

130 Davies, 'Rhetorical Inaction? Compliance and the Human Rights Council of the United Nations', 463; Redondo, 'The Universal Periodic Review of the UN Human Rights Council', 729.

131 HRC, 'Modalities and Practices for the Universal Periodic Review Process', 9 April 2008, UN Doc. 8/PRST/1, para. 7. This was a more flexible approach than the initial allocation by the President of 30 minutes for the presentation and 30 minutes for responses to questions.

132 Whose Ambassador was the Council President who had allocated the time period for state presentation of national reports.

133 Sweeney and Saito, 'An NGO Assessment of the New Mechanisms of the UN Human Rights Council', 209–10.

Criticisms of this practice did lead to some change, but it did not altogether abate. Time constraints, particularly where state presentations overran the allocated period, resulted in many states being unable to participate in the interactive dialogue.[134] Some reasons for this will be examined in the following subsections, particularly in terms of politicisation of the UPR and the various methods deployed to fill a state's allocated time in order to avoid criticisms being levied at the state under review.

Another issue was how reviewed states dealt with questions submitted through the troika. If states submitted written questions, the troika could amalgamate similar questions, or ask them in such an order as to allow various issues to be addressed. At the First Session, many states altogether ignored written questions submitted in advance. Therefore, by the Second Session most countries had abandoned the practice and such questions were almost exclusively deployed by Western states at subsequent sessions.[135] Indeed, even Western states sometimes took the floor to repeat the questions where the reviewed country had not allocated time to deal with written questions.[136] Many states did not allocate time for written questions, and even where states did do so such questions were far less likely to be answered by the reviewed state than questions posed from the floor. At the First and Second Sessions, for example, only the Netherlands, the United Kingdom, Japan and South Korea directly responded to written questions.[137] Ireland, noting the ineffectiveness in submitting written questions at the First Session, changed tack and asked questions from the floor during the second session.[138] Sweeney and Saito note that circumvention of the troika changed those states' role from being independent rapporteurs to 'simply rubberstamp[ing] the draft outcome reports' after the review.[139]

9.1.4.1 The initial sessions

The UPR Working Group's First Session was held in April 2008. The first review, of Bahrain, saw a tactic that had been previously deployed in Council sessions, whereby allied states fill the list of speakers in order to give positive responses to the state concerned. Such allies included Palestine, India, Pakistan, Qatar, Tunisia, the United Arab Emirates, Saudi Arabia, Turkey, Malaysia, Algeria, Libya and Cuba. Tunisia's review heard from so many of

---

134 Abebe, 'Of Shaming and Bargaining', 13.
135 International Service for Human Rights, 'Overview of the United Periodic Review in 2008', 2009, p. 39.
136 Abebe, 'Of Shaming and Bargaining', 13.
137 Sweeney and Saito, 'An NGO Assessment of the New Mechanisms of the UN Human Rights Council', 210.
138 See the compilation by UPR-info.org of state interventions related to human rights defenders (Online). Available HTTP: <http://www.upr-info.org/IMG/pdf/IA.HumanRights Defenders_S1-2.pdf> (accessed 22 July 2012).
139 Sweeney and Saito, 'An NGO Assessment of the New Mechanisms of the UN Human Rights Council', 210.

its allies[140] 'that it appeared an exercise in filibustering'.[141] This tactic undermined the process through blocking other states from asking questions or giving objective feedback. Moreover, it gave the impression that both reviewed states were beyond reproach and required few, if any, recommendations. The UPR's main objective, to 'improve of the human rights situation on the ground', was severely undermined, as was the credibility of the mechanism. Bahrain and Tunisia are OIC members. That group frequently employs a tactic whereby group statements are repeated by many members in order to give the impression that the position is widely held. Council sessions are limited in time, but not nearly as restricted as UPR sessions. The impact of this tactic was even stronger at the first UPR Session than during regular Council sessions. It resulted in few non-OIC members being able to take the floor during these two states' reviews.

Tunisia's report demonstrated the lack of finalised modalities. An argument ensued on where to record recommendations rejected by the reviewed state. States disagreed with listing rejected recommendations in the paragraph containing final conclusions and recommendations, as that would give rise to misperceptions. It was agreed instead that a separate paragraph would contain those recommendations rejected by the reviewed state.[142] That solution reflected the emphasis placed on achieving compromise in order to support the mechanism.

Another issue related to recommendations arose in regard to attribution to the state making them. Western countries, in particular, routinely made recommendations as part of their statements.[143] The African Group argued that including recommendations without attributing them to the recommending state gave the impression that it had been accepted by all working group members. This was especially problematic for politically sensitive issues such as recommendations on the right to sexual orientation. The solution provided a compromise acceptable to all. That allows factual reporting of proceedings rather than giving misleading perceptions.

The UPR Working Group's Second Session was held in May 2008. By the second UPR session, smaller states 'were less inclined to engage in interactive dialogues with states from regions other than their own'.[144] Less powerful states were perhaps disinterested in other regions' affairs, or reticent

---

140 The first 15 countries to speak in the interactive dialogue were Kuwait, Palestine, Pakistan, Philippines, Chad, Saudi Arabia, the Russian Federation, Slovenia, China, India, Madagascar, Ghana, Mauritania, Bangladesh and Angola, HRC Res. 8/21, 'Report of the Working Group on the Universal Periodic Review, Tunisia', 22 May 2008, UN Doc. A/HRC/8/21, paras. 12–26.

141 Sweeney and Saito, 'An NGO Assessment of the New Mechanisms of the UN Human Rights Council', 210.

142 Abebe, 'Of Shaming and Bargaining', 15.

143 *Ibid.*, 16.

144 Sweeney and Saito, 'An NGO Assessment of the New Mechanisms of the UN Human Rights Council', 211.

about offending more powerful states and thus impacting upon their national interests. Other than Morocco, Algeria and Egypt, all of whom were influential OIC members with large numbers of political allies, African states rarely took part in non-African interactive dialogues.[145] To a lesser degree, GRULAC and Asian states, themselves slightly more powerful than African nations, stuck to dialogues on their respective regional groups.[146] However, EU states, major players on the world stage, tended to join most interactive debates. Post-colonial theorists might claim that the contrast between the involvement of states from the Global North and Global South underscores that human rights are the preserve of developed countries and that those rights are used as a neo-colonial tool of oppression. It is therefore somewhat ironic that Abebe argues that the UPR demonstrates that the Council offers African states the opportunity to move from being subjects of a condemnatory system to being participants in the human rights forum.[147]

A pattern emerges whereby weaker states, mindful of the power politics at stake and the potential ramifications of criticising other states, withdrew from the process, whereas stronger states felt better placed to voice opinions. Sweeney and Saito argue that lack of participation might reflect some states' lack of interest in human rights.[148] That position would support the post-Marxist position that human rights hold little relevance for states from the Global South. While this may be true to some extent, many weaker states do join Council discussions at regular sessions on topics unrelated to their national or political interests. It seems more likely, from a realist perspective, that the UPR provides little incentive for weaker states to involve themselves in discussions which might affect other national interests. Unlike Council sessions, which are widely reported on and where taking a stance may further a state's reputation, the UPR sessions are less scrutinised and therefore criticisms earn little reward but carry a large risk to a state's foreign affairs. Another explanation, perhaps, is that economically stronger countries with larger Geneva-based delegations were better able to participate in a greater number of reviews. That explanation indicates that smaller or less economically developed states elected to attend some reviews at the expense of others, which, again, raises questions regarding political objectives and selectivity.

Reviews at the Working Group's Third Session, which took place in December 2008, continued many of the positive and the negative trends that

---

145 For example, in the review of Gabon, 13 of the 36 states that provided comments were from the African Group, whereas in the review of Peru, Algeria was the only African state to provide comments.

146 Of the GRULAC states, only Brazil, Mexico and Cuba tended to continually engage cross-regionally. Of the Asian Group, consistent cross-regional engagement was evident from Indonesia, the Philippines, Malaysia and Azerbaijan.

147 Abebe, 'Of Shaming and Bargaining', 3–4.

148 Sweeney and Saito, 'An NGO Assessment of the New Mechanisms of the UN Human Rights Council', 211.

had developed during the first two sessions. States under review generally were well-prepared and engaged with the process although, unsurprisingly, some states were more transparent or more willing to engage with critical questions. The key exception to this rule was Turkmenistan, which appeared unprepared for the review owing to both the report not being available in English and the delegation's failure to provide adequate responses to questions from the floor. Reviews of smaller or less developed states highlighted some of the practical difficulties posed by the process; Cape Verde presented its report orally[149] owing to a lack of resources,[150] while Tuvalu frequently referred to its lack of financial and human resources as the main factor for being unable to answer all of the questions asked during the review.[151]

A significant problem arose at the Third Session and subsequently continued throughout the first cycle; the number of delegations in the room and the number of states actively participating in the review significantly varied depending on which country was being reviewed. This impacted on the number of recommendations given, the length of the review, and the utility of the process. For example, 27 states participated in the review of the Bahamas,[152] 24 states took the floor during the review of Cape Verde,[153] and 22 states joined the interactive dialogue on Tuvalu.[154] Moreover, the number of delegations attending those reviews 'reached a new low'.[155] Comparisons can be drawn with other reviews at the same session, and even on the same days. In particular, the reviews of Israel and Colombia were standing-room only[156] and there was insufficient time for all states inscribed

---

149 Oral presentation of the national report was a new practice, but did not appear to detract from that state's preparation for, or engagement with, the review.

150 'Report of the Working Group on the Universal Periodic Review, Cape Verde', 12 January 2009, UN Doc A/HRC/10/81, paras 33–62.

151 HRC Res. 10/84, 'Report of the Working Group on the Universal Periodic Review, Tuvalu', 9 January 2009 UN Doc A/HRC/10/84, paras 21–66.

152 Algeria, Argentina, Australia, Bangladesh, Barbados, Botswana, Brazil, Canada, Chile, China, Cuba, Czech Republic, Djibouti, France, Germany, Ghana, Haiti, Italy, Jamaica, Latvia, Maldives, Mexico, Netherlands, Pakistan, Slovenia, Sweden, UK: HRC Res. 10/70, 'Report of the Working Group on the Universal Periodic Review, Bahamas', 7 January 2009, UN Doc A/HRC/10/70, para. 19.

153 Algeria, Angola, Argentina, Brazil, Cameroon, Canada, Chile, China, France, Germany, Italy, Latvia, Luxemburg, Maldives, Mexico, Morocco, Netherlands, Nigeria, Portugal, Senegal, Slovenia, South Africa, Sweden, UK: HRC Res. 10/81, 'Report of the Working Group on the Universal Periodic Review, Cape Verde', UN Doc A/HRC/10/81, paras 20–51.

154 Algeria, Australia, Brazil, Canada, China, Cuba, Czech Republic, France, Germany, Italy, Japan, Latvia, Maldives, Mexico, Morocco, Netherlands, New Zealand, Philippines, Slovenia, Switzerland, Turkey, UK, Zambia: HRC Res.10/84, 'Report of the Working Group on the Universal Periodic Review, Tuvalu', 9 January 2009, UN Doc A/HRC/10/84, paras 22–66.

155 ISHR, 'Overview of the Universal Periodic Review', 40.

156 *Ibid.*

on the speaker's list to be able to participate in the review.[157] Discrepancy between attendance at, and participation in, those reviews as compared with Bahamas, Cape Verde and Tuvalu might be attributable to the greater awareness of, and political reasons for focusing on, grave human rights violations in both Colombia[158] and Israel.[159] However, the same is not necessarily true of other states whose reviews at the Third Session were well-attended, including Serbia, Montenegro, Uzbekistan and the United Arab Emirates.

Interestingly, although 41 states[160] participated in the review of Serbia, 22 were from Europe. Similarly, of the 30 states[161] which chose actively to participate in Montenegro's review 19 were European. Those states provided critical comments, questions and recommendations to the countries being reviewed. All of the states inscribed on the speaker's list were able to participate in those two reviews; European domination of the interactive dialogue, therefore, indicates that states from other regions lacked interest in participating in those reviews, or were precluded from doing so by a lack of available resources. Members of other groups, however, sought to dominate reviews of their regional or political allies despite many other states from across the regional groups and political blocs attempting to participate in those reviews. Uzbekistan[162] and the United Arab Emirates[163] are both OIC members and, as with previous and subsequent UPR sessions, their reviews were largely taken up by comments from allies from that political bloc[164]

157 54 states participated in the review of Israel (HRC Res.10/76, 'Report of the Working Group on the Universal Periodic Review, Israel', 8 January 2009, UN Doc A/HRC/10/76, para. 19) and 43 in the review of Colombia (HRC Res. 10/82, 'Report of the Working Group on the Universal Periodic Review, Colombia', 9 January 2009, UN Doc A/HRC/10/82, para. 17).
158 cf. Amnesty International, *Annual Report 2009*, London: Amnesty International, 2010, pp. 108–12.
159 cf. *ibid.*, pp. 182–5.
160 Albania, Algeria, Argentina, Austria, Azerbaijan, Bangladesh, Bosnia and Herzegovina, Brazil, Canada, Chile, China, Croatia, Cuba, Czech Republic, Denmark, Finland, France, Germany, Ghana, Greece, Hungary, India, Ireland, Italy, Japan, Mexico, Netherlands, Norway, Philippines, Poland, Republic of Korea, Romania, Russian Federation, Slovakia, Slovenia, Spain, Sweden, Switzerland, Turkey, UK, Ukraine.
161 Albania, Algeria, Austria, Azerbaijan, Bangladesh, Bosnia and Herzegovina, Canada, Chile, China, Croatia, Czech Republic, France, Germany, Greece, Ireland, Italy, Japan, Luxembourg, Mexico, Netherlands, Norway, Poland, Russian Federation, Slovakia, Slovenia, Spain, Sweden, Turkey, UK, Ukraine.
162 Third Session of the Working Group of the Universal Periodic Review, 11 December 2008; HRC Res. 10/83, 'Report of the Working Group on the Universal Periodic Review, Uzbekistan', 11 March 2009, UN Doc A/HRC/10/83.
163 Third Session of the Working Group of the Universal Periodic Review, 9 December 2008; HRC Res. 10/75, 'Report of the Working Group on the Universal Periodic Review, United Arab Emirates', 12 January 2009, UN Doc A/HRC/10/75.
164 Afghanistan, Albania, Algeria, Azerbaijan, Bahrain, Bangladesh, Djibouti, Egypt, Indonesia, Iran, Jordan, Kuwait, Lebanon, Libya, Malaysia, Maldives, Morocco, Oman, Pakistan, Palestine, Qatar, Saudi Arabia, Senegal, Sudan, Syria, Turkey, United Arab Emirates, Uzbekistan, Yemen.

who sought to use the allotted time to provide laudatory comments rather than ask critical questions or provide recommendations. This tactic resulted in many countries inscribed on speaker's lists being unable to participate in reviews of OIC states owing to time constraints.

9.1.4.2 Second year of sessions

Many trends that emerged during the first year of UPR sessions became entrenched during the second year. Regionalism through shielding allied states continued to impact the utility of most of the reviews of both African Group and OIC members. Reviews of Cameroon,[165] Nigeria,[166] Chad,[167] Central African Republic,[168] and Eritrea[169] again saw neighbouring states and regional allies dominating the list of speakers and providing largely complimentary comments. The reviews of African states that did not follow this trend, notably of the Democratic Republic of Congo[170] and Cote d'Ivoire,[171] arguably were more difficult for states to use to pursue regional objectives owing to the gravity of those human rights situations stimulating a broader global interest about those countries. More than 50 states took part in the interactive dialogue for both of those reviews, including many Western countries[172] and some states from the Asian Group[173] and GRULAC.[174]

165 Fourth Session of the Working Group of the Universal Periodic Review, 5 February 2009; HRC Res. 11/21, 'Report of the Working Group on the Universal Periodic Review, Cameroon', 12 October 2009, UN Doc A/HRC/11/21.

166 Fourth Session of the Working Group of the Universal Periodic Review, 9 February 2009; HRC Res. 11/26, 'Report of the Working Group on the Universal Periodic Review, Nigeria', 5 October 2009, UN Doc A/HRC/11/26.

167 Fifth Session of the Working Group of the Universal Periodic Review, 5 May 2009; HRC Res. 12/5, 'Report of the Working Group on the Universal Periodic Review, Chad', 5 October 2009, UN Doc A/HRC/12/5.

168 Fifth Session of the Working Group of the Universal Periodic Review, 4 May 2009; HRC Res. 12/2, 'Report of the Working Group on the Universal Periodic Review, Central African Republic', 12 June 2009, UN Doc A/HRC/12/2.

169 Sixth Session of the Working Group of the Universal Periodic Review, 2 December 2009; HRC Res. 13/2, 'Report of the Working Group on the Universal Periodic Review, Eritrea', 4 January 2010, UN Doc A/HRC/13/2.

170 Sixth Session of the Working Group of the Universal Periodic Review, 3 December 2009; HRC Res. 13/8, 'Report of the Working Group on the Universal Periodic Review, Democratic Republic of the Congo', 4 January 2010, UN Doc A/HRC/13/8.

171 Sixth Session of the Working Group of the Universal Periodic Review, 7 December 2009; HRC Res. 13/9, 'Report of the Working Group on the Universal Periodic Review, Cote d'Ivoire', 4 January 2010, UN Doc A/HRC/13/9.

172 Australia, Austria, Belgium, Canada, Denmark, Finland, France, Germany, Greece, Ireland, Italy, Luxembourg, Netherlands, Norway, Spain, Sweden, Switzerland, UK, USA.

173 Bangladesh, China, Democratic Republic of Korea, India, Malaysia, Pakistan, Saudi Arabia, Vietnam.

174 Argentina, Brazil, Chile, Cuba, Mexico.

Reviews of Azerbaijan,[175] Bangladesh,[176] Jordan,[177] Malaysia,[178] Saudi Arabia[179] and Yemen,[180] were dominated by OIC states which gave laudatory comments and provided few critical questions or recommendations. The notable exception to this trend was the review of Afghanistan,[181] at which many critical questions were asked and recommendations provided, although mostly by Western states[182] – South Africa was the only African state to participate in the review, and Asian states mainly complimented their regional ally.[183]

Western states under review during the UPR's second year included Canada,[184] Germany,[185] New Zealand,[186] Norway[187] and Portugal.[188] With the

---

175 Fourth Session of the Working Group of the Universal Periodic Review, 4 February 2009; HRC Res. 11/20, 'Report of the Working Group on the Universal Periodic Review, Azerbaijan', 29 May 2009, UN Doc A/HRC/11/20.

176 Fourth Session of the Working Group of the Universal Periodic Review, 5 February 2009; HRC Res. 11/18, 'Report of the Working Group on the Universal Periodic Review, Bangladesh', 5 October 2009, UN Doc A/HRC/11/18.

177 Fourth Session of the Working Group of the Universal Periodic Review, 11 February 2009; HRC Res. 11/29, 'Report of the Working Group on the Universal Periodic Review, Jordan', 19 May 2009, UN Doc A/HRC/11/29.

178 Fourth Session of the Working Group of the Universal Periodic Review, 11 February 2009; HRC Res. 11/30, 'Report of the Working Group on the Universal Periodic Review, Malaysia', 5 October 2009, UN Doc A/HRC/11/30.

179 Fourth Session of the Working Group of the Universal Periodic Review, 6 February 2009; HRC Res. 11/23, 'Report of the Working Group on the Universal Periodic Review, Saudi Arabia', 4 March 2009, UN Doc A/HRC/11/23.

180 Fifth Session of the Working Group of the Universal Periodic Review, 11 May 2009; HRC Res. 12/13, 'Report of the Working Group on the Universal Periodic Review, Yemen', 5 June 2009, UN Doc A/HRC/12/13.

181 Fifth Session of the Working Group of the Universal Periodic Review, 7 May 2009; HRC Res. 12/9, 'Report of the Working Group on the Universal Periodic Review, Afghanistan', 20 July 2009, UN Doc A/HRC/12/9.

182 Australia, Austria, Belgium, Canada, Denmark, Finland, France, Germany, Greece, Iceland, Ireland, Norway, Netherlands, New Zealand, Poland, Spain, Sweden, Switzerland, UK, USA.

183 Bahrain, Bangladesh, Bhutan, China, Indonesia, Iran, Jordan, Lebanon, Malaysia, Nepal, Pakistan, Philippines, Republic of Korea, Saudi Arabia, Singapore, Sri Lanka, Uzbekistan.

184 Fourth Session of the Working Group of the Universal Periodic Review, 3 February 2009; HRC Res. 11/17, 'Report of the Working Group on the Universal Periodic Review, Canada', 4 October 2009, UN Doc A/HRC/11/17.

185 Fourth Session of the Working Group of the Universal Periodic Review, 2 February 2009; HRC Res. 11/15, 'Report of the Working Group on the Universal Periodic Review, Germany', 4 March 2009, UN Doc A/HRC/11/15.

186 Fifth Session of the Working Group of the Universal Periodic Review, 7 May 2009; HRC Res. 12/8, 'Report of the Working Group on the Universal Periodic Review, New Zealand', 4 June 2009, UN Doc A/HRC/12/8.

187 Sixth Session of the Working Group of the Universal Periodic Review, 2 December 2009, HRC Res. 13/5, 'Report of the Working Group on the Universal Periodic Review, Norway', 4 January 2010, UN Doc A/HRC/13/5.

188 Sixth Session of the Working Group of the Universal Periodic Review, 4 December 2009, HRC Res. 13/10, 'Report of the Working Group on the Universal Periodic Review, Portugal', 4 January 2010, UN Doc A/HRC/13/10.

exception of Canada, those reviews heard questions and comments that focused on very specific human rights issues; for New Zealand this was primarily in relation to human rights of indigenous people and women's rights, whereas for Germany, Portugal and Norway the primary focus was on rights of migrants and issues of racism and xenophobia. The reviews largely were conducted in a cooperative manner, with minimal politicisation or regionalism, and the outcomes were targeted recommendations aimed at improving specific human rights problems. Those reviews demonstrate the utility of the UPR in terms of promoting human rights within states which already have strong human rights records and where those states have non-politicised and non-contentious relationships with other UN members. Indeed, those reviews demonstrate that idealist aims underpinning the UPR are easier to achieve where conditions surrounding a review minimise the potential for politicisation. That conclusion is further supported by reviews of other, non-Western, states with stable human rights infrastructure and global political relations. In particular, the reviews of Uruguay[189] and Chile[190] were cooperative, non-politicised and aimed at protecting very specific human rights.

The review of Canada demonstrates that politicisation occurred, even of a Western state's review, where a country had previously challenged the dominant regional and political blocs at the Council. As previously explored,[191] Canada frequently opposed the OIC during Council discussions about Israel, often providing the sole dissenting vote on resolutions pertaining to that state. During the review of Canada,[192] 69 states were inscribed on the speaker's list. Of the 45 able to speak (owing to time constraints), many countries, particularly Western states, praised Canada's human rights record and noted specific concerns about the human rights of migrants, indigenous peoples, and xenophobia and racism. However, Algeria, Cuba, Egypt, Iran, Pakistan, and Syria used the review to criticise Canada's performance at the Human Rights Council and its withdrawal from the Durban Review Conference.[193] Those states accused Canada of violating the Council's founding principles of objectivity, non-selectivity and non-politicisation through its votes against resolutions on Israel. These comments undermined the purpose of the review – which was to focus on Canada's domestic human rights record. Five of those states are prominent OIC members – Cuba, the sixth, is strongly allied

---

189 Fifth Session of the Working Group of the Universal Periodic Review, 11 May 2009, HRC Res. 12/12, 'Report of the Working Group on the Universal Periodic Review, Uruguay', 4 June 2009, UN Doc A/HRC/12/12.

190 Fifth Session of the Working Group of the Universal Periodic Review, 8 May 2009, HRC Res. 12/10, 'Report of the Working Group on the Universal Periodic Review, Chile', 4 June 2009, UN Doc A/HRC/12/10.

191 Chapter 8, Section 8.3.4.

192 Fourth Session of the Working Group of the Universal Periodic Review, 3 February 2009; HRC Res. 11/17, 'Report of the Working Group on the Universal Periodic Review, Canada', 5 October 2009, UN Doc A/HRC/11/17.

193 *Ibid.*, paras 23, 27, 30, 54, 64, 74.

with that political bloc – and use of this tactic at the UPR mirrored the OIC's determination to use Council discussions to continue power struggles and pursue political objectives.

The reviews of China[194] and DPRK[195] heard many states voice serious concerns and make highly critical comments about the gross and systemic violations occurring within those countries. However, some states – including Cuba, Venezuela, Pakistan, Belarus, Myanmar, Libya, Iran, China, Zimbabwe, Palestine and Laos – not only failed to criticise but went further and praised those states. During the review of China, of 115 states inscribed on the speaker's list 60 were able to participate in the interactive dialogue.[196] Many states praised China's human rights record. Indeed, Smith notes that China's neighbours, in particular, heaped praise on China during the review:

> Russia commended China's role at the HRC and more generally in strengthening international human rights.[197] Bhutan commented that China 'places people first and seeks to ensure comprehensive, coordinated and sustainable development to build a harmonious society characterized by democracy, rule of law, equity and justice'.[198] Pakistan asserted that 'China does not require external advice on securing the rights of its people'.[199] Myanmar praised China's 'political will to promote and protect the human rights of the Chinese people'.[200] Moreover, Pakistan and Myanmar insisted that there had been politicisation of the review because of critical comments that it perceived as 'attacks on China's human rights record'.[201]

Regionalism through shielding allied states played a strong role at both of these reviews, resulting in a sharp contrast between strong criticisms of the country concerned and complimentary comments that altogether ignored the grave human rights abuses. Even critical comments of China were arguably affected by political concerns, with more states praising China's human rights achievements rather than criticising its grave abuses in Tibet. Realists might ascribe that phenomenon to China's global position and its political and

---

194 Fourth Session of the Working Group of the Universal Periodic Review, 9 February 2009, HRC Res. 11/25, 'Report of the Working Group on the Universal Periodic Review, China', 5 October 2009, UN Doc A/HRC/11/25.

195 Sixth Session of the Working Group of the Universal Periodic Review, 7 December 2009, HRC Res. 13/13, 'Report of the Working Group on the Universal Periodic Review, Democratic People's Republic of Korea', 4 January 2010, UN Doc A/HRC/13/13.

196 HRC Res. 11/25, 'Report of the Working Group on the Universal Periodic Review, China', UN Doc A/HRC/11/25, para. 26.

197 *Ibid.*, para. 34.

198 *Ibid.*, para. 35.

199 *Ibid.*, para. 88.

200 *Ibid.*, para. 94.

201 R.K.M. Smith, 'More of the Same or Something Different? Preliminary Observations on the Contribution of Universal Periodic Review with Reference to the Chinese Experience', *Chinese Journal of International Law*, Vol. 10 (3), 2011, 579.

economic power. Similar trends were seen in the reviews of Cuba[202] and Russia,[203] with stark contrast between laudatory comments of allied states[204] and criticisms from other countries.

9.1.4.3 Tactics undermining the UPR

Various tactics were used to deflect attention from sensitive issues or to protect states from particular scrutiny. In particular, regionalism was deployed within the UPR process in much the same way as it has throughout Council sessions and proceedings. Regionalism was once again particularly utilised by African and OIC members to protect allied states. Use of multiple positive statements, often filling the allocated time, undermined the review's ability to improve human rights situations within a state. Moreover, most statements contained both positive and critical comments and questions, with the positive aspects using valuable time that might better have been spent dealing with issues or offering practical advice. The first two sessions saw far more compliments than criticisms, with the percentage of positive comments by states far outweighing criticisms.[205] Commentators such as Sweeney and Saito[206] and Nowak et al.[207] note 'with great concern' that the report on Sri Lanka, a state with gross and systemic abuses of human rights,[208] heard more positive comments than critical interventions.[209]

Davies insists that states '"stack[ing]" [. . .] the review with friendly backers' undermines the founding principles of objectivity and transparency and precludes the UPR from fulfilling its mandate.[210] Indeed, Nowak et al.

---

202 Fourth Session of the Working Group of the Universal Periodic Review, 5 February 2009, HRC Res. 11/22, 'Report of the Working Group on the Universal Periodic Review, Cuba', 5 October 2009, UN Doc A/HRC/11/22.

203 Fourth Session of the Working Group of the Universal Periodic Review, 4 February 2009, HRC Res. 11/19, 'Report of the Working Group on the Universal Periodic Review, Russian Federation', 5 October 2009, UN Doc A/HRC/11/19.

204 Including Algeria, China, Cuba, DPRK, Egypt, Jordan, Pakistan, Saudi Arabia, Serbia, South Africa, Sri Lanka, United Arab Emirates, Uzbekistan, Venezuela, Vietnam, Zimbabwe.

205 In the case of Brazil, for example, positive comments were approximately 10 times more numerous than critical observations.

206 Sweeney and Saito, 'An NGO assessment of the new mechanisms of the UN Human Rights Council', 212.

207 Nowak et al., 'UN Human Rights Council in Crisis – Proposals to Enhance the Effectiveness of the Council', 46.

208 See, for example, Amnesty International, 'Sri Lanka: Silencing Dissent', 7 February 2008, Index Number: ASA 37/001/2008, examining ongoing gross and systemic violations occurring at the same time as Sri Lanka's UPR session.

209 HRC, 'Report of the Working Group on the Universal Periodic Review: Sri Lanka', 5 June 2008, UN Doc. A/HRC/8/46. For a summary of positive and critical statements, see (Online). Available HTTP: <http://www.ishr.ch/hrm/council/upr/upr_2nd_session_2008/upr_002_sri˙lanka_final.pdf>

210 Davies, 'Rhetorical Inaction? Compliance and the Human Rights Council of the United Nations', 463.

assert that this tactic obstructs the UPR's purpose.[211] Although the tactic continued throughout the first cycle, it increasingly became limited to reviews of African Group and OIC members. The voracity with which those groups deployed the tactic also increased throughout the cycle. By the Seventh Session, for example, the review of Qatar[212] heard such a great number of complimentary comments that, of the 48 states[213] able to speak, only six states asked critical questions.[214] A potential reform aimed at tackling this tactic, and one that draws upon idealism, would be to restrict oral statements to questions, criticisms or advice. Notably, the reviews of Iran[215] and Egypt[216] did hear many critical comments from states not regionally or politically allied with those countries. Seemingly – as previously occurred in relation to the Democratic Republic of Congo and Cote d'Ivoire[217] – greater effort is made by non-allied states to participate in, and preclude regional domination of, reviews of states about which there is greater awareness of gross and systemic human rights violations.

Another example of politicisation occurred through the OIC using 'cultural sensitivities' to undermine human rights. At the First Session, despite Ecuador not objecting to a recommendation on sexual discrimination during its review, Egypt argued that Ecuador could not accept the recommendation because sexual orientation did not fall within the terms of the review unless it was included in a particular state's 'voluntary pledges and commitments'.[218] That intervention undermined the UPR's central aim; effectively blocking the promotion of this right by diverting the discussion away from providing technical or advisory assistance. Egypt's underlying motivation appeared to be to ensure that issues of sexual discrimination would not be raised with

---

211 Nowak *et al.*, 'UN Human Rights Council in Crisis – Proposals to Enhance the Effectiveness of the Council', 46.

212 Seventh Session of the Working Group of the Universal Periodic Review, 8 February 2010, HRC Res. 14/2, 'Report of the Working Group on the Universal Periodic Review, Qatar', 15 March 2010, UN Doc A/HRC/14/2.

213 Algeria, Azerbaijan, Bahrain, Bangladesh, Belarus, Bosnia and Herzegovina, Brazil, Brunei Darussalam, Canada, Chile, Cuba, Djibouti, DPRK, Egypt, France, Hungary, Indonesia, Iran, Kazakhstan, Kuwait, Kyrgyzstan, Lebanon, Libya, Malaysia, Mexico, Morocco, Nepal, Nicaragua, Norway, Oman, Pakistan, Philippines, Russia, Saudi Arabia, Singapore, Slovenia, Sri Lanka, Spain, Sweden, Syria, Sudan, Tunisia, Turkey, United Arab Emirates, UK, Uzbekistan, Venezuela, Yemen.

214 Brazil, Canada, Norway, Spain, Sweden, UK.

215 Seventh Session of the Working Group of the Universal Periodic Review, 15 February 2010, HRC Res. 14/12, 'Report of the Working Group on the Universal Periodic Review, Islamic Republic of Iran', 15 March 2010, UN Doc A/HRC/14/12.

216 Seventh Session of the Working Group of the Universal Periodic Review, 17 February 2010, HRC Res. 14/17, 'Report of the Working Group on the Universal Periodic Review, Egypt', 26 March 2010, UN Doc A/HRC/14/17.

217 See Section 9.1.4.2.

218 For a summary of this debate, see ISHR, Monitor, Universal Periodic Review, 1st session Ecuador – Adoption of the report at 7–9 (Online). Available HTTP: <http://www.ishr.ch/hrm/council/upr/upr_1st_session_2008/upr_001_ecuador_final.pdf> (accessed 22 July 2012).

regard to itself or its OIC or African Group allies, many of which routinely discriminate on the grounds of gender or sexual orientation.[219] As occurs at the Council, 'cultural values' were deployed in an attempt to avoid scrutiny.

Sweeney and Saito[220] claim that the intervention indicates attempts may occur for states to reject recommendations on the basis that, as Pakistan argued, they do not concern 'universally recognised human rights principles'.[221] However, Pakistan's assertion can easily be refuted, for example using the UN Human Rights Committee's jurisprudence which has clearly accepted the universality of the right to sexual orientation.[222]

Egypt continued to raise the issue of sexual orientation. At the Third Session, it claimed that Western countries used recommendations on sexual orientation as a politicised and selective tool. During the UPR Working Group's adoption of the report on Israel, Egypt used the summary record of that review to demonstrate that Israel had not been asked about, nor provided with recommendations on, legitimising same-sex marriage.[223] Using this information, Egypt asserted that such recommendations were targeted only at Arab, African and Muslim countries.[224] However, those comments failed to acknowledge the contrast between the recognition and upholding of lesbian, bisexual, gay and transsexual (LBGT) rights in Israel and the grave violations of the LGBT communities' rights within Arab, African and Muslim states, which, arguably, was the reason why sexual orientation was not addressed during the review of Israel.

One method employed by states under review which sought to avoid scrutiny was for that country to ignore an issue altogether. States are not required to answer questions during the interactive dialogue, resulting in selective responses to the issues raised. Allowing states to avoid or ignore questions stems from the need for consent and cooperation. However, it arguably undermines

---

219 See, Chapter 1, Section 1.1.1.

220 Sweeney and Saito, 'An NGO assessment of the new mechanisms of the UN Human Rights Council', 212.

221 See 'Report of the Working Group on the Universal Periodic Review – Pakistan', 4 June 2008, UN Doc. A/HRC/8/42, para. 108, referring to recommendations in paras 23 (b) on repealing provisions criminalising non-marital consensual sex and failing to recognise marital rape recommendation made by Canada; 23 (f) on decriminalising defamation (Canada); 30 (b) on reviewing the death penalty with a view towards introducing a moratorium and abolishing it (United Kingdom); 30 (d) on repealing the Hadood and Zina Ordnances (United Kingdom); 43 (c) on declaring a moratorium on executions and moving towards abolition (Switzerland); 62 (b) on decriminalising adultery and non-marital consensual sex (the Czech Republic); and 62 (e) on prohibiting provisions of the Qisas and Diyat law in cases of honour killings (the Czech Republic).

222 See, for example, *Toonen v. Australia*, Communication No. 488/1992, 1994, UN Doc CCPR/C/50/D/488/1992, ruling that sexual orientation is protected under General Assembly Res. 2200A (XXI), 'International Covenant on Civil and Political Rights', 16 December 1966, UN Doc. A/6316 (1966), *entered into force* 23 March 1976, Articles 17(1) and 2(1).

223 ISHR, 'Overview of the Universal Periodic Review', 41.

224 *Ibid.*

the UPR's credibility. States often answered questions in clusters, thus allowing them to select questions. Some states[225] allowed so many questions within each cluster that they avoided the majority of issues raised. Sweeney and Saito note that in the Second Session Gabon took all of the questions at the end rather than in clusters, yet it too avoided addressing many issues raised during its review.[226] As recommendations have already been made by the time of the interactive dialogue, states have little reason to answer difficult or sensitive questions as it will not affect the review's outcome.[227]

States politicised proceedings during their own reviews by refusing to discuss certain human rights matters. Such refusals sometimes related to particular geographic areas: Israel refused to discuss human rights in the OPT;[228] Russia said that it would consider all 57 recommendations other than those made by Georgia,[229] which Russia deemed 'not relevant as they do not comply with the basis of the review'[230]; and China refused to discuss human rights matters or accept recommendations relating to Tibet.[231] Other refusals related to particular thematic rights, such as Afghanistan's explicit rejection of any recommendations on its use of the death penalty.[232] These examples all relate to contentious issues, again underscoring that the UPR is most effective for promoting non-contentious human rights.

Some states used reviews to raise political matters unrelated, or only tenuously connected, to the review of a country's human rights record. During the review of Cyprus,[233] comments by the Turkish delegate about the territorial dispute between those states[234] prompted the Working Group's Chairperson to remind the floor that human rights issues were the only appropriate topics to be discussed during the review. Raising unrelated topics occurred during other reviews, including those of Israel[235] and the US[236] and, indeed,

---

225 Including India, Brazil and Guatemala.
226 Sweeney and Saito, 'An NGO assessment of the new mechanisms of the UN Human Rights Council', 211.
227 *Ibid.*
228 ISHR, 'Overview of the Universal Periodic Review', 42.
229 HRC Res. 11/19, 'Report of the Working Group on the Universal Periodic Review, Russian Federation', UN Doc A/HRC/11/19, para. 54.
230 *Ibid.*, para. 86.
231 HRC Res. 11/25, 'Report of the Working Group on the Universal Periodic Review, China', UN Doc A/HRC/11/25, para. 117.
232 HRC Res. 12/9, 'Report of the Working Group on the Universal Periodic Review, Afghanistan', UN Doc A/HRC/12/9, para. 97.
233 Sixth Session of the Working Group of the Universal Periodic Review, 30 November 2009, HRC Res. 13/7, 'Report of the Working Group on the Universal Periodic Review, Cyprus', 4 January 2010, UN Doc A/HRC/13/7.
234 *Ibid.*, paras 38, 72, 73.
235 HRC Res. 10/76, 'Report of the Working Group on the Universal Periodic Review, Israel', UN Doc A/HRC/10/76.
236 Ninth Session of the Working Group of the Universal Periodic Review, 5 November 2010, HRC Res. 16/11, 'Report of the Working Group on the Universal Periodic Review, United States of America', 4 January 2011, UN Doc A/HRC/16/11.

mirrored tactics used during discussions within the Council. The review of Madagascar[237] was similarly used to highlight political matters unrelated to that state's human rights record, albeit in a wholly different fashion. African States refused to participate in the review, arguably owing to the African Union's suspension of Madagascar in 2009 following what it deemed to be a coup.[238] Use of UPR for these purposes arguably enable states to gain greater attention for unrelated political matters but, ultimately, undermined the purpose and objectives of the UPR.

Certain states asked the same questions at each interactive dialogue, which were often too broad to be of direct assistance to the review. The UK, for example, included a question on the role of civil society in the preparation of the national report, while Slovenia asked a general question on gender integration. Standard, broad questions were perhaps aimed at avoiding selectivity, but they risk undermining the review's objective of dealing with each state individually. Interestingly, Western states frequently asked these broad questions, perhaps to pre-empt the South's assertion that developed nations use human rights machinery as a neo-colonial tool of oppression against developing states.

Western states, despite their general power and strength, are in a minority at the Council. EU countries are particularly mindful to avoid conflict at the body, highlighting the realist explanations of proceedings at the Council and its mechanisms. Western states' approach to the UPR has perhaps been overly careful to avoid accusations of selectivity or criticism of developing nations. One serious implication of that tactic, according to Abebe, an Ethiopian delegate to the Council, is that countries may interpret this as meaning that there are no criticisms of their national human rights.[239] Interpreting lack of criticism as tacit approval may negatively affect a state's human rights, possibly resulting in a worse situation than if the review had not taken place.

9.2. Innovative mechanisms – Special Sessions

The Council's ability to deal with crises is central to the new body. However, Ghanea comments that negotiations on Special Sessions were somewhat sidelined in favour of discussions on peer review.[240] Special Sessions were designed to allow the Council the time and flexibility to meet outside of plenary sessions to discuss grave or crisis human rights situations, either country-specific or thematic.

237 Seventh Session of the Working Group of the Universal Periodic Review, 15 February 2010, HRC Res. 14/13, 'Report of the Working Group on the Universal Periodic Review, Madagascar', 26 March 2010, UN Doc A/HRC/14/13.
238 SADC, 'Communique of the Extraordinary Summit of SADC Heads of State and Government', Lozitha Royal Palace, Kingdom of Swaziland, 30 March 2009 (Online). Available HTTP: <http://www.sadc.int/index/browse/page/477> (accessed 22 July 2012).
239 Abebe, 'Of Shaming and Bargaining', 20.
240 Ghanea, 'From UN Commission on Human Rights to UN Human Rights Council', 703.

9.2.1 *Background*

Resolution 60/251 mandates that the Council 'be able to hold special sessions, when needed, at the request of a member of the Council with the support of one third of the membership of the Council'.[241] This was expanded upon in the IBP,[242] which sets out how requests for Special Sessions should be given; that the session be convened between two and five days after the request and should not exceed six days; attendance is open to Council members, concerned states, observers, NGOs, and other specified non-state parties; modalities for draft resolutions and decisions; the need to seek consensus wherever possible; and that participatory debate occur which is 'results oriented' with the outcomes able to be monitored and reported on.

Requiring one-third of Council members' support empowers dominant groups and alliances to use this mechanism to achieve political aims because the larger the group, the more easily the one-third threshold is achieved. Once again, this has manifested itself in the mechanism's use to keep the spotlight on Israel. This section will examine the Council's vastly disproportionate attention on Israel through Special Sessions. Themes that will be explored in relation to this mechanism include politicisation, selectivity and bias.

Of the Council's first twelve Special Sessions, ten were country-specific and two were thematic. Arguably, there are more country-specific than thematic crises situations. Developing states typically called for country-specific Special Sessions despite the South's general position against country-specific focus. Of the first twelve special sessions, half were convened on Israel, two addressed thematic issues, and one each dealt with Darfur, Myanmar, the Democratic Republic of Congo, and Sri Lanka. Schrijver insists that when the Palestinian plight is considered, Western observations that the Council excessively focuses on Israel is questionable.[243] However, owing to similar, if not worse, abuses ongoing elsewhere, Gaer argues that convening three Special Sessions on Israel in the Council's first six months raised serious concerns about the new body and its members.[244] Indeed, then Secretary-General Kofi Annan voiced his concerns at the Council's treatment of Israel in light of its silence on other grave situations.[245]

---

241 GA Res. 60/251, 'Human Rights Council', para. 10.

242 HRC Res. 5/1, 'Institution Building of the United Nations Human Rights Council', Part V, Chapter D, paras 121–128.

243 Schrijver, 'A New "Society of the Committed"', 820.

244 Gaer, 'A Voice Not an Echo: Universal Periodic Review and the UN Treaty Body System', 135–6.

245 See, for example, UN Press Release, 'Secretary General in Message to Human Rights Council Cautions against Focusing on Middle East at expense of Darfur, Other Grave Crises', 29 November 2006, UN Doc. SG/SM/10769-HR/4907. See, also, Speech by Kofi Annan, 8 December 2006, in which he stated 'we must realize the promise of the Human Rights Council which so far has clearly not justified the hopes that so many of us placed in it', Secretary-General, 8 December 2006, UN Doc. SG/SM/10788-HR/4909.

9.2.2 The Special Sessions

The First Special Session, on the human rights situation in the OPT, took place in July 2006 immediately after the Council's First Session. The Session was called by developing states or their allies,[246] such as Brazil and Russia, half of whom were OIC members. Many states took the floor over the two days, with the majority focusing on gross and systemic Israeli violations. South Africa, with its own history of gross and systemic human rights violations under *apartheid*, supported the Session, arguing that 'foreign domination is a denial of the right to [Palestinian] self-determination [and] fundamental freedoms and human rights'.[247] India's support for the Session was motivated by concerns about its own national security, with that country expressing 'grave concern at the deteriorating situation in West Asia'.[248] Sudan, perhaps seeking to deflect the spotlight away from its own abuses, argued that the 'Palestinian people should not be a sacrificial lamb caused by the silence of the international community'.[249] Cuba, Qatar, the Arab League, and OIC members all emphasised that inaction would affect the Council's credibility. Switzerland agreed with the OIC and its allies that violations in the OPT must be addressed, stressing that the body's credibility was at stake and reminding the Council of its mandate 'to respond to urgent situations of human rights'.[250]

Western states, other than Switzerland, while condemning Israeli violations, took a different position towards the convening of, and proceedings during, the Session. Canada criticised the one-sided proceedings, arguing that it 'cannot accept the focus of the Council only on Israel'. France criticised the Council for divisive proceedings,[251] insisting that Special Sessions should not be convened solely for political motives. The US expressed 'regret that we have to be here', arguing that Special Sessions 'should not face only one side of a conflict'.[252] Israel asserted that the Session was convened for political reasons, mirroring Commission practices, saying 'it only took two weeks to bring us to the old Commission culture'.[253]

246 Algeria; Azerbaijan; Bahrain; Bangladesh; Brazil; China; Cuba; Gabon; India; Indonesia; Jordan; Malaysia; Mali; Morocco; Pakistan; Russian Federation; Saudi Arabia; Senegal; South Africa; Sri Lanka; and Tunisia: HRC, 'Report on the First Special Session of The Human Rights Council', 18 July 2006, UN Doc. A/HRC/S-1/3.
247 South African delegate, 1st Special Session, 5 July 2006.
248 Indian delegate, 1st Special Session, 5 July 2006.
249 Sudanese delegate, 1st Special Session, 5 July 2006.
250 Swiss delegate, 1st Special Session, 5 July 2006.
251 French delegate, 1st Special Session, 5 July 2006.
252 American delegate, 1st Special Session, 5 July 2006.
253 Israeli delegate, 1st Special Session, 5 July 2006.

Finland (EU) requested a vote on the Session's draft resolution. The Resolution[254] was adopted by 29[255] votes to 11,[256] with 5 abstentions.[257] All Western countries voting against the Resolution, bar Switzerland who abstained. Brazil, Argentina and Uruguay emphasised that, despite their support for the resolution, they hoped the Council would not emulate the Commission by passing multiple resolutions on one situation.[258] Japan argued that the 'text is one-sided and non-constructive' saying 'this way of conducting business does not serve the Council or this particular issue'.[259] Pakistan (OIC) 'could not understand the rationale of those who opposed or abstained' expressing 'dismay that [. . .] some Council members have political considerations' which affected their vote.[260]

One month later, the Council convened its Second Special Session. It again focused on Israeli violations, this time within Lebanon. Of the states which called for the First Special Session, only Brazil, Gabon, India, Mali, and Sri Lanka did not call for the Second Special Session. All states calling for the Session[261] were OIC members, with three exceptions: Russia, a long-standing critic of Israel, particularly due to Israel's ties with America; Cuba, a strong OIC ally and fierce US critic; and South Africa, which strongly identified with the Palestinian cause. OIC states calling for Council action in Lebanon were joined by, amongst others, Argentina, Zambia, India, DPRK, and Ecuador. Cuba attacked the US and EU for supporting Israel, asserting that the Resolution should be adopted by consensus or overwhelming majority to 'send out a clear signal to the world'.[262] China commented that 'if the Council doesn't act, people will ask what is the point of the Council'.[263] Sudan attacked the US and the Security Council for investigating the situation in Darfur but not acting on Lebanon, although as discussed in Chapter 8 the investigation on Darfur was terminated.

254 HRC Res. S-1/Res.1, 'Human rights situation in the Occupied Palestinian Territory', 6 July 2006, UN Doc. A/HRC/Res/S-1/1.
255 Algeria, Argentina, Azerbaijan, Bahrain, Bangladesh, Brazil, China, Cuba, Ecuador, Ghana, Guatemala, India, Indonesia, Jordan, Malaysia, Mali, Mauritius, Morocco, Pakistan, Peru, Philippines, Russian Federation, Saudi Arabia, Senegal, South Africa, Sri Lanka, Tunisia, Uruguay, Zambia.
256 Canada, Czech Republic, Finland, France, Germany, Japan, Netherlands, Poland, Romania, Ukraine, United Kingdom of Great Britain and Northern Ireland.
257 Cameroon, Mexico, Nigeria, Republic of Korea, Switzerland.
258 Brazilian delegate, 1st Special Session, 5 July 2006.
259 Japanese delegate, 1st Special Session, 5 July 2006.
260 Pakistani delegate, 1st Special Session, 5 July 2006.
261 Algeria, Azerbaijan, Bahrain, Bangladesh, China, Cuba, Indonesia, Jordan, Malaysia, Morocco, Pakistan, Russian Federation, Saudi Arabia, Senegal, South Africa and Tunisia: HRC, 'Report of the Human Rights Council on its Second Special Session', 11 August 2006, UN Doc. A/HRC/S-2/2, Part II, para. 3.
262 Cuban delegate, 2nd Special Session, 11 August 2006.
263 Chinese delegate, 2nd Special Session, 11 August 2006.

Switzerland again supported the Session, although this time arguing for 'a non-discriminatory approach'.[264] Finland (EU) neither condemned nor supported the Session, but called for 'peaceful cooperation' and promotion of 'universal human rights without distinction'.[265] Australia was 'distraught by the one-sided nature of this session' arguing that holding a Special Session was unhelpful, particularly as the Security Council was dealing with the situation.[266] The US supported Australia's assertions, calling the Session 'unhelpful and potentially unproductive' and reminding the Council of the need for impartiality and non-selectivity.[267] The session's Resolution[268] was adopted by 27 votes[269] to 11,[270] with 8 abstentions.[271]

The Third Special Session, on Israeli violations in Beit Hanoun, took place in November 2006. States[272] calling for the Session were again from the South, OIC members, or allied states. Pakistan (OIC) stated:

> It is under exceptional circumstances that the OIC and the Arab League have requested this session. Some say that too frequent special sessions will devalue the Human Rights Council, but if the human rights machinery cannot respond to violations around the world it will devalue the Council. It is eerie how gross and systematic human rights violations take place before, during, and after Council Special Session relating to Israel. Convening the Council is not an abuse. Not convening the Council would be far worse.[273]

Other OIC states regretted the Council's failure to ensure its previous resolutions were implemented. Algeria (African Group) called on the Council 'to rise to the challenge of its mandate and confront these gross human rights violations'.[274] Switzerland again supported convening the Session, arguing that

264 Swiss delegate, 2nd Special Session, 11 August 2006.
265 Finnish delegate, 2nd Special Session, 11 August 2006.
266 Australian delegate, 2nd Special Session, 11 August 2006.
267 American delegate, 2nd Special Session, 11 August 2006.
268 HRC Res. S-2/1, 'The Grave Situation of Human Rights in Lebanon Caused by Israeli Military Operations', 11 August 2006, UN Doc. A/HRC/RES/S-2/1.
269 Algeria, Argentina, Azerbaijan, Bahrain, Bangladesh, Brazil, China, Cuba, Ecuador, India, Indonesia, Jordan, Malaysia, Mali, Mauritius, Mexico, Morocco, Pakistan, Peru, Russian Federation, Saudi Arabia, Senegal, South Africa, Sri Lanka, Tunisia, Uruguay, Zambia.
270 Canada, Czech Republic, Finland, France, Germany, Japan, Netherlands, Poland, Romania, Ukraine, United Kingdom of Great Britain and Northern Ireland.
271 Cameroon, Gabon, Ghana, Guatemala, Nigeria, Philippines, Republic of Korea, Switzerland.
272 Algeria, Azerbaijan, Bahrain, Bangladesh, Brazil, China, Cuba, Ghana, India, Indonesia, Jordan, Malaysia, Mauritius, Morocco, Nigeria, Pakistan, Philippines, Russian Federation, Saudi Arabia, Senegal, South Africa, Sri Lanka, Tunisia and Zambia: HRC, 'Report of the Human Rights Council on its Third Special Session', 15 November 2006, UN Doc. A/HRC/S-3/2, Part II, para. 3.
273 Pakistani delegate, 3rd Special Session, 15 November 2006.
274 Algerian delegate, 3rd Special Session, 15 November 2006.

it 'shows that we are willing to meet on acute world situations'.[275] Finland again demonstrated the EU's neutrality, neither supporting nor criticising the session. Canada and Australia repeated earlier positions deploring the Council for its lack of objectivity, impartiality, and balance. Both states reminded the Council of its founding principles, saying that the body's actions were futile without adherence to these principles. The Third Session's Resolution[276] was adopted by 32 votes[277] to 8,[278] with 6 abstentions.[279] Although Japan and Switzerland pointed to the Resolution's lack of balance, the OIC welcomed its adoption by a two-thirds majority, arguing that 'we can't all be wrong, can we?'[280]

The Fourth Special Session was convened on the human rights situation in Darfur. More states called for this session than other sessions, and for the first time states[281] calling for this session included countries from all regional groups. At this first session unrelated to Israel, Secretary-General Kofi Annan called on the Council to address problems outside of the Middle East. Unlike the sessions on Israel, various states, typically Sudan's allies from the OIC or the African Group, expressed support for the country concerned. Again, unlike previous sessions, Western states supported the Session. Palestine, Iran and Pakistan all used the Session to attack Israel, and to criticise Annan's 'partial' statement about the Middle East.

At the Fourth Special Session consensus was reached on the draft text. However, the final text was in the form of a decision[282] rather than a resolution, thus carrying far less weight than the previous sessions' outcomes. Nineteen Council members[283] spoke after the Decision's adoption, all lauding the Council for its cooperative, compromising, and congenial approach. Most

---

275 Swiss delegate, 3rd Special Session, 15 November 2006.

276 HRC Res. S-3/1, 'Human rights violations emanating from Israeli military incursions in the Occupied Palestinian Territory, including the recent one in northern Gaza and the assault on Beit Hanoun', 15 November 2006, UN Doc. A/HRC/RES/S-3/1.

277 Algeria, Argentina, Azerbaijan, Bahrain, Bangladesh, Brazil, China, Cuba, Djibouti, Ecuador, Gabon, Ghana, India, Indonesia, Jordan, Malaysia, Mali, Mauritius, Mexico, Morocco, Nigeria, Pakistan, Peru, Philippines, Russian Federation, Saudi Arabia, Senegal, South Africa, Sri Lanka, Tunisia, Uruguay, Zambia.

278 Canada, Czech Republic, Finland, Germany, Netherlands, Poland, Romania, United Kingdom of Great Britain and Northern Ireland.

279 France, Guatemala, Japan, Republic of Korea, Switzerland, Ukraine.

280 Pakistani delegate, 3rd Special Session, 15 November 2006.

281 Algeria, Brazil, Canada, the Czech Republic, Cuba, Ecuador, Finland, France, Gabon, Germany, Ghana, Guatemala, Japan, Mauritius, Mexico, Morocco, the Netherlands, Nigeria, Peru, Poland, the Republic of Korea, Romania, Russian Federation, South Africa, Switzerland, Tunisia, Ukraine, the United Kingdom of Great Britain and Northern Ireland, Uruguay and Zambia: HRC, 'Report of the Human Rights Council on its Fourth Special Session', 12–13 December 2006, UN Doc. A/HRC/S-4/5, Part II, para. 3.

282 HRC Decision S-4/101, 'Situation of Human Rights in Darfur', 13 December 2006, UN Doc. A/HRC/DEC/S-4/101.

283 Including 7 OIC countries, 5 EU countries, including Cuba, India, Russia, China, and Zambia.

were careful to say this was a happy moment for both the Council and the people of Darfur. However, India, Saudi Arabia, China, and Tunisia, amongst others, cared more that the consensus 'proved' the Council's legitimacy than about its impact on violations in Darfur.[284] The UK hoped that the Council would build on this constructive spirit to move away from solely focusing on the Middle East, and the President invited Council members to 'maintain this spirit when we deal with other situations'.[285]

The Fifth Special Session adopted a Resolution[286] on the situation in Myanmar by consensus. The Session took place after Myanmar's military junta violently repressed monks' peaceful demonstrations. The Resolution resulted in the Special Rapporteur on Myanmar's first invitation to visit the country since 2003.[287] The Sixth Special Session again focused on Israeli violations, this time in Gaza and Nablus. The Resolution[288] was adopted by 30 votes[289] to 1,[290] with 15 abstentions.[291] Canada was the sole dissenting voice, once again rejecting country-specific resolutions and emphasising the Council's founding principles. The Seventh Special Session was the first to deal with a thematic issue. It examined '[t]he negative impact on the realization of the right to food [. . .] caused inter alia by the soaring food prices' and its Resolution[292] was adopted by consensus. The Eighth Special Session also adopted its Resolution[293] by consensus, this time on the situation in the Democratic Republic of Congo. However, the Ninth Special Session, once again focused on Israeli violations. Its Resolution[294] was adopted by 33 votes[295]

284 All statements made at the 4th Special Session, 13 December 2006.

285 President Luis Alfonso de Alba (Mexico), 4th Special Session, 13 December 2006.

286 HRC Res. S-5/1. 'Situation of Human Rights in Myanmar', 2 October 2007, UN Doc. A/HRC/RES/S-5/1.

287 Callejon, 'Developments at the Human Rights Council in 2007', 340–41.

288 HRC Res. S-6/1. 'Human Rights Violations Emanating from Israeli Military Attacks and Incursions in the Occupied Palestinian Territory, Particularly in the Occupied Gaza Strip', 24 January 2008, UN Doc. A/HRC/RES/S-6/1.

289 Angola, Azerbaijan, Bangladesh, Bolivia, Brazil, China, Cuba, Djibouti, Egypt, India, Indonesia, Jordan, Madagascar, Malaysia, Mali, Mauritius, Mexico, Nicaragua, Nigeria, Pakistan, Peru, Philippines, Qatar, Russian Federation, Saudi Arabia, Senegal, South Africa, Sri Lanka, Uruguay, Zambia.

290 Canada.

291 Bosnia and Herzegovina, Cameroon, France, Germany, Ghana, Guatemala, Italy, Japan, Netherlands, Republic of Korea, Romania, Slovenia, Switzerland, Ukraine, United Kingdom of Great Britain and Northern Ireland.

292 HRC Res. S-7/1, 'The Negative Impact of the Worsening of the World Food Crisis on the Realization of the Right to Food for All', 22 May 2008, UN Doc. A/HRC/RES/S-7/1.

293 HRC Res. S-8/1, 'Situation of Human Rights in the East of the Democratic Republic of the Congo', 1 December 2008, UN Doc. A/HRC/RES/S-8/1.

294 HRC Res. S-9/1, 'The Grave Violations of Human Rights in the Occupied Palestinian Territory, Particularly Due to the Recent Israeli Military Attacks Against the Occupied Gaza Strip', 12 January 2009, UN Doc. A/HRC/RES/S-9/1.

295 Angola, Argentina, Azerbaijan, Bahrain, Bangladesh, Bolivia, Brazil, Burkina Faso, Chile, China, Cuba, Djibouti, Egypt, Gabon, Ghana, India, Indonesia, Jordan, Madagascar, Malaysia, Mauritius, Mexico, Nicaragua, Nigeria, Pakistan, Philippines, Qatar, Russian Federation, Saudi Arabia, Senegal, South Africa, Uruguay, Zambia.

to 1,[296] with 13 abstentions.[297] Canada again cast the sole dissenting vote. The Tenth Special Session dealt with the second thematic issue, the impact of the global financial crisis on human rights. Its Resolution[298] was adopted 31 votes[299] to 0, with 14 abstentions.[300] The Eleventh Special Session was convened on Sri Lanka. It took until 2009's massacre of Tamils for the Council to call the Session, despite Scannella and Splinter writing in 2007 of the 'growing deterioration' that required the Council's attention.[301] The Resolution[302] was adopted by 29 votes[303] to 12,[304] with 6 abstentions.[305] Those were the first dissenting votes cast on an issue other than Israeli violations. The Twelfth Special Session was again convened on Israel, and its Resolution[306] was adopted by 25 votes[307] to 6,[308] with 11 abstentions.[309]

9.2.3 Politicisation of special sessions

The first twelve Special Sessions were convened between 2006 and 2009. During this time, many gross and systemic human rights violations occurred

296 Canada.
297 Bosnia and Herzegovina, Cameroon, France, Germany, Italy, Japan, Netherlands, Republic of Korea, Slovakia, Slovenia, Switzerland, Ukraine, United Kingdom of Great Britain and Northern Ireland.
298 HRC Res. S-10/1, 'The Impact of the Global Economic and Financial Crises on the Universal Realization and Effective Enjoyment of Human Rights', 23 February 2009, UN Doc. A/HRC/RES/S-10/1.
299 Angola, Argentina, Azerbaijan, Bahrain, Bangladesh, Bolivia, Brazil, Burkina Faso, Cameroon, Chile, China, Cuba, Djibouti, Egypt, Ghana, India, Indonesia, Jordan, Madagascar, Malaysia, Mauritius, Nicaragua, Nigeria, Pakistan, Philippines, Qatar, Russian Federation, Saudi Arabia, Senegal, South Africa, Uruguay.
300 Bosnia and Herzegovina, Canada, France, Germany, Italy, Japan, Mexico, Netherlands, Republic of Korea, Slovakia, Slovenia, Switzerland, Ukraine, United Kingdom of Great Britain and Northern Ireland.
301 Arguably, political mistrust between states 'prevented Council members from cooperating effectively' to deal with the Sri Lankan human rights situation. Scannella and Splinter use that example to demonstrate 'the dangerous double standards' at the Council.
302 HRC Res. S-11/1, 'Assistance to Sri Lanka in the Promotion and Protection of Human Rights', 27 May 2009, UN Doc. A/HRC/RES/S-11/1.
303 Angola, Azerbaijan, Bahrain, Bangladesh, Bolivia (Plurinational State of), Brazil, Burkina Faso, Cameroon, China, Cuba, Djibouti, Egypt, Ghana, India, Indonesia, Jordan, Madagascar, Malaysia, Nicaragua, Nigeria, Pakistan, Philippines, Qatar, Russian Federation, Saudi Arabia, Senegal, South Africa, Uruguay, Zambia.
304 Bosnia and Herzegovina, Canada, Chile, France, Germany, Italy, Mexico, Netherlands, Slovakia, Slovenia, Switzerland, United Kingdom of Great Britain and Northern Ireland.
305 Argentina, Gabon, Japan, Mauritius, Republic of Korea, Ukraine.
306 HRC Res. S-12/1, 'The Human Rights Situation in the Occupied Palestinian Territory, Including East Jerusalem', 16 October 2009, UN Doc. A/HRC/RES/S-12/1.
307 Argentina, Bahrain, Bangladesh, Bolivia, Brazil, Chile, China, Cuba, Djibouti, Egypt, Ghana, India, Indonesia, Jordan, Mauritius, Nicaragua, Nigeria, Pakistan, Philippines, Qatar, Russian Federation, Saudi Arabia, Senegal, South Africa, Zambia.
308 Hungary, Italy, Netherlands, Slovakia, Ukraine, United States of America.
309 Belgium, Bosnia and Herzegovina, Burkina Faso, Cameroon, Gabon, Japan, Mexico, Norway, Republic of Korea, Slovenia, Uruguay.

that were not dealt with by this mechanism, or indeed at all by the Council. The violent repression of protests following Iran's 2009 Presidential elections was ignored by the Council despite well-documented human rights violations.[310] Similarly, grave violations occurring in China, particularly surrounding the Beijing Olympics in 2008, did not merit the convening of a Special Session despite widespread coverage of the human rights abuses.[311] Situations in these, and other, countries were not dealt with by the Council for political reasons. OIC members, including known grave abusers such as Iran, Libya, and Syria, were protected by their political and regional allies. Powerful states from the Global South, including China and Zimbabwe, as well as the South's allies, such as Russia and Venezuela, were also protected from scrutiny of their gross and systemic human rights violations.

While the Commission's bias was manifested in excessive resolutions against Israel,[312] the Council went further by using Special Sessions for selective and politicised aims. Countries such as the DPRK (North Korea), Zimbabwe, Russia and China, meanwhile, avoided scrutiny. An article on Zimbabwe in *The Economist* noted a main flaw regarding Special Sessions:

> True to form, the UN's recently revamped human rights council [. . .] which might have been expected to be taking keen interest in what is going on in Zimbabwe, has not even raised the issue. Unlike its discredited predecessor, the Commission on Human Rights, it has the power to call for an emergency session to address particularly egregious violations of human rights, for example in Zimbabwe. [. . .] In theory, calling an emergency session on Zimbabwe should not be so difficult [. . .] but with its 16 members, the Organisation of the Islamic Conference, supported by the 13 African members, has a stranglehold over the Council. Together, they repeatedly fend off moves to look into the human rights records of Muslim or African countries.[313]

Although the Council increasingly used this mechanism to respond to crises in 2010, with sessions on Haiti, Cote d'Ivoire, and Libya, those situations, as with the one in Sri Lanka, reached absolute crisis point before the body addressed them. Israel's human rights violations, on the other hand, were scrutinised regardless of whether they were an ongoing or crisis situation. Were this mechanism to be zero sum, with all grave and other situations able to be examined and to have time and resources devoted to them, then

---

310 See, for example, Amnesty International, 'Iran: Arrests and Deaths Continue as Authorities Tighten Grip', 14 July 2009, AI Index: MDE 13/072/2009.

311 See, for example, Amnesty International, 'People's Republic of China The Olympics Countdown – Broken Promises', July 2008, AI Index: ASA 17/089/2008.

312 One quarter of all Commission resolutions concerned that state.

313 Opinion, 'The United Nations and Zimbabwe: Crimes Against Humanity', *The Economist*, 26 June 2008.

undoubtedly the six sessions on Israel would be justified and necessary. However, in practice, the Council has time and resources to allocate even-handedly according to need.

Abebe comments that the African Group sought less emphasis on Special Sessions in light of the UPR's ability to deal with country-specific situations.[314] However, the Group supported country-specific action on Israel through the Council's Special Sessions. Moreover, whereas the African Group supported a weak and non-condemnatory text on Darfur, it supported strong and one-sided resolutions on Israel.

The EU's position at Special Sessions reflected its tendency for neutrality during politically sensitive Council proceedings. EU members did not call for Special Sessions to be convened on Israel, although they did call for sessions on other issues. Despite voting against or abstaining on resolutions about Israel, EU countries often remained silent or made passive and neutral statements during sessions. Other Western states did speak about politicisation, bias and selectivity, with Canada, Australia and the US taking strong positions on those issues. Indeed, Canada twice cast the sole dissenting vote against resolutions on Israel.

States from other groups did not adopt group positions on Special Sessions. Cuba, for example, pursued political objectives by allying itself with the OIC against Israel. Other Latin American states expressed various positions on Israel, even changing their positions at different sessions. While India cited its own national security as motivation for supporting Special Sessions on Israel, other Asian states at times abstained or voted against such resolutions. Realists might argue that many states pursued their own national policies, often not tied to the issue at hand. Japan, for example, voted with the West despite making statements supporting the opposite position. That form of politicisation is unsurprising given the Council's nature as an intergovernmental body. More worrisome is the use of collective weight to achieve political objectives where such aims do not affect a member's national politics.

9.3. Summary

The UPR and Special Sessions mechanisms were heralded as a break from the old body, and a method for overcoming the Commission's failings and fulfilling the Council's mandate. Exploration of these two mechanisms has, once again, demonstrated that the Council sought to fulfil its mandate but was obstructed by states seeking to use these mechanisms for political, biased and subjective aims. The form and design of these mechanisms allowed them to be hijacked by states, groups and blocs seeking to further political agendas. Arguably, without reform, these mechanisms will undoubtedly be further misused.

---

314 Abebe, 'Of Shaming and Bargaining', 32–3.

Conclusions may be drawn about the Council's use of these innovative mechanisms. I shall address the UPR and Special Sessions in relation to the Council's mandate, its founding principles, and politicisation of the body.

9.3.1 Mandate

UPR aims to identify areas of weakness upon which the Council may provide recommendations, assistance or advisory services to enable countries to better fulfil their human rights obligations. Many observers have been keen to herald the UPR's success. That view is unsurprising, as the mechanism is central to the Council's credibility. UPR has enabled fact-finding, dialogue and information sharing, but only to the extent that the states under review cooperated with the process. Recommendations on implementation of human rights and adherence to commitments and obligations have been made at all UPR sessions. The Council's promotion mandate was therefore fulfilled to some extent, with particular successes in relation to those states which would otherwise be ignored either due to their relatively benign human rights records or as a result of being shielded from scrutiny by allied states, groups or blocs. However, the process has been undermined by reviewed states either avoiding responding to criticisms or, indeed, preventing questions from being raised.

Full assessment of the utility of this mechanism cannot be made even after the first full cycle, owing to judgements being reserved until states begin to implement, or ignore, recommendations. The only true measure of success, according to Sweeney and Saito, is whether states implement the review's recommendations and report back on follow-up.[315] It is clear that the first cycle of UPR sessions did not go far enough to promote human rights. The reasons for this will be explored in relation to the politicisation of those sessions.

Special Sessions enabled the Council to take steps towards fulfilling its protection mandate through information sharing, providing a forum for dialogue, fact-finding, and recommendations. The body used those sessions primarily to deal with country-specific situations, but also convened sessions to discuss the impact of thematic issues on human rights. As such, these sessions did enable the body to fulfil its responsibility to address situations of human rights violations. However, the misuse of this mechanism to focus vastly disproportionate attention on Israel, combined with failure to convene sessions on other, often graver, situations in, for example, China or Iran, resulted in the body, once again, failing adequately to fulfil its protection mandate. Groups and blocs effectively blocked the Council from protecting human rights where the fulfilment of the body's mandate conflicted with regional or political objectives.

315 Sweeney and Saito, 'An NGO assessment of the new mechanisms of the UN Human Rights Council'.

9.3.2 *Founding principles*

UPR represents a compromise between radical and idealist proposals, and the need to encourage cooperation in order to ensure a universal, inclusive and cooperative mechanism. Focus on cooperation and dialogue resulted in states engaging with the UPR process, and the appearance of adherence to these principles. On closer examination, however, a number of states emphasised the need for cooperation in order to ignore questions asked or to avoid critical statements. The need for inclusiveness and for a state-led reviewing process to some extent impeded promotion of human rights. However, without such cooperation it is doubtful that the UPR would have fulfilled as many, let alone more, of the body's duties.

It has been argued that the UPR provides a mechanism that affords all states equal treatment,[316] but it is clear that equal treatment from states has not occurred in practice. Moreover, it is disproportionate for the Council to afford the same treatment and resources to, for example, Sweden and Somalia. Equal treatment appears to have been interpreted as devoting equal resources, rather than using the same benchmarks to review each state. In order to improve the effectiveness and credibility of the main UN human rights body, proportionate treatment must be afforded to states and their performance examined according to a limited number of benchmarks. Special Sessions, unlike the UPR, will necessarily involve some degree of selectivity and partiality as they are convened to focus on single human rights situations, whether country-specific or thematic. The mechanism was designed to ensure that violations within situations would be addressed by the Council in order to protect universal human rights standards. However, the selectivity involved in convening Special Sessions resulted in clear bias and partiality against Israel, with focus on that state's abuses to the exclusion of time and resources being devoted elsewhere. Indeed, discussions within Special Sessions and action taken at those sessions have been shown to have varied according to the subjective and partial aims of states, groups and blocs. The body clearly failed adequately to adhere to its founding principles both in the convening and conduct of Special Sessions.

9.3.3 *Politicisation*

A North–South divide has already impacted upon UPR sessions. Developing nations seek to avoid condemnation, instead focusing on practical advice and assistance in implementing recommendation, while Western countries focus on tailored, specific recommendations.[317] Gaer argues that lack of trust at the Council will impact on the UPR's effectiveness and ability to achieve its

---

316 Gaer, 'A Voice Not an Echo: Universal Periodic Review and the UN Treaty Body System', 138.
317 Abebe, 'Of Shaming and Bargaining', 31.

objectives.[318] The Council is already divided on politically sensitive issues, with ongoing tensions and mistrust between various groups and blocs. That atmosphere has affected, although not fully obstructed, the Council's proceedings and action on some sensitive human rights issues. As the UPR examines all states, including politically sensitive countries, the North–South divide will have some impact upon the mechanism.

UPR has been politicised in a number of ways. The mechanism has lacked even-handedness through its treatment of different states, particularly those countries singled out as 'enemies' of the main groups at the Council. The first cycle of sessions demonstrates regional tactics consistent with other Council proceedings whereby developing states, particularly OIC members and their allies in NAM and the African Group, protect each other through various methods. Those states took the floor to compliment allies, thus using the allotted time and blocking other states from asking questions or making recommendations. Similarly, states from the South have constantly emphasised lack of capacity for human rights protection and promotion in order to shield allies from criticism.

Sweeney and Saito note another potential political tactic arising from the UPR.[319] States have claimed, subsequent to the first UPR sessions, that country-specific mandates, discussions and resolutions are no longer required. Amongst others, this position has been taken by the DPRK, the Philippines and China.[320] Abebe comments that UPR should not be used to block Council discussions or action on grave situations of gross and systemic human rights abuses, nor should the review process be used by states to avoid other human rights scrutiny.[321] However, developing states have long sought to abolish country-specific resolutions, and despite failing to do so during the Council's creation, shifting the focus onto the UPR displays a worrying trend which may impact the Council's ability to take other forms of country-specific action.

Regionalism and group tactics that occurred during the UPR mirrored practices within the Council. Many other tactics adopted at UPR sessions were facilitated by the emphasis on cooperation and consent as the UPR's main bases. That allowed states to ignore human rights issues that were raised in reviews; to deflect attention away from gross and systemic violations; and to avoid considering recommendations. Despite this, some commentators view the UPR as a success. Carey comments that there has never previously been

---

318 Gaer, 'A Voice Not an Echo: Universal Periodic Review and the UN Treaty Body System', 138–9.

319 Sweeney and Saito, 'An NGO Assessment of the New Mechanisms of the UN Human Rights Council', 219.

320 See the debate around the extension of the mandate of the Special Rapporteur on the DPRK in ISHR, Daily Update, 27 March 2008, at 11–12 (Online). Available HTTP: <http://www.ishr.ch/hrm/council/dailyupdates/session_007/27_march_2008.pdf> (accessed 22 July 2012).

321 Abebe, 'Of Shaming and Bargaining', 31.

'an occasion when, in an organized and systematic fashion, a country bared its human rights record and then listened respectfully to polite but probing questions from other countries'.[322] Yet, it would be remiss to insist that the mere existence of the UPR is sufficient to render it a success. Instead, it is clear that the process must be reformed. Minimising the politicisation that occurred throughout the first cycle, ultimately, will be key to the UPR being able to fulfil its mandate.

Politicisation occurred throughout both the convening and conduct of Special Sessions. Special Sessions on human rights abuses committed by Israel in the OPT, Lebanon and Syria, furthered the OIC agenda of retaining focus on these abuses in order to keep international attention on that state in order to further the Palestinian cause. Moreover, such focus also resulted in less attention being paid to other regional human rights violations and grave or crisis situations.

Regional groups dominated proceedings at Special Sessions as they had done throughout regular Council sessions. The African Group, for example, continued to shield its regional ally, Sudan, throughout the Special Session focusing on the situation in Darfur. Collective positions were taken throughout almost all of the Special Sessions, with regional groups and political blocs seeking to further political objectives. Some groups and blocs focused on the need for human rights protection, but the same pattern emerged regarding states from the Global North which sought, during contentious sessions, to shield allies or to further unrelated political agendas.

322 Carey, 'The U.N. Human Rights Council', 460.

Conclusion

1. Assessment of the Council

Assessment of the Human Rights Council's formative years has demonstrated that the body is failing to fulfil its mandate, particularly in terms of protecting human rights. The Council has not achieved the idealist aims set forth in its constituent instrument, nor has it adhered to the founding principles that were designed to underpin and legitimise its proceedings and mechanisms. The Council, created to replace the failed Commission on Human Rights, has not overcome many of its predecessor's shortcomings. Although the Council has, to some extent, fulfilled its roles and functions, the body's ability to utilise them to discharge its mandate has been affected by a number of interconnected problems. This book did not focus on reform proposals but rather on identifying the problems facing the Council. However, reforms to the body, its form, its mechanisms and its proceedings are needed for the Council to fulfil its mandate. These problems were neither adequately addressed nor dealt with during the Council's 2011 internal assessment. Therefore, they will undoubtedly continue to undermine the body's work and credibility. Those problems include the body's composition and membership, politicisation, regionalism, and bias and selectivity.

Mandate. The Council's mandate is broadly divided into two parts: protecting and promoting human rights. The promotion mandate requires the body to assist states with implementing human rights and fulfilling their commitments and obligations. I have shown various ways in which the body sought to discharge this mandate. The assessment has, however, primarily focused on the protection mandate. Paragraph 4 of Resolution 60/251 requires the Council to address human rights situations. This paragraph is key for the body's protection mandate. The Council is given tools to address those situations through, for example, Special Sessions, fact-finding, and making recommendations.

I have assessed fulfilment of the protection mandate by examining which situations the Council chose to address, the manner in which they were addressed, and the extent to which the Council adhered to the principles of universality and even-handedness. The assessment has shown that disproportionate attention was focused on some states, such as Israel and the US, thus diverting time and resources away from other grave situations. Many grave situations were not addressed by the Council, for example in China, Zimbabwe and Russia. Moreover, even where the Council sought to discharge its protection mandate, it was at times impeded from doing so by states, groups or blocs shielding allies from scrutiny.

The body did fulfil its roles and functions in relation to fact-finding and information sharing, although states were able to block the Council from fulfilling these roles by refusing to cooperate with mandate holders, Working Groups and discussions within the body. The Council at times failed to provide formal recommendations on human rights protection, and was unable to ensure implementation of any recommendations made. Resolution 60/251 does not provide the Council with binding powers, thus negating its ability to do more than follow-up on implementation of recommendations and, exceptionally, to refer situations to the General Assembly or Security Council. As such, the body needed to discharge its mandate through other mechanisms, for example diplomatic pressure, but failed to do so even where vast efforts were put into place to ensure compromise agreements between groups, blocs and the state under discussion.

Although Resolution 60/251 only gave the Council non-binding powers, the body has been assessed in relation to its use of those powers to fulfil its mandate. Human rights fall under states' domestic jurisdiction other than in those exceptional cases where bodies such as the Security Council use binding powers, such as sanctions or the use of force, to ensure compliance with obligations. The Council's non-binding powers should, in theory, provide the basis for the body fulfilling its mandate. However, states abusing human rights often ignored the Council's recommendations, or failed to be swayed by diplomatic pressure, resulting in little change on the ground particularly in relation to grave or crisis situations.

Founding Principles. In order to combat the Commission's failings, and to balance the weakened reforms implemented at the new body, the Council's constituent instrument repeatedly mandated the body to adhere to the principles of impartiality, objectivity, non-selectivity and universality throughout its proceedings and work. I have assessed the body's adherence to these principles throughout its proceedings and work.

The Council has failed universally to protect and promote human rights, particularly through its ignoring, or being prevented from addressing, many grave human rights situations. The Council has, moreover, not overcome the Commission's selectivity and bias in addressing human rights. Israel occupies a vastly disproportionate amount of the Council's time and resources, as occurred at the Commission. Human rights violations by Israel in the Occupied Palestinian Territories are not disputed. However, the disproportionate focus on Israel within Council proceedings and mechanisms has been deliberately calculated to deflect the spotlight from similar, and often graver, human rights violations in other regions. The Secretary-General and the High

Commissioner for Human Rights were unable to convince Council members to avoid selectivity by giving proportionate attention to other human rights situations.

The founding principles also include cooperation, inclusiveness and dialogue, which aim to overcome the Commission's culture of naming, shaming and blaming. However, as has been demonstrated regarding the US, that culture is being repeated at the Council. Emphasis on cooperation has undermined the body's proceedings and mechanisms to the extent that states have refused to cooperate with the body or have used this principle to insist on weakened actions by the Council when seeking to protect or promote human rights. The Council has provided a forum for dialogue, but often that dialogue and information sharing has been impeded by groups and blocs intent on naming, shaming and blaming rather than seeking constructive dialogue.

Politicisation. Council proceedings and work have been undermined by politicisation from the outset. As an intergovernmental body, some politicisation was to be expected at the Council. However, national and regional political agendas have dominated Council proceedings, particularly on contentious or politically sensitive issues. States and groups deploy various tactics to further national or regional political objectives. Political aims have thus far directed the Council's work, with Council members shielding allies as well as attacking other states for political motives. Powerful alliances ensure constant Council focus on certain human rights issues, to the detriment of other pressing human rights concerns. Despite widespread criticism from UN staff, states and various observers, politicisation has only increased over the Council's formative years.

Regionalism. Many of the Council's attempts to fulfil its mandate have been undermined by states organising themselves by regional alliances. Regional and political groups have dominated the new body much like they dominated the Commission. Groups have placed national and collective agendas above the need for protecting and promoting human rights. Collective strength has been used to shield regional allies from Council scrutiny, or to focus the body's attention on issues collectively deemed important. Working in regional groups often results in use of the lowest common denominator, thus undermining the effectiveness of the Council's work.

The Council's composition is based on geographic representation, which does not take into account the cross-regional political blocs generally comprised of states from the South. Divisions along regional and political lines mirror those at the Commission during its final years. A North–South divide has increasingly developed during the post-Cold War era. Emerging states from across various regional and political alliances have supported each other's positions on contentious or politically sensitive issues. In particular, the African Group and the OIC have dominated Council proceedings, directing its work in accordance with collective agendas.

2. Moving forward

Many reforms proposals were not taken up at the Council's creation despite the clear need for the new body to overcome its predecessor's failings. This assessment has provided detailed evidence and analysis of the Council's failure to fulfil its mandate adequately. Having assessed the new body and identified the reasons for this failure, the conclusion can be drawn that the Council must be reformed in order for the body to effectively discharge its legal duties and achieve the aims for which it was created. Although I have not sought to offer reform proposals, the assessment has identified key areas in need of reform. It is hoped, albeit not expected, that the Council's internal review has provided impetus for reformation of the body. However, it is likely that the body will largely continue in its current form, and as such I will explore the need for reform in forthcoming scholarship.

Original Reform Proposals. The Commission's failings ultimately rendered it unable to fulfil its mandate. Discussions on the Council's creation focused on how best to overcome the pitfalls that had beset its predecessor. Radical reform proposals were not adopted, thus hampering the Council's ability to move beyond its predecessor. As the new body resembles its predecessor, albeit certain changes occurred and new mechanisms were created, it is not altogether unexpected that many of the same problems have arisen as plagued the Commission. States sought to keep the most radical reforms from being implemented, particularly those that would limit the Council's size and membership. Most importantly, states ensured that the body remained an intergovernmental forum. Allowing independent experts to replace state delegates would have radically altered the Council's composition, eliminating many of the issues that subsequently arose. Arguably, in light of this assessment, such reforms can be seen not as radical but rather as necessary for the body to have adhered to the legal duties and responsibilities ascribed to it.

Form and Design. The Council's form, as an intergovernmental body, is key for the body's legitimacy in the eyes of states and non-state actors, particularly those from the Global South who assert that human rights are used as a neo-colonial tool of oppression. However, that need for legitimacy must be balanced with the need for an effective body that is able to discharge its mandate. As such, the Council's form must be revisited, with a focus on whether a body consisting of independent experts, or indeed a different form altogether, would be better equipped to protect and promote human rights. The Council's design, with 47 member states all with equal votes, also serves to underpin the body's legitimacy. There again, the need for legitimacy must be balanced with the need for effectiveness. A smaller body would, arguably, be less politicised, and would be better able to discuss and take action on human rights issues.

Membership. It has been widely accepted that the final nail in the Commission's coffin was Libya's election as the body's Chairperson. This followed long-standing criticisms of known abusers sitting on the Commission as well as states seeking membership to avoid scrutiny of their own human rights record. Despite initial proposals that Council members should fulfil certain human rights criteria, the body's membership requirements focus on 'soft' criteria. Those requirements stemmed from the need for legitimacy and the adherence to Charter principles. Gross and systemic human rights abusers seemed undeterred by these 'soft' criteria from seeking membership, with countries such as China, Egypt, Saudi Arabia, Pakistan, Russia and Libya elected during the Council's formative years. The presence of known abusers undermines the Council's credibility. Moreover, with many of the same members, and thus similar delegations, as sat on the Commission during its final years, the new body is unlikely to depart radically from its predecessor's practices. The need for membership criteria, or indeed a method for preventing known grave abusers from being elected to the Council, must be revisited.

Proceedings. Under the current system, states dictate the Council's proceedings. This assessment has demonstrated that Council discussions have been repeatedly used by states, groups and blocs for political aims, or indeed have been hijacked for unrelated political agendas. There is clearly a need to reform the body's proceedings, and indeed its mechanisms, to ensure that discussions cannot be segued and can instead remain constructive and aimed towards protecting and promoting human rights. Reformation of the body's proceedings must focus on implementing effective mechanisms to reduce, or even eliminate, politicisation. There are various potential reforms, and to detail them would go beyond the scope of this project. However, for example, states could be prevented from giving individual statements unless they add to, or are different from, the group position given on their behalf. Another example would be to limit the time allocated to discussions under each agenda item in order to ensure time and resources are adequately shared out, and that Special Sessions are used to address situations requiring greater attention. Focus on reforming proceedings will be central to enabling the body better to fulfil its mandate and to adhere to its founding principles.

Powers. In its current form, and under Resolution 60/251, the Council does not have legally binding powers nor enforcement mechanisms to ensure implementation of its recommendations. States are unlikely to agree to the Council being given such powers as this would encroach on domestic jurisdiction. One solution, perhaps, would be to increase the body's ability to place pressure on states to comply with human rights obligations and commitments. A change to the Council's working culture, and an increased ability to place diplomatic or other pressure on abuser states, would go some way towards this aim. However, should the Council continue in the direction that this assessment has identified, the option of binding powers might be considered in order to combat the body's ineffective pursuit of its protection mandate.

3. Lessons to be learnt

The Council's problems are not only interconnected, but are also linked with problems facing other intergovernmental, international, and human rights bodies. Thus, this assessment is representative of broader problems within international institutions. Although comparison and contrast with other bodies goes beyond the scope of this work, parallels can be drawn which will enable better understanding of the context of problems facing the Council. The HRC was created with the specific intent and expectation that this body would overcome its predecessor's failings. That the body faces similar, and perhaps worse, problems to the Commission begs the question as to whether such failings can be overcome within a body of this form and design. State sovereignty has hampered the Council's ability to fulfil its mandate, particularly in light of its non-binding powers. Moreover, the nature of an intergovernmental body, especially of the Council's size, results in powerful groups or blocs dominating and directing proceedings, impeding the body's discharge of its mandate where necessary to further collective aims or agendas.

Throughout the assessment I have referred to UN human rights Committees as providing a benchmark for best practice when dealing with human rights issues. The Committees consist of expert delegates wholly independent from their sending state. Moreover, they deal with limited sets of rights which are applied on the basis of states' voluntary commitments to the relevant treaties. As such, these bodies are able to discharge their mandates far more effectively than the Council.

The Council's problems, based in large part on its form and composition, are reflected elsewhere within the UN and other intergovernmental bodies. The conclusion arguably can be drawn that radical reforms are, in fact, necessary in order to create a body which will effectively fulfil its mandate. International relations theories have been used to demonstrate the competing aims of states, groups and blocs within international organisations. In light of the number of UN member states and the power of various groups and blocs, the assessment of the Council perhaps underscores the need to re-evaluate the utility and effectiveness of intergovernmental bodies. Despite the Council being created in order to overcome the failings of its predecessor, the body has repeated many of those same mistakes, and lessons must be learnt in order for other similar institutions.

4. Final remarks

Council proceedings and mechanisms demonstrate that national and regional politics are of primary concern within the body. At times, such concerns are wholly unrelated to human rights. All areas of the new body have been undermined by selectivity, partiality, bias and politicisation, contradicting the Council's founding principles. While the Council's internal assessment identified its achievements, it is not sufficient for the body to fulfil its mandate on some human rights issues only. There have been achievements, mainly on non-contentious issues such as the rights to adequate housing and safe drinking water and sanitation. However, the body has failed to address many gross and systemic violations, while paying disproportionate attention to other issues, during its formative years. Even where situations have been addressed, action has at times been blocked or weakened for political reasons.

It is unlikely that the United Nations will disband this new body so soon after its creation. However, reforms could eliminate some, if not most, of the issues currently undermining the Council. As an intergovernmental body, the Council will remain a political body. Nevertheless, reforms to its procedural rules could go some way to achieving de-politicisation. The Council already lacks credibility among states, NGOs and observers, hampering its ability to protect and promote human rights. Without change, the legitimacy and credibility of the Council is likely to reflect that of the Commission.

Bibliography

Abbott, K.W., Keohane, R.O., Moravcsik, A., Slaughter, A.-M. and Snidal, D., 'The Concept of Legalization', *International Organization*, Vol. 54, No. 3, 2000, 401–19.

Abdulqawi, Y., *Standard-setting in UNESCO*, Leiden and Boston: Martinus Nijhoff Publishers, 2007.

Abebe, A.M., 'Of Shaming and Bargaining: African States and the Universal Periodic Review of the United Nations Human Rights Council', *Human Rights Law Review*, Vol. 9 (1), 2009, 1–35.

Abraham, M., *A New Chapter for Human Rights; A Handbook on Issues of Transition from the Commission on Human Rights to the Human Rights Council*, Geneva: ISHR and the Friedrich Ebert Stiftung, 2006.

Agence France-Presse, 'Prix Kadhafi des droits de l'homme', *Schweizerische Depesche-nagentur AG*, 30 September 2002.

Alston, P., 'The Commission on Human Rights', in P. Alston (ed.), *The United Nations and Human Rights, A Critical Appraisal*, Oxford: Clarendon Press, 1992, pp. 126–210.

Alston, P., 'The UN's Human Rights Record: From San Francisco to Vienna and Beyond', *Human Rights Quarterly*, Vol. 16 (2), 1994, 375–90.

Alston, P., *The United Nations and Human Rights: A Critical Appraisal*, Oxford: Clarendon Press, 1995.

Alston, P., 'Richard Lillich Memorial Lecture: Promoting the Accountability of Members of the New UN Human Rights Council', *Journal of Transnational Law and Policy*, Vol. 15, 2005–2006, 49–96.

Alston, P., 'Reconceiving the UN Human Rights Regime: Challenges Confronting the New UN Human Rights Council', *Melbourne Journal of International Law*, Vol. 7, 2006, 185–224.

Amerasinghe, C.F., *Principles of the Institutional Law of International Organizations*, Cambridge Studies in International and Comparative Law, Cambridge: Cambridge University Press, 2005.

Amnesty International, 'Meeting the Challenge: Transforming the Commission on Human Rights into a Human Rights Council', 12 April 2005, AI Index IOR 40/008/2005.

Amnesty International (AI), *Annual Report 2006*, London: Amnesty International, 2007.

Amnesty International (AI), *Annual Report 2007*, London: Amnesty International, 2008.

Amnesty International, 'Sri Lanka: Silencing dissent', 7 February 2008, Index Number: ASA 37/001/2008.

Amnesty International, 'People's Republic of China: The Olympics Countdown – Broken Promises', July 2008, AI Index: ASA 17/089/2008.

Amnesty International, 'Iran: Arrests and Deaths Continue as Authorities Tighten Grip', 14 July 2009, AI Index: MDE 13/072/2009.

Amnesty International (AI), *Annual Report 2009*, London: Amnesty International, 2010.

Anghie, A., *Imperialism, Sovereignty and the Making of International Law*, Cambridge: Cambridge University Press, 2004.

Archer, C., *International Organizations*, London: George Allen & Unwin, 1983.

Asia Watch, *Human Rights in Tibet*, Asia Watch Committee, 1988.

Aust, A., *Modern Treaty Law and Practice*, Cambridge: Cambridge University Press, 2000.

Avery, A., 'Hillary Clinton and the UN: How She Might Approach the Role of Secretary of State', 26 November 2008 (Online). HTTP: <http://unausa.org/Page.aspx?pid=923> (accessed 16 October 2012).

Badran, A.M., *Zionist Israel and Apartheid South Africa: Civil Society and Peace Building in Ethnic-National States*, London: Routledge, 2009.

Barnett, M.N. and Finnemore, M., *Rules for the World: International Organization in Global Politics*, Ithaca, NY: Cornell University Press, 2004.

Barraud, P., 'Mugabe Has History and Morality with Him,' *L'Hebdo*, August 22, 2002 (Online). Available HTTP: <http://translate.google.co.uk/translate?hl=en&sl=fr&u=http://www.hebdo.ch/laquomugabe_a_lhistoire_et_la_morale_avec_luiraquo_14088_.html&ei=1KzMTPXuKI2OjAeN563ZBw&sa=X&oi=translate&ct=result&resnum=1&ved=0CB0Q7gEwAA&prev=/search%3Fq%3DL%25E2%2580%2599Hebdo%2Bmugabe%2B2002%26hl%3De> (accessed 16 October 2012).

Barringer, F., 'U.N. Senses It Must Change, Fast, or Fade Away', *New York Times*, 19 September 2003, A.5 (Online). Available HTTP: <http://www.nytimes.com/2003/09/19/world/un-senses-it-must-change-fast-or-fade-away.html?pagewanted=all&src=pm> (accessed 16 October 2012).

Berger, M.T., 'After the Third World? History, Destiny and the Fate of Third Worldism', *Third World Quarterly*, Vol. 25 (1), 2004, 9–39.

Bernstorff, J.V., 'The Changing Fortunes of the Universal Declaration of Human Rights', *European Journal of International Law*, Vol. 19 (5), 2008, 903–24.

Bhabha, H., *The Location of Culture*, London: Routledge, 1994.

Birmingham, D., *The De-colonization of Africa*, London: Routledge, 1995.

Bishara, M., *Palestine/Israel: Peace or Apartheid: Occupation, Terrorism and the Future*, London: Zed Books, 2002.

Black, M., *The No-Nonsense Guide to International Development*, 2nd edn., Oxford: New Internationalist, 2007.

Bohm, A., 'Sie sind schwarz? Tut uns leid!', *Die Zeit* (Germany), 19 October 2006, p. 23.

Bolton, J.R., 'The Creation, Fall, Rise, and Fall of the United Nations', in Carpenter, T.G. (ed.), *Delusions of Grandeur: United Nations and Global Intervention*, Washington, DC: Cato Institute, 1997, pp. 45–59.

Bosch, M.M., *Votes in the UN General Assembly*, The Hague: Kluwer Law International, 1998.

Bowett, D.W., *The Law of International Institutions*, London: Stevens & Sons, 1963.

Boyle, K., 'The United Nations Human Rights Council: Power, Politics and Human Rights', *Northern Ireland Law Quarterly*, Vol. 60 (2), 2009, 121–33.

Brierly, J.L., *The Law of Nations*, Oxford: Oxford University Press, 1963.

Brooks, S. and Wohlforth, W., 'American Primacy in Perspective', *Foreign Affairs*, Vol. 81 (4), 2002, 19–33.

Brown, B.S., *The United States and the Politicization of the World Bank: Issues of International Law and Policy*, Publication of the Graduate Institute on International Studies, New York; London: Kegan Paul International, 1992.

Brownlie, I., *Principles of Public International Law*, 6th edn., Oxford: Oxford University Press, 2003.

Brülhart, W.A., 'From a Swiss Initiative to a United Nations Proposal (from 2003 until 2005)', in Müller, L. (ed.), *The First 365 Days of the United Nations Human Rights Council*, Switzerland: Baden, 2007, pp. 15–19.

Buhrer, J.C., 'Jean Ziegler Before the Bar', *Le Monde*, 26 July 1993.

Buhrer, J.C., 'UN Commission on Human Rights Loses All Credibility', *Reporters Without Borders*, (2003) (Online). Available HTTP: <http://www.rsf.org/IMG/article_PDF/UN-Commission-on-Human-rights.pdf> (accessed 16 October 2012).

Byrnes, A. and Charleworth, H., 'Action Urged on Statute', *The Canberra Times*, 22 May 2002.

Callejon, C., 'Developments at the Human Rights Council in 2007: A Reflection of its Ambivalence', *Human Rights Law Review*, Vol. 8 (2), 2008, 323–42.

Carey, J., 'The U.N. Human Rights Council: What Would Eleanor Roosevelt Say?', *ILSA Journal of International and Comparative Law*, Vol. 15 (2), 2008–2009, 459–70.

Carr, E.H., *Nationalism and After*, London: Macmillan, 1946.

Carr, E.H., *The Twenty Years' Crisis, 1919–1939: An Introduction to the Study of International Relations*, New York: St Martin's Press, 1964.

Chitkara, M.G., *Toxic Tibet Under Nuclear China*, New Delhi: APH Publishing, 1996.

Claude, I.L., *Swords into Ploughshares*, 4th edn., New York: Random House, 1971.

Copson, R.W., *The Congressional Black Caucus and Foreign Policy*, New York: Novinka Books, 2003.

Crook, J.R., 'United States Votes Against New UN Human Rights Council', *American Journal of International Law*, Vol. 100, 2006, 697–9.

Dalai Lama, *The Spirit of Tibet, Universal Heritage: Selected Speeches and Writings of HH the Dalai Lama XIV*, New Delhi: Allied Publishers, 1995.

Davies, M., 'Rhetorical Inaction? Compliance and the Human Rights Council of the United Nations', *Alternatives: Global, Local, Political*, Vol. 35, 2010, 49–468.

Davis, U., *Israel, an Apartheid State*, London: Zed Books, 1987.

Dembour, M.-B., 'Critiques', in Moeckli, D., Shah, S. and Sivakumaran, S. (eds.), *International Human Rights Law*, Oxford: Oxford University Press, 2010, pp. 64–86.

Dennis, M., 'Human Rights in 2002: The Annual Sessions of the UN Commission on Human Rights and the Economic and Social Council', *American Journal of International Law*, Vol. 97 (2), 2003, 364–86.

Dershowitz, A., *The Case Against Israel's Enemies: Exposing Jimmy Carter and Others Who Stand in the Way of Peace*, Hoboken, NJ: John Wiley, 2009.

Detter, I., 'The Effect of Resolutions of International Organizations', in Makarczyk, J. (ed.), *Theory of International Law at the Threshold of the 21st Century: Essays in Honour of K. Skubiszewski*, London: Kluwer Law, 1996, pp. 389–90.

Deutsch, K.W., *The Analysis of International Relations*, Englewood Cliffs, NJ: Prentice-Hall of India, 1989.

Diehl, P.F. and Du, C., *The Dynamics of International Law*, Cambridge: Cambridge University Press, 2010.

Donnelly, J., 'Human Rights at the United Nations 1955–85: The Question of Bias', *International Studies Quarterly*, Vol. 32 (3), 1988, 275–303.

Donnelly, J., *International Human Rights*, 2nd edn., Boulder, CO: Westview, 1998.

Doole, C., 'US Quits Human Rights Council?', *Human Rights Tribune*, 6 June 2008 (Online). Available HTTP: <http://www.humanrights-geneva.info/US-quits-Human-Rights-Council, 3184> (accessed 16 October 2012).

Doty, R.L., *Imperial Encounters: The Politics of Repression in North–South Relations*, Minneapolis, MN: Minnesota Press, 1962.

Downs, G., Rocke, D. and Barsoom, P., 'Is the Good News About Compliance Good News About Cooperation?', *International Organization*, Vol. 50 (3), 1996, 379–406.

Eade, D., *Capacity-Building: An Approach to People-centred Development*, Oxford: Oxfam UK & Ireland, 1997.

Eager, P.W., 'The Voice of the Congressional Black Caucus in American Foreign Policy', in Persons, G.A. (ed.), *The Expanding Boundaries of Black Politics*, New Brunswick, NJ: Transaction Publishers, 2007, pp. 271–91.

Editorial, 'The UN Today', *New York Times*, 10 February 1984, A27.

Editorial, 'The Church must not be complicit in gay persecution in Africa', *The Observer*, 23 May 2010.

Emmott, B., *Rivals: How the Power Struggle Between China, India, and Japan Will Shape Our Next Decade*, Boston, MA: Houghton Mifflin Harcourt, 2009.

Engels, F., *Anti-Duhring*, London: Lawrence & Wisshart Ltd, 1955.

Epstein, C., *The Power of Words in International Relations: Birth of an Anti-Whaling Discourse*, Cambridge, MA: Massachusetts Institute of Technology, 2008.

Evans, D., *Before the War: Reflections in a New Millennium*, Kelowna, BC, Canada: Wood Lake Publishing Inc., 2004.

Falk, R., 'Foreword', in Normand, R. and Zaidi, S. (eds.), *Human Rights at the UN: The Political History of Universal Justice*, Bloomington, IN: Indiana University Press, 2008.

Fandy, M., *Arab Media: Tools of the Government, Tools for the People?*, Darby, PA: Diane Publishing, 2008.

Farer, T.J. and Gaer, F.D., 'The UN and Human Rights: At the End of the Beginning', in Roberts, A. and Kingsbury, B. (eds.), *United Nations, Divided World*, 2nd edn., Oxford: Oxford University Press, 1993, pp. 240–96.

Fitzmaurice, M., 'Indigenous Whaling, Protection of the Environment, Intergenerational Rights and Environmental Ethics', *Yearbook of Polar Law*, Vol. 2, 2010, 253–77.

Franck, T.M., *Human Rights in Third World Perspective*, Dobbs Ferry, NY: Oceana Publications Inc, 1982.

Franck, T.M., 'Of Gnats and Camels: Is There a Double Standard at the United Nations?', *The American Journal of International Law*, Vol. 78 (4), 1984, 811–33.

Freedman, R., 'Improvement on the Commission?: The UN Human Rights Council's Inaction on Darfur', *University of California-Davis Journal of International Law and Policy*, Vol. 16 (1), 2009, 81–129.

Freedman, R., 'The United States and the Human Rights Council: An Early Assessment', *St Thomas Law Review*, Vol. 23 (1), 2010, 23–70.

Friedrich, C.J., *Trends of Federalists in Theory and Practice*, New York: Praeger, 1968.

Frum, D. and Perle, R., *An End To Evil: How To Win The War On Terror*, New York: Random House, 2003.

Gaer, F.D., 'A Voice not an Echo: Universal Periodic Review and the UN Treaty Body System', *Human Rights Law Review*, Vol. 7 (1), 2007, 109–39.

'Gaza Comments by Rights Expert Irresponsible – UN', *Reuters*, 7 July 2005.

Gearty, C., *Can Human Rights Survive?*, Cambridge: Cambridge University Press, 2006.

Gewirth, A., *Human Rights: Essays on Justification and Application*, London: University of Chicago Press, 1982.

Ghanea, N., 'From UN Commission on Human Rights to UN Human Rights Council: One Step Forwards or Two Steps Sideways?', *International and Comparative Law Quarterly*, Vol. 55 (3), 2006, 695–705.

Gibson, J.S., *International Organizations, Constitutional Law and Human Rights*, New York: Praeger Publishers, 1991.

Gill, S., *American Hegemony and the Trilateral Commission*, Cambridge: Cambridge University Press, 1992.

Gilman, B.A., *The Treatment of Israel by the United Nations: Hearing Before The Committee on International Relations, U.S. House of Representatives*, Darby, PA: Diane Pub. Co., 1999.

Goldstein, J. and Keohane, R.O. (eds.), *Ideas and Foreign Policy: Beliefs, Institutions and Political Change*, Ithaca, NY: Cornell University Press, 1993.

Goldstein, J., Kahler, M., Keohane, R.O. and Slaughter, A.-M., 'Legalization and World Politics', *International Organization*, Vol. 54 (3), 2000, 385–99.

Goodenough, P., 'UN Rights Expert Has Controversial Track Record', *CNSNews. com*, 26 April 2006 (Online). Available HTTP: <http://www.cnsnews.com/View ForeignBureaus.asp?Page=/ForeignBureaus/archive/200604/INT20060426b.html> (accessed 16 October 2012).

Goodrich, L.M., Hambro, E. and Simons, A.P., *Charter of the United Nations: Commentary and Documents*, New York: Columbia University Press, 1969.

Goonesekera, S., 'CEDAW: Reflections on the Framework', in Shivdas, M. and Coleman, S. (eds.), *Without Prejudice: CEDAW and the Determination of Women's Rights in a Legal and Cultural Context*, London: Commonwealth Secretariat, 2010, pp. 191–2.

Gorman, R.F., *Great Debates at the United Nations: An Encyclopedia of Fifty Key Issues 1945–2000*, Westport, CT: Greenwood Press, 2001.

Griffin, J., *On Human Rights*, Oxford: Oxford University Press, 2008.

Gutter, J., *Thematic Procedures of the United Nations Commission on Human Rights and International Law: In Search of a Sense of Community*, Antwerp: Intersentia, 2006.

Gutter, J., 'Special Procedures and the Human Rights Council: Achievements and Challenges Ahead', *Human Rights Law Review*, Vol. 7 (1), 2007, 93–107.

Haas, P.M., 'Introduction: Epistemic Communities and International Policy Co-ordination', *International Organization*, Vol. 46 (1), 1992, 1–35.

Hafner-Burton, E.M., 'Sticks and Stones: Naming and Shaming – the Human Rights Enforcement Problem', *International Organization*, Vol. 62, 2008, pp. 689–716.

Hamid, A.G. and Kulliyyah, A.I., 'Reservations to CEDAW and the Implementation of Islamic Family Law: Issues and Challenges', *Asian Journal of International Law*, Vol. 1 (3), 2006, 121–55.

Hampson, F.J., 'An Overview of the Reform of the UN Human Rights Machinery', *Human Rights Law Review*, Vol. 7 (1), 2007, 7–27.

Hannum, H., 'Reforming the Special Procedures and Mechanisms of the Commission on Human Rights', *Human Rights Law Review*, Vol. 7 (1), 2007, 73–92.

Harris, H., 'The Politics of Depoliticization: International Perspectives on the Human Rights Council', *Human Rights Brief*, Vol. 13 (3), 2006, 8–9.

Hassan, S.M. and Ray, C.E., *Darfur and the Crisis of Governance in Sudan*, Ithaca, NY: Cornell University Press, 2009.

Hatch, E., 'The Good Side of Cultural Relativism', *Journal of Anthropological Research*, Vol. 53, 1997, 371–81.

Havel, V., 'A Table for Tyrants', *New York Times*, 10 May 2008 (Online). Available HTTP: <http://www.nytimes.com/2009/05/11/opinion/11havel.html> (accessed 16 October 2012).

Heinze, E., 'Sexual Orientation and International Law: A Study in the Manufacture of Cross-Cultural Sensitivity', *Michigan Journal of International Law*, Vol. 22 (2), 2001, 283–309.

Heinze, E., 'Truth and Myth in Critical Race Theory and LatCrit: Human Rights and the Ethnocentrism of Anti-Ethnocentrism', *National Black Law Journal*, Vol. 20 (2), 2007, 107–62.

Heinze, E., 'Even-handedness and the Politics of Human Rights', *Harvard Human Rights Journal*, Vol. 21 (7), 2008, 7–46.

Heinze, E., 'The Reality and Hyperreality of Human Rights: Public Consciousness and the Mass Media', in Dickenson, R., Katselli, E., Murray, C. and Pedersen, O.W. (eds.), *Examining Critical Perspectives on Human Rights: The End of an Era?*, Cambridge: Cambridge University Press, 2011, pp. 193–216.

Heinze, E. and Freedman, R., 'Public Awareness of Human Rights: Distortions in the Mass Media', *International Journal of Human Rights*, Vol. 14 (4), 2010, 491–523.

Henkin, L., *How Nations Behave: Law and Foreign Policy*, New York: F.A. Praeger, 1968.

Henkin, L., 'U.S. Ratification of Human Rights Conventions: The Ghost of Senator Bricker', *The American Journal of International Law*, Vol. 89 (2), 1995, 341–50.

Hicks, P., 'How to Put U.N. Rights Council Back on Track', *The Forward*, 3 November 2006 (Online). Available HTTP: <http://www.forward.com/articles/how-to-put-un-rights-council-back-on-track/> (accessed 16 October 2012).

Hobson, J., *The State and International Relations*, Cambridge: Cambridge University Press, 2000.

Huguenin, P., 'Le Nobel de Kadhafi' (Kadhafi's Nobel), *L'Hebdo*, 27 April 1989.

Human Rights Watch, 'UN Human Rights Body in Serious Decline', *Human Rights News (US)*, 25 April 2003.

Human Rights Watch, 'Sudan – Events of 2007', in *World Report 2008* (Online). Available HTTP: <http://www.hrw.org/englishwr2k8/docs/2008/01/31/sudan17759.htm> (accessed 16 October 2012).

Humphrey, J.P., *Human Rights and the United Nations: A Great Adventure*, New York: Transnational Publishers Inc., 1984.

Ibhawoh, B., *Imperialism and Human Rights: Colonial Discourses of Rights and Liberties in African History*, Albany, NY: SUNY Press, 2008.

Ignatieff, M., *American Exceptionalism and Human Rights*, Princeton, NJ: Princeton University Press, 2005.

International Service for Human Rights (ISHR), 'Overview of the Universal Periodic Review in 2008', (2009) (Online). Available HTTP: <http://www.ishr.ch/upr-monitor/analytical-overviews> (accessed 16 October 2012).

Jackson, R.G.A., *A Study of the Capacity of the United Nations Development System* (2 volumes), Geneva: United Nations, 1969.

Jacoby, T.A., *Bridging the Barrier: Israeli Unilateral Disengagement*, Aldershot: Ashgate Publishing Ltd, 2007.

Jeanneret, M., 'United Nations: Jean Ziegler at the Heart of a New Polemic,' *Le Matin*, 24 April 2006.

Johnson, A., 'Appointment With Farce', *The Guardian*, 5 April 2008.

Jolly, R., Emmerij, L. and Weiss, T.G., *UN Ideas That Changed The World*, Bloomington, IN: Indiana University Press, 2009.

Kahler, M., 'The Causes and Consequences of Legalization', *International Organization*, Vol. 54 (3), 2000, 661–83.

Kaiser, K., 'The Interaction of Regional Subsystems. Some Preliminary Notes on Recurrent Patterns and the Role of Superpowers', *World Politics*, Vol. 21 (1), 1968, 84–107.

Kälin, W. and Jimenez, C., 'Reform of the UN Commission on Human Rights', Study Commissioned by the Swiss Ministry of Foreign Affairs (Political Division IV), Geneva: University of Bern, 30 August 2003.

Kälin, W. and Kunzli, J., *The Law of International Human Rights Protection*, Oxford: Oxford University Press, 2009.

Kälin, W., Jimenez, C., Künzli, J. and Baldegger, M., 'The Human Rights Council and Country Situations: Framework, Challenges and Models', Study commissioned by the Swiss Ministry of Foreign Affairs, Geneva: Institute of Public Law, University of Bern, 2006.

Kaplan, L.S., *NATO Divided, NATO United: The Evolution of an Alliance*, Westport, CT: Greenwood Publishing Group, 2004.

Kausikan, B., 'Asia's Different Standards', *Foreign Policy*, Vol. 92, 1993, 24–41.

Kausikan, B., 'A Universal Definition of Human Rights Ignores Cultural Diversity', in Williams, M.E. (ed.), *Human Rights: Opposing Viewpoints*, Greenhaven Press Inc., 1998, pp. 21–24.

Kennedy, D., 'The Move to Institutions', *Cardozo Law Review*, Vol. 8, 1987, 841–988.

Keohane, R.O., *After Hegemony: Cooperation and Discord in the World Political Economy*, Princeton, NJ: Princeton University Press, 1984.

Keohane, R.O., *International Institutions and State Power*, Boulder, CO: Westview Press, 1989.

Keohane, R.O. and Nye, J.S., 'World Politics and the International Economic System', in Bergsten, C.F. (ed.), *The Future of the International Economic Order: An Agenda for Research*, Lexington, KY: Lexington Books, 1973.

Keohane, R.O. and Nye, J.S., *Power and Independence*, 3rd edn., New York: Longman, 2001.

Khaliq, U., *Ethical Dimensions of the Foreign Policy of the European Union: A Legal Appraisal*, Cambridge: Cambridge University Press, 2008.

Kingsbury, B., 'The Concept of Compliance as a Function of Competing Conceptions of International Law', in Weiss, E.B. (ed.), *International Compliance with Nonbinding Accords*, Washington, DC: American Society of International Law, 1997, pp. 49–80.

Kissinger, H., 'NATO At The Crossroads; NATO's Uncertain Future In A Troubled Alliance', *San Diego Union-Tribune*, 1 December 2002.

Klabbers, J., *Introduction to International Institutional Law*, Cambridge: Cambridge University Press, 2002.

Krasner, S.D., *International Regimes*, Ithaca, NY: Cornell University Press, 1983.

Lal, D., *Indo-Tibet-China Conflict*, New Delhi: Gyan Publishing House, 2008.

Laor, Y., 'Israel's Apartheid is Worse than South Africa's', *Haaretz*, 1 November 2008 (Online). Available HTTP: <http://www.haaretz.com/print-edition/opinion/israel-s-apartheid-is-worse-than-south-africa-s-1.4590> (accessed 16 October 2012).

Lauterpacht, H., *The Function of Law in the International Community*, Oxford: Oxford University Press, 1933.

Lauterpacht, H., *International Law and Human Rights*, London: Stevens & Sons Limited, 1950.

Lebovic, J.H. and Voeten, E., 'The Politics of Shame: The Condemnation of Country Human Rights Practices in UNCHR', *International Studies Quarterly*, Vol. 50 (4), 2006, 861–88.

Lelyveld, J., 'Jimmy Carter and Apartheid', *The New York Review of Books*, 29 March 2007 (Online). Available HTTP: <http://www.nybooks.com/articles/archives/2007/mar/29/jimmy-carter-and-apartheid/> (accessed 16 October 2012).

Lempinen, M., *The United Nations Commission on Human Rights and the Different Treatment of Governments*, Abo: Abo Akademi University Press, 2005.

Leopold, E., 'Sudan Elected to UN Rights Group, US Walks Out', *Reuters*, 5 May 2004 (Online). Available HTTP: <http://www.talktalk.co.uk/news/world/reuters/2004/05/04/sudanelectedtounrightsgroupuswalksout.html> (accessed 16 October 2012).

Lijnzaad, L., *Reservations to UN-Human Rights Treaties: Ratify and Ruin?*, Dordrecht: Martinus Nijhoff Publishers, 1995.

Limbach, J., *Judicial Independence: Law and Practice of Appointments to the European Court of Human Rights*, London: Interrights, 2003.

Lobe, J., 'US: Obama Urged to Strengthen Ties with UN', *Inter Press Services*, 19 November 2008 (Online). Available HTTP: <http://ipsnews.net/news.asp?idnews=44780> (accessed 16 October 2012).

Lombaerde, P.D. and Schulz, M. (eds.), *The EU and World Regionalism: The Makeability of Regions in the 21st Century*, Aldershot: Ashgate Publishing Ltd, 2009.

Loudon, A., 'Gaddafi Human Rights Prize for Two Dock Strike Wives', *Daily Mail*, 4 September 1997.

Lundestad, G., *East, West, North, South: Major Developments on International Politics Since 1945*, Oxford: Oxford University Press, 1999.

Lyons, G.M., Baldwin, D.A. and McNemar, D.W., 'The "Politicization" Issue in the UN Specialized Agencies', *Proceedings of the Academy of Political Science*, Vol. 32 (4), 1977, 81–92.

McArthur, S., '91 Hostages Freed from Iraq Arrive Back in Europe', *Reuters News*, 22 November 1990.

McCormick, J.M. and Kihl, Y.W., 'Intergovernmental Organizations and Foreign Policy Behaviour: Some Empirical Findings', *American Political Science Review*, Vol. 73 (2), 1979, 494–504.

McCorquodale, R. and Fairbrother, R., 'Globalization and Human Rights', *Human Rights Quarterly*, Vol. 21 (3), 1999, 735–66.

McCorquodale, R. and Orosz, N., *Tibet, The Position in International Law: Report of the Conference of International Lawyers on Issues Relating to Self-Determination and Independence for Tibet, London 6–10 January 1993*, Chicago, IL: Serindia Publications Inc., 1994.

McDermott, A., *The New Politics of Financing the UN*, Basingstoke and New York: Palgrave Macmillan, 2000.

McGoldrick, D., *The UN Human Rights Committee: Its Role in the Development of the International Covenant on Civil and Political Rights*, Oxford: Oxford University Press, 1994.

McGoldrick, D., 'Political and Legal Responses to the ICC', in McGoldrick, D., Rowe, P. and Donnelly, E (eds.), *The Permanent International Criminal Court*, Oxford: Hart, 2004, pp. 389–459.

McGreal, C., 'Worlds Apart', *The Guardian*, 6 February 2006 (Online). Available HTTP: <http://www.guardian.co.uk/world/2006/feb/06/southafrica.israel> (accessed 16 October 2012).

McNeal, R.H., *Lenin, Stalin, Khrushchev: Voices of Bolshevism*, Englewood Cliffs, NJ: Prentice Hall, 1963.

Mapondera, G. and Smith, D., 'Human rights campaigners attack Malawi gay couple conviction', *The Guardian*, 19 May 2010.

Marx, K. and Engels. F., *The Communist Manifesto*, Oxford: Oxford University Press, [1888] 2008.

Matas, D., *No More: The Battle Against Human Rights Violations*, Toronto: Dundum Press Ltd, 1994.

Maurer, P., 'About the Negotiation Process in New York (from 2005 until 2006): Of Ants, Caterpillars and Butterflies', in Müller, L. (ed.), *The First 365 Days of the United Nations Human Rights Council*, Switzerland: Baden, 2007, pp. 33–6.

Mearsheimer, J., 'The False Promise of International Institutions', *International Security*, Vol. 19 (3), 1995, 5–49.

Mertus, J., *The United Nations and Human Rights: A Guide for a New Era*, Abingdon: Taylor & Francis, 2009.

Meyer, A.G., *Leninism*, Cambridge, MA: Harvard University Press, 1957.

Meyer, P., 'The International Bill: A Brief History', in Williams, P. (ed.), *The International Bill of Rights*, Glen Ellen, CA: Entwhistle Books, 1981.

Mitrany, D., *A Working Peace System*, Chicago, IL: Quadrangle, 1966.

Mitrany, D., *The Functional Theory of Politics*, London: St. Martin's Press, 1976.

Monshipouri, M., 'The Search for International Human Rights and Justice: Coming to Terms with the New Global Realities', *Human Rights Quarterly*, Vol. 23 (2), 2001, 370–401.

Moravcsik, A., 'The Origins of Human Rights Regimes: Democratic Delegation in Postwar Europe', *International Organization*, Vol. 54 (2), 2000, 217–52.

Morgenthau, H.J., *Politics Among Nations*, New York: Alfred A. Knopf, 1960.

Morgenthau, H.J., *Politics among Nations: The Struggle for Power and Peace*, New York: McGraw-Hill, 1993.

Moskowitz, M., *The Roots and Reaches of United Nations Actions and Decisions*, Alphen aan den Rijn, the Netherlands: Sijthoff & Noordhoff, 1980.

Moss, L.C., 'Will the Human Rights Council have Better Membership than the Commission on Human Rights?', *Human Rights Brief*, Vol. 13 (3), 2006, 10–11.

Mullik, B.N., *The Chinese Betrayal: My Years with Nehru*, Bombay and New York: Allied Publishers, 1971.

Muravchik, J., 'Qaddafi's Good Friend at the U.N.', *The Weekly Standard*, Vol. 11, No. 33, 15 May 2005 (Online). Available HTTP: <http://www.weeklystandard.com/Content/Public/Articles/000/000/012/198ikivt.asp> (accessed 16 October 2012).

Myrdal, G., 'Realities and Illusions in Regard to Inter-Governmental Organizations', in *Hobhouse Memorial Lecture*, Oxford: Oxford University Press, 1955.

Nathwani, N., 'Religious Cartoons and Human Rights', *European Human Rights Law Review*, Vol. 4, 2008, 488–507.

Nicol, D., 'Interregional Co-ordination Within the United Nations: The Role of the Commonwealth', in Andemicael, B. (ed.), *Regionalism and the United Nations*, Dobbs Ferry, NY: Oceana Publications Inc, 1979, pp. 95–144.

Nifosi, I., *The UN Special Procedures in the Field of Human Rights*, Antwerp: Intersentia, 2005.

Normand, R. and Zaidi, S., *Human Rights at the UN: The Political History of Universal Justice*, Bloomington, IN: Indiana University Press, 2008.

Nowak, M., 'Country-Oriented Human Rights Protection by the UN Commission on Human Rights and its Sub-Commission', *Netherlands Yearbook of International Law*, Vol. 22, 1991, pp. 39–90.

Nowak, M., Birk, M., Crittin, T. and Kozma, J., 'UN Human Rights Council in Crisis – Proposals to Enhance the Effectiveness of the Council', in Benedek, W., Benoit-Rohmer, F., Karl, W. and Nowak, M. (eds.), *European Yearbook on Human Rights*, Vienna: European Academic Press, 2011, pp. 41–84.

Nye, J.S., 'UNCTAD: Poor Nations' Pressure Group', in Cox, R.W. and Jacobson, H.K. (eds.), *The Anatomy of Influence: Decision Making in International Organization*, New Haven, CT and London: Yale University Press, 1973, pp. 334–70.

Oberleitner, G., *Global Human Rights Institutions*, Cambridge: Polity Press, 2007.

O'Brien, C.C. and Topolski, F., *The UN – Sacred Drama*, London: Hutchinson, 1968.

Odum, H.W., 'A Sociological Approach to the Study and Practice of American Regionalism', *Social Forces*, Vol. 20 (4), 1942, 425–36.

Opinion, 'Vote For Justice, Embarrassment For US', *People's Daily (China)*, 4 May 2001 (Online). Available HTTP: <http://english.people.com.cn/english/200105/04/eng20010504_69258.html> (accessed 16 October 2012).

Opinion, 'The United Nations and Zimbabwe: Crimes Against Humanity', *The Economist*, 26 June 2008.

Osakwe, C., *The Participation of the Soviet Union in Universal International Organizations*, Leiden: A.W. Sijthoff International Publishing Company, 1972.

Osgood, R.E. and Tucker, R.W., *Force, Order and Justice*, Baltimore, MD: Johns Hopkins University Press, 1967.

Palling, B., 'Gaddafi Funds Peace Prize', *The Independent*, 25 April 1989.

Pappe, I., *Peoples Apart: Israel, South Africa and the Apartheid Question*, London: I.B. Tauris, 2011.

Parmar, S., 'The Challenge of "Defamation of Religions" to Freedom of Expression and the International Human Rights', *European Human Rights Law Review*, Vol. 3, 2009, 353–75.

Parsons, A., 'The UN and National Interests of States', in Roberts, A. and Kingsbury, B. (eds.), *United Nations, Divided World*, 2nd edn., Oxford: Oxford University Press, 1993, pp. 104–24.

Pashukanis, E.B., in Beirne, P. and Sharlet, R. (eds.), *Pashukanis: Selected Writings on Marxism and Law*, London: London Academic Press, 1980.

Patten, C., 'Globalization and the Law', *European Human Rights Law Review*, Vol. 6, 2004, 6–13.

Perelman, M., 'U.N. Official Slammed for Criticism of Israel', *The Forward*, 9 December 2005 (Online). Available HTTP: <http://www.forward.com/articles/1729/> (accessed 16 October 2012).

Pleming, S., 'US Foreign Policy Experts Give Obama UN Advice', *Reuters*, 19 November 2008 (Online). Available HTTP: <http://www.reuters.com/article/politicsNews/idUSTRE4AI7WX20081120> (accessed 16 October 2012).

Preston, W., Herman, E.S. and Schiller, H.I., *Hope and Folly: The United Nations and UNESCO*, Minneapolis, MN: University of Minnesota Press, 1989.

Rahmani-Ocora, L., 'Giving the Emperor Real Clothes: The UN Human Rights Council', *Global Governance*, Vol. 12 (1), 2006, pp. 15–20.

Ramcharan, B.G., 'Strategies for the International Protection of Human Rights in the 1990s', in Claude, R.P. and Weston, B.H. (eds.), *Human Rights and the International Community: Issues and Action*, Philadelphia, PA: University of Pennsylvania Press, 1992, pp. 271–83.

Ramcharan, B.G., *The UN Human Rights Council*, London: Routledge, 2011.

Redondo, E.D., 'The Universal Periodic Review of the UN Human Rights Council: An Assessment of the First Session', *Chinese Journal of International Law*, Vol. 7 (3), 2008, 721–34.

Reuter, P., *International Institutions*, London: Allen & Unwin, 1958.

Rice, X., 'Gay activists attack Ugandan preacher's porn slideshow', *The Guardian*, 19 February 2010.

Risse, T., 'Lets Argue! Communicative Action in World Politics', *International Organization*, Vol. 54 (1), 2000, 1–39.

Rittberger, V. and Zangl, B., *International Organization: Polity, Politics and Policies*, Houndsmills: Palgrave Macmillan, 2006.

Roberts, A. and Kingsbury, B. (eds.), *United Nations, Divided World*, 2nd edn., Oxford: Oxford University Press, 1993.

Robinson, M., 'Human Rights: Challenges for the 21st Century', *First Annual Dag Hammarskjöld Lecture*, Uppsala, Sweden, 1 October 1998.

Rombouts, H., *Victims Organizations and the Politics of Reparations: A Case Study on Rwanda*, London: Intersentia, 2004.

Roosevelt, F.D. and Churchill, W., *The Atlantic charter: the eight-point declaration of President Roosevelt and Prime Minister Churchill, August 14, 1941*, Commission to study the organization of peace, 1941.

Roth, K., 'Despots Pretending to Spot and Shame Despots', *New York Times*, 17 April 2001 (Online). Available HTTP: <http://www.nytimes.com/2001/04/17/opinion/17iht-edroth_ed2_.html?pagewanted=1> (accessed 16 October 2012).

Rovenger, J., 'ANALYSIS: Obama vs. McCain on U.S.–U.N. Relations', Citizens for Global Solutions, 15 June 2008 (Online). Available HTTP: <http://www.globalsolutions.org/in_the_news/analysis_obama_vs_mccain_u_s_u_n_relations> (accessed 16 October 2012).

Rubenberg, C., *Israel and the American National Interest: A Critical Examination*, Urbana, IL: University of Illinois Press, 1986.

Rudolf, B., 'The Thematic Rapporteurs and Working Groups of the United Nations Commission on Human Rights', *Max Planck Yearbook of United Nations Law*, Vol. 4, 2000, 289–329.

Rugh, W.A., *Arab Mass Media: Newspapers, Radio and Television in Arab Politics*, Westport, CT: Praeger Publishers, 2004.

Russett, B.M., *International Regions and the International System: A Study in Political Ecology*, Chicago, IL: Rand-McNally, 1967.

Sabine, G.H., *A History of Political Theory*, London: George G. Harrap & Co., 1964.

Said, E., *Orientalism*, London: Routledge, 1978.

Sakr, N., *Arab Media and Political Renewal: Community, Legitimacy and Public Life*, London: I.B. Tauris, 2007.

Sanders, E., 'Is the Darfur Bloodshed Genocide? Opinions Differ', *LA Times*, 4 May 2009.

Sands, P., 'After Pinochet: The Role of National Courts', in Sands, P. (ed.), *From Nuremberg to The Hague*, Cambridge: Cambridge University Press, 2002, pp. 68–108.

Sands, P. and Klein, P., *Bowett's Law of International Institutions*, London: Sweet & Maxwell, 2001.

Scannella, P. and Splinter, P., 'The United Nations Human Rights Council: A Promise to be Fulfilled', *Human Rights Law Review*, Vol. 7 (1), 2007, 41–72.

Schermers, H.G., *International Institutional Law*, Leiden: Sijthoff, 1972.

Schermers, H.G. and Blokkers, N.M., *International Institutional Law*, 3rd edn., Dordrecht: Martinus Nijhoff, 1995.

Schoenbaum, T.J., *International Relations – The Path Not Taken: Using International Law to Promote World Peace and Security*, Cambridge: Cambridge University Press, 2006.

Schrijver, N., 'The UN Human Rights Council: A New "Society of the Committed" or Just Old Wine in New Bottles', *Leiden Journal of International Law*, Vol. 20 (4), 2007, 809–23.

Sewell, J.P., *Functionalism and World Politics*, Princeton, NJ: Princeton University Press, 1966.

Shaw, M.N., *International Law*, 5th edn., Cambridge: Cambridge University Press, 2003.

Shaw, M.N., *International Law*, 6th edn., Cambridge: Cambridge University Press, 2008.

Shivdas, M. and Coleman, S. (eds.), *Without Prejudice: CEDAW and the Determination of Women's Rights in a Legal and Cultural Context*, London: Commonwealth Secretariat, 2010.

Shultz, R.H., *The Soviet Union and Revolutionary Warfare: Principles, Practices, and Regional Comparisons*, Stanford University, CA: Hoover Press, 1988.

Simma, B. (ed.), *The Charter of the United Nations: A Commentary*, Oxford: Oxford University Press, 1995.

Simmons, B.A., 'International Law and International Relations: Scholarship at the Intersection of Principles and Politics', *American Society of International Law Proceedings*, Vol. 95, 2001, 271–9.

Slaughter, A.-M., 'International Law and International Relations', *Hague Academy of International Law*, Vol. 285, 2001, 9–250.

Sloan, B., 'General Assembly Resolutions Revisited, (Forty Years After)', *British Yearbook of International Law*, Vol. 58, 1987, 39–150.

Smith, C.B., *Politics and Process and the United Nations: The Global Dance*, Boulder, CO: Lynne Rienner, 2006.

Smith, M.J., *Realist Thought from Weber to Kissinger*, Baton Rouge, LA: Louisiana State University Press, 1986.

Smith, R.K.M., 'More of the Same or Something Different? Preliminary Observations on the Contribution of Universal Periodic Review with Reference to the Chinese Experience', *Chinese Journal of International Law*, Vol. 10 (3), 2011, 565–86.

Smithers, (Sir) P., 'Towards Greater Coherence Among Intergovernmental Organizations Through Governmental Control', in Andemicael, B. (ed.), *Regionalism and the United Nations*, Dobbs Ferry, NY: Oceana Publications Inc, 1979, pp. 13–93.

Stalin, J.V., 'The Foundations of Leninism' (1933), in *Problems of Leninism*, Peking: Foreign Languages Press, 1976, pp. 1–116.

Steinberg, R.H., *The Greening of Trade Law? International Trade Organizations and Environmental Issues*, Lanham, MD: Rowman & Littlefield Publishers Inc., 2002.

Steiner, H.J., Alston, P. and Goodman, R., *International Human Rights In Context*, 3rd edn., Oxford: Oxford University Press, 2008.

Subedi, S.P., Wheatley, S., Mukherjee, A. and Ngane, S., 'Special Issue: The Role of the Special Rapporteurs of the United Nations Human Rights Council in the Development and Promotion of International Human Rights Norms', *The International Journal of Human Rights*, Vol. 15 (2), 2011, 155–61.

Sweeney, G. and Saito, Y., 'An NGO Assessment of the New Mechanisms of the UN Human Rights Council', *Human Rights Law Review*, Vol. 9 (2), 2009, 203–23.

Tammes, A.J.P., 'Decisions of International Organs as a Source of International Law', *Recueil des Cours*, Vol. 94, 1958-II, 261–364.

Terlinghen, Y., 'The UN Human Rights Council: A New Era in UN Human Rights Work?', *Ethics & International Affairs*, Vol. 21 (2), 2007, 167–78.

Thakur, R., *What is Equitable Geographical Distribution in the 21st Century?*, New York: United Nations University, 1999.

Tolley, H., *The U.N. Commission on Human Rights*, Boulder, CO: Westview Press, 1987.

Totten, S., *Genocide in Darfur: Investigating the Atrocities in the Sudan*, London: Routledge, 2006.

Tunkin, G.I., *Theory of International Law*, Cambridge, MA: Harvard University Press, 1974.

Tyagi, Y., *The UN Human Rights Committee: Practice and Procedure*, Cambridge: Cambridge University Press, 2011.

United Nations Department of Public Information (New York), *Yearbook of the United Nations 1991, Vol.45*, Dordrecht: Martinus Nijhoff Publishers, 1992.

Van Boeven, Th.C. and Coomans, F., *Human Rights From Exclusion to Inclusion: Principles and Practice*, The Hague: Martinus Nijhoff Publishers, 2000.

Vasquez, J.A., 'Colouring it Morgenthau: New Evidence for an Old Thesis on Quantitative International Politics', *British Journal of International Studies*, Vol. 5 (3), 1979, 210–28.

Vengoechea-Barrios, J., 'The Universal Periodic Review: A New Hope for International Human Rights Law or a Reformulation of Errors of the Past?', *International Law: revista colombiana de derecho internacional*, Vol. 12, 2008, 101–16.

Wallerstein, I., *The Modern-World System*, New York: Academic Press, 1974.

Watson, R., 'Bush Deploys Hawk as New UN Envoy', *The Times*, 8 March 2005 (Online). Available HTTP: <http://www.timesonline.co.uk/tol/news/world/us_and_americas/article421888.ece> (accessed 16 October 2012).

Weiss, T.G., *What's Wrong with the United Nations and How to Fix It*, Cambridge: Polity Press, 2008.

Weiss, T.G., Carayannis, T., Emmerij, L. and Jolly, R., *UN Voices: The Struggle for Development and Social Justice*, Bloomington, IN: Indiana University Press, 2005.

Wenger, A., Nuenlist, C. and Locher, A., *Transforming NATO in the Cold War: Challenges Beyond Deterrence in the 1960s*, London: Taylor & Francis, 2007.

Wheeler, R., 'The United Nations Commission on Human Rights, 1982–1997: A Study of "Targeted" Resolutions', *Canadian Journal of Political Science*, Vol. 32 (1), 1999, 75–101.

Wilson, J.Q. and DiIulio, J.J., *American Government: Institutions and Policies*, 7th edn., Boston, MA: Houghton Mifflin Harcourt, 1997.

Wilson, W., *President Wilson's Great Speeches and Other History Making Documents*, Chicago, IL: Stanton and Van Vliet, 1917/18.

Wolfers, A., 'The Actors in International Politics', in Wolfers, A. (ed.), *Discord and Collaboration: Essays on International Politics*, Baltimore, MD: Johns Hopkins Press, 1962.

Worsley, P., *The Third World*, London: Weidenfeld and Nicolson, 1964.

Youngs, R., *The European Union and the Promotion of Democracy*, Oxford: Oxford University Press, 2001.

Ziegler, J., *L'empire de la honte* ('The Empire of Shame'), Paris: Fayard, 2005.

Ziring, L., Riggs, R.E. and Plano, J.C., *The United Nations International Organization and World Politics*, 2nd edn., Belmont, CA: Wadsworth, 1994.

Zweifel, T.D., *International Organizations and Democracy*, Boulder: Lynne Rienner, 2006.

Index

Please note that page numbers relating to Notes will have the letter 'n' following the page number. HRC stands for 'Human Rights Council'.

Printed in Great Britain
by Amazon